Italy
at the Polls,
1979

AEI'S AT THE POLLS STUDIES

The American Enterprise Institute
has initiated this series in order to promote
an understanding of the electoral process as it functions in
democracies around the world. The series will include studies
of at least two national elections in each of nineteen countries
on five continents, by scholars from the United States and
abroad who are recognized as experts in their field.
More information on the titles in this series can
be found at the back of this book.

Italy at the Polls, 1979

A Study of the Parliamentary Elections

American Enterprise Institute for Public Policy Research
Washington and London

Library of Congress Cataloging in Publication Data
Main entry under title:

Italy at the polls, 1979

    (AEI studies ; 321)
    Includes index.
    1. Italy. Parlamento—Elections—Addresses, essays,
lectures. 2. Elections—Italy—Addresses, essays,
lectures. 3. Italy—Politics and government—1945–
—Addresses, essays, lectures. I. Penniman, Howard Rae,
1916–   . II Series.
JN5609.I89   325.945'0927   81-8106
ISBN 0-8447-3440-3   AACR2
ISBN 0-8447-3441-1 (pbk.)

AEI Studies 321

Contents

Abbreviations

AO	Avanguardia Operaia, Workers Vanguard
DC	Democrazia Cristiana, Christian Democratic party
DN	Democrazia Nazionale, National Democracy
DP	Democrazia Proletaria, Proletarian Democracy
LC	Lotta Continua, Continuous Struggle
MSI	Movimento Sociale Italiano, Italian Social Movement
MSI-DN	Movimento Sociale Italiano-Destra Nazionale, Italian Social Movement-National Right
NSU	Nuova Sinistra Unità, United New Left
PCI	Partito Comunista Italiano, Italian Communist party
PDUP	Partito di Unità Proletaria, Party of Proletarian Unity
PLI	Partito Liberale Italiano, Italian Liberal party
PR	Partito Radicale, Radical party
PRI	Partito Repubblicano Italiano, Italian Republican party
PSDI	Partito Socialista Democratico Italiano, Italian Social Democratic party
PSI	Partito Socialista Italiano, Italian Socialist party
PSIUP	Partito Socialista Italiano di Unità Proletaria, Socialist party of Proletarian Unity
SVP	Südtyroler Volkspartei, South Tyrolean People's party
UV	Unione Valdostana, Valdostian Union

Preface

Italy at the Polls, 1979: A Study of the Parliamentary Elections is another in the continuing series of studies of national elections in selected democratic countries published by the American Enterprise Institute (AEI). Underlying the series is the belief that public policy makers and students of elections in each democracy can profit from a knowledge of electoral practices in a wide variety of other democracies. The greater their understanding of the political consequences of the conduct of elections in other countries, the deeper their insights into the impact of electoral rules and practices at home.

As of mid-1981 the *At the Polls* series includes books on at least one election in Australia, Canada, France, West Germany, Greece, India, Ireland, Israel, Italy, Japan, New Zealand, three of the four continental Scandinavian democracies, the United Kingdom, and Venezuela. Volumes on more recent elections in Canada, France, West Germany, India, Greece, and Japan are nearing completion, and books on elections in Belgium, Colombia, Jamaica, Luxembourg, the Netherlands, Portugal, and Spain are in progress or planned. AEI has also published two studies of referendums and *Democracy at the Polls: A Comparative Study of Competitive National Elections*, on the conduct of elections in twenty-eight democracies. A volume on the election of representatives from nine countries to the European Parliament will appear in the winter of 1981–1982. Finally, a new group of books will approach aspects of electoral politics cross-nationally. Volumes under way on left-wing parties in Western Europe, women in national politics, public financing of election campaigns and political parties, and candidate selection and its impact on party systems will combine essays on particular countries already published in the series with a new analysis of the similarities and differences among the countries covered. A complete list of the books in the series can be found at the back of this volume.

The 1979 Italian elections witnessed more than the usual number of changes in the nation's political life, but the "dominant party system" remained intact. As Samuel H. Barnes explains, this is a system where "elections do not determine, at least in the short run, who will form the Government" because "the dominant party is assumed before the election." In Italy this has always been the Christian Democrats (DC), the only party to lead a Western national government for the entire period since the end of the Second World War. Support for the DC has remained so stable that in the past five elections only 0.8 percentage points has separated the party's largest and smallest shares of the popular vote, while its strength in the Chamber of Deputies has stayed between 260 and 267 seats.

But even if the party that will lead the Government is known in advance, Barnes argues that Italian elections "identify which parties are necessary and, sometimes, willing coalition partners." The 1976 elections, for example, gave the Communist party (PCI) 34.4 percent of the votes and 228 seats, which virtually dictated its participation in the Government. As a result, the PCI became the first major European Communist party to share national legislative leadership since the French Communists were expelled from the cabinet nearly three decades earlier. In addition, PCI deputies were elected to the presidency of the Chamber of Deputies and to the chairmanship of eight of its committees. In 1979, however, the PCI suffered its first decline in votes in a national election since the war. Its share of the votes dropped in every province in the country. Between 1976 and 1979, Joseph LaPalombara notes in his chapter on the PCI, the party's membership had declined and some supporters had become less compliant. Giacomo Sani's data suggest that the party was least able to integrate into its electorate voters who had first backed it in 1976 in the areas where its gains had been greatest. Further, as several authors point out, the PCI's influence within the trade union movement had been declining since 1969. Barnes concludes that, "while the election of 1979 by no means ensured that Italy could govern without the PCI, it did seem to push further into the future the time when the PCI, alone or with left partners, could assume control of the Italian Government."

The PCI's electoral losses redounded to the benefit not so much of the DC or the Socialist party (PSI) as of the small parties of the center and the left, which increased their combined share of the vote from 17.1 to 21.4 percent and their chamber seats from 82 to 105. This reversed the pattern of 1976, when parties other than the PCI and the DC had lost votes and seats. In 1979 the Radical party (PR), the most successful of the smaller parties, as Joseph LaPalombara points out, seemed to score well in those regions where the erosion of the PCI vote was heaviest. The PR more than trebled its share of the vote and the size of its parliamentary delegation—according to Robert Leonardi, largely because the party and its charismatic leader, Marco Pannella, adopted uncompromising policy positions of a kind that are available only to politicians unencumbered by the practical considerations that come with holding public office. Drawing on "a mixture of radical chic and anticommunism [they] castigated the PCI for its adherence to Leninist doctrine while at the same time attacking it for having dropped its revolutionary goals in its headlong lunge to work out an agreement with the DC." Between the 1976 and 1979 elections the PR tried to force public confrontations on divisive issues. It managed to bring to referendum a proposal to revoke a public order law and one to repeal legislation for public financing of political campaigns. Sidney Tarrow says the "Radicals, with some exaggeration, claimed a major victory" in the referendums, not because either measure was repealed but because the Communists had to reverse "their earlier opposition to the public order law [and thereby] suffered a symbolic defeat."

The PSI, Italy's third largest party, profited little from the PCI's losses. This, Gianfranco Pasquino suggests, means that if anything remains of the notion of a "socialist area," it "must refer to a large pool of leftist voters few of whom are inclined to support the PSI consistently—the truly floating . . . voters of the left. . . . If the 1979 elections contain a lesson for the leaders of the PSI it is that for some time to come the future will be brighter than the past." Since the PSI has long been "by far the smallest Southern European Socialist party," this is not saying a great deal.

Some major changes in campaign practices in 1979 resulted from quite independent developments in mass communications. William E. Porter describes the rise of independent radio and television stations, which now provide Italian viewers with a very wide choice of information and entertainment. For the first time candidates and parties used these largely unregulated stations on a significant scale. An important side effect of this development was the reduction in the number of outdoor rallies and the size of their audience. Enrico Berlinguer, the Communist leader, for example, "made only fourteen speeches at political rallies but participated in some thirty interviews, press conferences, and roundtables—double the number for 1976." This development is by no means an exclusively Italian phenomenon. For some years parties in most democracies have recognized that they can reach far more people with far less effort by one television and radio broadcast than by a dozen massive public meetings. When used at all, rallies today provide colorful backdrops for political television shows.

A high proportion of the essays in this volume, after noting the disruptive forces in Italian society, still point to stabilizing developments. The quality of reporting in the media has improved; new parties have been accepted into the governing majority; and, while terrorism continues, fewer citizens identify with the terrorists. The 1979 elections themselves provided evidence of increasing stability in the country once called the "sick man of Europe."

The contributors to this volume are Samuel H. Barnes, professor of political science and program director of the center for Political Studies of the Institute for Social Research at the University of Michigan; Karen Beckwith, visiting instructor at Oakland University; Joseph LaPalombara, Arnold Wolfers Professor of Political Science and professor of international management at Yale University; Robert Leonardi, associate professor of political science at DePaul University; Patrick McCarthy, associate professor of political science at Haverford College; Gianfranco Pasquino, professor of political science at the University of Bologna and editor of the journal *Il Mulino*; William E. Porter, professor of journalism at the University of Michigan, Ann Arbor; Giacomo Sani, professor of political science, Ohio State University; Richard M. Scammon, director of the Elections Research Center, Washington, D.C.; Sidney Tarrow, professor of government, Cornell University; and Douglas A. Wertman, a political analyst at the United States International Communication Agency. In addition to writing a chapter and an appendix, Douglas Wertman kindly answered countless questions that arose in the editing of this book.

HOWARD R. PENNIMAN
American Enterprise Institute

1

Three Years of Italian Democracy

Sidney Tarrow

On June 20, 1976, Italy traversed a major milestone. On that day, there was a national legislative election brought on by the defection of the Socialists from a Christian Democratic-led Government, in a context of violence, economic crisis, and political confusion. As a result of that election, the Communists would ultimately have to be included in the majority for the first time since 1947.* The election would leave much unsettled, but one thing was certain: as Samuel Barnes has written, the election "demonstrated that the overwhelming majority of Italians were determined to abide by the existing rules of the game, that there [was] considerable consensus on the nature and functioning of these rules, and that there was no payoff for parties and individuals that sought to alter them."[1]

Three years later, Italy was again at the polls. This time, it was the Communists—who by now had lent their support to two successive Christian Democratic Governments—who brought on the election, amid continuing violence, economic difficulties, and left-wing dissatisfaction. The democratic process would survive the Communists' re-

---

I wish to express my thanks to the contributors to P. Lange and S. Tarrow, eds., *Italy in Transition: Conflict and Consensus* (London: Frank Cass, 1980), also published as a special issue of *West European Politics*, vol. 2 (October 1979), many of whose articles are cited or quoted herein. I owe a special debt to Peter Lange for his advice during the preparation of this chapter, and to Gianfranco Pasquino and Michele Salvati for comments on an earlier version.

*EDITOR'S NOTE: For an explanation of the process of Government formation in Italy and definitions of terms like "opposition," "majority," and "working majority," see appendix A.

[1] Samuel Barnes, "The Consequences of the Elections: An Interpretation," in Howard R. Penniman, ed., *Italy at the Polls: The Parliamentary Elections of 1976* (Washington, D.C.: American Enterprise Institute, 1977), p. 327.

turn to opposition, as it had their support for the Government. But if democracy in Italy was alive and well, why then were new elections necessary, and when, if ever, would the country overcome its permanent aura of crisis and uncertainty? Had the three-year experiment of Christian Democratic–Communist collaboration only proved that elections in Italy are no more than a Hobson's choice between unstable democracy with the Communists in opposition—and the Communists in power with no democracy at all?[2]

In this chapter, I will argue that this interpretation is more pessimistic than the tumultuous events of 1976–1979 would justify. I hope to show that the reality behind the headlines was that of a political class reestablishing its authority and trying to find a balance between the needs of governance and demands from the society. The role of the Communist party (PCI) in this delicate balancing act— which took place under conditions of economic uncertainty, heavy foreign scrutiny, and a near breakdown of civil order—was equivocal but necessary. That of the Christian Democrats (DC) was equally necessary but more equivocal still. That the experiment was not a failure can be seen in the reduction of turbulence and in some modest economic improvements and reforms. But it was less than a success: violence continued and no more stable solution would follow the election of 1979.

In reviewing the events of the 1976–1979 period, three major questions can be asked. First, why did Communist–Christian Democratic collaboration appear a necessity to almost all sectors of the political class, as well as to business and labor? Second, what were the major strains on the majority, both from inside the coalition and from without that would cause it to fall? Third, what was the balance sheet, both in terms of problems inherited from the past and in terms of Italy's evolution as a democracy? Has Italy, as some observers feel, merely gone from crisis to crisis, or has it gone from crisis toward transition to a new political order? After reviewing the events of the period and outlining the strains on the majority, I will return to this theme and argue that—at least for the period in question— Italy was not a "republic without government," but a nation "surviving by governing."[3]

---

[2] Joseph LaPalombara, "Italian Elections as Hobson's Choice," in *Italy at the Polls, 1976*, p. 1.

[3] Percy A. Allum, *Italy—Republic without Government?* (New York: Norton, 1973); Giuseppe Di Palma, *Surviving without Governing: The Italian Parties in Parliament* (Berkeley and Los Angeles: University of California Press, 1977).

Before and After 1976

In the light of events both before and after June 1976, a loyal reader of the Italian press might find the cautious optimism just expressed somewhat surprising. It was during this period that Italy had gained a reputation as the "sick man of Europe." In a book published in 1975 John Earle wrote:

> The most cursory glance suggests that the motive forces in national life have lost momentum, or that their movement is downhill. Governments do not govern, but struggle to survive. The politicians, if we judge by their achievements, seldom rise above mediocrity and inefficiency. Men of stature are rare. Is the country on the verge of revolution, or of a complete breakdown in society?[4]

As we shall see, there were alternatives besides breakdown and revolution. But there is no denying that both before and after 1976 Italy's problems approached what Peter Lange has called a "crisis of accumulation."[5] The hallmark of the crisis in both periods is that it invested economy, society, and political system at the same time. But whether it was a *single* organic crisis—a seamless web of inseparable contradictions, none of which could be solved without posing the problem of replacing the system—is another question.

In his convenient summary of the events leading up to the 1976 elections in the last *Italy at the Polls*, Joseph LaPalombara listed five politically relevant trends:[6]

1. Corruption and clientelism. The mid-1970s were the heyday of political scandals in Italy, with their center in the governing Christian Democratic party. Corruption and clientelism were seen by many as pillars of the DC's system of power, implying that the ruling party had to be removed from Government for the system to be cleansed.

2. Radicalization and terrorism. In the factories, schools, and streets, there were continuing aftershocks of the worker and student

---

[4] John Earle, *Italy in the 1970s* (London: David and Charles, 1975), p. 9.

[5] Peter Lange, "Crisis and Consent, Change and Compromise: Dilemmas of Italian Communism in the 1970s," in Peter Lange and Sidney Tarrow, eds., *Italy in Transition: Conflict and Consensus* (London: Frank Cass, 1980); also published as a special issue of *West European Politics*, vol. 2 (October 1979), p. 122; also see Carlo Donolo, *Mutamento o transizione?* [Change or transition?] (Bologna: Il Mulino, 1977).

[6] LaPalombara, "Italian Elections as Hobson's Choice," pp. 2-13.

movements of 1968–1970, with the additional problem that the young were no longer willing to grant an unquestioning mandate to the major parties. On the extremes, terrorism generated insecurity right up to the 1976 election.

3. *Economic crisis.* Because of rising production costs, fueled both by the big wage gains of the earlier period and by the international economic crisis of 1973–1974, Italy in 1976 had high unemployment, an unstable currency, and raging inflation; this had left the country in debt internationally, raising questions about the effects of external factors on internal politics.

4. *The failure of reform.* The Government—weak, unstable, and scandal-ridden—lacked an efficient bureaucracy, army, and police force with which to confront these problems. Neither administrative reform, educational reform, nor the reform of the loss-ridden public sector appeared possible without a more basic reform of the state, which in turn was retarded by the DC's reliance on patronage to preserve its system of power.

5. *Fear of communism.* These first four—corruption and terrorism, economic crisis, and reform of the state—were the themes that the Communist party, the country's major opposition, hammered away at in the campaign of 1976. The PCI had just gained credit for a successful campaign to legalize divorce in 1974, followed by an electoral surge in local and regional elections in 1975. So real did the Communist threat appear to be in 1976 that many feared a repetition of the "Christ or communism" election of 1948. For some, as LaPalombara concluded, "the worst possible outcome [was] that PCI participation in the cabinet would lead to a Chilean scenario."[7]

With the benefit of hindsight, we can see that a Chilean scenario was never very likely, if only because the failure of the left in Chile had been seen as an "antimodel" by PCI strategists since 1973.[8] From that year on, the Communists—with some internal dissent and ambiva-

---

[7] Ibid., p. 13. LaPalombara goes on to define a Chilean scenario thus: "the flight of capital would accelerate, the Government would prove unable to control wages or inflation, strikes would multiply, international financial institutions would withdraw credit, Italy might be subjected to a *cordon sanitaire* by countries hostile to the Communists, the country would collapse, and a dictatorial regime would emerge to restore order."

[8] For acute discussions of the development of this line, see Lange, "Crisis and Consent, Change and Compromise," pp. 116-121, and Stephen Hellman, "The PCI in Transition: The Origins of the Historic Compromise" (Paper delivered at the Annual Meeting of the American Political Science Association, Chicago, September 1976), partially published in his "The Longest Campaign: Communist Party Strategy and the Elections of 1976," in Penniman, ed., *Italy at the Polls, 1976*, chap. 5.

lence, it is true—had sought a coalition with the DC, the small parties of the center, and the Socialists in what they called a "historic compromise" between the major forces of Italian politics. In the face of such a strategy, not even the most strident anticommunist could picture the PCI with a knife between its teeth, bent on destroying the fabric of democracy. The danger that conservatives saw was that, though Berlinguer might be sincere in his professions of democratic faith, the force of events would lead the PCI, once in the majority, toward more threatening tactics.[9]

The 1976 Elections and After. The results of the 1976 election were too ambiguous to support either the Communists' best hopes or their enemies' worst fears. "If there was a winner in these elections," wrote LaPalombara, "it was the DC," which emerged with the same 38.7 percent of the vote it had won in 1972. Yet the losers were not the Communists; with 34.4 percent of the vote, they had increased their total over 1972 by over seven percentage points and their representation in the Chamber by forty-nine seats. The real losers were "all of the parties—Radicals, Socialists, Democratic Socialists, Republicans, and even the . . . Liberals—that have tried to find viable space between the two giants."[10] This increased polarization led many to fear a left-right confrontation and others to be concerned with the dangers of a "conciliar republic"—a cartel of Catholics and Communists that would exclude the lay forces in the context of a more and more heavily "organized" democracy.

In the weeks that followed, the DC made clear that it had no intention of including in the cabinet, or even in its formal majority, a Communist party that had not yet proved its democratic credentials. Yet several aspects of the vote appeared to augur greater Communist strength in the future and, as a result, to increase the PCI's pressure for inclusion in the Government. First, there was a generational thrust in the electorate which seemed to work in the Communists' favor. As LaPalombara observed, "the parties of the center and the right suffered greater attrition of supporters through death than parties of the left; the parties of the left were more successful than any others in attracting new voters."[11] Second, the 1976 results confirmed and

[9] For a reasoned conservative argument see Giovanni Sartori, "Calculating the Risk," in Austin Ranney and Giovanni Sartori, eds., *Eurocommunism: The Italian Case* (Washington, D.C.: American Enterprise Institute, 1978).

[10] LaPalombara, "Italian Elections as Hobson's Choice," pp. 31, 34.

[11] Ibid., p. 36. Sani's succinct statement of the generational thesis has been published in Italian as "Ricambio elettorale, mutamenti sociali e preferenze politiche" [Electoral renewal, social changes, and political preferences], in Luigi

reinforced the national character of the PCI electorate, as could be seen in the increase in its vote in the South and in the almost equal distribution of the votes of the two main parties in all the major geographic regions.[12] Third, Communist gains in the 1975 local and regional elections and the subsequent control over most of the big cities by the left, would, it could be supposed, inevitably allow the PCI to "capture" many more voters in the future from these cities.

On the other hand, the global distribution of the electorate between left, right, and center had not changed substantially;[13] the South could be a notoriously fickle electoral reservoir, as the PCI had learned in the past;[14] and generational change would only benefit the Communists if young people followed their parents' habit of party loyalty and stayed in the Communist fold after they had once voted for the PCI. There was evidence that the younger voters of the 1970s, unlike their parents in the 1950s and 1960s, had the education and the personal autonomy to remain independent "issue voters" in the future.[15]

If electoral ambiguities were not enough, the international constraints should have alerted observers that no political earthquake was probable. Broadsides from Washington and subtler messages from Bonn made it clear that Italy's allies and creditors were not prepared to go along with political changes that threatened a change of camp on the exposed southern flank of NATO.[16] The continued gravity of

---

Graziano and Sidney Tarrow, eds., *La crisi italiana* [The Italian crisis], vol. 1 (Turin: Einaudi, 1979), pp. 303-328.

[12] LaPalombara, "Italian Elections as Hobson's Choice," p. 37; for a more detailed analysis based upon aggregate data, see Giacomo Sani, "The Italian Electorate in the Mid-1970s: Beyond Tradition?" in Penniman, ed., *Italy at the Polls, 1976*, pp. 89-98.

[13] Giacomo Sani, "Political Traditions as Contextual Variables," *American Journal of Political Science*, vol. 20 (August 1976), pp. 375-406.

[14] Sidney Tarrow, *Peasant Communism in Southern Italy* (New Haven: Yale University Press, 1967), chap. 7.

[15] Arturo Parisi and Gianfranco Pasquino, "Changes in Italian Electoral Behavior: The Relationships between Parties and Voters," in Lange and Tarrow, eds., *Italy in Transition*, pp. 13–23, provide a reasoned critique of, and alternative to, the "generational" thesis of changing Italian electoral behavior, one which depends more on qualitative changes in the voters' motivations than upon quantitative changes in the behavior of various age cohorts in the electorate.

[16] The warnings from Washington went into gear with a statement issued by the State Department on April 6, 1977; they continued into January 1978, when Ambassador Richard Gardner's return to Washington provided the occasion for a major policy review and warning to the Italian Government that the United States would not look kindly upon PCI participation in the government of one of its allies. Bonn was more circumspect, and Chancellor Schmidt at one point advised Washington that its policy goals were more likely to be met if it stopped overtly interfering in Italian affairs.

the economic situation, heightened by a major currency crisis in early 1976, also warned against sudden changes in political direction.[17] And the Socialists—who had brought on the 1976 election—were by no means reliable partners in a Communist strategy that tended to relegate them to the status of second-string allies.

Faced by such constraints, the Communists were not inclined to press their electoral advantage to the point of overt conflict with the DC over entry into the Government in 1976. Placated by formal consultation in the formation of a Government by Giulio Andreotti and satisfied with the choice of Communist Pietro Ingrao as president of the Chamber and a number of committee chairmanships, the PCI abstained in the vote investing Andreotti's all-DC cabinet, carefully calling for a Government of "democratic and national solidarity . . . within the framework of the present-day domestic and international balance of forces."[18] The PSI was rebuffed in its call for an alternative of the left, and the small parties of the center-left (PSDI and PRI) and the moderate right (PLI) acquiesced in a continued DC hold on power in return for permanent consultation—along with the Communists and Socialists—in the making of Government policy.

The Andreotti Formula. The Andreotti formula—which in other countries would have been ruled out as too precarious—survived for for almost three years. It provided something for each of the major political and social actors and a period of social peace and economic revival for Italy.

For the DC, it provided a respite from the torrent of criticism the party had weathered since the beginning of the 1970s on the issues of divorce, scandal, economic mismanagement, and incompetence in defeating terrorism. With Andreotti in the Government and moderates Aldo Moro and Benigno Zaccagnini in the party organization, the DC's delicate internal balance was preserved as well. It was the Moro-Zaccagnini group that had arranged the party's agreement with the other parties, an agreement that would threaten the DC's right wing unless some respectable figure could be found to

---

[17] The 1976 crisis is dealt with succinctly in its economic aspects by Raymond Lubitz in an unpublished paper, "The Italian Economic Crisis of the 1970s" (International Finance Discussion Paper no. 120, June 1978), pp. 26-32. For an analysis that tries to balance economic with political factors, see Michele Salvati, "Muddling Through: Economics and Politics in Italy—1969-1979," in Lange and Tarrow, eds., *Italy in Transition*, pp. 38-39.

[18] Gerardo Chiaromonte, "Il governo e il PCI" [The Government and the PCI], *Rinascita*, August 6, 1976, p. 1.

defend its interests. Andreotti, with his strong ties to the Vatican, his independent political base, and his reputation for firm flexibility, had been prime minister twice before and was made to order as a counterweight to the dominance of Moro and Zaccagnini in the party directorate.

The Andreotti solution also served the interests of the Communists, who needed a sign that their overture to the Christian Democrats was bearing fruit. They found it in the new legitimacy accorded them in the legislature, and in Andreotti's rigorous recourse to the heads of the six parties of his working majority (the DC, PCI, PSI, PSDI, PRI, and PLI) before each new policy initiative went to Parliament. The PCI was consulted on major appointments—an advantage that it soon pressed in the state-run radio and television network— and gained DC cooperation in governing a number of local and regional governments through the formula of the *giunta aperta*, the open cabinet.

However, the PCI did not want too much legitimation too soon, both because its ordinary members and the trade unions were wary of what the critics called *entrismo*, and because the party had a genuine fear of frightening the bourgeoisie into taking its capital out of Italy. The base's ambivalence about the whole experiment and the leaders' fear of a crumbling economy and the chaos that would follow led the Communists to support an honest conservative who would consult them, in preference to a more left-oriented but less reliable Government that would try to deliver too much too soon. They were satisfied for the moment with consultation on policy, abstention in Parliament, and the symbolic legitimation they had craved for nearly three decades.

The Andreotti solution also excluded the Socialists from the cabinet, but this served their interests too. The PSI had brought on the 1976 election in the hope of reversing the long-term fall in the party's fortunes. When this proved mistaken, a new leadership group—the "generation of forty year-olds"—took over, sweeping out the old leaders of the resistance generation, instituting changes in party rules, and, under a new secretary-general, Bettino Craxi, launching a campaign to establish a new PSI "identity" between the two larger mass parties. However, Craxi's majority, which was composed of an ill-assorted combination of left and right-wing factions, was weak, and he needed time to establish both the new line and his own authority. As David Hine writes, Craxi

> needed a period in which the main center of power in the
> party would remain the party organization itself, and not

the ministries and parastate agencies which offered a reservoir of patronage through which individual leaders could obtain party members and preference votes independently of the apparatus.[19]

In addition, the convergence of the PCI and the DC gave Craxi license to criticize both. Paradoxically, the PSI could pose as "autonomous" in contrast to the two major forces in a Government the Socialists were supposed to be supporting![20]

Given the agreement of the three major parties, the smaller "lay" parties of the center and center-right had little choice. The Liberals (PLI), who had lost heavily in 1976, could consider themselves lucky to be included in Andreotti's "programmatic majority," a fact that they owed largely to his desire to calm the fears of business. As for the center Republicans (PRI) and the Social Democrats (PSDI), they were impressed with the usefulness of involving the Communists in economic policy while keeping them out of the Government. Republican leader Ugo La Malfa, for years a searing critic of the Communists, even eventually supported the PCI's inclusion in the majority, on the ground that this would have a moderating influence on organized labor.

Andreotti's game was more complex, which is why he refused to allow the Communists the formal entry into the Government that they eventually demanded. For as well as involving the PCI in an austerity coalition and satisfying the smaller parties that he did not seek permanent DC monopoly, Andreotti had the conservative factions of his own party to worry about, not to mention the international financial community, on which Italy was dependent, and the United States. The latter made it clear that it would not tolerate Communist ministers in the Government when its newly chosen ambassador, Richard Gardner, came home for consultations following the fall of Andreotti's first Government in early 1978. What resulted was an abrupt, but ultimately successful, State Department statement declaring: "The United States and Italy share profound democratic values and interests, and we do not believe that the

---

[19] David Hine, "Surviving or Reviving? The Italian Socialist Party under Craxi," in Lange and Tarrow, eds., *Italy in Transition*, p. 140. Also see Gianfranco Pasquino's chapter in this volume. For an explanation of "preference votes," see chapter 2, fn. 3, in this volume.

[20] Hines writes: "the P.S.I., as a pivotal party, seems to do better when the two larger parties are converging than when they are polarized. In the former case, the Party can afford to stand aloof and hope to win support from a variety of different groups opposed to the collusion of the giants." "Surviving or Reviving?" p. 140.

Communists share those values and interests."[21] The second Andreotti Government, which admitted the PCI into the majority but not into the Government, was at least in part a response to Washington's pressure and to the domestic sectors of opinion that remained, despite everything, fundamentally pro-American.[22]

A new relationship with the major productive forces—business and labor—was another important element in the Andreotti formula. Beginning in the late 1960s, labor had been intransigent in its negotiations with government, but between 1976 and 1979 its strategy evolved, and episodic cooperation became possible. With exceptions to be described below, there was a revival of production and of international competitiveness for Italian industry during these years, due in no small part to the inclusion of the parties of the left in the majority, but also to Andreotti's attempt to bring organized labor closer to economic policy making.

For different reasons, business after 1976 regained some of its confidence in the Italian state's capacity to run the economy. Desperately in need of capital, and paralyzed by a bitter heritage of labor conflict, business in 1976 was prepared to cooperate with a Government whose majority included the Communists in exchange for a calmer industrial climate and for Government help in restructuring obsolete and labor-intensive industries. The presence of respected "technicians" in the Andreotti Government and at the helm of the Bank of Italy also helped to restore industry's shaken confidence. Improved business confidence and labor's cooperative attitude were the factors most responsible for the relative social peace and the modest economic recovery that, between them, helped to reverse Italians' sense that their country was going down the drain.

These were the conditions which would make possible the relative political stability of the three years from 1976 to 1979. Gianfranco Pasquino writes, "One single prime minister, Giulio Andreotti, was able to survive (and, for that matter, to thrive) through the creation of three different types of Governments."[23] All three had all-DC cabinets. The first (technically, the third Andreotti Government) enjoyed the abstention of the other parties with the exception of the very extreme right and left; after July 1977 it operated under a "programmatic accord" hammered out by the secretaries of the six

[21] State Department official statement, January 12, 1978.

[22] Robert D. Putnam, "Italian Foreign Policy: The Emergent Consensus," in Penniman, ed., *Italy at the Polls, 1976*, pp. 308-312.

[23] Gianfranco Pasquino, "In Search of a Stable Governmental Coalition: The Italian Parliamentary Elections of 1979," Occasional Paper, School of Advanced International Studies, Bologna (1980), p. 1.

major parties. This Government lasted 536 days, almost *twice* the length of the average postwar Italian Government. It was forced to resign in January 1978, when the PCI demanded a formal role in the Government. This triggered the long governmental crisis that ended in March 1978 with the PCI in the majority but not in the cabinet.

This second Government formed after the 1976 elections (the fourth Andreotti Government) lasted for less than a year—the most turbulent in Italy's postwar history—and finally fell because of the Communists' renewed demands for cabinet posts. After a long governmental crisis marked by the failure of a compromise proposal to admit "technicians" acceptable to the PCI into the cabinet, Andreotti formed a somewhat broader Government in March 1979, whose real purpose was to prepare the way for new elections; the PCI was outside the majority and the small parties of the center were in the Government.[24]

The stratagem worked. In June 1979, there would be major gains for the smaller parties, a stable position for the DC, and a large electoral setback for the Communists, who declined from their electoral pinnacle of 1976 to just over 30 percent of the vote and 201 seats in the Chamber, a loss of twenty-seven seats. The PCI, as LaPalombara observes in this volume, lost among younger voters, among the urban working class, in the South, and among a number of "single issue" constituencies; in addition, many of the protest voters who cast blank or invalid ballots were probably former party supporters.[25] The Communists had made errors during the Andreotti years, as their leaders were quick to concede and as numerous authors pointed out. But beneath the political hurly-burly, there were societal and structural factors that made the PCI's tactical errors only secondary. These we will discuss under the headings of changes in the electorate, the labor movement, and the terrorist phenomenon, before examining the collapse of the Andreotti formula and turning to a general assessment of what the 1976–1979 period meant for the future of Italian politics.

Voters, Unions, Terrorists

As must already be clear, 1976 marked a political turnover in Italy. Old shibboleths were shattered and new political formulas invented. The three years that followed were similarly turbulent: three Governments came and went; a head of state resigned under a cloud of scan-

---

[24] Ibid., p. 3.
[25] See LaPalombara's chapter in this volume.

dal; a prominent political leader was kidnapped and brutally murdered; and strains within the PCI finally brought on new elections. But under the roiled surface of a political system adapting to the electoral "earthquakes" of 1975 and 1976, Italian society was hardening in a new mold that combined elements of change and tradition. These structural factors go further toward explaining the outcome of the 1979 election than the errors of the Communists, the shrewdness of the Andreotti formula, or the occasional unsolicited intervention of American policy makers.

The Electorate. The first half of the 1970s was a period of social turmoil in Italy, and it was this that had led to the electoral "earthquakes" of 1975 and 1976. The level of politicization was immensely high during the early 1970s—in schools and factories, in local government, and in the streets. Permanent and decentralized industrial conflict made life difficult for union leaders as well as management, and areas of Italian life that had been insulated from politics in the past—like the family—were frequently split by generational and political conflict. Entire occupational and educational sectors were in a state of near-permanent committee of the whole—*assemblearismo*, as critics called it—with devastating effects on patience, productivity, and social peace.[26]

After 1976, the curve of popular mobilization turned sharply downward, and many of the grass-roots institutions that had been created to reflect it—neighborhood councils, parents' associations in the schools, faculty assemblies in the universities—began to suffer a decline in participation and a routinization as stultifying as that of the institutions they had been created to replace. This demobilization was the harbinger of a conservative trend in the electorate.

At the same time, the youth vote that had helped to carry the left toward participation in the majority in 1976 began to show signs of independence and dispersion. Still heavily influenced by the anti-institutional ideology of the "movement" of the early 1970s, many young people continued to participate in manifestations of dissent after 1976, but now directed as much against the Communists as against their conservative allies. (The fact that the major manifestation of the young people's revolt during this period took place in Bologna, a Communist stronghold, is significant.) At the same time, the tiny Radical party (PR), under the charismatic leadership of Marco Pannella, began to stir, attracting the votes of the discontented with

[26] Giuseppe Di Palma, "The Available State: Problems of Reform," in Lange and Tarrow, eds., *Italy in Transition*, pp. 161-164.

a sweeping denunciation of the collusion (*ammucchiata*) of the institutional parties.

The combination of the demobilization of most of Italian society and the continued electoral mobility of youth hit the Communists hardest. This was evident as early as 1977 and 1978, when two rounds of partial elections showed not only a decline for the PCI, but growth for the DC, recovery for the PSI and the minor parties, and the emergence in several areas of local and regionalist lists. Its losses in the South disturbed the PCI most of all, since in 1976 the party had registered nearly even support in all the geographic regions. Local and regional PCI leaders soon began to suffer the typical symptom of crisis in Communist parties—criticism and self-criticism in the party press.[27]

If the local elections showed that the Communist advance had been reversed, two referendum campaigns in June 1978 proved that *all* the major parties had problems. Much of the political debate in the first half of 1978 was dominated by the attempt of the Radicals to put a number of potentially divisive referendums on the ballot.[28] The major parties, acting in close concert, succeeded in cutting down the raft of Radical proposals to two, but each was potentially explosive: first, a proposal to revoke the tough law on public order that had been passed in 1975 (over Communist opposition) to fight terrorism; and, second, a proposal to strike down the law establishing public financing of political parties, to which the "institutional" parties were understandably committed.

Coming in the midst of a wave of terrorism in the spring of 1978, the proposal to revoke the public order law was bound to fail, and, indeed, the results showed that over three-fourths of the public supported the law. But in the midst of a continuing economic crisis, when

[27] The PCI's first response was to hedge about the extent of its electoral losses in 1978 and to scoff at "those commentators who attribute to the electoral sample . . . an absolute value that can be generalized to the entire country, and even pull out of an electronic brain the results of fantasmagoric political elections." Adalberto Minucci, "Prima e dopo il voto" [Before and after the vote], as well as Celso Ghini, "Analisi del primo voto dopo il 16 marzo" [Analysis of the first vote after March 16], both in *Rinascita*, May 19, 1978, pp. 1-2, 3-4. However, a more reflective—and therefore pessimistic—interpretation came two weeks later from Paolo Franchi who observed that the DC leadership had emerged more powerful from the Moro affair and that the local elections showed the existence of a fluctuating vote moving from left to right. See his "In che cosa cambia la DC?" [In what way has the DC changed?], *Rinascita*, May 26, 1978, pp. 3-4.

[28] On the phenomenon of the "new" Radical party, see Massimo Teodori, Piero Ignazi, and Angelo Panebianco, *I nuovi radicali* [The new Radicals] (Milan: A. Mondadori, 1977).

the Government was campaigning for "austerity," the proposal to end public financing did much better; only 56 percent of the electorate voted in favor of retaining the law even though all the institutional parties supported it.[29] The Radicals, with some exaggeration, claimed a major victory. The Communists, who had reversed their earlier opposition to the public order law, suffered a symbolic defeat, especially on public financing, qualified only by the fact that both Radical proposals were more easily defeated in areas of PCI strength than elsewhere.

The referendums too hurt all the major parties, however. "Not all of those who wanted to repeal the laws could be located on the left of the political spectrum," observes Pasquino. "If a lesson has to be learned from the June 1978 referendums, its basic content regards the dissatisfaction of large sections of the electorate and their inclination to slip away from the grip of the major parties."[30] Although this threat existed for the DC as well, the governing party's core electorate appeared to be stable, while the PCI's biggest gains had come from younger and southern voters whose party loyalty was not yet established and who could be more readily influenced by the issues of the moment than their compatriots.

The Labor Movement. There were other strains on the majority which came from Italian society. In the early 1970s, the Italian labor movement had become more unified politically—a process that considerably increased its bargaining power with management—and more decentralized internally, with factory committees open to all the workers in a firm replacing more narrowly based union structures.[31] The mid-1970s saw a partial recentralization of power within each national confederation, while interconfederal unity remained more or less at the level it had reached by 1975. While these trends—recentralization and interconfederal unity—strengthened the Government's hand in dealing with the economy, there were counterpressures, both at the base and at the summit of the labor movement, which made it im-

---

[29] On the referendum results, see Arturo Parisi and Maurizio Rossi, "Le relazioni partiti-elettori: quale lezione?" [Party-voter relations: What is the lesson?], Il Mulino (July-August 1978), pp. 503-547, and Gianfranco Pasquino, "Referendum: l'analisi del voto" [Referendum: Analysis of the vote], Mondo Operaio (July-August 1978), pp. 18-24.

[30] Pasquino, "In Search of a Stable Governmental Coalition," pp. 3-4.

[31] Marino Regini, "Changing Relationships between Labor Unions and the State in Italy: Towards a Neo-Corporatist System?" in G. Lehmbruch and P. Schmitter, eds., Variations in the Pattern of Corporatist Policy-Formation (London: Sage Publications, forthcoming).

possible for either management or the Government to discount the possibility of a renewal of working-class militance.

The high point of labor's cooperative attitude toward the Andreotti Government came in early 1978, when an interconfederal conference at the EUR convention center in Rome endorsed the Government's austerity program. It was in connection with this meeting, carefully prepared but broadly contested, that Luciano Lama, leader of the Italian General Confederation of Workers (CGIL), pointed out that wage increases cannot be regarded as a variable independent of productivity. But the EUR platform also revealed the cracks in labor's unity, as leaders of the Catholic-led Italian Confederation of Workers' Unions (CISL) and even some Socialist and Communist CGIL leaders called for the labor movement to put greater pressure on a Government whose economic policy had, so far, done little to meet labor's demands.

However, examining strike statistics, we see that these were straws in the wind, not general trends. From 177 million man-hours lost in 1976, industrial action declined to 15 million hours lost in 1977 and to 71 million in 1978.[32] However, the unions were in a quandary about how to carry out their traditional functions under a wage system in which most wage increases were the result of automatic indexation—the so-called *scala mobile*. They thus began to demand more public investment and increased employment, trying in this way to appeal to what Marino Regini calls their "secondary constituency"—the unemployed, youth, and the South [33]—while supporting a Government that called for austerity.

At the same time, the labor confederations had great difficulty holding their members in check in the face of the so-called autonomous unions' refusal to go along with wage restraint. There was also tension between the CGIL and the other two main confederations about the extent of the former's subservience to the PCI. And there were a number of cases of industrial violence, including one—at the Alfa Romeo plant outside of Milan—in which the confederations had to send militants to the factory gate to protect workers reporting for overtime.

The most politically disruptive labor dispute, which took place in early 1978, also showed that the strains were structural. It was between paramedical workers and the state, which, through the

[32] Organization for Economic Cooperation and Development, *Main Economic Indicators* (August 1979), pp. 110-113.

[33] Marino Regini, "Labour Unions, Industrial Action and Politics," in Lange and Tarrow, eds., *Italy in Transition*, pp. 60-61. Also Salvati, "Muddling Through," pp. 44-45.

regional governments, finances most of Italy's hospital system. The wages of these public employees had continually lagged behind still rampant inflation. But salaries in the public sector were one of the few tools with which the Government could attack inflation directly, and despite the wavering of the regional governments, the Ministry of Health refused to raise them—until two of the regions gave in. In the confrontation that followed, the health minister was forced to resign and the Communists—faced with the determination of the hospital staffs and the distress of their patients—compromised their previously firm support for austerity. The Andreotti Government emerged almost intact, but the PCI was weakened by the obvious contradiction between the wage restraint its representatives called for in the CGIL and the party's vacillation before the aroused hospital workers. The Communist dilemma was revealed in a survey of PCI workers: only a bare majority felt that the party's commitment to the factory was still sufficient.[34]

It was mainly labor pressure on the PCI—and the unease of working-class oriented leaders within the party—that led the Communists to put pressure on Andreotti in January 1978 for cabinet seats. In the extended negotiations which followed, labor's demands for structural reform and increased public investment in the South were given broad public airing.[35] But in the end, as LaPalombara observes in this volume, the concessions made to the trade unions were largely cosmetic, and there was "abundant evidence that all of the trade unions, including the CGIL, were fundamentally unsatisfied with the policy directions proposed by Andreotti."[36] The structural strains within the labor movement were an underlying cause of the PCI's problems, and thus of the eventual collapse of the Andreotti formula.

Terrorism. It was the increasing attacks against law and order that most sorely tested the Andreotti majority. The decline in popular political mobilization from the first half of the decade had a number of negative consequences, most forbidding among them the separation between the "institutional" extreme left—parties like Lotta Continua (Continuous Struggle) and Avanguardia Operaia (Working-class Vanguard)—and a violent fringe that increasingly clustered around the Red Brigades and other professional terrorist organizations. The pro-

---

[34] R. Mannheimer, M. Rodrigues, and C. Sebastiani, *Gli operai comunisti* [The Communist workers] (Rome: Editori Riuniti, 1979), p. 110.

[35] See Vittorio Siva, "E i sindacati non sono certo teneri" [And the trade unions are not tender], *La Repubblica*, February 17, 1978, p. 3.

[36] See chapter 4, p. 123.

fessionalization of violent protest symbolized the isolation of the extremists in a society that was weary of mobilization; but it also brought out the extreme weakness of the party system, the police, and the army, which would test the fragile fabric of what is, after all, a young democratic state.

Already in 1976, a wave of kidnappings, bombings, and political shootings threatened to destroy civil order. Soon after the 1976 election, a reorganization of the security services revealed widespread disaffection, competition between services, and duplication of activities in the fight against terrorism. The reorganization was not yet complete when the strategy of the regime's opponents took a different tack. Instead of attacking the prominent, they began to single out men at the middle levels of power: in management, journalism, prison administration, and even the trade unions. If even an ordinary citizen could not feel secure walking from his front door to his car, either civil society would crumble of its own weight or the regime would be forced into a degree of repression that would strip away any semblance of the rule of law.[37]

It was a tribute to the coolness under fire of the political class that a truly repressive policy was not instituted during most of the three-year period. However—partly because the structure of the security services was still shaky—police incompetence led repeatedly to violence as demonstrations were broken up and suspects arrested. In Bologna in March 1977 an extreme-left youth demonstration frightened the police into killing a demonstrator. The army was called in, and the Communist mayor, Renato Zangheri, urged vigilance against extremism. In this atmosphere, the city's left-wing administration had to suffer the humiliation of an even larger left-wing demonstration under the windows of city hall in the "model" city of Italy's Red Belt.[38]

Both police incompetence and calls for "vigilance" came to a head in the kidnapping in broad daylight and the eventual murder of DC President Aldo Moro by the Red Brigades in the spring of 1978. In the six weeks between the kidnapping in March and the murder, the DC held firm in the face of the agony of its leader, but the most intense pressure against compromising with the terrorists came from the PCI. The Communists were scathing in their criticism of anyone who dared to talk of a flexible approach to Moro's captors; they also

[37] A turning point was the murder of the vice-director of Turin's respected *La Stampa* in November 1977. See *Corriere della Sera*, November 30, 1977, p. 1.
[38] The shrillness of the PCI response can be glimpsed in an interview given by Mayor Zangheri entitled "Perché Bologna?" [Why Bologna?], *Rinascita*, March 18, 1977.

called for greater internal party discipline. Only Bettino Craxi's Socialists urged a "more humanitarian" approach and priority on saving Moro's life.[39]

Although Aldo Moro was president of the Christian Democratic party, his murder was an attack aimed at the PCI, for he was on his way to Parliament to speak in favor of the installation of the fourth Andreotti Government when he was seized. Writes Peter Lange:

> The conjunction of the two events was neither accidental nor without its ironies. The entrance of the PCI into the majority was the apogee of success for the policy of accommodation and national unity which the PCI had been pursuing for a number of years. . . . The terrorism, in contrast, represented the most extreme form of discontent with the politics of unity and with the compromises and at best half measures of reform which could be expected to result.[40]

Though all the parties of the majority were placed under extreme strain by the Moro affair, it was the PCI that suffered the worst blows. For the Communists could not win. Had they called for flexibility in dealing with the Red Brigades, they would have invited the accusation of being soft on terrorism. But their actual policy was no more successful. Cooperating with the police and calling for "revolutionary vigilance" against extremists alienated fearful liberals and failed to placate conservatives, while leaving the party's working-class base indifferent. When a shift to the right is in motion, the old rule still applies that parties of the left cannot stop it by shifting to the right themselves.

Andreotti's Collapse and the Election Campaign

These were the strains underlying the three years of Andreotti's prime ministership: an electorate that was, for the most part, demobilized and, with respect to its younger and southern cohorts, unpredictable; a labor movement in uneasy symbiosis with the Government and a thorn in the side of the PCI; and a terrorist fringe that eroded the left each time it attacked the establishment. Because the PCI was in the line of fire of each of these forces, it was the Communists who brought Andreotti down. Bridging the major ideological fault line in Italian politics had been possible only in the conditions of the mid-1970s. As the decade evolved, the strains beneath the surface became too

[39] See Gianfranco Pasquino's chapter in this volume for the PSI's strategy during the Moro affair.
[40] Peter Lange, "Crisis and Consent," p. 110.

strong for such a fragile and complicated political formula to survive. In fact, as I shall show below, Andreotti's very *success* made both him and his formula expendable, especially for those elements in the party system which had never been happy with either. These came together before and after the June 1979 elections to revive a form of government which had been discredited during the early 1970s: a coalition between the parties of the center-left—including the Socialists—and the DC.

The PCI: From Compromise to "Constructive Opposition." It was the Communists who precipitated the election when their compromises on the formation of the fourth Andreotti Government brought no relief from internal and trade union pressures and when, following the Moro affair, they began to experience heightened attacks from their partners as well. Though the move toward opposition began at a Central Committee meeting in the summer of 1978 and continued through the fall of that year, it culminated at the party's fifteenth congress in March 1979. In the meantime, the fourth Andreotti Government had fallen and the fifth—really only a Government of transition—had been formed.

Why did the Communists wait so long to launch their campaign for the 1979 election? They did so partly because they did not want to pull out in the atmosphere of national unity that had been created during the Moro affair; partly because they needed an issue on which the DC was arguably hurting the interests of the workers; and partly because a party congress was needed to recompose the fabric of party unity before party leaders could feel confident going into what promised to be a searing electoral campaign.

But there were penalties for delay. In the first place, the fifteenth congress had been built up for many observers as an occasion at which the PCI would answer its political critics and clarify its theoretical stands on a number of key problems relating to Leninism, democracy, reform versus revolution, and so on. In the atmosphere of an impending election campaign, such issues could not be seriously debated, lest—as in the Spanish Communist party not long before—they reveal the divergences among party militants on these central issues.

The second major cost of delay was that Andreotti, knowing an election to be imminent, had the time to form a Government of transition which included the two minor center parties, permitting the latter to go into the election as parties of both Government and opposition—Government with Andreotti and opposition to the Communists! The gains of the PSDI could partly be explained in this way.

The fifteenth congress also failed to clear up the ambiguities in the PCI's general line.[41] The underlying strategy of the "historic compromise" was nowhere revised in the congress documents, although more prominence was given to the party's historic alliance with the Socialists than to its failing alliance with political Catholicism. As for the party's internal life, though criticisms were launched at the Soviet Union, democratic centralism remained largely untouched as the basis of the party's organization. The PCI went into the 1979 election on the attack, denouncing its former allies for failing to meet their programmatic commitments and for their political anticommunism, yet offering no clear opposition program or alternative coalition that would send the DC into opposition. Though its tone was more strident than before, the PCI was unwilling to sacrifice its basic strategic commitment to compromise for the sake of tactical electoral gains. The efficacy of its campaign was thus weakened, and its leaders failed to regain the image of militance needed to arrest their party's decline.

The DC: From "Confronto" to Confrontation. Although it was the PCI that precipitated the 1979 elections, Andreotti's fall was brought about by his success. Andreotti had gained the support of moderates within and outside his party because of the unusual gravity of Italy's crisis in 1976 and because he was supported by the Moro-Zaccagnini coalition in the party organization. When Moro died, one of the main pillars of this edifice collapsed. But even apart from the Moro affair, Andreotti's success in reversing an apparently inexorable economic decline sealed the fate of his formula and of his own political fortunes for the time being. In the long run, the fact that Andreotti enjoyed the unique collaboration of the parties of the "constitutional spectrum," the cooperation of business and labor, and the passive agreement of Italy's international creditors would have profound implications for the future. But in the short run, his success had the opposite effect: it emboldened both conservatives and moderates to seek alternative governmental formulas and isolated Andreotti within his party and the Communists on the left.

This can best be seen in the DC's attitude to economic policy. As Peter Lange writes, "the DC seemed increasingly ready to risk confrontation rather than make any more concessions to the PCI."[42] The trend came to a head between September and the end of the year,

---

[41] See the draft theses of the congress, published in *The Italian Communists* (Special Issue), 1978.
[42] Lange, "Crisis and Consent," p. 127.

when Treasury Minister Filippo Maria Pandolfi convinced the Government to push for Italian entry into the European Monetary System under terms that seemed to require a ceiling on real wages for at least three years.[43] This challenge to the labor movement could not go unanswered by the Communists, despite Andreotti's efforts to find a compromise that would allow them to stay in his majority. Here was the major policy issue that the PCI needed on which to go into opposition.

Events were more complicated inside the DC where—despite the ascendancy of the Moro-Zaccagnini faction at the 1976 party congress—an anti-Zaccagnini coalition had maintained its strength in the party organization. By the summer of 1978, with Moro gone and the PCI in disarray, "there was a growing desire of a number of DC leaders for a departure from the strategy Moro had designed," as Douglas Wertman shows in his chapter in this volume.[44] While Andreotti was calling for a mere *confronto* (comparison and competition of ideas) between the DC and the Communists, the right wanted to return to real confrontation, to "a correct distinction between the roles of majority and minority,"[45] a line that they stressed with increasing stridency as the election approached. That the DC chose to run a classical anticommunist campaign reflects the growing influence of these groups within the party as the country's economic picture brightened and the need for continued PCI support declined.[46]

The Socialists: From Alternative to "Autonomy." The evolution of the PSI was less straightforward. The politics of the situation was that of a classical intermediate party caught between two large parties whose collaboration threatened its survival. While the PSI's collaboration was desired by both the PCI and the DC as long as their own cooperation lasted, strictly speaking it could be dispensed with (as the Socialists learned to their bitterness) in key policy areas. The big decisions were made over their heads.

Where the PSI's collaboration *would* be essential was in a center-left Government of the type that had governed Italy during most of the 1960s. The party's problem was that it had been tainted with both reformism and ineffectiveness during that experience and had been loudly denouncing it ever since. No Socialist leader who wanted

---

[43] Salvati, "Muddling Through," pp. 42-43.

[44] See chapter 3, p. 84.

[45] Ibid., and the article cited in footnote 33 in that chapter.

[46] See Gianfranco Pasquino's "Italian Christian Democracy: A Party for All Seasons," in Lange and Tarrow, eds., *Italy in Transition*, pp. 91, 105-108, for an excellent summary of the factional currents in the DC during this period.

21

to survive politically could afford to call for a repeat performance of the center-left, but neither could he ignore that his own party's future would be more secure with the PCI back in opposition than with the Communists cooperating with the DC. Like it or not, the PSI was obliged to try to expand its own political space at the expense of the PCI.

The opening rounds in this attack—as befits so intellectual a party—were theoretical. Well before the Moro affair, a group of PSI intellectuals had begun a debate with the PCI on the compatibility of the PCI's version of Marxism with democracy.[47] In early 1978, many of these contributed to a "Project for a Socialist Alternative," prepared for the March 1978 party congress. The project, in David Hine's words,

> represented the response of the new leadership to the challenge of Eurocommunism . . . calling upon the PCI to show its full legitimacy by denouncing the communist states of Eastern Europe, working with the PSI towards an alternation in power in the framework of competitive pluralism, and renouncing the . . . essentially anti-competitive historic compromise strategy.[48]

Unfortunately for this bold effort, the project was overwhelmed by the Moro affair and by the referendums of June. But Craxi renewed the attack following the PSI's successful performance in the May 1978 local elections in an *Espresso* article in which he condemned "the philosophical thread linking the Jacobin tradition of élitist, centralizing authoritarianism with the Leninist route to power."[49] This was a classical attack on the PCI from the right. But Craxi also attacked from the left, "presenting the PCI as too moderate, both in its stances on political-economic policy and on public order."[50]

Though Craxi could hardly admit it, there was a congruence between his attacks on the PCI and the more subtle changes at work in the DC: both tended to ease the Communists out of the majority (this was largely accomplished by the end of 1978) and led toward a renewal, in suitably updated form, of the alliance between the DC and the PSI that had been the dominant governmental formula during most of the 1960s.

---

[47] For a sample of the debate, see F. Coen, ed., *Egemonia e democrazia* [Hegemony and democracy] (Rome: Quaderni de Mondoperaio, 1977), and the articles in *Rinascita* from September 1976 through February 1977 on the subject.

[48] Hine, "Surviving or Reviving?" p. 138.

[49] Ibid., p. 139. Craxi's article appears in *l'Espresso* of August 27, 1978.

[50] Lange, "Crisis and Consent," p. 128.

But the Socialists could not run an electoral campaign on the theme of the center-left; it would have meant alienating the left wing of the party and many of its nostalgically radical voters. They chose instead the campaign theme of "governability," proclaiming fidelity to the Communist-Socialist alliance but denouncing the Andreotti formula in terms that condemned the two major parties in equal measure. "The only promise that the DC and the PCI make to the voters is to produce all over again the ungovernability of the country by prolonging . . . their mutual vetoes and mutual ultimatums," said a Socialist leader.[51] The Socialists' failure to maintain the momentum of 1977 and 1978 in the 1979 elections may have been due in part to the lassitude of a campaign based on so uninspiring a theme as "governability."

The Minor Parties: Pygmies among Giants or Mice among Elephants?
Whenever the larger parties cannot agree on their direction, Robert Leonardi points out in chapter 6 in this volume, the small parties gain in importance. This was clearly the case as the 1976–1979 period came to an end, especially with respect to the smaller lay parties, the Liberals, Republicans, and Social Democrats, and the big surprise of the 1979 election campaign, the Radicals. Although a clear picture is hard to obtain for all four of these parties, in general, their position and their gains and losses added fuel to the impetus to return to some version of the center-left formula.

This was most obvious for the Liberals, who had left the Andreotti coalition in March 1978, calling for an end to Communist participation in the majority. By early 1979, the Liberals had been joined in this theme by the Social Democrats, who hoped to establish a new kind of center-left Government which the lay parties would prevent from once again being dominated by the DC. It was in order to bring such a Government about that PSDI secretary Pietro Longo launched the trial balloon of a Socialist prime minister. But he made little headway, even with the Socialists, until after the elections had been held.

The Republicans took much longer to come around to the idea that a center-left Government might replace the Andreotti formula. In fact, Republican leader La Malfa had called for the Communists' participation in the Government earlier in the Andreotti period, on the theory that only in this way would the PCI's influence over the workers be used to restrain wage demands. When La Malfa died

[51] The words are those of a close confederate of Craxi, Claudio Martelli, in an interview published in *Corriere della Sera*, June 2, 1979, p. 2.

shortly before the 1979 election, his party drifted into a kind of "silent majority" campaign, calling for a reaffirmation of the market economy and a restructuring of the role of Parliament. But it was strategically oriented toward a center-left solution too, as events soon after the election were to show.

The only one of the minor lay parties *not* oriented toward a center-left formula, either openly or covertly, was the Radical party, which argued during the 1979 campaign that "the governing parties from the Communists to the Christian Democrats were insensitive to society's needs and as a result were destroying any semblance of social order and justice."[52] It sought an increase in Radical votes so that the PCI would "renounce its historic compromise strategy and join the PR and other leftist forces in forging a leftist alternative." This goal was obviously at cross-purposes with those of the Communists, who refused to even admit that the Radicals were part of the left. Their losses were widely interpreted to have been caused by the Radicals' widespread appeal to young people, the disaffected, and workers embittered by the PCI's recent collaboration with the DC. Whatever the cause, the Radicals fought an extremely effective campaign, intelligently utilizing both Pannella's charisma and the newly liberalized media and winning enough seats to remain visible in Parliament after the elections.

The Campaign. The election campaign of 1979 was a lackluster one, in part because the themes of the major parties were uninspired, but in part because the public was simply exhausted after the repeated elections and crises of the previous few years. Both public television and the growing number of private stations were deluged with election news and debates, and the traditional meetings in city piazzas had a much lower attendance than at any time in the past.

A curiosity of the campaign was that the issues were for a time obscured by jockeying among the parties over the election date. Italy was scheduled to hold its first direct election to the European Parliament on the second weekend in June. The Socialist strategy all along had been to hold off on new legislative elections until after the European elections—presumably producing a favorable Socialist vote throughout Europe that would help the PSI to fight the Italian election under the "European" banner as colleagues of the more powerful socialist parties of northern Europe. But the PSI's hope was utopian, given the Communists' determination to hold a national election as

---

[52] This quotation and that in the next sentence are from chapter 6, on which I have drawn repeatedly in this section.

soon as possible after their congress and the DC's power to schedule it when it liked. And so, after a three-year period of almost continual crises, elections, referendums, terrorist attacks, and scandals, Italy went to the polls in 1979 for two weekends in a row, a timetable which further confused an already complicated electoral season and a wearied electorate.

The results should by now be clear and will, in any case, be exhaustively treated in the chapters that follow. The PCI suffered major losses in both the national and the European elections; the DC vote was stable in the first and went down in the second; the Socialists were disappointed, maintaining their poll from 1976 in the national elections and increasing it only slightly in the European ones; and the big percentage winners were the smaller lay parties, especially the Radicals, but also the Liberals and Social Democrats, who had in common with the Radicals only that they were small, lay, and had argued against the collusion of the larger parties since well before the election. The extreme right maintained its roughly 6 percent of the electorate in both elections.

Though there was no enthusiasm in any camp for a return to a center-left Government, there was no longer a majority for the Andreotti formula, either among the parties of the center-left or in the DC, where the anti-Zaccagnini forces soon regained control of the party organization. The PCI emerged from the election refusing any cooperation except on its terms: a Government with Communist ministers. The minor parties jockeyed for position in the eventual center-left coalition that would emerge after a brief "transition" under Christian Democrat Francesco Cossiga. And the Socialists went through a major leadership crisis which reduced the power of Bettino Craxi in the party organization but still left him in a position to "represent the working class" in the Government that was formed by the Republicans and Christian Democrats in early 1980. Andreotti remained very much in the wings, a favorite speaker at DC conferences but a man whose very success in reweaving the shredded fabric of national life between 1976 and 1979 had made him, for the moment, redundant in the party and in the country.

Three Years of Italian Democracy

What had the Andreotti years accomplished? "The balance sheet of this bipolar system," claimed a Socialist leader in the 1979 campaign, is "not at all flattering: two years of immobilism, one of confrontation."[53] As against this partisan condemnation, we have Michele Sal-

[53] From Martelli interview, *Corriere della Sera*, June 2, 1979, p. 2.

25

vati's judgment that "the period from the end of 1976 to the beginning of 1979 saw one of the most stable governmental formations of the whole decade," one which permitted the Italian economy to be stabilized and directed.[54]

Was the experiment a failure or a success? Was the Andreotti formula—which can be summarized as one hand outstretched to the Communists while the other held them at bay—something more than a political success for the Christian Democrats, which it assuredly was? It is too soon for a balanced judgment to be put forward on what is, in any case, a highly subjective question. But in concluding, I will argue that the period 1976–1979 had positive results for three features of the Italian scene that go well beyond the political standing of the governing party: the nature and dynamics of the Italian crisis; the relations between the state and the Communist party; and expectations about the power of Italian democracy to survive under stress.

Unravelling the Crisis. Between 1969 and 1973, Italian society underwent a general convulsion that—as in other Western democracies— was jointly due to increased labor militance and to largely middle-class demands for participation.[55] The uniqueness of Italy's crisis arose from the fact that the results of the 1969–1973 period had not yet been assimilated when the burdens of its 1974–1976 financial crises were encountered.[56] The result was a number of contradictory strains and pressures which the Government—itself weakened by scandals and recent electoral reversals—could not absorb without an expansion of its political base. The center-left was simply too unstable a formula to cope simultaneously with a social and an economic crisis of such magnitude.

Was the Italian crisis of these years an "organic" one: that is, a crisis that cannot be solved without posing the problem of the replacement of an entire social system?[57] The experience of the period answers "no." The crisis of a system is organic when its various strands cannot be separated from one another without posing the problem of the replacement of the system itself. But when a political class gains the unity necessary to unravel the knot of crisis into its

---

[54] Salvati, "Muddling Through," p. 44.

[55] For the argument that there were really two simultaneous protest movements in Italy in the early 1970s, see my "The Italian Party System between Crisis and Transition," *American Journal of Political Science*, vol. 21 (May 1977), pp. 193-224.

[56] A good account of the 1973-1974 crisis is found in Lubitch, "The Italian Economic Crises," pp. 21-25.

[57] Donolo, *Mutamento o transizione*.

various strands, each of these can be isolated and dealt with through political compromise, policy change, and reform. In the short run, the effect of this operation is contradictory: as the apparently insoluble crisis evaporates, actual policy problems increase, for it is only after the politicians achieve enough unity to break the crisis down into its components that problems assume a form that can be confronted by ordinary administration. It is at this stage that the administrative weaknesses of a system come into play and that the political wizardry of a political class cannot substitute for a state machinery that remains to be reformed.

How do these observations apply to Italy between 1976 and 1979? Of LaPalombara's five politically relevant trends most important in 1976, fear of communism has received most attention, for obvious reasons. But the unravelling of Italy's crisis eased some problems, enlarged others, and put still others on the back burner for future Governments to cope with. Summarizing a complex period all too briefly, we can see the following developments:

Corruption and Clientelism. As the almost anticlimatic fall of President Giovanni Leone showed, the public had had its fill of scandal. A war on corruption like the one waged in Italy between 1974 and 1976 is never wholly a response to the objective evils of the corrupt; it is also based on the politicians' and the press's willingness to turn the public's diffuse distrust of public officials into directed moral outrage.[58]

After the Andreotti Government was formed in 1976, both the press and the Communists changed their tune. The press was as sensational as ever, but its attention gradually shifted from the peccadilloes of the politicians to the problems of the regime—while the Communists, whose columnists and cartoonists had had a field day denouncing corruption before 1976, now began to find unsuspected virtues in the DC.[59] The self-censoring of the country's major left-wing force after June 1976 was one of the developments that made it possible for the country to turn to other issues.

[58] William E. Porter, "The Mass Media in the Italian Elections," in Penniman, ed., *Italy at the Polls, 1976*, p. 270.

[59] For example, in an article by a noted Communist historian of the South, one learns that "one of the merits of the DC was to have confronted the question of the South . . . in terms that attempted to be both 'strategic' and 'national' . . . in contrast with the localistic and subaltern tradition of the political life of the South." Rosario Villari, "Il rinnovamento della DC e la democrazia nel Sud" [The revival of the DC and democracy in the South], in *Rinascita*, October 8, 1976, p. 6.

The left's war against politically inspired appointments and agencies also took a turn after 1976. The Andreotti Government ushered in a system under which the major parties would openly arrive at agreements on important government appointments—hardly meritocracy, but an improvement over the obscurity which had surrounded such appointments in the past. As for government agencies, some progress was made in reducing the number of so-called useless agencies, which served as patronage fiefs for the DC. Since rapid progress in the war on clientelism would threaten the survival of the coalition itself, this was one area in which reform was swept under the rug. Nevertheless, the bases of recruitment were somewhat broadened.[60]

Terrorism and Radicalization. Apart from its purely political consequences, the Moro affair taught three lessons: first, it showed how isolated the Red Brigades were from the rest of the extreme left; second, in the outpouring of sympathy for the Moro family, it showed that—despite the changes of the previous decade—the ideal of the Catholic family was still alive; and third, it showed how feeble the Italian administrative apparatus was when faced by an extraordinary threat like urban terrorism.

But the Moro affair, the nadir of the attempt to stop terrorism, was also the acme of the unity of the political parties. Afterwards, as we have seen, this unity crumbled, but while it lasted, its role in preserving Italy as a fundamentally democratic system was crucial, and its decline was accompanied both by greater restrictions on the civil rights of citizens[61] and by an improvement of the strike record of the security services in finding "nests" of Red Brigade members. Countries with a longer record of constitutional democracy than Italy's have been known to exercise fewer curbs on police and intelligence services when faced by threats to domestic order that, in retrospect, were less grave than the threat Italy faced during the years 1976–1979.

Economic Problems and Reform. As the war against clientelism and corruption waned and as terrorism isolated the extremists from both the official and the extraparliamentary left, the air of permanent crisis

---

[60] "In addition," writes Pasquino, "the DC has made some steps away from too close a relationship with various State agencies. The relationship still exists, but it is more flexible." "A Party for All Seasons," p. 102.

[61] The most striking examples were the virtual police siege of the University of Calabria and the arrests of Toni Negri and a group of intellectuals in Padua on charges that, in part, rested on Negri's alleged ideological influence on the terrorists.

began to disperse, and a number of discrete policy problems appeared on the agenda. Some of these have been mentioned in passing—like the independent unions' rejection of wage restraint and the Government's decision to enter the European Monetary System. But it was in the general areas of economic management and the reform of the state that the dissipation of the atmosphere of permanent crisis revealed how weak were the Government's policy-making tools.

In its short-term economic management, the Government was aided by having fairly stable and broad political backing. It had three priorities: reestablishing the international stability of Italian currency, reducing inflation, and inducing employment-creating investment. How successful was the Government in meeting these three goals?

It was clearly most successful in meeting its first priority, for the balance of payments went into the black by the third quarter of 1977; it was less successful in fighting inflation, although the public sector deficit was lowered from 7.3 percent of gross domestic product in 1975 to 4.8 percent in 1977; and it was least successful of all in reducing unemployment—or rather, it was successful in keeping down investment, and thus employment—even after the credit squeeze was eased in 1977.[62]

This vicious circle of inflation-stabilization-unemployment-lack of investment illustrates the dilemma of the Andreotti Government. The successful solution of each concrete policy problem would exacerbate other problems and create political strains in the coalition. The credit squeeze and currency stabilization of 1976 were successful at the cost of low investment and continued high unemployment. The latter could not be improved in the face of business's caution without injecting large amounts of public money into the economy. This would surely hobble the fight against inflation unless it were accompanied either by a reduction in the state deficit or by a decision to allow business to redeploy part of the existing labor force in new and more efficient firms. Both were politically difficult because of the composition of the coalition that had brought political stability in the first place.

The Failure of Reform. Viewing repeated failures of bureaucratic reform, some observers have concluded that there is no majority support in Italy for reforming the state.[63] It is probably more accu-

---

[62] The data in this paragraph are given in Salvati, "Muddling Through," pp. 41-42.
[63] Di Palma, "The Available State," pp. 163-164.

rate to argue that there are different majorities for different *types* of reform[64] and that reconstituting a modern bureaucratic state requires a concurrent and not a simple majority.

Certainly, the 1976–1979 period saw no fundamental reform of the state. But this does not mean that policy or institutional reforms were absent. On the contrary, during this period a number of key reforms passed through Parliament or were implemented by the bureaucracy. The delegation of powers and functions to the new regional governments was most important.[65] More dramatic in its immediate impact was the implementation of a major reform in the tax system, which greatly increased state revenues through direct taxation. Most controversial of all—and still not implemented in its entirety—was the complicated *equo canone* (fair rent) law that was passed by Parliament in 1977 at a time when the housing market was deteriorating and many tenants and homeowners faced real hardship.

These policy reforms demonstrated the responsiveness of the Government to the people's real needs, but they also illustrated the difficulty of implementing parliamentary reforms in the face of an unreformed bureaucracy and local government system and the difficulty of reforming a bureaucracy that had been built along partisan lines during the 1950s and 1960s. As Di Palma rhetorically asks, "Can a Christian Democracy losing organized support and governing grip" preside over the task of reforming the state—"be in effect its own surgeon—without cutting vital connections in the short but decisive range?"[66]

The events of 1976–1979 did not make any single reform of the state appear essential but—on the contrary—revealed the contradictory nature of the problems the country faced and the constituencies whose interests had to be sacrificed if each reform were to be pushed to its conclusion. In this context, a thoroughgoing reform of the state did not occur, but neither did a relapse into heightened politicization and inertia. By following a coherent economic line for three years, by drawing labor and the private sector closer to the government, by making a few key policy reforms, and by engaging the cooperation of the Communists in unravelling the knot of crisis, the Andreotti Governments preserved the state they inherited.

[64] This is my argument in "The Italian Party System between Crisis and Transition," pp. 208, 220.

[65] See my "Decentramento incompiuto o centralismo restaurato?" [Incomplete decentralization or restored centralization?], in *Rivista Italiana di Scienza Politica*, vol. 9 (Fall 1979), pp. 229-261.

[66] Di Palma, "The Available State," pp. 156-157.

The Problems of the Communists. Much has been written about the nature of the "communist problem" in Italy, and in closing I only wish to add a few remarks to what has been said elsewhere. There is a tendency outside of Italy to characterize the PCI's role in the Andreotti years in purely tactical terms—in one author's words, as a "function of its proximity to state power."[67] It is true that the PCI had power in mind when it set out to support the Andreotti formula—if it had not, it would not be in the business of politics. But the decision was a logical extension of the strategy to which the Communists have been committed for most of the postwar period— a strategy of transformation of the society through gradual structural reform within and through the democratic process and through political and institutional alliances reaching well beyond the traditional alliance targets of Leninist parties.[68] This search for alliances quickens every time the PCI views itself, the Italian political system, or both, as being in imminent danger. This was true in the early 1970s as a middle-class backlash resulted from labor's gains of the preceding years, and it was true again in the mid-1970s when the Italian crisis seemed to be a knot of inseparable and insoluble problems with no way out short of an authoritarian solution. The Communists helped to untie the knot.

This is not to say that the PCI was not interested in power in 1976, but it took the Italian crisis seriously enough to extend its historic alliance strategy beyond its capacity to hold together its increasingly diverse and independent following—not to mention the trade unions and the rest of the left. It was through the tortured and tumultuous relationship between the PCI and the Andreotti Governments that the "communist problem" transformed itself into the problems of the Communists. Or rather, problems the PCI had always had grew larger and more unsettling as the party was held at bay by a governmental formula that gave the PCI only an uncertain influence on policy and a politically intangible legitimation.[69]

The Communists' problems should by now be clear: relations with the party base and with the trade unions; the untenable alternatives of softness on terrorism and support for repression; the choice

---

[67] Sartori, "Calculating the Risk," p. 171.

[68] Discussions of postwar PCI domestic strategy are found in Donald L. M. Blackmer, "Continuity and Change in Postwar Italian Communism," Stephen Hellman, "The PCI's Alliance Strategy and the Case of the Middle Classes," and Sidney Tarrow, "Communism in Italy and France: Adaptation and Change," in Blackmer and Tarrow, eds., *Communism in Italy and France* (Princeton: Princeton University Press, 1975).

[69] This point is driven home in Joseph LaPalombara's chapter in this volume.

between a "natural" but insufficient left-wing ally—the Socialist party—and a powerful but "unnatural" one—the DC; the insoluble dilemma of democracy or Leninism, no longer to be brushed aside with sterile references to the party's Gramscian tradition; finally, the choice of programmatic priorities, which, in the simple days of total opposition, could be settled demagogically, without fear of the party's being one day obliged to put them into practice.

The experience forced the party to rethink and clarify a number of choices that had been obscured by events and by party leaders over the past few years, beginning with its very membership in the international communist movement and including its strategy of alliances, its relation with the trade unions, and its economic program. The PCI reaffirmed its commitment to international communism; it once more gave priority to the historical link with the Socialists but did not close the door to the DC; and in the economic area it turned back from a populist dispersiveness to a bolder defense of the interests of labor. To Communists who wanted to come to power with appeals of all kinds to all kinds of people and alliances across the board, the period was no doubt a defeat; but to those who wanted to seek power on the basis of clear party choices and more solid alliances, the defeat was a victory.

Was the PCI's experience of power—if it was indeed power that it experienced—in some way worth it? From the point of view of the system, the answer depends upon how serious the threat to its survival was taken to be in 1976. Many people, from the Communists to the Liberals, thought it serious enough to justify the political risks that were taken, though others did not. From the point of view of the Communists, who were hardly unaware of the risks—and who were severely criticized by their French comrades for taking them—there were greater risks in remaining in splendid isolation than in struggling for influence within the majority. This alone testifies to the seriousness of the crisis that paralyzed Italian society at that time.

From the point of view of the other parties, the experience was certainly worthwhile. For the Christian Democrats, it made clear that their mandate to govern was not made in heaven and would not continue to be renewed indefinitely, regardless of their behavior. The Socialists were forced to choose an identity—that of what party leader Craxi called a "European" socialist party—though with the PSI surprises are always likely. From the point of view of the minor parties, it led to their renewed importance in the system and—in the case of the Radicals—to a revitalized role. And from the point of view of all the parties, it was probably worthwhile having to bargain across a table almost daily with the leaders of the country's major working-class party, something they may have to do again in the not-too-distant future. Whatever we may think happens to democracy when Communist parties join coalitions (and the 1976–1979 period in Italy was not negative in this regard), it was certainly *not* a sign of democratic vitality that the country's second-largest party, which now governs more people in local governments throughout the country than any other party, was long excluded by definition from participating in the national Government.

The history of the 1976–1979 period could be written as a descending curve of PCI support for the Government and of support within the PCI for its leaders' moderate policies. But it can also be seen two other ways, both of which I hope to have illustrated in this chapter: as the ascending curve of collaboration between major producer groups and political forces with a Government that succeeded in reweaving the country's damaged civil fabric and staging an economic recovery; and as the steady course, in the face of unprecedented strains, of a political system that—for all its inefficiency, instability, and immobility—remained a democracy.

2

Italian Voters, 1976-1979

Giacomo Sani

Few periods in recent Italian history have witnessed as many significant events as the second part of the 1970s. Among the most important developments of the 1974–1979 period the following stand out: the confirmation of the divorce law and the legalization of abortion; the acquisition by the parties of the left of a predominant position in the government of all major Italian cities; the forced resignation of a president of the republic amidst the rumor of his involvement in the Lockheed scandal; the entry of the Communist party into a Government majority even if without formal participation in the cabinet; the election of a prominent Socialist leader to the position of president of the republic; the emergence in 1976 and the consolidation in 1979 of a new political force, the Radical party; the continuing high levels of political violence symbolized by the murder of Christian Democratic leader Aldo Moro; and finally the appearance of political groups challenging the Communist party from the left.

The protagonists were, of course, the political elites. But the mass public did its part as well. In the relatively short span of five years Italian citizens were called to the polls six times in nationwide elections. In 1974 the occasion was a referendum on whether or not to repeal the recently introduced legislation on divorce. A year later the voters' task was to elect regional, provincial, and municipal councils throughout the country. In June 1976 the electors went to the polls to elect a new Parliament. In 1978 there were two referendums dealing with the issue of the public financing of parties and with recently adopted measures against terrorist activities. On June 3, 1979, the people were again asked to vote for the renewal of the Chamber of Deputies and of the Senate. Finally, a week later they had a chance to select the Italian representatives to the European Parliament.

In recent times it has been fashionable among political observers and commentators to talk of a change in the mood of the country. It has been said that after the surge in participation of the early part of the decade there has been a trend, especially among the younger generations, toward a "return to the private sphere," a more marked concern with the personal aspects of life—job, family, income, personal relations—and a lessened degree of involvement and interest in public life.[1] Since the phase of mass political activism had coincided with an increase in the strength of the left in the elections of the mid-1970s, one might legitimately wonder what impact this recent trend toward the private sphere has had and will have on the level of support for the different political groups. Thus, the question is: Did the cycle inaugurated in 1974 with the referendum on divorce come to an end with the parliamentary elections of 1979?

This chapter examines the electoral trends of the late 1970s with this question in mind. After a brief examination of some of the characteristics of the campaign, of participation rates, and of the returns, attention will be focused on patterns of stability and change in the different areas of the country.

The Parties and the Campaign

Traditionally, Italian electors have been offered a variety of choices in the voting booth, and in 1979 they had even more alternatives than usual: eleven parties presented lists of candidates throughout the country, and in a number of districts the election was contested by local or regional groups as well.[2] The national parties and their symbols which appeared on the ballots are listed in figure 2–1. As one can see, leftist voters had a considerable number of options. In addition to the traditional forces such as the Communist party (PCI) and the Socialist party (PSI), lists were presented by the Radical party (PR), the party of Proletarian Unity (PDUP), and the United

---

[1] The "return to the private sphere" (il riflusso) has been the subject of extensive commentaries in recent times. On its likely political consequences, see for example, Giorgio Galli in Panorama, June 6, 1979, p. 39, and Paolo Nasso in Il Settimanale, May 16, 1979, p. 11.

[2] Traditionally, local lists have been a significant factor only in limited areas such as the regions of Aosta and Trentino Alto Adige. In more recent times lists of candidates not affiliated with the national parties have attracted voters' support in some districts of the northeast. In 1979 the Il Melone list received 30.8 percent of the vote in the province of Trieste, and local lists did fairly well in the provinces of Gorizia (4.6 percent) and Udine (6.0 percent).

FIGURE 2–1
Symbols of Italian Parties Contesting the 1979 Election in All Districts

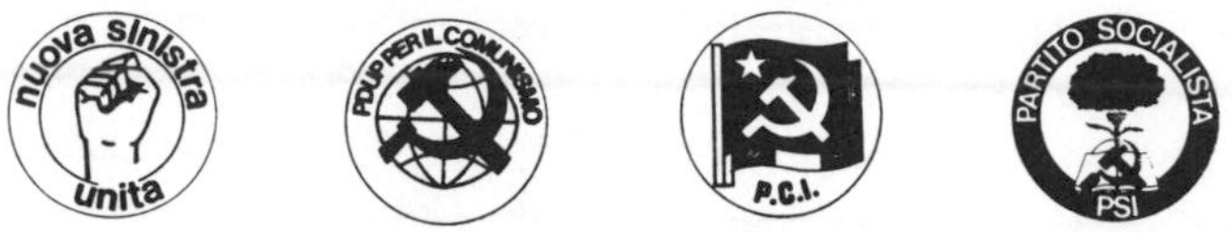

NSU   Nuova Sinistra Unita (United New Left)
PDUP   Partito di Unità Proletaria (Proletarian Unity party)
PCI   Partito Comunista Italiano (Italian Communist party)
PSI   Partito Socialista Italiano (Italian Socialist party)

PSDI   Partito Socialista Democratico Italiano (Italian Socialdemocratic
        party)
PRI   Partito Repubblicano Italiano (Italian Republican party)
DC   Democrazia Cristiana (Christian Democratic party)
PLI   Partito Liberale Italiano (Italian Liberal party)

MSI   Movimento Sociale Italiano (Italian Social Movement)
DN   Democrazia Nazionale (National Democracy)
PR   Partito Radicale (Radical party)

New Left (NSU). These last two parties had contested the 1976 election together under the label of Proletarian Democracy (DP). There were no changes among the centrist parties: Social Democrats (PSDI), Republicans (PRI), Christian Democrats (DC), and Liberals (PLI) have been on the Italian political scene since the beginning of the postwar period. Last, on the right we find in addition to the neo-Fascist party (Italian Social Movement, MSI), a list of candidates presented under the label National Democracy (DN) by a group that had broken away from the MSI since the preceding election. In summary, the voters were presented with two more options in 1979 than in 1976. However, neither of the two new groups represented a true novelty.

The positions taken by the parties in the 1976–1979 period and their stands before the election are discussed at length in other chapters of this volume. Here I will present only some general observations on the campaign.

Proportional representation systems tend to deemphasize individual candidates. The sheer number of names appearing on the lists in a typical multimember district makes it unlikely that any individual candidate who is not a well-known party figure will stand out. Partly in consequence, only about half of the voters take advantage of their right to choose among the candidates of a given list by casting "preference votes."[3] While parties remained much more salient than candidates in 1979, the focus on the latter seemed somewhat greater than it had been previously. At least in some parties, individual candidates made a considerable effort to contact voters by mailings or handouts in public places, and paid advertisements for candidates appeared in daily newspapers and weekly magazines, usually featuring a photograph and a short slogan.

A more significant novelty was the adoption of a propaganda technique well known to the American public—the purchase of time for spot advertisements on private radio and television. This development was made possible by a landmark decision of the Constitutional Court in the mid-1970s that had opened the way for private broadcasting in Italy in limited areas. It had already played a role in the 1976 campaign,[4] but in 1979 the private stations were much better prepared to handle the demand for political advertisements, and many candidates exploited this new avenue because it was both suitable for

[3] For a good summary of the Italian electoral system see the chapter by Douglas Wertman, "The Italian Electoral Process: The Election of June 1976," in Howard R. Penniman, ed., *Italy at the Polls: The Parliamentary Election of 1976* (Washington, D.C.: American Enterprise Institute, 1977), pp. 41-80. On preference voting, Wertman says: "Each voter, if he chooses to do so, may cast from one to four preference votes in districts with sixteen or more seats and from one to three preference votes in districts with fifteen seats or fewer. The preference votes may be cast only for candidates of the party the voter has selected. The voter indicates his preferences by writing, in the space provided on the ballot, the name or number on the party list of each candidate. If in marking his ballot a voter designates only a party and does not cast preference votes, it is not assumed that he supports the order on the party list; only preference votes directly cast for each candidate count in his total. In recent Chamber elections approximately 30 percent of the Italian electors have cast preference votes. . . . Preference voting has major implications for the style of Italian political campaigns" (p. 48). See also the Chamber ballot reproduced in appendix B.

[4] The role of private stations in the 1976 campaign is discussed in William E. Porter, "The Mass Media in the Italian Elections of 1976," in Penniman, ed., *Italy at the Polls, 1976*, pp. 259-286. For information about the 1979 campaign, see *Il Settimanale*, May 23, 1979, pp. 18-20, and *Panorama*, May 15, 1979, pp. 60-62.

reaching a limited local audience and cheaper than other channels.[5] The impact of this alternative on campaign style and on the voters' decisions is hard to estimate. It is clear, however, that spots, interviews, and debates served to give little-known office-seekers greater exposure to the electorate than ever before.

The success of the private stations and their capture of a share of the political market might be due in part to the rather stiff and stale nature of the political programs broadcast during the campaign by the state-owned radio and television network, RAI (Radio-Televisione Italiana). The broadcasts directly geared to the election (the "Tribune Elettorali") were designed and produced by the parties in 1979, and they continued to attract very large audiences. The public network estimates that on the average almost 6 million people watched these programs. While this is an impressive figure, a study by a firm specializing in audience measurement indicates that the average audience figure is misleading since there is a considerable drop of attention during the broadcast. Typically an initial audience of 11 million dwindled to a mere 2.4 million by the end of the program some sixty minutes later.[6] Whether the audience declines because the programs are boring, as some critics contend, is difficult to establish, but it is safe to say that the parties' official political presentations fail to keep the voters glued to their radio and TV sets.[7]

A number of themes surfaced during the campaign, among them the energy crisis, the persistence of political violence, the condition of the economy, particularly the problems of inflation and unemployment, the implementation of the reform of the health care system, the overcrowding of the universities, and the reform of secondary education.[8] But the central emphasis of the debate was not on these policy areas; rather, it was on the question of "future alignments" —which coalitions the outcome of the election would make possible or unviable. The electoral contest of 1979 was seen by many as a referendum on the single issue of whether the Communist party was to be a full member of a governmental coalition with its share of cabinet posts. On the eve of the election, PCI general secretary

[5] A number of candidates of different parties explain why they preferred the new medium in *Panorama*, May 22, 1979, pp. 48-49.

[6] The estimates of audience size were reported in *Panorama*, May 22, 1979, p. 44. It should be pointed out that the figures refer to all political broadcasts in the first few months of 1979 including those before the beginning of the campaign.

[7] On the reasons for the lack of appeal of the broadcasts produced by the RAI-TV network see *Panorama*, May 22, 1979, p. 44.

[8] For an overview of the parties' positions with respect to twelve policy areas see *Corriere della Sera*, June 2, 1979, pp. 16-17.

Enrico Berlinguer stated the basic alternative facing the electorate in these terms:

> This is the choice facing the voter today. Either a return to the past which would represent a step backward for the workers . . . and which would mean more disorder, inefficiencies, injustices, or a courageous step toward the future based on the enormous and vital energies of the workers, of the middle classes, of the young generations, of women, of all those who are ready to commit themselves to serious, just and progressive policies.[9]

For his part, only a few days before, the general secretary of the DC had made clear that his party counted on the electoral outcome to block the Communists' access to the cabinet. "All sincere democrats," said Zaccagnini, "must have an interest in possible ideological changes within the PCI." But he went on to say that recent pronouncements by the PCI in favor of democracy and NATO

> did not change the final goal of the Communist Party. . . . a goal which is profoundly different from the kind of democratic society that we want to build and to preserve. Therefore we say to the Communists: if the majority of Italians really want the kind of society that you propose they will have to give you the necessary votes. But you cannot ask us . . . to help you with our support or to open for you the door to the cabinet.[10]

Spokesmen for the other parties almost always betrayed the same preoccupation with alternative coalition schemes. The Socialists argued that a strengthening of their support base, "altering in a significant manner the balance of forces within the left," would give the PSI the leverage it needed to break the impasse and bring about a new alignment.[11] Secretary Craxi offered the electorate a "contract," promising governmental stability if the PSI's strength were adequately boosted.[12] On both the right and the left the target was the coalition of "national solidarity" which had prevailed during the 1976–1979 period and which was based on a fragile and uneasy agreement between DC and PCI. The groups of the "new left" (PR, PDUP, NSU) attacked the Communists and their historic compromise

[9] *Corriere della Sera*, June 2, 1979, p. 1.
[10] Interview with Benito Zaccagnini, *Il Giornale*, May 26, 1979, p. 1.
[11] *Corriere della Sera*, June 2, 1979, p. 1.
[12] Interview with Bettino Craxi, *Il Settimanale*, June 6, 1979, pp. 12-13 (published before the election).

strategy. On the opposite front, the MSI and the DN argued that only a strengthening of committed anticommunist forces could free the Christian Democrats from "Communist blackmail" and make possible a centrist or a center-right coalition.

Since significant changes in the relative strength of the parties were unlikely, some observers felt that an election fought over future coalition alignments was a "useless" one.[13] And some of the public opinion polls seemed to prove that they were right. One of the major surveys reported a month before the election predicted a marginal increase for the DC (1.2 percentage points), a decline for the Communists (3.4 points), a surge in the strength of the Radicals (5 points), and essential stability for the other forces.[14] Projections from a later poll published toward the end of May placed the DC above the 40 percent mark and gave the PR 3 percent of the vote.[15]

Among the findings that provoked most discussion was the high percentage of undecided voters—about 20 percent of the respondents queried. While some experts dismissed the figure as unrealistically high and attributable to people's reluctance to make their politics known, others argued that it reflected genuine and widespread uncertainty among the voters.[16] They also argued that the contingent of "floating voters" had grown in recent years. As one sociologist put it, "public opinion is much less ideological, less dogmatic, and hence the person with an average education has become more prone to 'floating.'"[17] Others pointed out that the indecision of a larger percentage of voters was a consequence of the shrinking distance between parties: they suggested that shifts in voting behavior were likely not only to become more common but also to involve a wider part of the political spectrum. In the past floaters had moved basically from a political group to one adjacent to it on the left-right continuum; in the late 1970s, it was argued, they might very well move

---

[13] Many shared the view that the election would be useless. Some argued that the only purpose the election served was to downplay the election for the European Parliament and therefore to damage the Socialists. On this point see the chapter by Gianfranco Pasquino in this volume.

[14] Some of the findings from the poll carried out by the Demoskopea Institute of Milan were published in the issues of *Panorama* of May 8, 1979 (pp. 43-46) and May 15, 1979 (pp. 52-56).

[15] Projections based on a late poll carried out by the Doxa Institute appeared in *La Repubblica*, May 29, 1979, p. 1.

[16] One skeptic was the PCI's electoral expert Celso Ghini. His comment on the poll was: "I cannot believe that there are 8 million voters who have not made up their minds." *Il Settimanale*, May 16, 1979, p. 12.

[17] Sabino Acquaviva, quoted in *Il Settimanale*, May 16, 1979, p. 11.

from one portion of the spectrum to another.[18] Perhaps these observers erred in attributing to the electorate characteristics that are typical of a much smaller group of educated, well-informed voters, and probably the number of truly undecided voters really was smaller than the pollsters' figure suggested. However, it also seems likely that indecision and uncertainty on the part of the voters was higher in 1979 than in the past, and this could account for the increase in the number of people who chose not to go to the polls on election day.

The Election

The Turnout. With the addition of the three cohorts of young voters born in 1959, 1960, and 1961, the number of eligible electors reached a record 42.2 million in June 1979. Some 36.4 million of these, being twenty-five years of age or older, were also eligible to vote for the Senate. The new growth of the electorate between 1976 and 1979 stood at approximately 4.5 percent—a figure that is very similar to those of previous elections, with the notable exception of 1976 when the growth of the electorate was due in part to the lowering of the voting age.[19]

In the first thirty years of the postwar period, turnout levels in Italy were very high: between 92 and 94 percent of the people fulfilled their obligation to vote. In June 1979 the turnout rate, while remaining quite high by comparative standards, decreased somewhat: approximately one elector in ten chose not to vote. In addition, approximately 1.6 million of those who did go to the polls failed to cast a valid ballot, and an equally large number rendered their ballots invalid by marking them improperly. Altogether, 13.5 percent of the eligible electors failed to contribute to the outcome of the election by casting invalid votes. Several observers emphasized this fact and pointed out that the "party" of the nonvoters (5.6 million) would be easily the third-largest political force in the country after the DC and the PCI. It was also suggested that the decline in participation was a symptom of malaise, an indication of growing disaffection from the political system. One observer spoke of a growing distance between "those who cast the votes and those who receive them"— namely, the politicians.[20] A well-known sociologist argued that the

[18] On this point see the comments attributed to political scientist Giuliano Urbani, *Il Settimanale*, May 16, 1979, p. 11.

[19] Changes in the composition of the Italian electorate are discussed in my essay "The Italian Electorate in the Mid Seventies: Beyond Tradition?" in Penniman, ed., *Italy at the Polls, 1976*, pp. 81-122.

[20] Giorgio Battistini, *La Repubblica*, June 5, 1979, p. 7.

decline in participation would probably have been greater were it not for the fact that "many people believed that not voting is a crime."[21] Another stated that "the members of the Italian political class have never looked more alike to one another. The same faces, the same words, the same hypocrisies," and he added, "How can one blame those who did not vote?"[22] A well-known commentator, Luigi Barzini, said: "One must conclude that the millions who did not vote or who cast a blank ballot are mostly disillusioned people who for some years believed that everything could be solved by magic with the help of some acrobatic parliamentary alliances and with some ingenious laws that would eliminate once and forever the most serious problems of the country."[23] There was also agreement among observers on the fact that lower participation rates could have had an impact on the outcome of the election. The losses of the PCI, for example, were attributed in part to a mood of disenchantment especially among the younger cohorts of voters. We will explore this point later on, but first it is useful to consider in somewhat greater detail the changes in the rates of participation.

The decline in turnout appears to have been a general phenomenon in the sense that it took place in every region. Data for the ninety-four provinces show that participation declined from a mean of 93.1 percent to a mean of 89.6 percent in 1979. The same data tell us that there was little change between the two elections in terms of the rank ordering of provinces for turnout: the correlation between the participation rates in the two elections is extremely high (+.97). The second point to be made is that the decline in participation was not the same in the different areas of the country. The drop in participation was somewhat more pronounced in those regions where turnout rates have traditionally been low. For example, in Molise the rate declined from 85.4 to 74.7 percent and in Sicily from 86.4 to 80.3 percent, whereas in the Veneto area the drop was only 2.7 percentage points and in Lombardy 2.9 points. Analysis of turnout rates at the provincial level shows that there is a nonnegligible correlation between the drop in participation in 1979 and the level of participation in 1976 (r = .74). As a result, the "distance" between the different areas of the country from the standpoint of participation has increased. In 1976, for example, the regions of Emilia Romagna and Calabria were separated by a spread of 12 points in turnout rates; in 1979 the gap grew to 19 points. And

[21] Francesco Alberoni, *Corriere della Sera*, June 6, 1979, p. 3.
[22] Alessandro Pizzorno, *Corriere della Sera*, June 6, 1979, p. 3.
[23] Luigi Barzini, *Corriere della Sera*, June 8, 1979, p. 1.

the same is true if we consider figures at a lower level of aggregation. It is no accident that in these examples we have juxtaposed northern and southern regions. Traditionally, participation rates have been higher in the North. These recent trends suggest that the well-known gap between North and South has been increasing in recent years.

It seems likely that, as in the past, patterns of migration had something to do with turnout rates. It is common for workers to maintain their residence in one city while working in another part of the country or abroad, and since the right to vote can be exercised only in the place of residence and voting by mail is not allowed, participation rates in the provinces of residence of migrant workers have suffered. This pattern is most common in the South, but it also affects some northern provinces such as Udine.[24] Another possible reason for the decline in the turnout rate might be that the mild legal-administrative sanctions for not voting have lost their force.[25]

Some commentators have suggested that abstention was particularly pronounced among the younger cohorts of voters. They point out that in some areas turnout rates in the Chamber election were lower than in the Senate election, and the younger electors can vote only in the first. While it is quite clear that this discrepancy did exist in some areas—specifically in Milan and Naples[26]—it is doubtful that it occurred throughout Italy. Comparison of turnout rates for the two elections fails to reveal, for the country as a whole, any significant difference. There remains the possibility that turnout affected the returns and, in particular, that it depressed the level of support for the PCI. We shall return to this question after a general overview of the outcome.

The Returns. When the votes were counted it became clear that the verdict rendered by the voters had done little to resolve the impasse the Italian political system had reached in the mid-1970s. A stable and viable coalition seemed as remote as ever (see table 2–1). The headline in the prestigious Milan daily *Corriere della Sera* proclaimed:

[24] Electoral participation in the province of Udine declined by four percentage points.

[25] The names of people who, without justification, have failed to vote are posted outside the city hall in their commune of residence, and "Did not vote" is stamped on their *certificato di buona condotta*, a document (now infrequently used) for which a citizen can apply and which he may be required to present, for example, when seeking certain jobs.

[26] The difference between turnout rates in the elections for the Chamber and for the Senate was 0.8 points in Milan and 0.3 points in Naples. *La Repubblica*, June 5, 1979, p. 7.

TABLE 2–1

CHANGE IN PARTY STRENGTH, CHAMBER OF DEPUTIES ELECTIONS,
1976–1979

(percent and percentage points)

Party	Share of the Vote		Change
	1976	1979	
PDUP-NSU	1.5	2.2	+0.7
PCI	34.4	30.4	−4.0
PSI	9.6	9.8	+0.2
PR	1.1	3.4	+2.3
Total left	46.6	45.8	−0.8
PSDI	3.4	3.8	+0.4
PRI	3.1	3.0	−0.1
DC	38.7	38.3	−0.4
SVP	0.5	0.6	+0.1
PLI	1.3	1.9	+0.6
Total center	47.0	47.6	+0.6
DN	—	0.6	+0.6
MSI	6.1	5.3	−0.8
Total right	6.1	5.9	−0.2
Other	0.3	0.7	+0.4

SOURCE: Compiled by the author from official statistics reported in the press.

"It Will Be Increasingly Difficult to Govern." Turin's *La Stampa* described the returns as "complex and contradictory."[27] The Communists acknowledged their setback, but Secretary-General Berlinguer observed that the party had retained much of the ground it had gained in 1976—not bad considering the "massive and concentric attacks" launched against his party in the three preceding years. And he could point out that the "Communist question" was yet to be resolved.[28] The Christian Democrats, predictably enough, stressed the Communists' defeat and used it to console themselves for their poor showing; the Socialists' disappointment was plain.[29]

In the aftermath of the election cartoonists zeroed in on the Communists' decline and on the surge of the Radical party. The DC

[27] *Corriere della Sera* and *La Stampa*, June 6, 1979.
[28] *L'Unità*, June 5, 1979, p. 1.
[29] *Avanti!*, June 5, 1979.

published a cartoon of Marco Pannella, the Radical leader, with Popeye's body, drinking from a can labeled with the PCI's hammer and sickle.[30] The front cover of a large-circulation newsmagazine showed an anguished Berlinguer carrying a huge cross inscribed with the DC symbol and sporting a crown of thorns and red roses like the rose in the Radical party's symbol.[31] Columnists, political scientists, and observers generally focused on changes within the left. This was natural enough since the changes in the share of the vote going to the PCI and the PR, while not stunning or unexpected, stood out against the stable trends for the other parties. There can be little doubt that stability was the prevailing note of the returns. The figures in table 2–1 tell the story.

In the first place, if we look at the three clusters into which the Italian parties are customarily grouped, it is easy to see that the variations were minimal. The left declined from 46.6 to 45.8 percent, the center gained marginally, and the erosion of the right was a very modest −0.2 percentage points. In terms of broad tendencies and nationwide aggregations of votes, it is quite clear that 1979 brought little change. This remains true, for the most part, even when we look at individual parties. The strength of nine parties—DC, PSI, PSDI, PRI, PLI, MSI-DN, and PDUP-NSU—changed by less than 1 percentage point. Indeed, disregarding the sign of the variations, we find that the mean gain/loss for *all* of the Italian parties including the PCI and the PR, was approximately 0.9 percentage points.[32] And for the Senate, the degree of stability was even higher: the largest variation was a decline of 2.3 percentage points for the Communist party.

To be sure, these conclusions are valid only at the national level. When we consider trends at a lower level of aggregation—the region, or even more the province—we expect voting behavior to be less stable. This is indeed the case. While roughly one-third of the provinces were characterized by a considerable degree of stability, in the others the balance of forces in the strength of the parties had altered considerably. Thus, in the provinces of La Spezia, Bergano, Cremona, Ferrara, and Modena the amount of change brought about by the 1979 election was below the national figure. On the other hand, in Naples, Reggio Calabria, Caltanisetta, Enna, and others the mean gain/loss for the parties was clearly out of line with the trend at the

---

[30] *Il Popolo*, June 8, 1979, p. 2.

[31] *Panorama*, June 12, 1979.

[32] The measure of overall change is obtained by adding the absolute values of the variations and dividing by the number of parties involved.

national level. More generally, the analysis shows that changes were minimal in the central regions, higher in the North, and highest in the South. Since one of the possible sources of change in the strength of the parties is the rate of electoral participation, one might wonder whether the two were statistically linked in 1979. Indeed, the correlation between changes in the level of participation and our measure of change is −.44, which, would suggest that turnout affected the outcome of the election, especially in the South, through the differential propensity to vote of different groups of partisans. Whether in addition to the statistical link there is a causal link is not so clear. It is quite possible that the correlation is the result of the fact that the South posted both a greater decline in participation and a greater amount of change due to the voters' higher propensity to shift from election to election, a phenomenon that has been noted throughout the postwar period.[33] But it might be useful to stress that were it not for the South the stability of the Italian electorate would be even higher than it already is.

Stability and Change. The conclusions just reached apply to change in general and say very little about individual parties. We know that in terms of figures aggregated at the national level variations in party strength were, except for the PCI and the PR, quite modest. But this does not necessarily mean that the fate of each party at the provincial level remained the same. Stability at the national level can hide significant local variations. For example, we know that the Socialist party received basically the same share of the vote in 1979 that it had received three years before. But did this support come from the same areas of the country, or has the regional distribution of Socialist votes changed?

Analysis of the returns at the provincial level shows that the PSI actually posted a loss in forty-two of the ninety-four provinces. In twenty-five of these the losses were, of course, minimal, but in seventeen others they were not negligible considering the Socialists' normal share of the popular vote. Thus in the provinces of Belluno and Gorizia a loss of about 4 percentage points represented a one-third reduction in the size of the Socialist electorate. Naturally, the opposite also occurred: in the remaining fifty-two provinces the PSI posted gains, in some cases over 2.0 percentage points (in Messina

---

[33] The higher levels of electoral instability in the South have been well documented. See for example, Giorgio Galli, et al., *Il Comportamento Elettorale in Italia* [Electoral behavior in Italy] (Bologna: Il Mulino, 1968); Sidney Tarrow, *Peasant Communism in Southern Italy* (New Haven: Yale University Press, 1967).

TABLE 2–2

MEAN SHARE OF THE VOTE FOR THE PSI IN THREE GROUPS
OF PROVINCES, 1972, 1976, AND 1979

(percent and percentage points)

Area	PSI Share of the Vote			Change 1976–1979
	1972	1976	1979	
Northern provinces	11.0	10.8	10.0	−0.8
Red Belt provinces	8.7	9.6	9.4	−0.2
Southern provinces	8.7	8.8	9.6	+0.8

SOURCE: Computed by the author from provincial returns published in the press.

and Salerno, for example). In sum, analysis of the returns at the provincial level indicates that the trend for the PSI was by no means uniform. Rather, there was a degree of variability considerably greater than one might suppose from looking at the national returns.

Turning now to a second aspect of the problem we might ask whether there were regional variations in the changes in the Socialists' strength. And indeed there were: the PSI suffered losses primarily in the northern and central regions and gained in the South. As table 2–2 shows, this is not an entirely new trend: in fact the decline in the North, however slight, dates from 1972. Quite clearly the distribution of the Socialists' strength in the different areas of the country is becoming more even: the difference between North and South that existed in 1972 has almost completely disappeared. This trend toward uniformity raises questions in view of the PSI's aspiration to attract the support of the more modern segments of the population. Not only is the party not making progress in the country as a whole, but it is advancing in the more backward areas while gradually losing ground in the more modern ones.

In the case of the DC, too, apparent stability at the national level (−0.4 percentage points) hides a fair amount of variability. The Christian Democrats posted losses in approximately two-thirds of the provinces. In nineteen provinces the decline was modest (less than 1 percentage point), in twenty-eight provinces it was between 0 and 2 percentage points, and in sixteen it exceeded 2 points. But

TABLE 2–3

MEAN SHARE OF THE VOTE FOR THE DC IN THREE GROUPS
OF PROVINCES, 1972, 1976, AND 1979

(percent and percentage points)

Area	DC Share of the Vote			Change 1976–1979
	1972	1976	1979	
Northern provinces	43.3	42.1	40.1	−2.0
Red Belt provinces	31.2	31.9	30.7	−1.2
Southern provinces	42.8	42.2	43.7	+1.5

SOURCE: Computed by the author from provincial returns published in the press.

the DC gained as well. In fact, in sixteen provinces the gains were above the 2 percentage point mark. It is important to note that, here again, the pattern of gains and losses was not random. Christian Democratic losses were concentrated largely in the northern and central regions. It was the party's relative success in the continental South that allowed it to limit its overall decline to a fraction of a percentage point (see table 2–3).

In the aftermath of the election the success of the small centrist parties received considerable attention. One reason for this might be the fact that even a small increase in its percentage of the popular vote looms as a large gain for a small party. It might also be that the PLI's recovery seemed miraculous after the trends of the decade. In 1976 the Liberals appeared to be on the verge of extinction, and their comeback in 1979 was unexpected. Similarly, in the case of the PSDI the outcome surprised observers, who had counted on the Social Democrats' decline. Party leader Pietro Longo was both bitter and triumphant in denouncing the pollsters' dire predictions.[34] Nevertheless, the influence of the small centrist groups remains modest in all areas of the country. The combined growth of the PSDI, the PLI, and the PRI amounted to a mean of 1 percentage point in the northern provinces and 0.8 points in the South. The Liberals fared somewhat better in the North and the Social Democrats in the South (see table 2–4).

[34] Longo's unhappiness is recorded in *Panorama*, June 12, 1979, p. 50. A similar statement appeared in *Il Settimanale*, June 13, 1979, p. 15.

TABLE 2–4

MEAN CHANGE IN THE PSDI, PRI, PLI, AND MSI-DN SHARES OF
THE VOTE, IN THREE GROUPS OF PROVINCES, 1976–1979
(percentage points)

Area	PSDI	PRI	PLI	MSI-DN
Northern provinces	+0.4	−0.3	+0.9	+0.2
Red Belt provinces	+0.1	0	+0.4	0
Southern provinces	+0.6	0	+0.2	−0.7

SOURCE: Computed by the author from provincial returns published in the press.

Perhaps the most surprising of this last set of figures is the overall gain registered in the North by the right-wing lists of the MSI and DN. Here is a political force that has been cut off from the mainstream of Italian political life and whose democratic legitimacy has been repeatedly denied by all other political groups. Yet, thirty-five years after the demise of a regime toward which the MSI is openly sympathetic, the right has enough sway to secure gains in such cities of the industrial North as Turin (+0.5 points), Milan (+0.3 points), Vernona (+0.4 points), and Venice (+0.3 points). If one needed new evidence to document the persistence of political traditions in Italy, the returns of 1979 would certainly provide it.

The Left: Old and New

Discussion of the trends in the Communist and Radical vote has been left for last for two reasons. First, the variation in the strength of these two forces was more pronounced than that of other parties. Second, although the outcome was positive for one and negative for the other, the trends for these two parties have one characteristic in common: they were uniform in all ninety-four provinces. There are also grounds for including in this discussion an analysis of the returns for the two smaller parties of the far left, the PDUP and the NSU, since they too gained popular support in almost all parts of the country.

The press reported that the leaders of the Radical party were disappointed by the returns. Perhaps their expectations were based on overoptimistic estimates. Radical leader Pannella reportedly was expecting the surge for his party to reach 25 percent. How far this reflected Pannella's real views and how far his unorthodox and flamboyant political style is not clear,[35] but by any objective reading of Italian electoral history the PR leaders should have been pleased with the returns. To find a comparable surge in the fortunes of a small party one must go back to the beginning of the postwar period. Since then, the electorate has never rewarded the efforts of new small parties to gain an electoral foothold.

The Radicals' success was general in that it occurred in all parts of the country. However, there were areas where they did particularly well and others where their gains were modest. The PR's strength rose significantly in Rome (+5.1 points), Naples (+4.7 points), Palermo (+4.6 points), Milan (+4.5 points), Venice (+4.4 points), Turin (+4.3 points), and other cities. The party's gains were more modest in the less urbanized, less industrialized, peripheral areas, particularly in the south. In provinces such as Avellino, Benevento, Caserta, Agrigento, and Potenza the Radicals' gains reached only the 1 percentage point mark.

Between these two extremes we find the large majority of the provinces; because of this, the dispersion of values around the mean is rather modest.[36] In evaluating the size of the increment in the PR's strength one should always keep in mind the fact that the support the party enjoyed after the 1976 election was minimal in most areas. When we take this baseline into account, even a modest gain, say 1.5 points, represents in many cases a doubling of the party's strength. And in some cases the increase of 2 to 4 percentage points registered in 1979 constituted a threefold or even a fourfold increase in the Radicals' strength.

Last, it is important to note that especially in the large metropolitan areas where its gains have been noticeable, the PR is now the fourth-largest political force (as in the cities of Turin, Milan, Genoa, Venice, Florence, and Bologna), that in others it competes with the Socialists and the neo-Fascists for third place (Rome), and finally that in other cities such as Naples and Palermo the Radicals are running neck and neck with the Socialists.

The success of this newer component of the Italian left is even more remarkable in that it occurred concurrently with the gains posted by the other two small formations of the far left, the PDUP and the NSU. Ever since the Communist party adopted the "historic

---

[35] *Panorama*, May 15, 1979, p. 60.
[36] The standard deviation of the gains for the Radicals is 0.8.

compromise" strategy in the early 1970s, scholars and observers have been speculating on the likelihood that a political force might emerge and challenge the PCI on its left.[37] In the two elections preceding that of 1979 several groups played this role. In 1972 the lists of candidates presented by the PCI dissenters of the Il Manifesto group and by the MPL (Movimento Politico dei Lavoratori) received about 250,000 votes. In the parliamentary elections of 1976 the Democrazia Proletaria group managed to double that figure, and by 1979 the PDUP and NSU lists received almost 800,000 votes. This is still a small share of the vote (2.2 percent), and thus the challenge to the PCI is not for the moment a serious one. Furthermore, in spite of the reference to unity in their names, the PDUP and the NSU are badly split. Their inability to put together a joint list of candidates cost them a few seats in Parliament and deprived the NSU of any parliamentary representation. Nevertheless, the emergence and consolidation in the 1970s of an electoral bloc, however small, that did not exist in the 1940s, 1950s, or 1960s should not be underestimated. For one thing, the far left did particularly well in 1979 in the working-class belts surrounding industrial cities such as Milan and Turin, a fact that has not escaped the attention of the Communists.[38] For another, support for the PDUP and the NSU, like support for the Radicals, is not localized in circumscribed areas but appears to be diffused throughout the national territory. It would seem that in every province there is a contingent of voters who are unhappy with the posture taken by the Communist party in recent years and who, given a choice, do not hesitate to prefer leaders and candidates proposing a different course of action.

Analysis of the returns at the provincial level indicates that the PDUP and the NSU have done relatively better in areas where the Radicals did less well, and vice versa.[39] It would thus appear that these two forces appeal to not too different segments of the electorate and thus they complement each other in attracting dissatisfied leftist voters. Evidence from survey data helps in uncovering one of the reasons for this. As table 2–5 shows, Radicals and new left voters are similar in some of their socioeconomic characteristics. They tend to be young, to have a better than average education, and to have a fairly high proportion of white-collar occupations. These traits,

[37] For some comments on this point see my essay, "The Changing Role of the PCI" in David E. Albright, ed., *Communism and the Political Systems in Western Europe* (Boulder, Colorado: Westview Press, 1979), pp. 43-94, especially pp. 73-82.
[38] See the statement by Angelo Bolaffi in *Rinascita*, June 8, 1979, p. 10.
[39] There is a −.36 correlation between 1976-1979 changes for the PR and for the PDUP-NSU.

TABLE 2–5

SOCIOECONOMIC CHARACTERISTICS OF LEFTIST VOTERS, 1979

(percent)

Characteristic	Party Preference			
	PDUP-NSU	PR	PCI	PSI
Age				
Under 35	72	63	38	31
Education				
Some higher education	62	48	23	30
Profession				
Self-employed	11	13	12	13
White-collar	22	20	11	14
Blue-collar	26	18	28	22
Students	16	8	5	4
Retired and housewives	25	44	47	41

SOURCE: Demoskopea Survey reported in *Panorama* (Milan), May 8, 1979, p. 43.

especially age and education, also serve to differentiate them sharply from the traditional parties of the left and particularly from the Communist voters. For the moment, the threat posed by the new left to the old is not serious. However, the fact that the new forces seem to have a wider appeal among young voters indicates that they have a potential for consolidation and further growth.

The decline of the PCI was the chief focus of attention in the aftermath of the election. Though expected by some, it was a novelty in Italian electoral history: never before in the postwar period had the Communist party "lost" an election.[40] Moreover, a loss of 4 percentage points, given the general stability of the Italian system, was likely to be considered substantial. The PCI's share of the popular vote declined in all provinces. In some the losses were minimal, in others they were more pronounced, but the decline was general. In approximately 25 percent of the provinces the losses were above the 5 percentage point mark and in another 25 percent they stood between 3 and 5 points. The regions in which the PCI's decline was modest were in the Red Belt, the party's traditional stronghold. In Emilia-Romagna the party declined from 48.5 to 47.4 percent; in Tuscany

[40] At the national level in the postwar period there had never before been a decline in the PCI's percentage of the vote. Of course, in many districts the party has experienced an occasional downturn.

its loss was 1.7 points; in Umbria 1.8 points, and in the Marches 1.9 points. On the other hand, the losses in the South were heavier. The Communists lost 7.4 percentage points in Campania, 6.4 points in Sicily, 6.3 points in Calabria, and 5 points in Puglia. The contrast between the Center and the South is actually softened when the data are aggregated at the regional level. Inspection of the returns at a lower level of aggregation—the province—shows the existence of a wide gulf between some provinces of the Red Belt and some provinces of the South. For example, in Arezzo and Siena PCI losses were 0.7 points and 0.9 points, respectively; in Naples the drop was 9.3 points, in Catania 8.0 points, and in Cosenza 7.0 points. These figures refer to the province as a whole. More detailed analysis of returns within provinces shows that actually PCI losses were somewhat greater in large cities and metropolitan areas than elsewhere.

Comparison of the returns for 1976 and 1979 suggests a linkage between the surge of the mid-1970s and the decline that took place three years later. In 1976 the strength of the Communist party grew in all provinces by a considerable margin. In some areas this increase was a nice addition to an already strong support base. Thus in Emilia-Romagna the gain of 4.5 percentage points reinforced an already high baseline of 44 percent (see table 2–6); the pattern was similar in Tuscany and Umbria. On the other hand, in many provinces, particularly in the South, the 1976 increase was disproportionately large given the level of support the party enjoyed in 1972. Again from table 2–6 we can see that in Molise the change from 17.3 to 26 percent represented an increase of about 50 percent over the 1972 baseline; similarly, in Sardinia the gains constituted an increase of 35.4 percent. This suggests that popular support for the PCI after 1976 had two components: a steady base of loyal voters who had been with the party prior to 1976 and a contingent of new Communist voters who had turned to the PCI for the first time in 1976.

The problem of the party after 1976 was to consolidate its base of support among the second group of voters—what we might call the "soft fringe" of the PCI vote in 1976. In other words, the task for the party and its organization was to convert what might have been a temporary or episodic electoral choice into a sense of identification with the party. It had done this successfully in previous times, as the gradual increase in popular support for the PCI during the postwar period attests. But in the aftermath of the 1976 election, the task was made more difficult by several factors. First, the increase in support had been quite sharp, and the number of voters to be reached was rather large. Second, the task was to be carried out during a political phase that saw the PCI move away from its opposition stance and

TABLE 2–6
PCI VOTE, BY REGION, 1972, 1976, AND 1979
(percent)

Region	1972	1976	1972–76 Increase as Percent of 1972 Vote	1979	1976–79 Decrease as Percent of 1976 Vote
Piedmont	26.3	35.4	+35.0	30.6	−13.8
Lombardy	23.8	31.6	+32.9	28.4	−10.0
Liguria	31.6	39.1	+23.7	36.0	− 7.8
Veneto	17.3	23.8	+37.1	21.7	− 8.5
Friuli V.G.	20.2	26.6	+31.9	23.7	−11.0
Trentino A.A.	7.6	13.2	+73.2	11.1	−16.2
Emilia-Romagna	44.0	48.5	+10.3	47.4	− 2.4
Tuscany	42.2	47.5	+12.7	45.8	− 3.6
Marches	32.8	39.9	+21.5	38.1	− 4.6
Umbria	41.7	47.3	+13.4	45.5	− 3.7
Latium	27.1	35.9	+32.4	30.2	−16.0
Abruzzo	27.0	34.9	+29.5	31.1	−10.9
Molise	17.3	26.0	+49.8	21.5	−17.1
Campania	22.7	32.3	+42.2	24.9	−23.0
Apulia	25.7	31.7	+23.4	26.7	−15.7
Basilicata	24.9	33.3	+33.6	28.9	−13.2
Calabria	25.9	33.0	+27.3	26.7	−19.2
Sardinia	26.3	35.6	+35.4	31.7	−10.8
Sicily	21.3	27.5	+29.4	21.1	−23.5

SOURCE: Computed by the author from regional returns published in the press.

assume a quasi-governmental role, with all the stresses and strains that such a transition implied. Last, there was little or no increase in the capabilities of the agency that was to perform the task: there is no indication that the organization of the party expanded in order to cope with the new load; and the slight decline in membership reported at the fifteenth PCI congress, two months before the election, was not a reassuring sign.

Given these conditions, it was likely that the party would be more successful in retaining its 1976 following in areas where the soft fringe of voters was small relative to the core of solid support, and vice versa—that the party might find it difficult to retain its following in those areas where the increase had been dramatic in 1976.

This interpretation is supported by analysis of the distribution of returns at the provincial level in 1972, 1976, and 1979. There is a

FIGURE 2–2
RELATIONSHIP BETWEEN PCI LOSSES IN 1979 AND PCI GAINS IN 1976,
BY REGION

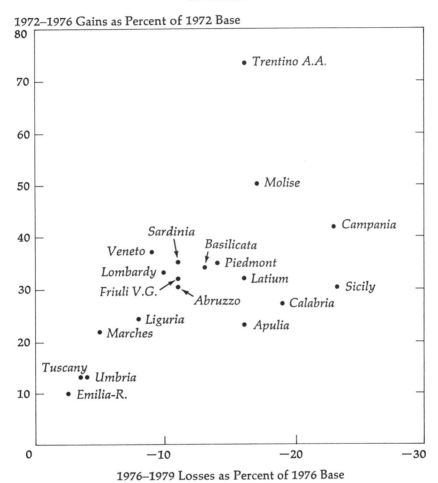

1972–1976 Gains as Percent of 1972 Base

1976–1979 Losses as Percent of 1976 Base

marked correspondence between the pattern of gains made in 1976 and the pattern of losses suffered in 1979. This means that the size of the advances made in the first period is a good predictor of the size of the decline in the second period. The point is quite apparent from the third and fifth columns of table 2–6, and is brought out even more clearly by the scattergram in figure 2–2. I have used here regional level data for simplicity of presentation, but the conclusion does not change if provincial level data are used.

But where did these "volatile" voters go, and what led them to reject the choice they had made in 1976? A number of answers to these questions were advanced by observers in the aftermath of the election, and they are discussed and evaluated in detail in the chapters that follow. Here I shall focus only on two possible causes of the losses the Communists suffered.

The first interpretation stresses abstentionism as a factor that contributed to the decline of the PCI. It could be argued that among the people who chose not to go to the polls there was a disproportionately high percentage of electors who had voted for the PCI in 1976. In 1979 these voters either failed to return to their communes of residence or they felt that they could not meaningfully vote for any party. Perhaps some were people whose vote for the PCI in 1976 had been an act of protest; possibly they were people who had believed that things would change were the PCI to play a more significant role and whose expectations had been frustrated by the events of the 1976–1979 period.

The plausibility of this interpretation would be strengthened if one found that the drop in electoral participation closely paralleled the decline in support for the PCI. And this turns out to be the case. There is a correlation of 0.49 over the set of ninety-four provinces between 1976–1979 change in turnout and 1976–1979 change in percent of the vote for the Communist party. At first, this finding lends support to the notion that lower turnout levels hurt the PCI. However, closer inspection of the data shows that the correlation is due, in large part, to the juxtaposition of two sets of provinces: those of the north-central regions where the drop in participation was modest and the losses of the PCI were small and moderate, and the southern provinces where the decline in participation was more pronounced and the decline of the PCI was more marked. When we consider these two sets of provinces separately, it turns out that the correlation vanishes altogether for the first group and becomes much smaller for the second group. This suggests that the impact of lower participation rates on the decline of the PCI was not as significant as one might have thought, or at least that the linkage between the two phenomena was not systematic.

The second interpretation focuses on the electoral behavior of the young. It has been argued by some commentators that one of the causes of the PCI's decline was to be found in the difficulty the party encountered in recruiting and retaining the support of young voters. Communist leaders have recognized this problem and have singled out 1977 as the year in which the relationship between young people and the party reached a turning point.[41] Proponents of this interpretation have relied for evidence mostly on the difference in the PCI share of the vote in the election for the Chamber and the election for the Senate (30.4 percent versus 31.5 percent). Since there are seven cohorts of voters who are eligible to cast a ballot only in the first election, it is argued that a comparison of returns for the two elections can allow us to make some inferences about the political orientations of the younger cohorts. This kind of comparison is fraught with all sorts of difficulties, as scholars have repeatedly pointed out.[42] In making it, one must ignore the possibility (not entirely remote) of ticket-splitting by some voters and assume a similar level of participation in the two elections. An even more important limitation is the fact that some small parties do not present their own list of candidates for the Senate. In 1979, for example, the PDUP did not have its own candidates for the Senate, and party leaders encouraged their voters to support Communist candidates. Thus, when we look at the two sets of returns we are really in a quandary as to how to interpret them (see table 2-7). If we treat the Chamber-Senate difference as evidence of higher support for the PCI among the older electors we are left to wonder what happened to the PDUP voters. On the other hand, if we assume that PDUP electors did vote for the PCI in the race for the Senate, we have evidence that support for the Communists was lower among the younger cohorts.

Other and better evidence bearing on this same point is provided by the figures in table 2-8. These are estimates of the distribution of partisan preferences in the seven younger cohorts and among electors twenty-five and older. These estimates were computed by the author from survey findings on the age composition of different parties' support. It might be objected that this evidence is not very reliable: after all, the pollsters overestimated the level of support for the Radicals, and they even predicted an increase in the vote for the Christian Democrats that never materialized. While this is a sensible objection,

---

41 Fabio Mussi, "What Happened in 1977?" *Rinascita*, June 8, 1979, pp. 11-13. For a discussion of trends in PCI membership, voters/members ratio, and organizational strength, and of the relationship between the party and the "movement" generally, see Marzio Barbagli and Piergiorgio Corbetta, "Partito e Movimento" [Party and movement] in *Inchiesta*, vol. 8 (January-February 1978).

42 See for example, Mattei Dogan, "Confutazione di un metodo di analisi del voto giovanile" [Confutation of a method for analyzing the youth vote] in Mattei Dogan and Orazio M. Petracca, eds., *Partiti Politici e Strutture Sociali in Italia* [Political parties and social structure in Italy] (Milan: Comunita, 1968), pp. 481-490.

TABLE 2–7
PCI VOTE, SENATE AND CHAMBER ELECTIONS, BY REGION, 1979
(percent)

Region	Senate, PCI	Chamber	
		PCI and PDUP	PCI
Piedmont	31.9	32.3	30.6
Lombardy	29.4	30.4	28.4
Liguria	36.2	36.0	36.9
Trentino A.A.	11.5	12.0	11.1
Veneto	22.6	23.1	21.7
Friuli	23.9	24.8	23.7
Emilia-Romagna	48.2	48.4	47.4
Tuscany	46.6	46.2	45.8
Marches	39.0	39.7	38.1
Umbria	46.3	46.6	45.5
Latium	30.8	31.2	30.2
Abruzzo	31.7	32.1	31.1
Molise	22.8	23.3	21.5
Apulia	27.7	27.8	26.7
Campania	26.2	26.2	24.9
Basilicata	29.0	30.8	28.9
Calabria	28.5	28.5	26.7
Sardinia	32.1	33.0	31.7
Sicily	22.4	22.2	21.1

SOURCE: Computed by the author from regional returns published in the press.

one could point out that our estimate of party preference among the older cohorts fits the Senate returns rather well. Thus we have reason to believe that the estimate for the younger cohorts is not too far off the mark.

A number of points can be made on the basis of these figures. First, parties of the left continue to receive a majority of the preferences of young voters. It is important to note that the percent favoring the left (57.9) is very close to estimates made by this writer and others on the basis of evidence collected in 1974 and 1975.[43] Second, the figures indicate that the PCI is still doing somewhat better among the younger cohorts than in the rest of the electorate. From this point

[43] Giacomo Sani, "Le elezioni degli anni settanta, terremoto o evoluzione?" [The elections of the 1970s: earthquake or evolution?], in *Rivista Italiana di Scienza Politica*, vol. 2, no. 2 (August 1976), pp. 261-288.

TABLE 2–8

ESTIMATES OF PARTY PREFERENCE AMONG YOUNGER AND OLDER VOTERS
(percent)

Party	Age Group		Senate Vote, 1979
	18–24	25 and over	
PDUP-NSU-PR	15.1	4.4	2.6
PCI	32.7	30.7	31.5
PSI	10.1	11.1	10.4
Total left	57.9	46.2	44.5
PSDI-PRI-PLI	4.5	7.5	9.8
DC	30.9	41.5	38.8
MSI-DN	6.7	4.7	6.3
Total center-right	42.1	53.7	54.9

SOURCE: Calculated by the author from the results of a voting intention survey carried out by the Demoskopea Institute and published in *Panorama*, May 8, 1979, p. 43.

of view the contrast with the DC is still marked. While it might very well be that the Christian Democrats have recovered some of the ground lost in the past, the age composition of its support group continues to be unbalanced. Last, it is quite clear that the small parties of the left had a disproportionately high level of support among the younger cohorts of voters in 1979. It is here, within these generations, that the PDUP, the NSU, and the Radicals constitute a challenge for the PCI, and for the Socialists as well.

Three Patterns of Returns

Our discussion of the 1979 returns has shown that the outcome of the election for the different parties was not uniform over the national territory. Socialists and Christian Democrats lost ground in the North and recouped it in the South. The Communists posted losses in all areas, but their rate of decline was hardly uniform. The Radicals gained across the board, but their gains were least pronounced in the districts in which the PCI suffered major losses.[44] Given these trends, it would not be very useful to search for a single pattern of change in

[44] The mean gain of the PR was 2.7 percentage points in the northern provinces, 1.6 points in the central regions, and 1.9 points in the South. The mean loss of the PCI was 3.0 percentage points in the North, 1.5 points in the Red Belt, and 5.3 points in the South.

TABLE 2–9

THREE PATTERNS OF ELECTORAL RETURNS: CHANGE IN THE VOTE,
1976–1979

(percentage points)

Province	PDUP NSU	PCI	PSI	PR	PSDI	PRI	DC	PLI	MSI-DN
PATTERN I									
Savona	+0.5	−4.0	+0.6	+2.9	+0.6	−0.1	−2.1	+1.5	+0.1
Grosseto	+0.7	−1.8	+0.5	+1.6	+0.3	−0.3	−1.6	+0.3	+0.1
PATTERN II									
Vercelli	+1.4	−5.3	−0.2	+1.6	+1.0	0	−1.0	+2.0	+0.3
Pavia	+0.9	−3.5	−1.1	+1.9	+0.8	−0.4	+0.1	+1.1	+0.1
PATTERN III									
Cosenza	+1.1	−7.0	+1.3	+1.6	+1.9	+0.3	+1.0	+0.1	−0.6
Caltanisetta	+2.0	−8.9	+0.3	+1.6	+1.0	+0.8	+5.0	+0.4	−2.8

SOURCE: Computed by the author from provincial returns published in the press.

the strength of the parties that would hold nationwide. To make sense of the election it is more profitable to attempt to identify the two or three patterns of variations that emerged most often (see table 2–9).

The first of these patterns can be illustrated by the returns for the province of Savona. Here we have a situation in which the Communists' losses were fully compensated by the gains of the other leftist parties, so that the overall strength of the left between the 1976 and 1979 elections remained unchanged. In this case the most plausible interpretation is an internal flow of voters within the left. Naturally, the figures do not prove that PCI voters switched to the Radicals and the PDUP; the figures are net variations and, in principle, they could reflect a number of alternative combinations involving complex exchanges of votes among parties. Nevertheless, this interpretation is both plausible and consistent with the returns. A slight variation of this pattern is illustrated by the figures for the province of Grosseto, where the Communist losses were more than compensated by the advances of the other leftist parties, so that we are led to infer a shift toward the left of a smaller number of centrist voters, in addition to an internal shift within the left.

A second pattern is illustrated by the returns for the province of Vercelli. Here the gains of the Radicals, the PDUP, the NSU, and the

PSI were not large enough to offset the losses suffered by the PCI. The most probable interpretation of this pattern is that in addition to a shift within the left there was an outflow of leftist voters toward the centrist parties, specifically the PSDI and the PLI. One should also note that PCI decline could have been accounted for to some extent by the drop in participation rates.[45]

The outcomes in the provinces of Cosenza and Caltanisetta illustrate a third pattern. In these cases only one-third of the Communist losses can be accounted for by the gains of the other leftist parties. To make sense of these results one must assume that between 1976 and 1979 there was a great deal of electoral mobility and that shifts in voting choices involved all segments of the political spectrum. The amount and the direction of the changes in the parties' strength lead us to the supposition that in these provinces the defections from the PCI benefited not only the Radicals, the new leftists, and the Socialists, but the Social Democrats and Christian Democrats as well.

We can now ask which of these three typical configurations predominated in the different areas of the country and how well these modal patterns fit the actual distributions of returns.

The simplest case is that of the Red Belt, the area that coincides with four regions of north-central Italy which traditionally have been a stronghold of the left. Here in 1979 there was a limited erosion of the support for the PCI, often accompanied by slight losses for the Socialists and a concurrent growth of PR, PDUP, and NSU support. Analysis indicates that in the twenty-three provinces of this area the first of our three patterns is the predominant one. As one can see from figure 2–3, there is a definite linear correspondence between the size of the combined losses incurred by the PCI and the PSI, and the size of the gains for the other leftist forces. Were it not for the provinces of Lucca and Massa (which, interestingly enough, have always been atypical) the correlation would be quite pronounced.[46] In sum, the returns in the Red Belt can satisfactorily be accounted for in terms of a flow of PCI voters toward the Radicals and the two formations of the new left.

As we move to consider the situation in the North we find that there is no single dominant pattern. In the thirty-two northern provinces we find two predominant distributions. The first is the one

[45] In spite of an increase in the size of the electorate, 10,000 fewer votes were cast in this province in 1979 than in 1976. Quite possibly these included a high percentage of potential PCI votes.
[46] Lucca has traditionally been a "white" island in the "red" region of Tuscany, and typologies of provinces by students of electoral behavior have traditionally placed it outside the Red Belt.

FIGURE 2–3
Relationship between PCI-PSI Losses and PR, PDUP, and NSU Gains in the Red Belt Provinces, 1979

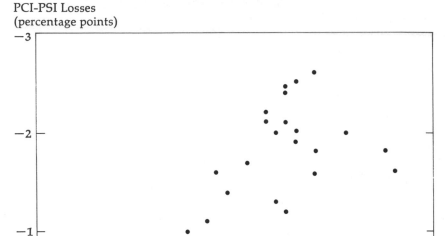

PCI-PSI Losses
(percentage points)

PR-PDUP-NSU Gains (percentage points)

that occurs in the Red Belt; that is, situations in which the Communists' losses can be accounted for in terms of the gains of the Radicals and the new left forces. This obtains in about 60 percent of these provinces. However, in the remaining 40 percent or so, a "compensatory" flow within the left does not entirely account for the outcome. In these areas the gains of the smaller leftist parties are not enough to compensate for the losses of the PCI, which are often accompanied by a decline of the Socialists as well. Since the Christian Democrats and the Republicans did not do very well, one is led to conclude that part of the losses of the traditional parties of the left represented an outflow of voters in favor of the Social Democrats and, possibly, the Liberals.

Last, in the South we find an even more complex situation. Our first and second patterns summarize reasonably well the returns for approximately 65 percent of the thirty-three southern provinces. But there remain one-third of the southern provinces for which we must turn to the last of the configurations discussed above.

Given the nature of the data analyzed, no firm conclusions are warranted. The evidence reviewed confirms that no single pattern of returns fits the realities of 1979 for Italy as a whole. The question, Where did the Communist votes go? has at least three answers.[47]

Conclusions

Judging from many of the comments made after the 1979 election one would have to conclude that the political consequences of the contest depend as much on how the country's critical elites choose to interpret the returns as they do on objective changes in the parties' strength. Those who contend that June 3 represented the beginning of a new phase emphasize the decline of the PCI and tend to ignore the fact that the overall strength of the left remained largely unchanged. To be sure, the left is not a homogeneous bloc, and its adversaries can take some comfort from its increasing fragmentation. Yet if we are to provide an answer to the question raised at the beginning of this chapter, we have to conclude that there is little evidence for the proposition that the cycle inaugurated in 1974 has come to an end. While it may be true that there has been a "return to the private sphere," it is clear that its impact on mass political orientations has been minimal. Perhaps young people spend less time demonstrating and more time disco dancing; tradition in dress styles and reading habits may have revived. But these changes have hardly affected people's choices in the voting booth. The wave of conservatism—or the new centrism—that many observers anticipated did not materialize.

The major and perhaps the only novelty introduced by the election of 1979 is the consolidation of new forces within the left at the expense of the traditional parties. The 1970s ended without major changes in broad political alignments but with a reward for those groups that in the middle of the decade had emerged as the carriers of a new political style.

---

[47] The first pattern was predominant in fifty-three provinces, the second in twenty-two, and the third in eleven.

3

The Christian Democrats: Masters of Survival

Douglas A. Wertman

The Christian Democratic party (DC) has been the leading party in Italy for more than thirty-five years. Each of the thirty-nine Governments since December 10, 1945, when Alcide De Gasperi first became prime minister, has been headed by a Christian Democrat, and the great bulk of the ministerial and undersecretary posts in these governments have been filled by Christian Democrats.[1] In addition, the DC has benefited from the largest share of the spoils, placing Christian Democrats in many key positions in the national bureaucracy, the judiciary, the large public corporations, and other public agencies, for example, in the fields of agriculture and the development of the South. Few parties have dominated a democratic political system in the post-World War II period as have the Christian Democrats in Italy. Now that the Congress party in India and the Labor party in Israel have tasted defeat, only the DC and Japan's Liberal Democratic party have held power continuously over the past twenty-five years.

Except in the confrontation election of 1948, when it won 48.5 percent of the vote in the Chamber of Deputies elections and established its position as the dominant party, the DC, while always remaining the largest party, has not come close to having its own

---

This chapter was written while the author was teaching at Franklin and Marshall College. The views expressed herein are those of the author and do not necessarily represent the views of the International Communication Agency or the U.S. Government.

[1] Christian Democrats have held 73.7 percent (691 out of 937) of the cabinet positions in the thirty-nine Governments from De Gasperi's first to Forlani's. Fourteen of the thirty-nine have been *monocolore* (one-party) Governments; if only the twenty-five Governments which included the DC and at least one other party are counted, the DC held 62.0 percent (361 out of 582) of the cabinet positions.

majority in Parliament. Despite this, the DC was able to adapt to changing political conditions and to maintain its dominance through a series of different political formulas. These were the Popular Front (including the PCI and the other parties of the anti-Fascist resistance) until 1947, the centrist coalition (with the three small lay parties, the PRI, the PLI, and the PSDI) during the 1950s, and the center-left (which extended the centrist coalition, minus the Liberals, to include the Socialists) from 1963 until its collapse in early 1976 (with an interlude in 1972–1973 for a DC-PSDI-PLI center-right Government). The special nature of the DC's hold on state power in its many forms, as well as the DC's role as the representative of some of the most important conservative forces in Italy, was, in effect, recognized by the PCI in its adoption of the "historic compromise" strategy in the 1970s.[2]

Since 1963 the DC's aggregate national support in parliamentary elections has been more stable than that of any other Italian party or any other large political party in Western Europe. In the Chamber of Deputies elections over the past sixteen years, the DC has won 38.3 percent in 1963, 39.1 percent in 1968, 38.7 percent in 1972, 38.7 percent in 1976, and 38.3 percent in 1979.[3] However, the DC's hold on governmental power has not been as stable in the past five years as it was before the 1974–1976 crisis. After the defeat of its antidivorce position in the May 1974 referendum and the party's loss of approximately 3 percentage points in the 1975 regional and provincial elections (coupled with substantial gains by the left), the DC was on the defensive. The Communist party, meanwhile, had closed the nationwide gap between the DC and itself from 11.6 percentage points in 1972 to 3.2 points in 1975, and there appeared to be a serious possibility that the PCI would surpass the DC as the largest Italian party in the 1976 elections. Aided by the fear of a Communist victory, the DC recovered enough in 1976 to take exactly the same proportion of the vote it had won in the 1972 elections and to widen slightly its margin over the PCI, to 4.3 percentage points. In the psychological climate of 1976, this was perceived as a victory. In the

[2] Stephen Hellman, "The Longest Campaign: Communist Party Strategy and the Elections of 1976," in Howard R. Penniman, ed., *Italy at the Polls: The Parliamentary Elections of 1976* (Washington, D.C.: American Enterprise Institute, 1977), pp. 165-168 and p. 177.

[3] Among the four major Western European countries, the largest parties closest to the DC in terms of electoral stability since the early 1960s are the French Communist party (with a range of 20.0 percent to 22.5 percent between 1962 and 1978) and the West German CDU/CSU (with a range of 44.9 percent to 48.6 percent between 1961 and 1976).

three years that followed, while there was an uncertain political situation in which no governmental formula was clearly acceptable to any majority in Parliament, the DC was able to maintain its hold on power through a succession of arduously negotiated agreements and to resist the demands of the Communist party for full governmental participation. It was the DC that was on the offensive in 1978 and 1979 (as a result of its victory in the May 1978 local elections and its strong showings in the polls); it had rebounded from its period of greatest crisis—while the PCI faced serious problems. The PCI suffered substantial losses in the 1979 elections, as most polls and observers had predicted it would, but the biggest surprise of these elections was that the DC did not win the major victory many expected; instead it suffered slight losses: 0.4 percentage points in the Chamber of Deputies vote and 0.6 points in the Senate elections. Nevertheless, the DC was able to increase its margin over the PCI to 7.9 percentage points. Though the DC is certainly not as dominant as it was before 1974, it remains in power—and the overall political situation remains unsettled.

The Nature of the DC

The DC's Development: 1943–1976. The DC, founded in 1943, was a new party at the end of World War II, though it had an antecedent in the Italian Popular party of 1919–1926. In the 1946 Constituent Assembly elections the DC gained 35.2 percent of the vote (compared with 20.7 percent for the PSI and 18.9 percent for the PCI); this was nearly 15 percentage points more than the Popular party had achieved in the last pre-Fascist elections in 1919 and 1921. The DC's success can be explained by the support—based above all on anticommunism—of the church, the United States, and the bourgeoisie, as well as by the fact that women were given the right to vote for the first time in 1946; in addition, the weakened position of the Liberals allowed the DC to penetrate (or coopt) many of the traditional clienteles in the South.[4]

The first phase of the DC's development, from 1945 until 1954, was dominated by Alcide De Gasperi (prime minister in eight consecutive Governments during those years) and others from this first generation of DC leaders, many of whom had been active in the Popular party. The DC's organization was very weak, and De Gasperi

[4] For a discussion of the creation of the DC in the 1943-1945 period, see Gianfranco Pasquino, "Crisi della DC e evoluzione del sistema politico" [The crisis of the DC and the evolution of the political system], *Rivista Italiana di Scienza Politica*, vol. 5 (December 1975), pp. 445-449.

depended heavily on the infrastructure of the Catholic church and the Catholic subculture to mobilize support for the DC. De Gasperi's goal clearly was to build the Christian Democratic party into a force which would have a solid interclass electorate, including a strong popular or working-class/lower-class component, and would for a long time dominate the Italian political system.

Of crucial importance in understanding both De Gasperi's political strategy and the DC's domination of the postwar political system is the nature of the largest opposition party, the Italian Communist party. For most of the postwar period, Italy has been, in effect, a "special democracy." This concept developed from De Gasperi's emphasis, which has been continued by subsequent DC leaders, on opposing the extremes of left and right as threats to the Italian democratic system and maintaining the DC in some kind of centrist position by stressing its "centrality" as the protector and keystone of Italian democracy.[5] In other words, "Her Majesty's Loyal Opposition" has not existed because many both inside and outside Italy have perceived the major opposition party as not "loyal" to the democratic system and not a legitimate or acceptable alternative to, or possible coalition partner of, the DC. The PCI was strong enough to be a threat and, thereby, to help the DC aggregate anticommunist support and maintain its dominance. At least until 1975, however, it was not strong enough to challenge the DC's dominance as the main Government party or its resistance to cooperation with the PCI. Anticommunism has always been an important factor in the DC's electoral support and was clearly the most prominent theme of its electoral campaigns in both 1976 and 1979.

The Christian Democrats lost more than eight percentage points in the 1953 elections. This substantially weakened De Gasperi's position and led to the rise of the second generation of DC leaders, many of whom are still major figures in the party twenty-five years later. Amintore Fanfani, who was the party secretary from 1954 until 1959, began a major effort to build the party organization and to reduce the DC's reliance on the church. Fanfani was partially successful in developing a more solid party structure (though organizational weakness is still a problem for the DC today), but the DC continued to rely greatly on the church and the Catholic subculture. This new emphasis on the party's organization, coinciding with the second generation's arrival at the top positions of power, was one of the chief causes of the proliferation and organization of factions within

[5] See Ruggero Orfei, *L'occupazione del potere* [The occupation of power] (Milan: Longanesi and Co., 1976), pp. 5-15.

the DC. By the late 1950s and early 1960s, factional conflict had become the dominant feature of intraparty decision making as well as of the allocation of positions of power within the DC, the Government, the bureaucracy, and the public corporations. A handful of individuals such as Fanfani (1954–1959 and 1973–1975) and Aldo Moro (1963–1968 and 1976–1978), have been the most important leaders over the past twenty-five years and the central figures during particular phases, but no single leader has been able to dominate the party as De Gasperi did in the first phase of the DC's life.

The electoral and political weakness of the centrist formula (dating from the 1953 elections) and the accompanying concern in the DC that a more stable Government coalition was necessary, the deepening split between the Communists and the Socialists, the Socialists' developing acceptance of the major features of Italian foreign policy (especially membership in the EEC and NATO), the papacy of John XXIII, and the support by several factions within the DC for a more reformist program led the DC in the late 1950s and early 1960s toward the "opening to the left." The Liberals went into opposition and the Government coalition was extended to the left by the addition of the Italian Socialist party. This acted to solidify further the DC's hold on power by widening the base of the Government. It also helped the DC keep the Communist party on the margins of the political system at the national level (at least until the mid-1970s). The PSI's entry into the Government did not bring a major change in the nature of the DC's rule; a few reforms were enacted over the next several years, but perhaps the chief outcome was the PSI's adaptation to participation in the division of the spoils— the positions of power within the Government, the bureaucracy, and the public corporations.[6]

While the DC has been the major governing force since 1945 and has filled many important positions in the state bureaucracy and other public agencies with Christian Democrats, it has largely undertaken an "occupation of power" without enacting substantial economic, social, political, or bureaucratic reforms.[7] The DC's inability (and, in part, unwillingness) to enact a coherent reform program during its thirty-five years in power is due to a variety of factors. First, the conservative groups within the DC electorate, including the Small

---

[6] For a discussion of the Italian Socialist party, see Gianfranco Pasquino, "The Italian Socialist Party: An Irreversible Decline?" in Penniman, ed., *Italy at the Polls, 1976*, pp. 183-227.

[7] The now very popular phrase "occupation of power" is the title of Ruggero Orfei's work *L'occupazione del potere.*

Farmers Confederation and much of the bourgeois component, have resisted reform, making it difficult to reach consensus in support of any reform program among the different social groups in a party whose electorate was and is the most "interclassist" of all Italian parties. Second, because of its permanence as the dominant party, there has been a lack of accountability. Not until the mid-1970s did the DC face any strong challenge which might stimulate it to enact reforms. When there is no alternation in power, there is much less incentive to make changes and much greater room for the abuse of public resources. Third, most observers have argued that there is widespread inefficiency in the Italian bureaucracy; this has been aggravated because of its "colonization" by the DC. The DC's "occupation of power" and its use of the bureaucracy, the special public agencies, and the public corporations for clientelistic purposes were fully developed in the middle and late 1950s with (1) the coming to power within the party of the second generation of leaders, who made a conscious effort to solidify the DC's hold on these state institutions, (2) the growth of factionalism within the DC, (3) the expansion and centralization of the public sector of the economy, especially through the institution of the National Hydrocarbons Trust (ENI) in 1953 and of the Ministry of State Industrial Holdings in 1956, and (4) the struggle for positions of power among the four parties participating in the center-left.[8] Patronage, at both the national and local levels, has been one of the tools used by the DC to maintain its power and by individual leaders to retain their share of power within the DC. Three additional factors which have frustrated reform are the immobilism which results when governments last on the average less than one year, the factionalism within the DC which makes effective policy making very difficult, and the lack of substantial turnover in the DC leadership group for almost twenty-five years.

While Italy was going through the economic boom of the 1950s and early 1960s and resources were expanding, the nature of DC rule created relatively few immediate problems; however, by the late 1960s the "colonization" of the bureaucracy was entrenched, eco-

---

[8] The National Hydrocarbons Trust was created in 1953 to centralize in one agency the management of state activities in the hydrocarbons field, including petroleum, natural gas, coal, etc. The State Industrial Holdings Ministry was set up in 1956 to provide overall direction and coordination of corporations wholly or partially owned by the Italian state. For a discussion of the development of the Ministry of State Industrial Holdings see Giuliano Amato, "Il ruolo dell' Esecutivo nel governo delle Partecipazioni statali" [The role of the executive in the governing of state participations] in *Il governo democratico dell'economia* [The democratic governing of the economy] (Bari: De Donato, 1976), pp. 135-147.

nomic and social crises were at hand, and the student protests and university occupations of 1968 and labor's "Hot Autumn" of 1969 had stimulated an atmosphere of mass mobilization. Under these conditions the DC's system of power made it much more difficult to deal with Italy's problems. There was a developing public sense in Italy that many of the problems were to a substantial degree a result of government inaction, maladministration at both the national and local levels, and corruption. Its public image badly damaged, the DC suffered losses in the 1975 regional elections that undoubtedly reflected profound dissatisfaction. In his postelection analysis Aldo Moro argued that a part of its electorate had become "tired" of the DC.[9]

The crisis of the party was apparent by the 1974–1975 period. First, there was the major defeat for the DC's antidivorce position in the May 1974 referendum. Second-time party secretary Amintore Fanfani led the campaign; his attempt to play on the voters' anti-communism was far from successful since the prodivorce group included anticommunist parties such as the PLI and the PSDI and since the control of the Government was not at stake. The referendum accentuated the conflict within the Catholic community and clearly showed that the church, from top to bottom, was much more divided over involvement in Italian politics than it had been in earlier decades.[10] Second, there were the DC's losses and the left's gains in the regional and provincial elections of June 1975; the gap between the DC and the PCI after these elections was only 3.2 percentage points, down from a margin of 11.6 points after the 1972 parliamentary elections.[11]

The anticommunism (and the stress on polarization as an electoral tool) that dominated the 1975 DC campaign led by Fanfani posed a basic dilemma for Prime Minister Aldo Moro: they moved the DC toward the right at a time when he needed the support of the PSI to

[9] For excerpts of Moro's speech, see Aniello Coppola, *Moro* (Milan: Feltrinelli, 1976), pp. 138-144.

[10] For a discussion of the referendum, see Martin Clark, David Hine, and R.E.M. Irving, "Divorce-Italian Style," *Parliamentary Affairs*, vol. 27, no. 4 (Autumn 1974), pp. 333-358.

[11] In comparing the ninety-two (of ninety-four) provinces where elections took place on June 15, 1975, with the results for the same ninety-two provinces in the 1972 parliamentary elections, one finds that the PCI gained 4.9 points (from 27.5 percent to 32.4 percent), while the DC lost 3.1 points (from 38.7 percent to 35.6 percent). For an explanation of these results, see Giacomo Sani, "Secular Trends and Party Realignments in Italy: The 1975 Election" (Paper delivered at the Annual Meeting of the American Political Science Association, San Francisco, California, September 1975).

maintain the Government. The PSI, which felt itself and the left as a whole to be in a much stronger position as a result of the 1975 elections, wanted to bring the PCI into some kind of relationship with the Government majority and was clearly moving in the second half of 1975 toward a break with the center-left formula. In his analysis of the elections, Moro argued that it was necessary, given the message the DC had received in 1975 and the crisis nature of Italy's problems, to develop some kind of dialogue or constructive relationship between the Government majority and the Communist opposition, but he also said that this relationship had to stop short of Communist participation in the majority.[12] Moro's speech clearly shows the early development of his political strategy, which the DC followed in the 1976–1979 period.

Much of the blame for the DC losses in the regional elections was placed on Fanfani, who, shortly after these elections, failed to receive a vote of confidence from the DC National Council and resigned. His replacement, Benigno Zaccagnini, chosen as an interim secretary, quickly became much more than a transitional figure; instead he became the figure around whom two coalitions formed prior to the DC congress of March 1976. The pro-Zaccagnini coalition (though it included many traditional party figures such as Mariano Rumor, Emilio Colombo, and Antonino Gullotti who could not be seen as convinced supporters of significant party reform) certainly included many people who believed that there was a real need for reform of the DC—to overcome the excesses of factionalism and to bring the Catholic working class, Catholic youth, and the dissident Catholics closer to the party again but also simply to permit the party to stay in power. If the DC considered the PCI an unacceptable partner, it must undertake a genuine revitalization and become the alternative to itself.

The anti-Zaccagnini group, though it adopted the rhetoric of "revitalization," was largely opposed to significant reform and was much more cautious about self-criticism, which it saw as playing into the hands of the PCI and PSI with their attacks on DC hegemony in the postwar political system. The pro-Zaccagnini group won by a very small margin at the Congress (and Zaccagnini was reelected party secretary), but the anti-Zaccagnini coalition eventually achieved a slim majority in both the DC National Council and the National Executive Committee.[13] Ultimately the efforts of Zaccagnini and

---

[12] Coppola, *Moro*, pp. 138-144.

[13] The DC National Executive Committee, which may meet weekly or a little less often, is composed of many of the top factional leaders and is responsible for

others at *rifondazione* (refounding) of the DC were frustrated by opposition from many of the long-standing factional chiefs—and by the DC's recovery in the 1976 elections.[14]

The death of the center-left came in early 1976 when the Socialists put pressure on the DC for either a new Government which would include the PCI along with the parties of the center-left or at least a changed majority, with the Communists giving external support to the new Government. The resulting Government crisis and the DC opposition to the Socialist proposals eventually led to the establishment of a Government, like its predecessor headed by Moro, which had very shaky parliamentary support. The Socialists, at their party congress in March 1976, adopted the "leftist alternative" as their official party strategy and at a minimum called for some kind of relationship of the PCI to the DC-led Government; these demands made early elections necessary. The elections were fought in a climate of confrontation. The dual possibility of the PCI surpassing the DC as the largest party and of a leftist majority seemed very real (though the PCI had officially adopted the "historic compromise" strategy in 1975); the DC was clearly on the defensive and appeared to be headed for another defeat. However, to the surprise of most observers and contrary to the predictions of the polls, the DC recovered from its 1975 losses to maintain the 38.7 percent of the vote it had won in the last parliamentary elections, in 1972. The DC gained about 3 percentage points from 1975, winning back in the political elections some of the voters it had lost in the administrative elections and attracting some new support at the expense of the PSDI (which lost 1.7 percentage points compared with 1972), the PLI (which lost 2.6 points), and the MSI (which lost 2.6 points).[15] Again, the key was anticommunism: when the threat of the Communist

---

setting much of the party strategy, particularly since the National Council (which has more than 200 members compared with the 43 on the National Executive Committee) only meets two or three times during the year.

[14] Some changes or innovations were made—such as the institution of DC-related organizations in workplaces (Gruppi di Impegno Politico) and DC festivals (Feste d'Amicizia) and the modification of party statutes to attempt to lessen the artificial inflation of party membership—but they fall well short of a refounding of the DC.

[15] On the DC vote in 1976, see Giacomo Sani, "The Italian Electorate in the Mid-1970s: Beyond Tradition?" in Penniman, ed., *Italy at the Polls, 1976*, pp. 95-97 and pp. 108-109; and Arturo Parisi and Gianfranco Pasquino, "20 giugno: struttura politica e comportamento elettorale" [June 20: political structure and electoral behavior], in Arturo Parisi and Gianfranco Pasquino, eds., *Continuità e mutamento elettorale in Italia* [Electoral continuity and change in Italy] (Bologna: Il Mulino, 1977), pp. 34-60.

party's surpassing the DC seemed real, the DC, seen as the protector of Italy's democratic institutions, could recover from its 1975 losses.

The PCI rose to 34.4 percent (a gain of 2 points compared with 1975 and 7.2 points compared with 1972), but the gap between the DC and the PCI widened, from 3.2 to 4.3 points. The PCI was becoming even stronger numerically, but the DC had made an important recovery both numerically and psychologically. As a result of this election, there was no clear governmental formula supported by a majority in Parliament; this lack of a stable parliamentary majority and the Communist party's demand for full governmental participation remained the dominant problems throughout the life of the Parliament elected in June 1976.

The Electoral Support of the DC. Despite the many changes in Italian society in the past two decades and the increased dissatisfaction in the 1970s with the nature of DC rule and the party's inability to enact a reformist program, the DC has been able to maintain itself at virtually the same level in the five parliamentary elections since 1963. Yet surveys have shown that the DC has received by far the largest share of the public's blame for the Italian political and economic crisis of the 1970s.[16] In a January 1975 survey not only was the DC by far the most frequently named by all respondents as having the major responsibility for the crisis, but it was also the most frequently named by DC respondents; 29.1 percent of the DC respondents said that the DC must bear the major responsibility for the crisis, and this proportion went up to 45.9 percent of the DC respondents who named a party as responsible.[17] Marradi concluded that "among those who made strong accusations of incapacity and corruption against the DC, more than just a few admit that they voted for it, often adding explicitly as a reason the guarantee the DC offers for the maintenance of liberty, tranquility or simply the status quo."[18] Clearly a substantial degree of the DC's support is based on factors not directly related to its governmental performance.

Four explanations are most significant in understanding the Christian Democrats' electoral base: (1) the religious factor, (2)

[16] Giampaolo Fabris, *Il comportamento politico degli italiani* [The political behavior of the Italians] (Milan: Franco Angeli Editore, 1977), pp. 80-83 and pp. 166-167. Alberto Marradi, "Immagini di massa della DC e del PCI," [Popular images of the DC and the PCI], in Alberto Martinelli and Gianfranco Pasquino, eds., *La politica nell'Italia che cambia* [Politics in a changing Italy] (Milan: Feltrinelli, 1978), pp. 66-103.

[17] Fabris, *Il comportamento politico*, pp. 80-83.

[18] Marradi, "Immagini di massa," p. 84.

strong female support, (3) appeals based on anticommunism in particular and antiextremism in general as well as on the role of the DC as the main protector of Italy's democratic institutions and liberties, and (4) clientelism.[19] Despite the changes in Italian society in the 1960s and 1970s, there have not been major modifications in the composition of the DC electorate over the past several elections. First, the Catholic church and the Catholic subculture played a central role both culturally and organizationally in the formation and electoral success of the DC, and the religious factor clearly continues to be significant for the party despite the lesser commitment of the church to the DC, the lesser support for the DC and/or diminished strength of the major organizations of the Catholic subculture, and the shrinking pool of those who attend church regularly. In fact, the DC electorate contains a much higher proportion of people who attend church regularly than the electorate of any other party; a survey done in late 1975 showed that, while 62.7 percent of the DC respondents attended church weekly or almost weekly, only 24.0 percent of all the other respondents did so; no other single party had more than 33.3 percent of its respondents attending church weekly or almost weekly.[20] However, the secularization of society (the proportion of Italians saying that they had attended mass the previous Sunday declined from 69 percent in a 1956 survey to 36.6 percent in a 1976 survey), the decreasing strength of the Catholic subculture as a whole, and the church's lesser commitment to the DC, which was very apparent in the 1979 campaign, all appear to be irreversible trends; though these developments have not yet made a major impact on support for the DC, they will, slowly, and will present a problem for the party. This does not mean, of course, that the DC's electoral strength will eventually collapse, since the party has other sources of support and is clearly much more than simply a Catholic party.

The DC's female support continues at very nearly the same level it has maintained in the entire postwar period—a level that makes the DC electorate, in its sex composition, very different from

---

[19] For more detailed discussions of the DC electorate see Douglas Wertman, "The Electorate of Religiously-Based Political Parties: The Case of the Italian Christian Democratic Party" (Ph.D. dissertation, Department of Political Science, The Ohio State University, August 1974); and Gianfranco Pasquino, "Italian Christian Democracy: A Party for All Seasons?" *West European Politics*, vol. 2, no. 3 (October 1979), pp. 88-109.

[20] Sani, "The Italian Electorate," p. 111. In a survey done in April 1976, 70 percent of the DC respondents said that they had been to mass the previous Sunday, while the parties with the next highest proportions had 44 percent and 32 percent of their respondents saying that they had attended mass the previous Sunday. Fabris, *Il comportamento politico*, p. 50.

TABLE 3–1

FEMALE PROPORTION OF THE ELECTORATE OF ITALIAN PARTIES, 1975–1980
(percent)

Survey Date	DC	PCI	PSI	PSDI	PRI	PLI	MSI	PR	DP/PDUP	Total Sample
November–December 1975	61.4	49.5	47.0	37.5	32.6	43.3	38.6		35.9[a]	51.4
Mid-1976	61.0	41.0	40.0	46.0	34.0	47.0	35.0	—	—	51.9
July 1977	60.8	47.6	40.0	56.2	42.6	41.7	35.8	50.0	31.0	51.8
April 1979	60.0	48.0	52.0	—	50.0	—	37.0	48.0	49.0	—
June 1980	60.5	45.2	41.7	46.1	43.7	50.0	35.7	—	47.6	—

Dash (—): Information not available.

[a] Small parties of the left given together.

SOURCE: The November–December 1975 data appear in Giacomo Sani, "The Italian Electorate in the Mid-1970s: Beyond Tradition?" in Howard R. Penniman, ed., *Italy at the Polls: The Parliamentary Elections of 1976* (Washington, D.C.: American Enterprise Institute, 1977), p. 111. The mid-1976 data (which are a result of a composite of five surveys done over a five month period in mid-1976) and the July 1977 data were both given to me by DOXA. The April 1979 survey, done by Demoskopea, was reported in *Panorama*, May 8, 1979, p. 43. The June 1980 survey, conducted by Demoskopea, was reported in *Panorama*, June 23, 1980, p. 47.

that of any other Italian party. As table 3–1 shows, five surveys done between late 1975 and June 1980 indicate that the DC has been consistently much more dependent on female support than any other party; in fact, only a few parties (and then in only one survey out of five) have had as much as 50 percent of their support from women. On the basis of thirteen surveys done between 1947 and 1980, it can be concluded that the DC's electorate has always been at least 60 percent female. An indication that this female predominance is likely to continue, at least for a while longer, comes from a July 1977 survey,[21] which showed a very similar sex distribution among young, middle-aged, and older DC voters: 63.3 percent of the DC voters aged eighteen to thirty-four were women, 59.1 percent of those aged thirty-five to fifty-four were women, and 60.8 percent of those fifty-five and older were women. The most important reason for this high level of female support for the DC is the greater degree of church attendance among women; studies using survey data from 1972 and 1975 have clearly shown that when one eliminates the impact of different levels of church attendance among men and women there is a much smaller difference in their electoral behavior.[22]

As we have already noted in discussing De Gasperi's political strategy, the dominance of the DC in the Italian political system, and the election campaigns of 1976 and 1979, anticommunism, combined with the DC's emphasis on its role as the protector of Italy's democratic institutions, has been and continues to be an important source of support for the DC. This has been especially true in times of direct confrontation, such as 1976, when it was the central factor in the DC's recovery from its 1975 losses. Though anticommunism has diminished somewhat in the electorate as a whole, it still exerts a strong influence on a substantial number of voters. Anticommunism has been important to the DC both because of the party's ties with the church and because of its support from a significant number of middle-class and upper-class voters (sometimes, as in 1976, defectors from the Liberal party or the Social Democratic party). This anticommunism also acts as a constraint on what DC leaders can do; apart from their own feelings, the DC leaders did not want to grant full legitimacy to the PCI in the 1976–1979 period by allowing it to have full participation in the Government because this could have seriously hurt one of their major bases of support.

---

[21] I would like to thank DOXA for providing me with the data from the July 1977 survey.

[22] See Wertman, "The Electorate of Religiously-Based Political Parties," pp. 149-152, and Sani, "The Italian Electorate," pp. 113-114.

Finally, the DC system of clientelism at the national and local levels also plays a role in its electoral support; however, its impact cannot very easily be measured and may vary substantially from one part of Italy to another. Studies by Allum and Caciagli, for example, have shown the importance of clientelism for the DC in the cities of Naples and Catania respectively, but, as Pasquino argues, "nowhere is clientelism alone the basis of the strength of the party." [23] Clientelism is one part of the whole picture of DC electoral support, but, while certainly not underestimating its importance, one should not over-emphasize it, as some have, to the near exclusion of the religious, female, and anticommunist factors in the DC electoral base.

Factionalism, New Forces in the DC, and Intraparty Decision Making. Particularly since the mid-1950s, factionalism has been the central feature of decision making within the DC and of the division of important positions of power within the party and the Government. This factional character of the DC remains in 1981—despite the attempts at "refounding" the DC in the 1975–1976 period, when criticism of the "logic of tribal chieftains" was frequent, and despite the strong dissatisfaction with factionalism expressed in late 1980 by a large number of younger DC members of Parliament from all factions. There are today at least ten identifiable factions in the DC.[24] There have been many changes in the past twenty-five years in the factional composition of the DC, but there has also been a great deal

[23] Pasquino, "Italian Christian Democracy," p. 94. See also P. A. Allum, *Politics and Society in Postwar Italy* (Cambridge: Cambridge University Press, 1973). Mario Caciagli, *Democrazia Cristiana e Potere nel Mezzogiorno: il sistema democristiano a Catania* [Christian Democracy and power in Southern Italy: the Christian Democratic system in Catania] (Florence: Guaraldi Editore S.P.A., 1977).

[24] Despite the shifting of alliances between 1976 and 1980, there was little change in the strength of the major DC factions between the Thirteenth DC National Congress in March 1976 and the Fourteenth National Congress held in January 1980, as shown in the percentage of delegates from each faction:

	13th National Congress	14th National Congress
Base	10	13
Morotei	10	6
Gullotti	3	3
Dorotei	23	23
Andreottiani	9	13
Fanfaniani	12	13
Dissident Fanfaniani	6	1
Rumoriani	5	4
Colombiani	7	5
Forze Nuove	13	9
Nuove Forze	—	7
Proposta	—	2

of continuity in the individuals who have been top factional leaders. Some factions, such as Base and the Fanfaniani, have remained separate factions for most of the period, while others, such as the Dorotei, the Andreottiani, Colombiani, and Rumoriani, have been involved in a number of mergers and splits.[25] Decisions on the tactics and alliances of each faction are usually made by a small group of its top chiefs.

The DC factions are clearly recognized within and outside the party; they are commonly discussed by name in the Italian press, and the individual leaders and members of Parliament are often identified in the press by their factional membership. Most of the factions have their own press agency or weekly or monthly publication, or cultural or study center, which becomes an electoral machine fighting for preference votes for the faction's members during parliamentary elections. Though they are centered in the regions or provinces of their major leaders, at least the biggest factions have roots which go down to the regional, provincial, and even communal level throughout the country. And factions often hold their own national and local meetings.[26] The tools individual leaders use to maintain their faction's power as well as their own power within the faction include: (1) the control of a substantial part of the party membership/party organization within their home region or province, which is crucial to a faction's strength at the national congress; (2) the holding of top party positions; and (3) the holding of positions within the Government and, through them, the ability to distribute patronage. The major role of clientelism in the maintenance of factional power suggests why the ministries, such as State Industrial Holdings or Post and Telecommunications, which control a large amount of patronage, are considered very important by DC leaders when cabinets are formed.[27]

[25] Since the 1979 elections, a formal split has taken place in Forze Nuove between Carlo Donat Cattin, leader of Forze Nuove, who has taken a strongly anti-communist position and has been very critical of Zaccagnini, and Guido Bodrato, one of Zaccagnini's closest advisors. A number of undersecretaries, deputies, senators, regional elected officials, and party officials have also split from Donat Cattin in support of Bodrato and Zaccagnini. This new faction, led by Bodrato, has taken the name Nuove Forze.

[26] For a detailed theoretical discussion of factionalism and its causes, see Giovanni Sartori, ed., *Correnti, Frazioni, e Fazioni nei Partiti Politici* [Currents, fractions, and factions in the political parties] (Bologna: Il Mulino, 1973), and Alan S. Zuckerman, *The Politics of Faction: Christian Democratic Rule in Italy* (New Haven: Yale University Press, 1979).

[27] State Industrial Holdings and Post and Telecommunications are, along with four other cabinet positions (prime minister and ministers of interior, agriculture, and public instruction), those most frequently controlled by Christian Democrats in coalition cabinets.

Though a few DC independents—individuals not directly attached to a faction—have been ministers in the Governments between 1976 and 1979, most of the ministerial and undersecretary posts go to representatives of the organized factions. As table 3–2 shows, factionalism still plays the central role in the distribution of cabinet and undersecretary posts as well as in the allocation of the positions of power within the party itself. This distribution of party and Government positions to the factions is based upon the strength of each faction at the most recent national congress of the DC.[28]

Another development that shows the continued importance of the factions in intraparty decision making was the setting up of a new party institution, the enlarged Office of the Secretariat, in April 1979. Because of the numerous intricate negotiations on programs and Governments in the post-1976 period, the DC delegation—the party secretary, the vice-secretaries, the president of the DC National Council, and the leaders of the DC groups in the Chamber of Deputies and the Senate—has played a central role on the basis of the decisions made by the National Executive Committee. The delegation usually represents the DC in meetings with the leaders of other parties and in the negotiations over the formation of a new Government. In late March 1979 Zaccagnini decided that, since four of the six members of the delegation were from factions by then hostile to Zaccagnini and his political strategy, he would nominate two additional vice-secretaries, Ciriaco De Mita and Antonino Gullotti, who were favorable to his views, to create a better balance within the DC delegation. At a meeting of the DC National Executive Committee on April 5, 1979, there was substantial opposition to Zaccagnini's proposal, especially from the leaders of those factions who were not directly or, in their view, sufficiently represented within the DC delegation (which would play a central role in directing the DC campaign on a daily basis). It was finally agreed that there would be the two additional vice-secretaries, but that there would also be a newly created Office of the Secretariat which would direct the party day to day during the campaign and which would include all the

---

[28] One other consideration which is taken into account in the division of cabinet positions among DC factions is the importance of each position. According to Massimiliano Cencelli, a DC functionary who admits to having prepared a manual which is used by party leaders in the distribution of cabinet and undersecretary posts, "Mathematics is not based on opinion; it is sufficient to calculate the percentage of the votes at the Congress and to update the importance of each ministry." (The relative importance of ministries may change over time as they acquire or lose functions.) *Panorama*, March 21, 1978, p. 17. The same kind of division of ministerial and undersecretary positions among the factions has taken place in the formation of Governments since the 1979 election.

TABLE 3–2

FACTIONAL COMPOSITION OF DC PARTY ORGANS AND OF DC MEMBERSHIP IN GOVERNMENTS, 1976–1979

(percent)

Faction	National Party Congress[a] (March 1976)	National Council (Elected March 1976)	National Executive Committee (Elected April 1976)	Enlarged Office of Secretariat (April 1979)	Andreotti #4 (March 1978–Jan. 1979)		Andreotti #5 (March 1979–Aug. 1979)	Cossiga #1 (Aug. 1979–April 1980)	
					Cabinet	Under-secretaries[b]	Cabinet	Cabinet	Under-secretaries[b]
Dorotei	23.0	20.8	26.2	20.0	19.0	31.9	21.4	23.5	28.0
Andreottiani	9.0	6.7	7.1	6.7	9.5	8.5	14.3	11.8	4.7
Fanfaniani	12.0	9.2	14.3	13.3	14.3	14.9	14.3	11.8	14.0
Dissident Fanfaniani	6.0	5.0	4.8	6.7	0.0	0.0	0.0	0.0	0.0
Colombiani	7.0	6.7	4.8	6.7	4.8	0.0	7.1	0.0	2.3

Rumor/ Gullotti	9.0	8.3	7.1	13.3	4.8	8.5	0.0	0.0	4.7
Morotei	10.0	8.3	14.3	13.3	9.5	10.6	14.3	5.9	14.0
Base	10.0	10.0	7.1	13.3	14.3	8.5	14.3	17.6	4.7
Forze Nuove	13.0	11.7	9.5	6.7	9.5	12.8	7.1	5.9	16.3
Independents/ diverse groups	—	13.4	4.7	0.0	14.3	0.0	7.1	23.5	0.0
Unidentified as to faction	0.0	0.0	0.0	0.0	0.0	4.3	0.0	0.0	16.3
N		(120)	(43)	(15)	(21)	(47)	(14)	(17)	(43)

Dash (—): Data not available.

[a] These figures are approximate.

[b] Sometimes a faction is compensated for a smaller proportion of the cabinet membership with a larger proportion of the undersecretary positions.

SOURCE: Party Congress, *Corriere della Sera*, March 18, 1976, p. 2; National Council, *Corriere della Sera*, March 25, 1976, p. 2; National Executive Committee, *Corriere della Sera*, April 15, 1976, p. 2; Enlarged Office of the Secretariat, *La Stampa*, April 6, 1979; cabinet and undersecretary positions, information gathered by the author from a variety of sources.

members of the DC delegation plus seven additional individuals to create a better factional balance and to assure representation in this office to all factions. Therefore, to the two Dorotei, two Base members, one Fanfaniano, one Gullottiano, one Forze Nuove member, and one Moroteo/Zaccagniniano in the delegation were added a third Doroteo, a second Fanfaniano, a second Moroteo/Zaccagniniano, and one individual each from the factions headed respectively by Andreotti, Rumor, and Colombo as well as the independent Fanfaniano group.[29]

To a large extent the top leadership which gained power in the DC in 1954 (men like Andreotti, Fanfani, Colombo, Rumor, and Piccoli) still plays the key role in determining DC policy. A third generation of leaders, such as Arnaldo Forlani, Antonio Bisaglia, and Ciriaco De Mita, have been integrated into the top leadership group after working their way up by the traditional factional paths, but there has not been any substantial turnover at the top levels since 1954.

Since the mid-1970s a number of new forces have developed within the DC.[30] (1) A conservative, strongly anticommunist, lay-oriented group, whose membership includes Massimo De Carolis and Luigi Rossi di Montelera, formed a faction named Iniziativa Democratica in June 1978. (2) In many ways similar politically to Iniziativa Democratica, another group, Proposta, also grew out of the "group of 100" DC members of Parliament who sent a letter to Zaccagnini in early 1978 opposing Communist entry into the majority. Proposta's members include Gerardo Bianco, Vito Scalia, Mario Segni, Roberto Mazzotta, and others who have left one of the traditional factions. It has had one of its leaders in the cabinet in two of the three Governments since the 1979 election. At the same time, however, it is rather weak within the party infrastructure and is not as well organized as are the traditional factions. Proposta had 2 percent of the delegates at the DC national congress in January 1980. (3) Communion and Liberation is primarily a student movement of approximately 100,000 members organized around several hundred religious communities. The most dynamic force within the Catholic subculture today, it is interested in a reemphasis on religious values in

---

[29] *La Stampa*, April 6, 1979, and *La Repubblica*, April 6, 1979.
[30] Discussions of these new forces appear in Massimo De Carolis, "The Christian Democratic Party Today," in Austin Ranney and Giovanni Sartori, eds., *Eurocommunism: The Italian Case* (Washington, D.C.: American Enterprise Institute, 1978), pp. 153-155, and Giancarlo Galli, *Il Piave Democristiano: I protagonisti della DC che cambia* [The Christian Democratic Piave: The protagonists of the changing DC] (Milan: Longanesi and Co., 1978).

Italian society and in the DC and has a few deputies in the DC parliamentary group. (4) Finally, a technocratically oriented group associated with Umberto Agnelli has emerged (though Agnelli himself decided not to run for reelection to the Senate in 1979).[31] These new forces each have some representation within the DC Chamber and Senate groups and have broader support on some issues, such as opposition to further cooperation with the Communists, from rank-and-file members of the established factions. These groups are also interesting because they give a picture of the newest developments within the DC political and cultural world, but, apart from a few limited successes, they have been unable thus far to accede to major positions of power in the party where party strategy is decided. Party strategy is still made by the leaders of the established factions who have long dominated the top party organs.[32]

The DC and Italian Politics Between the 1976 and 1979 Elections

DC Political Strategy. The 1976–1979 period in Italian politics was dominated by the lack of any stable parliamentary majority and by the demands of the Communist party, which were resisted by the Christian Democratic party, for full governmental participation. On several occasions during this period, the Communists (supported, at times even pushed, by other parties and other social forces in Italy) became dissatisfied with the status quo and proposed a closer relationship between themselves and the Christian Democrats, the ultimate goal being the historic compromise. At each point the Christian Democrats presented counterproposals, which were agreed upon only after very long and very difficult discussions within the DC leadership and parliamentary groups and were an effort to yield as little as possible. The 1976–1979 period showed the political agility and creativity of the DC leadership in its "politics of small steps." The DC, in fact, did develop a series of new formulas which enabled it, while making some concessions to the PCI, to minimize the changes in the "political picture" at each step (particularly in the PCI's relationship to the Governments led by the DC) or at least to

[31] On the formation of Iniziativa Democratica, see *Corriere della Sera*, June 25, 1978, p. 2, and *La Repubblica*, June 25, 1978, p. 3. On Proposta, see *La Stampa*, September 23, 1979, p. 5.

[32] The few successes of these new forces so far include the victory of Gerardo Bianco over Giovanni Galloni, who is one of Zaccagnini's top advisers, after the 1979 election for the position of head of the DC group in the Chamber of Deputies, and the inclusion of Vito Scalia, a leader of Proposta, in the Cossiga Government formed in August 1979.

create the impression that there had not been meaningful change. This was especially important to the DC leadership because of the crucial role of anticommunism as a DC electoral appeal. The interest of the PCI was, of course, the opposite: it wanted to create the impression that things really had changed at each step along the way. However, by 1979, the "politics of small steps" appeared to have worked to the advantage of the DC and to the disadvantage of the PCI; the Communists, still outside the Government, were in serious political difficulty, while the DC had remained in power for an additional three years and seemed to be in a very strong political position.

After June 1976 there was substantial opposition within the DC to any kind of cooperation with the PCI; in addition to their political and ideological objections, many within the DC were afraid that each concession only brought closer the day when they would have to accept the historic compromise. During the 1976–1979 period two opposing tendencies formed within the DC on the question of political strategy, and the conflict between them became more intense with each further development in DC-PCI relations. In particular, the Government crisis in early 1978 played a major role in the full development of these two opposing coalitions. The debate at the DC National Council meeting in late July 1978 showed that by then there was a growing desire of a number of DC leaders for a departure from the strategy Moro had designed, which put priority on developing DC-PCI relations short of a joint Government coalition. For example, Attilio Ruffini, a leading Doroteo, argued for a return to "a correct distinction between the roles of majority and minority."[33] However, since no alternative was immediately available, this meeting resulted in a general confirmation of the existing governmental formula as well as a continuation of the DC's firm refusal to accept full PCI participation in a coalition Government with the DC.[34]

The two opposing coalitions within the DC, which continued to be in strong conflict over party strategy in the 1979 campaign, at the January 1980 DC national congress and after, differ particularly on the issue of the relationship between the DC and the PCI. The strategy of Aldo Moro—supported by Zaccagnini and what remains of the Moroteo faction, Andreotti (who headed the Governments based on this strategy), most of the Base faction, and some within Forze Nuove—argued that, because of the emergency situation resulting from the economic crisis and the lack of a stable parliamentary

[33] *Corriere della Sera*, July 31, 1978, pp. 1-2.
[34] Ibid.

majority, it was necessary to provide the widest base of support for the Government. Moro's strategy was based on the belief that all-out conflict between the two major political forces (as well as early elections) would only create greater problems in a very fragile situation. Therefore, further cooperation between the DC and the PCI, which has strong popular support as well as important influence with some of the unions and other social forces, should be cultivated.[35] The opposing strategy—supported by Fanfani, Forlani, Donat Cattin and members of his Forze Nuove, Bisaglia and many from the Dorotei faction, and most of the new forces in the DC parliamentary delegation, including the De Carolis group, Proposta, and Communion and Liberation—is based on the hope that the Italian Socialist party will again be the DC's major partner and on the premise that the PCI is a political force antithetical to the DC. What this group proposes is not exactly a return to the center-left formula, which the PSI would not accept, but some kind of new political relationship between the DC and the PSI. In 1979 some within this group proposed that the prime ministership be offered to the PSI as an incentive for partnership with the DC.

An important question about these two groupings is whether there are ultimately substantive political differences between them or simply tactical differences over the best way to maintain the centrality and power of the DC within the Italian political system. Clearly, both oppose a joint DC-PCI Government and both would continue the DC as a major governmental force. However, this is certainly not the whole picture; there is clearly a substantial difference in political values, for example, between some in Base who welcome cooperation with the PCI, on the one hand, and the strongly anticommunist "group of 100" on the other. Moro's strategy was a means of shoring up the DC in the face of its losses in 1975 and the political ambiguity resulting from the 1976 elections, but it was also an attempt to find a way to deal with the Italian political and economic crises in a changed social and political reality. In summary, while the differences between these groupings are in part tactical ones, it is an oversimplification to explain the differences between these two tendencies exclusively in terms of tactics.[36]

[35] For a detailed discussion by Aldo Moro of his political strategy and its underlying assumptions, see the excerpts of his speech to the DC deputies and senators on February 28, 1978, in *Panorama*, March 21, 1978, pp. 38-39.

[36] A different view is taken by Giorgio Galli in his articles "Bianco é il volto della DC" [Bianco is the face of the DC], *Panorama*, July 16, 1979, p. 31, and "Il vero obiettivo della DC" [The real objective of the DC], *Panorama*, July 2, 1979, p. 27.

The Succession of Agreements and Negotiations. Within several weeks after the 1976 elections, there was agreement among the six parties of the "constitutional arc"[37] that the PCI, for the first time in almost thirty years, would be given an important role in the running of Parliament, including the presidency of the Chamber of Deputies and the chairmanships of eight of the twenty-six parliamentary committees. Despite the ambiguous political situation, a Government was formed surprisingly quickly. It was composed only of Christian Democrats and was headed by Giulio Andreotti. This Government, whose program was fairly general and was not based on joint consultation among the parties, was supported directly on the vote of confidence only by the DC (and the tiny South Tyrolean People's party), while the Communists, Socialists, Social Democrats, Republicans, Liberals, and "independents of the left" all abstained in the vote of confidence that allowed the Government to live. Zaccagnini argued that this Government provided a truce or a pause for reflection during which Italy could at least have a fully functioning Government but that it did not represent a political accord: the Communists had abstained not as the result of an explicit agreement but rather by their own free choice to play a responsible role in an emergency. The Communists, for their part, portrayed this decision as an important step toward the historic compromise. When Andreotti presented his Government, he did not, as is normally done, ask for confidence; instead, he requested only "confirmation" or "non-no confidence" in a "spirit of collaboration" at a time of crisis.[38]

By March 1977 the Communists, as well as the Socialists, Social Democrats, and Republicans, were dissatisfied. They were helping to keep in office a Government in which they had no direct voice and over whose program (which failed to satisfy them) they had not been consulted. This led to three months of negotiations which produced a programmatic agreement among the six parties of the constitutional arc. In these negotiations the DC sought agreement on the program without any change in the political relationships, while the Communists' goal was entry to the majority as well as a voice in a new program. The compromise reached in July 1977 had three main features: (1) the programmatic agreement, which included some concrete proposals, some general statements on matters where agreement was more difficult, and some "agreements to disagree," for example, on

---

[37] These six parties, the Christian Democrats, the Communists, the Socialists, the Social Democrats, the Republicans, and the Liberals, worked together in the anti-Fascist resistance during World War II and then in the Government from 1944 until 1947.

[38] *Corriere della Sera*, August 5, 1976, pp. 1-2.

the question of whether the union that the policemen would now be allowed to form would be independent or would be permitted to affiliate with the CGIL-CISL-UIL unitary federation; (2) the continuance of the Andreotti Government without change (considered very important by the DC as a means of minimizing change in the "political picture"), but with a commitment to enact the provisions of the agreement into law and to consult with the six parties which had jointly drawn up the program; and (3) a vote in the Chamber of Deputies by the six parties in support of a unitary motion which summarized the programmatic agreement. This motion passed easily, but many DC deputies (possibly more than 100 out of 263) either voted against it, abstained, or were intentionally absent as a sign of their disapproval of the new relationship with the PCI.[39] While the Communist party did not get either a new Government or entry into the majority, it could at least claim that it had entered the "area" of government, since it had had a direct role, along with the other five parties, in the negotiation of the program, in the joint summit meetings of the top leaders of the six parties (symbolically important and the first of their kind in almost thirty years), and in the introduction and passage of the motion in the Chamber of Deputies which showed the six parties' commitment to the program.

Though this programmatic agreement had taken more than three months to negotiate in the spring and summer of 1977, there was great dissatisfaction with it by the end of the year within several of the parties because they believed that it provided them insufficient political control and that the program was not being enacted either fully or quickly enough by the Andreotti Government. The Communists did not start the round of criticisms which led to the Government crisis; the first pressures came from other parties, especially the Republicans and the Socialists, and from some of the unions. In early December the metalworkers staged a large demonstration in Rome, and about the same time the Socialists announced their support for a "Government of emergency" which would include all the parties of the constitutional arc. By mid-December the Communists too were calling for a "Government of democratic solidarity."[40] Andreotti resigned in mid-January as a result of these pressures, but within three days he was again named by President Giovanni Leone to try to form a new Government.

---

[39] The vote in the Chamber of Deputies on the final motion was 442 in favor, 87 against, and 16 abstaining, with 85 absent. The total strength of the parties officially opposing the programmatic agreement was only 45.

[40] *Corriere della Sera*, December 16, 1977, p. 1.

The DC firmly rejected the Communist proposal for full Government participation, but in addition there was much opposition within the DC to *any* collaboration with the PCI beyond the programmatic agreement.[41] Many of the top DC leaders opposed any new types of cooperation with the PCI, but opposition was especially strong within the DC parliamentary group. An ad hoc grouping of deputies from the new forces within the DC as well as from several of the established factions, especially the Dorotei and the Fanfaniani, sent a letter to Zaccagnini calling for DC opposition to any new steps in collaboration with the PCI; they were nicknamed the "group of 100." A survey of DC members of the Chamber of Deputies taken in January 1978 gives another good indication of the strength of the opposition to new kinds of collaboration between the DC and the PCI.[42] Of the 263 DC deputies, 205 (excluding the top DC leaders and those who could not be reached) were asked: "Are you favorable to or against the entrance of the Communist party into the majority?" Of the 205, 64.4 percent were against, 18.5 percent were favorable, and 17.1 percent were not sure or would not answer.[43] It was clear from the beginning of this Government crisis that any solution would require difficult negotiations not only among the parties but also within the DC.

By early February there was some movement within both the DC and the PCI. The Communists made it clear that they would accept something less than a "Government of emergency" but that it had to be at minimum an "explicit, recognized, jointly contracted majority." Within the DC it appeared that Moro, Zaccagnini, and Andreotti were trying to lead their party to an acceptance of a "programmatic majority," which would include Communist support for the

[41] The American government also put pressure on the DC by issuing a policy statement on January 12, 1978, which opposed Communist participation in the Government in Italy or anywhere else in Western Europe, though the statement also said that it was ultimately up to the Italians themselves to make the decision about the composition of their Government. Of course, the DC did not have to be pushed to oppose Communist participation in the Government.

[42] Stefano Malatesta, "Tanti modi di dire no" [Many ways to say no], *Panorama*, January 24, 1978, pp. 38-40.

[43] I want to thank Stefano Malatesta of *Panorama* for allowing me to look at the original statements of all of the DC deputies who were interviewed. The following answers to the question about PCI participation in the majority illustrate the depth of opposition of some DC deputies to further collaboration with the PCI: (1) Paolo Bonomi, the aging leader of the Small Farmers Confederation, "I am 100 percent against because I am an anticommunist deep in my bones, and I fight all forms of collaboration with the Communists"; (2) Aristide Tesini, "My vision of society is antithetical to that of the PCI. I would be a traitor to my past"; (3) Bruno Vicenzi, "I entered the DC in 1945 because of its anticommunist position; I would deny myself"; and (4) Carlo Stella, "Freedom divides us from the PCI; you cannot reconcile our principles with those of Marxism."

new Government on the vote of confidence. In early February the DC National Executive Committee issued a policy statement which seemed to be moving the DC in this direction, but which was still rather ambiguous because of the continuing conflict within the DC.[44] It called for: (1) a new Government with a program jointly drawn up by all the participating parties (though it did not speak directly of Communist entry into the majority); (2) agreement among the parties that there would not be a new Government crisis until after the end of President Leone's "white semester" in late 1978;[45] and (3) inclusion of all *six* parties in the new arrangement, since the DC wanted to protect itself on the right, that is, among its middle-class and upper-class anticommunist support, through the continued involvement of the Liberals. After very intense conflict within the DC over the next month, the entry of the Communists into the majority was accepted very grudgingly by most of the DC leadership and by many (though far from all) within the DC parliamentary delegation. The success of these two months of negotiations was largely due to the mediation of Aldo Moro between the demands of the Communists for full Government participation and the opposition of many within the DC to any relationship which went beyond the programmatic agreement of July 1977. Moro was clearly the main architect of this solution, winning support for it within the DC.[46]

The agreement, which was finally reached in early March 1978, consisted of: (1) Communist entry into the majority for the first time, together with the DC, the PSI, the PSDI, and the PRI (the Liberals went into opposition),[47] and (2) another "pure" *monocolore* Govern-

---

[44] For the text, see *Il Popolo*, February 5, 1978, p. 1.

[45] During the last six months of his seven-year term, the president of the Italian republic does not have the power to dissolve Parliament and call new elections as he does during his first six and one-half years in office; President Giovanni Leone's "white semester" (or last six months in office) would have been the second half of 1978. The Christian Democrats wanted to avoid a Government crisis during this time when the possibility of a dissolution of Parliament was unavailable. Ultimately, Leone was forced to resign in June 1978 because of charges about his abuse of power for personal benefit.

[46] Of particular importance was Moro's role in overcoming at least some of the opposition within the DC parliamentary group; his speech to the parliamentary group on February 28, 1978, in which he set forth his reasons for accepting Communist entry into the majority, played a very crucial role in the final resolution of the Government crisis.

[47] In a letter of March 7, 1978, sent to Andreotti, PLI Secretary Valerio Zanone criticized the new majority, which he argued was "composed of parties which are divergent and contrasting in both their immediate and future views." Zanone also said: "The DC and the PCI, after thirty years of opposing roles, find themselves together in a Government majority whose program, in our opinion, is less significant than its political implications. In such a situation the PLI

ment consisting only of DC ministers. One of the most interesting things about this new step was the different ways the Communists and Christian Democrats explained it. The Communists argued that their vote for the Government represented a major change in the "political picture" since it meant their entry into a "political majority" with the Christian Democrats and the three other parties. The Christian Democrats, who were very concerned about not alienating their electorate (and even more so after the Liberals' decision to go into opposition), tried to minimize the importance of the Communists' support for the new Government by arguing that this was a "parliamentary programmatic majority." The DC, they said, had accepted Communist support for a Government based on a specific program. This was not a "political majority," such as centrism or the center-left, because there was no common philosophy for the long-term development of society, but another truce in an emergency situation designed to prevent early elections.[48]

While the Communists made no claim of veto power over cabinet appointments in the new Government, they made it clear through repeated criticisms in the party newspaper *Unità* and elsewhere that a number of DC ministers were in their view not competent to serve in the cabinet (Donat Cattin and Bisaglia were the prime targets) and that they expected some real change in the personnel of the new cabinet. However, of the twenty-one members of the new cabinet, eleven held the same positions as in the previous cabinet, eight had served in the cabinet before but in different positions, and only two were new. In other words, there was virtually no change; the DC succeeded in retaining even the ministers most criticized by the PCI as well as a *monocolore* Government. The parliamentary debate on the new Government that would normally have taken place would have shown the dissatisfaction of many Christian Democrats (over the majority), Communists (over the cabinet and the program), and others (especially over the program), but it did not occur because of the kidnapping of Aldo Moro by the Red Brigades on March 16, 1978. Moro was seized while he was on his way to the Chamber of Deputies for the opening of the debate on the motion of confidence in the new Government. Within sixteen hours the Chamber and the Senate both gave a vote of confidence to the Government.

---

must assume the essential role of democratic opposition. . . ." Zanone was clearly trying to maximize the political embarrassment of the DC. *Corriere della Sera*, March 8, 1978, p. 1.

[48] For a discussion of the various political terms used during the crisis, see Maurizio De Luca, "Minivocabolario della crisi" [Mini-dictionary of the crisis], *Panorama*, February 14, 1978, pp. 42-43.

Throughout the nearly two months that Aldo Moro was held before he was killed both the Christian Democrats and the Communists refused to make concessions to the Red Brigades in return for his release. The DC's political position was clearly strengthened in the wake of the Moro kidnapping, while the Communists, however strongly they attacked the Red Brigades, were hurt by this new instance of terrorism of the left. In the administrative elections of May 14, 1978, which were held less than a week after Moro was killed and in which voting took place in communes containing about 5 percent of the Italian electorate, the Christian Democrats won 42.5 percent of the vote (compared with 38.9 percent in these same places in the 1976 elections), while the Communists received 26.9 percent (9.1 percentage points less than they had won in these communes in the 1976 elections).[49] By May 1978, therefore, the DC was in a substantially stronger position than it had been at any time since before 1974, while the Communists had lost their momentum of 1975 and 1976.[50]

By mid-1978, as we have seen, a number of leaders and factions within the DC were expressing dissatisfaction with the relationship more and more openly. The resolution passed by the DC National Council in late July 1978 marked at least a temporary acceptance of the existing governmental formula, but it was also clear that many in the DC were no longer afraid of the possibility of early elections.

By the last months of 1978 the PCI was becoming increasingly dissatisfied. It shared responsibility (and, therefore, blame) for Government policies and had a certain degree of "negative power"—power to prevent at least some things from being done—but had not made a significant gain in its effective, positive power in the nearly two and one-half years since the 1976 elections. The Communist leadership, because of the PCI's weakened political position, decided to intensify its pressure on the Government.[51] There were a number of specific

---

[49] Proportional representation is used in all communal elections in communes with at least 5,000 residents; 255 such communes, with a total of approximately 2 million voters, held elections on May 14, 1978.

[50] Data from DOXA surveys done at six points between December 1976 and May 1979 show that May 1978 was, in fact, the high point for the DC; in December 1976, it had 40.5 percent; in July 1977, 38.5 percent; in May 1978, 46.5 percent; in January 1979, 43 percent; in March 1979, 42 percent; and in May 1979, 43.5 percent. L'Espresso, June 3, 1979, p. 18.

[51] Some indications of the PCI's political problems were its substantial losses in the local elections in 1978, the dissatisfaction among the party rank and file, the slight decline in recruitment of new members (especially among the young), and the polls which showed the PCI losing at least three or four percentage points in national elections and the Christian Democrats gaining at least three points.

programmatic disagreements in the last months in 1978; the two most controversial related to Italian membership in the European Monetary System and the nominations to several top positions in the state industries. On these two questions, the first in mid-December and the second in early January, the Communists for the first time voted *against* the Andreotti Government. Clearly, these votes were a general indication of the PCI's feeling that it had not been sufficiently consulted by the Government on these as well as many other issues.

By late January 1979 the PCI decided that the only way it could have a direct role in policy making was through full governmental participation. It made clear its intention to leave the majority, and in less than a week Andreotti resigned; this was the beginning of a Government crisis which lasted seven months, included six unsuccessful attempts to form a new Government, and was punctuated by parliamentary elections.

Between January and March there were three attempts to form a Government—the first and the third by Andreotti and the second by Ugo La Malfa of the Italian Republican party, the *first* non-DC leader since 1945 to be given a chance to try to form a Government. However, when the PCI's firm demands for full Government participation and the DC's firm opposition met head on, there was very little margin for compromise on an intermediate solution. The PCI was unwilling to accept the DC's offer of mere consultation over personnel (within the framework of a Government which would not include the PCI), and the DC was unwilling to accept the entry of the "independents of the left" (who are elected on the PCI lists) in a Government led by either La Malfa or Andreotti. The DC's "politics of small steps" had lasted for more than two and a half years through a succession of agreements, but when the PCI reaffirmed its "either Government or opposition" position at its fifteenth party congress in late March 1979, the only recourse was a general election. At this point the DC was clearly not afraid of early elections, which it thought would work to its benefit.

The DC Campaign in 1979

There are six considerations of particular interest with respect to the DC in the 1979 campaign: (1) the expectations that the DC would make electoral gains, (2) the DC's effort to make the 1979 election into a referendum on Communist participation in the Government, (3) the polemics between the DC and the PCI over terrorism, (4) the divisions within the DC over its future political strategy, (5) the lack of a major turnover resulting from the candidate selection process, and (6) the absence of any strong church intervention in support of the DC.

Expectations About the DC. The DC entered the election campaign in April 1979 in a much stronger position and with much higher expectations than was true in the 1976 elections; the results of the local elections in 1978 and 1979 and the various national surveys done during that time suggested that the DC would make some gains, and possibly even large ones.[52] The first poll published during the campaign (in early May) indicated that the DC would win 40 percent (compared with 38.7 percent in 1976) while the PCI would take 31 percent (a loss of 3.4 points from its 1976 results).[53] The possibility of DC stability or slight losses was not really given serious consideration by most during the 1979 campaign. The DC could, therefore, hope for a margin over the Communists after the 1979 election which would be only slightly smaller than what it had had after the 1972 election. Certainly more of the public expected its position to improve in 1979 than was true in 1976. In two national surveys in 1976 and late 1978 respondents were asked: "Do you think that in the next elections the DC (PCI) will have more votes or fewer votes than it had in the last elections?" In late 1978, a third of the Italians thought that the DC would improve in the next elections; only 11 percent believed this in April 1976. While in the late 1978 survey 26 percent expected DC losses, this was only half of the 53 percent who thought this in April 1976. The public's impressions about the PCI's chances changed in the opposite direction between 1976 and 1978 (see table 3–3).

The Major DC Campaign Themes. The DC campaign in 1979 centered on the same theme which had dominated its campaign in 1976: anticommunism. In 1976 it had been the fear of the Communists' passing the DC to become the largest party; in 1979 the DC tried to make the election as much as possible into a referendum on its opposition to Communist entry into the Government together with the DC. The DC also criticized the Communists for being the ones who had broken with the "politics of national solidarity" and had forced the calling of early elections. In addition, the DC leaders attempted to explain, particularly to the DC electorate, the distinction between cooperation with the PCI of the kind it had espoused since 1976 and a joint Government coalition. This was in part an effort to retain one of the shakiest sectors of its electorate, the middle-class

---

[52] However, the DC did not show the same large gains in the local and regional elections of late 1978 and early 1979 that it had in the May 1978 elections.

[53] This was a survey done by Demoskopea in the first half of April and first reported in *Panorama*, May 8, 1979, p. 41.

TABLE 3-3

EXPECTATIONS ABOUT THE ELECTORAL CHANCES OF THE DC AND THE PCI,
APRIL 1976 AND DECEMBER 1978
(percent)

In Next Election Party Will Win:	April 1976		December 1978	
	DC	PCI	DC	PCI
More votes	11.3	55.6	34.3	27.5
Same	22.4	18.8	30.4	28.2
Fewer votes	53.2	10.4	25.9	32.7
No answer	13.0	15.3	9.4	11.7
Total	100.0	100.0	100.0	100.0

SURVEY QUESTION: "Do you think that in the next elections the DC (PCI) will have more votes or fewer votes than it had in the last elections?"
SOURCE: DOXA surveys reported in *L'Espresso*, January 21, 1979, pp. 9-12.

and upper-class voters who might go to the Liberals (and many of whom had probably come to the DC from the Liberals in 1976).

The DC's concentration on anticommunism was apparent from the first days of the campaign. In an interview published on April 5, Flaminio Piccoli, the president of the DC National Council, stated: "We will never enter the Government with the Communist party."[54] The same day Zaccagnini argued that the DC could not accept a joint Government coalition with the PCI because this could create "the conditions for the transformation of the society and the state in a way which cannot be reconciled with our conception of democracy, pluralism, and civil commonwealth."[55]

The anticommunist theme was clearly expressed in the DC's electoral program, which was approved by the DC National Council on April 21:

> In addition to their profound divergence on the ideological and philosophical plane, the PCI and the DC have models of society which are clearly different and opposed. The PCI was responsible for ending the politics of national solidarity when, forcing the truce established among the political forces to deal with the emergency and save the legislature, it interpreted it as an instrument for introducing socialist transformations in Italian society. Our refusal to form a Govern-

[54] *La Repubblica*, April 5, 1979, p. 1.
[55] *La Stampa*, April 6, 1979.

ment with the PCI is based on these reasons. We repeat: this is a solemn commitment that we make to our voters.[56]

As the campaign entered its final weeks, the attacks on the PCI became even more intense. The DC leaders made their maximum effort to heighten anticommunist consciousness and fear within the electorate and to mobilize them behind the DC. On May 24, Zaccagnini raised what he considered the ominous possibility (very unlikely given the survey results) of the Communists' surpassing the DC or of the left's winning a majority and argued that, though the election results were not a sure thing, "the people do not realize the importance of these elections."[57] On May 29, Zaccagnini once again questioned the PCI's democratic credentials, contending: "The Communists want a classless society. Now this means the removal of differences, of debate, of interchange. And once this utopia were realized, there would not be the instruments for a rethinking which are present in a concrete form in our democracy in the possibility of change in the majority."[58]

The other major (and closely related) theme of the DC campaign was that the DC over the previous thirty-three years had served as the "keystone" protecting the democratic institutions and freedoms in Italy and was, therefore, the main target of the terrorist groups. One of the DC campaign posters showed a picture of Aldo Moro and read: "There are those who gave their life for liberty; help us to defend it." During the campaign a new series of terrorist attacks against the offices and personnel of the DC occurred. The most serious of these was an attack by the Red Brigades on the Rome city headquarters of the party on May 3.[59] The DC reacted very strongly to this attack and claimed in its newspaper, *Il Popolo*, that the DC "is the indispensable force guaranteeing the peaceful evolution of Italy."[60]

During the campaign there were frequent DC-PCI polemics over the responsibility for and causes of terrorism in Italy. On May 6, *Il Popolo* argued that "there is an objective relationship between the intensification of terrorist assaults and the ever more pressing request

---

[56] Ibid., April 22, 1979, p. 1.

[57] *La Repubblica*, May 25, 1979, p. 3.

[58] Ibid., May 30, 1979, p. 3.

[59] In this attack a group of more than ten Red Brigades terrorists held the Rome city headquarters of the DC for approximately fifteen minutes and set off a number of bombs before making their escape (during which one policeman was killed and two others were wounded).

[60] *La Repubblica*, May 4, 1979, p. 4.

of the Communist party to arrive in power." In response to Communist statements that *Il Popolo* claimed implied a relationship between the terrorist actions and the electoral success of the DC, the writer insisted that these attacks on the DC were efforts "not to help it in the elections but rather to destroy the connecting tissue of our democracy." This article also contended that the PCI had been "slow in realizing the dangers of terrorism, slow in recognizing the need for adequate defensive preparations."[61] The Communists, who were clearly vulnerable on the issue of terrorism of the left despite their strong refusal to consider concessions during the Moro kidnapping, later suggested, at least indirectly, that the rise of terrorism was in part the result of the nature of DC rule in postwar Italy as well as of the inability of DC-led Governments to deal with it effectively. The Christian Democrats responded that the blame for terrorism rested with "others," a category which clearly was meant to include the PCI.[62] In his last speech of the campaign, Zaccagnini again presented the issue of terrorism in a dramatic way; he argued that the DC was a nonviolent party, proclaiming, "If our flags are bloodied, it is not with the blood of our enemies, but with that of our martyrs."[63]

Despite the general unity within the DC on the broad themes of anticommunism and the DC as the "keystone" of Italian democracy, the old divisions over the party's political strategy continued during the campaign. After a long, contentious debate at the DC National Council meeting of April 20–21, 1979, the final document, which was supported by nearly everyone present (De Carolis and a few others objected), represented a very difficult compromise between the two contending positions. There was a firm statement of the DC's opposition to a joint DC-PCI Government; also a reaffirmation of the strategy of "national solidarity" as it had been up to that point, though not a definitive commitment to this strategy for after the elections. The possibility of cooperation only with the Socialist party and the three small lay parties was left open, especially if the Communists continued to refuse any solution short of either Government or opposition.[64]

Despite these efforts to present an image of unity, the DC came across during the campaign as a party deeply divided and uncertain over its political strategy, though how far this was a matter of substantive differences was not clear. Christian Democratic spokesmen

[61] *La Stampa*, May 6, 1979, p. 14.
[62] *La Repubblica*, May 23, 1979, p. 2.
[63] Ibid., June 2, 1979, p. 2.
[64] *La Stampa*, April 22, 1979, p. 1.

made strongly differing statements and sometimes even direct, personal attacks on each other during the campaign. Fanfani, Bisaglia, and others often explicitly argued for emphasis on a closer relationship with the PSI, and referred to the possibility of a Socialist prime minister, while Zaccagnini and his supporters continued to speak of renewing the formula of March 1978 to January 1979, with the Communists in the majority. However, Zaccagnini did also say that if the Communists continued to reject this and to demand full Government participation, some other formula for a new Government would have to be considered.[65]

Candidate Selection. Though in the 1979 campaign Berlinguer, Craxi, and others frequently criticized DC hegemony and the nature of DC rule over the previous thirty-three years, and though the DC had not undertaken major reform of its intraparty structure or governmental personnel, this was not as central an issue in 1979 as it had been in 1976. (In the 1976 campaign one prominent DC poster showed a picture of Zaccagnini with the slogan "The new DC has already begun"; and there was concern about creating a substantial turnover in the DC parliamentary delegation.)[66] There was dissatisfaction with the DC and its governmental performance within the electorate (including the DC electorate), and it ultimately hurt the party, but the DC did not feel itself to be on the defensive about this as it had in 1976.

In 1979, 92 percent of the incumbent DC deputies and senators were renominated to run for one or both of the chambers of the Italian Parliament;[67] this compares with 74.5 percent of DC deputies and senators who were renominated in 1976. The greater turnover of the DC parliamentary delegation in 1976 (the highest since 1948) and the short period since the last elections were in part responsible for the high proportion of DC members renominated in 1979, but this

---

[65] *La Repubblica*, May 27-28, 1979, p. 2. Berlinguer's half-serious description of the differences within the DC about the PCI was: "The most reactionary Christian Democrats say the Communists eat children; the more open-minded Christian Democrats say we still eat children; the most open-minded say, unfortunately we still eat children." *Economist*, June 9, 1979, p. 53.

[66] In his last speech of the 1979 campaign, for example, Berlinguer again emphasized this theme, arguing that the "real risk of these elections is that this arrogant, closed, clientelistic DC will be rewarded in some way." *La Repubblica*, June 2, 1979, p. 2.

[67] If one includes the nine incumbent DC members of the Italian Parliament who were nominated in the DC lists for the European Parliament elections of June 10 but were not renominated for the Italian Parliament, the proportion renominated increases to 94 percent.

high level of renomination was basically a return to the pattern that had prevailed prior to 1976.[68] The process of drawing up the candidate lists was no less confusing or time-consuming than in 1976, but the concern about revitalization was not a major factor.[69]

The Church in the 1979 Campaign. The Italian Bishops' Conference met shortly before the elections of both 1976 and 1979. In 1976, Pope Paul VI addressed the meeting and issued a strong condemnation of communism, a call for Catholics to be "more united than ever" (an obvious endorsement of the DC), and a forceful indictment of the Catholics running as independent candidates on PCI lists. By contrast, John Paul II—elected in 1978, and the first non-Italian pope in more than 400 years—chose not to intervene directly in the 1979 campaign. The statement issued by the Italian Bishops' Conference after its May 1979 meeting did not include the traditional pro-DC phrase urging the "unity of Catholics" in the elections. In its cautious approach, it was more like the bishops' statements of the late 1960s/ early 1970s than those issued after after the resurgence of anti-communism in the mid-1970s. The 1979 communiqué did not mention the DC, the abortion law, Marxism, or communism and was only indirectly supportive of the DC: "Not every political choice is compatible with the Gospel," it said. "Coherence today excludes support for all political candidates and programs which propose solutions in conflict with Christian principles on questions such as civil and religious freedom and the respect for human life and the family."[70] The Italian church of the late 1970s and Pope John Paul II were clearly not ready to make the kind of commitment to the Christian Democrats that the church had made in the 1940s and 1950s or, to a certain degree, in the mid-1970s.

---

[68] Maurizio Cotta, "Il rinnovamento del personale parlamentare democristiano" [The renewal of Christian Democratic parliamentary personnel], *Il Mulino*, vol. 27 (September-October 1978), p. 732.

[69] The DC candidate selection process for the Chamber of Deputies and the Senate begins at the provincial level and ends with four or five days of continuous, last-minute discussions in the National Executive Committee. Most names for the Chamber of Deputies and the Senate come from the provincial and regional level, but the National Executive Committee keeps some spaces on the Chamber lists as well as usually twenty to twenty-five very safe Senate seats to allocate itself. In addition, the National Executive Committee decides upon the *capolista* (head of the list) for each Chamber of Deputies district and sometimes overrules local party leaders on nominations, especially for safe Senate seats. For a more detailed discussion of the DC candidate selection process, see Douglas Wertman, "The Italian Electoral Process: The Elections of June 1976," in Penniman, ed., *Italy at the Polls, 1976*, pp. 54-65.

[70] *La Stampa*, May 19, 1979, p. 2.

The Results

The 1979 elections followed expectations in several ways—in particular, the PCI losses (4.0 percentage points in the Chamber of Deputies) and the Radical party gains (2.3 points in the Chamber). The biggest surprise was the DC's failure to make any gains. In 1976, when the DC had been expected to lose, its success in maintaining its 1972 level had been perceived as a victory; in 1979, when it was expected to gain, its slight loss was perceived as very disappointing. In spite of the PCI's losses, the DC's strong psychological position prior to the elections was not reinforced.[71] Also surprising was the recovery of the Liberals and the Social Democrats (while the Republicans remained stationary); for the first time since 1963, the three small lay parties as a group improved their position in the parliamentary elections.

In 1979 the polls all overestimated the DC vote and underestimated the total for the three small parties (the reverse of 1976, when they had underestimated the DC's showing and overestimated the lay parties').[72] One reason may have been that a higher proportion of the undecided electors (especially those wavering between the DC and the PLI or between the DC and the PSDI) voted for the DC in 1976 because of their anticommunist fears, while in 1979 a higher proportion of these undecided voters went to the PLI or the PSDI because it was their traditional party and/or because their disaffection toward the DC was more salient than their anticommunism.

The DC suffered losses in the Northwest, the Northeast, and the Center (or Red Belt), which were largely balanced by gains in most of the provinces of the continental South and the island of Sicily.[73] The heaviest DC losses were in northwestern Italy and, in particular, in its three largest cities, with losses of 4.2 points in Milan, 2.9 points in Turin, and 2.6 points in Genoa. A substantial portion of these votes lost by the DC in the cities of the Northwest undoubtedly went to the PLI; many of these may, in fact, have been PLI voters returning to their pre-1976 party.[74] In contrast with the large PLI gains in the

[71] In their postelection analyses, the DC leaders tried to put the best face on the results by arguing that they had not really expected to make major gains and were satisfied with the outcome because they had basically maintained their parliamentary strength. (They lost only 0.4 percentage points and one seat in the Chamber of Deputies, and lost 0.6 points, but gained three seats, in the Senate.)

[72] An analysis of the polls and the election results in 1976 can be found in Sani, "The Italian Electorate," pp. 87-89.

[73] The DC made gains in thirty-one of the thirty-five provinces in the continental South and Sicily, but lost votes in all four provinces of Sardinia.

[74] This conclusion is based on aggregate data at the province, city, and senatorial-district levels as well as partial neighborhood-level data from the cities of Milan and Turin.

Northwest, the PLI made only very small gains in the South (and actually had marginal losses in several of the southern districts in the Chamber of Deputies elections). The DC electorate in 1979 became somewhat more southern and, in particular, less northwestern; this was the biggest change in the regional composition of the DC during any of the three elections of the 1970s.

Despite its best efforts, the DC failed to whip up the same level of anticommunist fear within the electorate that it had in 1976; most voters believed that there was very little, if any, chance that the PCI would outpoll the DC or that the left would win a majority.[75] In effect, the DC was in too strong a position psychologically—it had recovered too well since its crisis (while the PCI had lost its momentum and was in difficulty)—to retain many of the voters that it had gained primarily on the basis of anticommunism in 1976 and in the immediate aftermath of the Moro kidnapping in 1978. Anticommunism remained a major source of support for the DC, but a number of voters saw the issue in less dramatic terms than in 1976 and no longer felt it necessary to support the party which presented the strongest "bulwark against communism." The DC clearly lost some votes "loaned" from the small parties in 1976. There may also have been some voters who thought that the DC had gone too far in cooperating with the PCI and had real concern about the future strategy of the DC, whatever the DC leaders said in the campaign; the PLI must have gained among this group of voters by moving into opposition in March 1978.

With the lower intensity of anticommunist fear and the strengthened position of the DC in the 1978–1979 period, a number of voters may have felt it important that the DC *not* be rewarded for its performance over the previous thirty-three years. In 1979 dissatisfaction with the DC was a central consideration to some voters (especially some of those who had left the PLI or the PSDI for the DC in 1976) when the question was not whether the DC would have more votes than the PCI, but rather how many more votes. This negative view of the DC was reinforced by the disagreements and different emphases of the spokesmen for what appeared to be a divided, faction-ridden party.

The elections did not result in a clear victory for any particular faction or group of factions within the DC; the distribution of preference votes for the major leaders and the pattern of defeats among the incumbents running for reelection conveyed no consistent political message and did not result in substantial changes in the strength of

---

[75] As mentioned earlier, Zaccagnini recognized this when he said, "The people do not realize the importance of these elections." *La Repubblica,* May 25, 1979, p. 3.

the various factions within the DC parliamentary group.[76] The percentage of incumbent DC deputies defeated in 1979 (14.6 percent) was very close to the average for elections since 1963.[77]

The results of the European elections (held one week after the national elections) tended to confirm or accentuate developments in the national elections. Both the PCI and the DC suffered losses: the PCI dropped a further 0.8 points to 29.6 percent and the DC 1.8 points to 36.5 percent. The major winners were (1) the Socialists, who, after their disappointment in the national elections, gained 1.2 points in the European elections, and (2) the Liberals, who won 3.6 percent (nearly three times their total in 1976 and almost double their 1.9 percent in the 1979 national elections) and were clearly the major beneficiary of the DC losses, especially in northwestern and central Italy. The DC failed to make gains in what should have been very favorable terrain for a party with a long tradition of consistent support for European integration; since control of the Government was not directly at stake, the DC's anticommunism may have been a less compelling attraction than it is in parliamentary elections.

The DC's overall strength has been remarkably stable in the past five national elections, varying only between 38.8 percent and 39.1 percent of the vote. In addition, the available survey data suggest that no substantial changes in the composition of the DC electorate occurred in 1979. Over the next decade, however, there is likely to be a slow erosion in the DC's bases of support. The DC cannot count indefinitely on a stable electorate tied to it by religion and anticommunism, which are largely independent of governmental performance.

---

[76] Factional strength in the DC delegation in the Chamber of Deputies showed very little change. Forze Nuove had 11.0 percent of the DC delegation in 1976 and 11.1 percent in 1979; Base had 9.5 percent in 1976 and 1979; the Morotei/Zaccagniniani had 9.1 percent in 1976 and 11.8 percent in 1979; the Fanfaniani had 13.3 percent in 1976 and 13.7 percent in 1979; the Andreottiani, the biggest gainers, had 6.9 percent in 1976 and 9.5 percent in 1979; Rumor, Colombo, and Gullotti together had 8.0 percent in 1976 and 5.7 percent in 1979; the Dorotei had 25.9 percent in 1976 and 30.9 percent in 1979 (their gain appears artificially high because many of those in the 1976 election whose faction I could not fully identify probably come from the Dorotei); and the De Carolis group and other conservative forces had 5.7 percent in 1976 and 7.6 percent in 1979. For 1976, 10.6 percent of the DC group were not identified by faction, while the factional membership of all was identified in 1979. The 1976 data were put together by the author from numerous sources, while the 1979 data come from Corriere della Sera, June 7, 1979, p. 2.

[77] Two characteristics of the incumbent deputies defeated in 1979 stand out, in addition to factional membership, which was especially important in some areas of Italy: most were among the lowest preference-vote winners in 1976, and most were first-term deputies running for reelection (62.9 percent of the incumbents defeated in 1979 had first been elected to the Chamber in 1976).

The 1979 national and European elections suggest that there is almost a self-correcting mechanism at work within a portion of the electorate, which can be motivated by anticommunism to support the Christian Democrats when it perceives a serious threat, but which is unwilling to see them do well enough to return to their pre-1974 dominance. It is likely to be very difficult for the DC to go much beyond its current level in national elections and to acquire significant new support on more than a temporary basis (as it did in May 1978). In summary, the DC will probably neither suffer a major collapse nor make major gains in parliamentary elections in the near future, but the long-term trends should be more troubling to the DC leadership.

Conclusion

The Government crisis that began in January 1979 was certainly not resolved by the 1979 elections. They produced no clear political majority, and the uncertainty that had existed since June 1976 continued. Since the two major parties had returned to directly opposing positions on the issue of PCI participation in Government, the political situation was probably even more difficult and more confused in 1979 than in the period immediately following the 1976 elections. Fewer intermediate options remained open, and the likelihood of the two major parties' agreeing on them (at least for a while) was less than had been true after the 1976 elections. After three unsuccessful attempts to form a Government (by Andreotti, PSI Secretary Bettino Craxi, and Filippo Maria Pandolfi of the DC) and very serious conflict among the parties, Francesco Cossiga of the DC (who was aided by President Sandro Pertini's warning that he might consider resigning if no solution were quickly achieved) was finally able to put together a "Government of truce." It included the DC, the PLI, and the PSDI, plus two technicians from the socialist "political area." This Government was supported on the vote of confidence by the parties having ministers; the PRI and the PSI allowed it to live through their abstentions while the PCI returned to opposition. Since then, the Christian Democrats and the Socialists have been able to cooperate enough to form two Governments (in April 1980 and in October 1980) which have included both of these parties as well as others, but there is still a real tension, as seen in the controversy surrounding the D'Urso kidnapping, between them as well as within the Christian Democratic and Socialist parties. There is certainly no sense that an enduring solution to Italy's political instability has been achieved in the Cossiga and Forlani Governments; early elections again seem a real possibility.

Thanks to anticommunism in 1976 and to the "politics of small steps" between 1976 and 1979, the DC was able to recover from its crisis of 1974–1976. Nevertheless, at a time when it was expected to do well, it met slight losses in the 1979 national elections and larger losses in the European elections. Still the largest Italian party, it will undoubtedly remain a central governing force and will hold on to much of its multifaceted power. But the DC has not recaptured and is not likely to recapture its pre-crisis hegemony; it is even possible, though not immediately likely, that after protracted conflict and negotiations Italy will see its first non-DC prime minister since 1945.

4

Two Steps Forward, One Step Back: The PCI's Struggle for Legitimacy

Joseph LaPalombara

The electoral outcome of June 20, 1976, was, to put it mildly, a mixed blessing for the Italian Communist party (PCI). On the one hand, a long-term strategy theorized by Antonio Gramsci and pressed forward by Enrico Berlinguer, and by Palmiro Togliatti before him, seemed on the verge of bearing fruit.[1] The long march toward political legitimacy and a formal share in governmental power seemed almost concluded. Those in the party who had welcomed Togliatti's *Svolta di Salerno* of 1944 and his *Yalta Testament* twenty years later; those who—even in the face of genuine doubts and considerable internal party tensions —had lined up behind Berlinguer's "historic compromise," the most recent and controversial articulation of the party's long-term strategy, could view the 1976 electoral outcome with considerable satisfaction.

The author wishes to thank Giorgio Napolitano, Sidney Tarrow, and the editor of this volume for advice which, where followed, has no doubt improved the quality of this chapter.

[1] Antonio Gramsci, together with Palmiro Togliatti, Umberto Terracini, and Amadeo Bordiga, founded the PCI in 1921. Enrico Berlinguer, the PCI's current secretary general, has led the party since 1972. Gramsci died in a Fascist prison, where he wrote most of the works on which his belated recognition (even by his own party) as a major theorist of Marxism-Leninism is based. I do not suggest that the views of either Gramsci or Togliatti are fully reconcilable with those of Berlinguer, Giorgio Amendola, and others who have articulated the PCI's more recent positions on such matters as the dictatorship of the proletariat, working-class hegemony, political pluralism, the historic compromise, or Euro-communism. The point is that historic compromise in particular is less of an innovation than many have thought. As Peter Lange, among others, has made abundantly clear, the PCI's "strategic themes" have been wrapped in ambiguity, no doubt intentionally. See P. Lange, "Il PCI e i possibili esiti della crisi italiana" [PCI and the possible outcomes of the Italian crisis] in L. Graziano and S. Tarrow, eds., *La crisi Italiana* [The Italian crisis] (Turin: Einaudi, 1979), vol. 2, pp. 657-718. Cf. the excellent statement by Donald M. Blackmer, "Continuity and Change in Postwar Italian Communism," in Donald M. Blackmer and Sidney Tarrow, eds., *Communism in Italy and France* (Princeton: Princeton University Press, 1975), pp. 21-68.

After all, the PCI's steady but painfully slow electoral growth had taken an unexpected giant step in the local elections of 1975 and an even more impressive leap forward in the national elections a year later. For many of these PCI leaders and members, the party's "governmental vocation" seemed on the threshold of fulfillment.[2]

In reflecting on the 1976 results, even such an open critic of Berlinguer's "soft" line as Luigi Longo was moved to ask, "Have we therefore come on the end of an epoch?" He replied: "We can safely say yes, although it is clear that we are not today at a decisive turning point. More precisely, we are moving on a new terrain that offers possibility for further advance and makes a return to old equilibriums extremely difficult."[3]

Early Complications

If the nectar of victory was heady stuff in June 1976, it was destined to turn bitter in a relatively short time. The party's euphoria over securing not only the presidency of the Chamber of Deputies but also the chair of eight powerful legislative committees was soon converted into depression as it became apparent that these positions and, indeed, the legislature itself were surely not the commanding heights of the Italian political system. As one distinguished PCI leader put it in a personal and rueful comment, "We entered the control room, that's true, and we found a lot of buttons there. But the buttons weren't connected to anything!"

It is a mistake to think that the PCI leadership moved onto the postelectoral terrain unaware of the problems and risks involved. From the vantage point of 1979, Giorgio Napolitano, the PCI's second in command, has written, "Right from the beginning we had a sharp understanding of the problems and perils that the Communist party, and the entire working-class movement, would have to face in order to bring the new experience to a positive outcome." He adds that for anyone, inside or outside the party, to "discover" these problems and perils now, as if they had not been identified earlier, is to fall into the trap of making appear entirely too simple a number of reflections and analyses that were much more complex.[4] In effect, the PCI understood in 1976 that it was embarking on a complicated venture.

[2] A short, perceptive overview of the PCI's postwar strategy is offered by Gianfranco Pasquino, *The P.C.I.: A Party with a Governmental Vocation* (Bologna: The Johns Hopkins School of Advanced International Studies, Occasional Paper, February 1978).

[3] Luigi Longo, "Party Initiative," *The Italian Communists*, no. 4-5 (August-October 1976), p. 34.

[4] Giorgio Napolitano, *In mezzo al guado* [In the middle of the stream] (Rome: Editori Riuniti, 1979), p. xvii. The reader should note that the title of this book

A year before the 1976 elections, the PCI's marked improvement in local elections had brought complications. Faced with the twin needs to govern (with Socialists or others) most of Italy's major cities and to integrate into the party a large number of new-found voters, the PCI leadership realized that they were short-handed in disciplined and experienced cadres. Before the party could digest these new responsibilities and deal with its new voters, it was handed in 1976 the largest share of the votes it had ever won.

If some within the PCI fixed their gaze on the silver lining, more thoughtful leaders understood the clouds. The party's rise was inextricably bound up with Italian and international politics, as well as with the internal tensions and contradictions of the PCI itself. New questions arose; older ones had clearly become more complex or dramatic. How would the more intransigently anticommunist factions within the DC react to the PCI's startling electoral prowess? What about the leaders of key European states, to say nothing of the United States? How would the more doctrinaire party members respond to the leadership's accelerated efforts to enter into coalition with the Christian Democrats, the symbol of the very bourgeois state the party was committed to transform? What kinds of organizational party changes were required by the fact that hundreds of thousands of new voters had marked the PCI circle on the ballot? How could the party ensure that its new electoral adherents in what Tarrow calls the politically fickle South[5] would support the party in future elections? Did the party leaders have a sufficient understanding of how Italian society, as well as the Italian electorate, might be changing and what these changes required of a party devoted to being, simultaneously and somewhat contradictorily, "a party of struggle and of Government"?[6]

---

defies easy translation. Napolitano no doubt took the title from one or more writers who compared the PCI, after 1976, to an army caught halfway across a river it is trying to ford.

[5] See Tarrow's introductory chapter in this volume. For a typically more sanguine Communist view of how well the PCI was doing in the South, see G. Quercini, "Non c'e solo disgregazione" [There isn't just disunity], *Rinascita*, vol. 33 (March 3, 1976), pp. 11-12.

[6] This description of the PCI is the product of its own sloganeers; it represents an effort to reconcile what many of the party's most ardent supporters consider to be not reconcilable. The possible dangers in this formulation were often cited by Luigi Longo. Although he accepts the Gramscian strategy of broad party alliances as a means for bringing about the peaceful and democratic transformation of the capitalist state in a socialist direction, he has warned that, because the PCI is only one part of this broad alliance, it must be at pains to remain a "battling" or "struggling" party as opposed to "a party of Government." See Longo's speech to the PCI's twelfth congress in PCI, *Xii Congresso del PCI* (Rome: Editori Riuniti, 1969).

The next phase of the PCI's march toward power was fraught with uncertainty. Not merely the content or the substance of the party's proposals but also their pacing would be critical in a country where timing is such a prominent aspect of a highly nuanced political process. What to demand of the DC and other parties, when to demand it, and on the basis of what considerations became the PCI's overriding concerns the morning after the 1976 electoral results were known.

Despite their general awareness of these conditions, PCI leaders seemed to play things somewhat by ear when they weren't following the strategies and tactics that had served them so well in the past. Their basic premise was that expressed by Luigi Longo in the remark quoted earlier and underscored by Giorgio Napolitano in his post mortem on 1976–1979:[7] Because the 1976 election had introduced something new in Italian politics, it was unthinkable that one could return to things as they were prior to the party's great leap forward. This being so, the Christian Democrats would be compelled to acknowledge, first, that Italy could not be successfully governed without the active participation of the PCI; and, second, that if the PCI were to participate in a Government of national unity, in whatever form, it would require some concessions in return. In effect, it seemed to the party, as Hellman suggests, that "the barriers began to crumble" and that "the 1976 election was a referendum on whether the Communists should enter the Italian Government."[8]

Several concrete events may well have encouraged the party in its pragmatic, one-step-at-a-time posture. Capturing the presidency of the Chamber of Deputies and the chairmanships of parliamentary committees was one such event. Another was the fact that, far from acting on its campaign promise not to strike any deals with the Communists, the DC wound up soliciting the party's abstention on the Giulio Andreotti investiture vote. This step was widely and correctly interpreted as representing an important turn in the attitude of Italy's leading party toward the PCI. When the third Andreotti Government was formed, in August 1976, it was with the certain knowledge that the PCI would continue to press for concessions that would justify its decision not to vote against a Government in which it would have no part.

Berlinguer knew that the party was walking into a political mine-

---

[7] Napolitano, *Guado*, p. vii.

[8] Stephen Hellman, "The Longest Campaign: Communist Party Strategy and the Election of 1976," in Howard R. Penniman, ed., *Italy at the Polls: The Parliamentary Elections of 1976* (Washington, D.C.: American Enterprise Institute. 1977), pp. 155-156.

field. Stinging criticisms of the party's decision were heard as soon as it was made. They came not only from minor parties on the PCI's left, but from within the party as well. Thus, Berlinguer's speech on the investiture vote underscored that the abstention was a tentative step, not a blank check to the Christian Democrats.[9] Two months later, addressing the party's Central Committee, he said:

> Our attitude toward the Government is not one of support, as some people have maliciously claimed. We limit ourselves to supporting on a case by case basis, but loyally and responsibly, only those measures which we feel are correct and necessary. However, we do not identify with the government, indeed, quite the contrary.[10]

Berlinguer evoked the need for *responsibility*. The PCI must eschew gratuitous diffidence toward the Christian Democrats. In an obvious reference to those within his own party who might favor intransigence toward a bourgeois Government, he cautioned:

> Certainly our present situation exposes us to risks; but this does not mean we can pull back or indulge in nostalgia for past situations (which is obviously not to exclude that it may become necessary to return to opposition). We must see the risks, but we must face them and overcome them. We must go forward . . . overcoming in our own ranks all inertia, inefficiency and bureaucratic attitudes, today more intolerable than ever; and, above all, thinking and working more and more with the mentality, rigor and capacities of a Government force.[11]

In the first few months following the elections, some events seemed to validate and fortify Berlinguer's strategy, while others did not. For example, Ugo La Malfa, the distinguished leader of the Republican party (PRI), came out boldly in favor of the historic compromise. He argued that the failures of the parties of the center and the severity of Italy's economic and social problems made PCI participation in the Government an "ineluctable" fact of contemporary Italian history. La Malfa's startling change of heart caused a political furor, even within his own party. The Socialists, as well as other lay democratic parties, raised the specter of *integralismo*—an Italy clamped in

[9] Berlinguer's speech explaining why the PCI was abstaining, reproduced in *The Italian Communists*, no. 4-5 (August-October 1976), pp. 3-27.

[10] Enrico Berlinguer, "The P.C.I.'s Proposals and the Goals of Its Struggle" (Report to the Central Committee, October 18, 1976), *The Italian Communists*, no. 4-5 (August-October 1976), p. 71.

[11] Ibid., p. 77.

the authoritarian vise by a private agreement between DC and PCI, the country's largest parties. The Socialists in particular, always and understandably fearful of being squeezed out by the PCI, protested alleged under-the-table dealings between the two parties and reiterated their conviction that formulas other than the historic compromise should be explored.

Within the DC itself, La Malfa's statement brought panic to the hearts of those in the center and on the right who had never really approved of the Moro-Zaccagnini search for ways of accommodating the Communists. These DC leaders not only refused to consider the 1976 elections a referendum on the issue of PCI participation; they reminded everyone that the DC had fought the last campaign on the central issue of anticommunism. In short, La Malfa's statement served to mobilize those political forces prepared to make last-ditch stands against any implementation of the historic compromise.[12]

The Socialist posture on this issue was particularly complicated. The PSI itself was and remains internally divided over the issue of whether, when, and under what circumstances the PCI should be admitted to formal governmental responsibility. One strategy for slowing down the historic compromise had been to insist on the "Socialist alternative," that is, a coalition Government of the PCI and PSI. That strategy not only would confront the Communists with complex problems if it were flatly refused; it also postponed to an improbable future the time when a PCI–PSI electoral majority would materialize. The Socialist alternative was in any event fundamentally at odds with a major tenet of the historic compromise, namely, that the left in Italy should not try to govern alone, even were it to secure a majority of the votes and legislative seats.[13]

Once Bettino Craxi assumed the PSI leadership, the Socialist strategy vis-à-vis the PCI was articulated along four interrelated dimensions. First, oppose the historic compromise, on grounds that it threatens a PCI-DC deal, to the exclusion of other democratic parties, especially the PSI. Second, placate the PCI by demanding a broad-

[12] See the pages of *L'Unità*, *Avanti!*, *La Voce Repubblicana*, and *Il Popolo* for the period August-September 1976. A very good summary of the issue and of reactions to La Malfa's initiative is found in *Il Mondo*, September 1, 1976, pp. 10-15. It should be stressed that, in his articulation of the historic compromise, Berlinguer has never suggested that it would involve a two-party Government of the DC and the PCI. Nevertheless, many of Italy's political leaders either believe that this would be the case or find it politically expedient to raise this specter.

[13] For the earliest elucidation of the historic compromise, see *Rinascita* (October 5, 1973). Cf. Joseph LaPalombara, "Italian Elections as Hobson's Choice," in Penniman, ed., *Italy at the Polls, 1976*, pp. 14-16.

spectrum "Government of national emergency" that would include the PCI. Third, maintain credibility on the left by refusing (except in conditions of *extremia ratio*) to enter a Government with the DC from which the PCI is excluded. Fourth, mount a "friendly" ideological debate with the PCI, compelling the latter to spell out whether it has a theory of the socialist democratic state and, if so, whether the theory is compatible with the PCI's Leninist residues and its vaunted commitment to pluralism.[14]

By the beginning of 1977, Berlinguer found himself having to fight on many fronts simultaneously. Internally, the need to work through the contradictions implicit in being a "party of struggle and of Government" grew exponentially as members of the Central Committee began reacting to evidence of restiveness at the party's base.[15] Externally, Berlinguer found himself complaining about "sorties" against the PCI from certain DC leaders, and reassuring the PSI that his party was not in fact making sub rosa policies or deals with the Christian Democrats.[16]

Concurrently with these defensive efforts, PCI leaders had to worry about declining party membership, pressures for internal organizational changes, deteriorating relationships with the trade unions, as well as tense and complex relations with the Soviet Union and Communist bloc countries growing out of Berlinguer's strategy of Eurocommunism.

Two aspects of the party's tribulations between 1976 and 1979 warrant special attention—the party's relationship to the trade unions, on the one hand, and its local leaders and membership, on the other.

Austerity and the Trade Unions. Predictably, the Andreotti Government solicited PCI support for a program of austerity designed to cope with problems like investment, production, wages, inflation, a weak

---

[14] This is not the place to explore the PSI's ideological campaign against the PCI, which the latter construed as anything but amicable. The debate began innocently enough with several important articles published by Norberto Bobbio in *La Stampa*, September 21, 1976, p. 3; September 22, 1976, p. 3; November 28, 1976, p. 3; and December 1, 1976, p. 3. See also the pages of *Mondo Operaio* during 1977-1978. Bobbio's pointed questions addressed to the PCI appeared in *Mondo Operaio* under the following titles: "Esiste una dottrina marxista dello stato?" [Does there exist a Marxian doctrine of the state?] (August-September 1975), pp. 24-31; and "Quali alternativi alla democrazia rapprestativa?" [What alternatives to representative democracy?] (October 1975), pp. 40-48.

[15] See, for example, the revealing presentation of Gianni Cervetti to the PCI Central Committee meeting of December 1976, reproduced in *L'Unità*, December 14, 1976, p. 9.

[16] Cf. Berlinguer's article in *Rinascita*, December 10, 1976.

currency, and the balance of payments. Among other controversial issues, the Government wished to curtail and to modify the "escalator clause," which, many economists correctly believed, tended to push wages ahead of actual increases in the cost of living.[17] For Italian organized labor, the escalator clause, *la scala mobile*, has long been a sacred cow, a symbol of labor's new-found prowess, not to be man-handled or even touched by the politicians.

The policy of austerity opened an acrimonious debate within the PCI, and between the PCI and the unions, that persisted throughout the period between elections. As early as October, Giorgio Amendola took a tough-minded position before the Central Committee that earned him an unsympathetic, not to say hostile, response from most of his colleagues.[18] Amendola claimed that the Government could not pretend simultaneously to encourage greater investment and produc-tion *and* reduce inflation. Others in the party insisted that such a policy was not only possible but indispensable.

Ugo La Malfa, long an opponent of economic wishful thinking, unleashed a barrage of hard-nosed economic advice. The escalator clause had to be cut; Italy could not continue to spend more than it was producing; organized labor would have to accept a temporary relinquishment of some of its gains. "We can't be transformed," he said, "into an everlastingly compassionate doctor who permits a disease to devour the patient." As La Malfa said, "There are no alter-natives: It is necessary that sacrifices be tolerated by the entire mass of Italians." The left, in his view, could not continue its old practice of bending over backward not to antagonize the trade unions, not to insist that the unions stop pursuing wage and related demands that took little account of Italy's objective economic and productive capaci-ties.[19]

The October 1976 Central Committee meeting was widely inter-preted as a careful exploration of the Berlinguer strategy.[20] Berlin-guer's speech to the Committee revealed that he would try to steer a difficult middle road, accepting the need for austerity, on the one hand, but trying to anticipate and to dampen attacks from party

[17] On the need to put the brakes on the "escalator clause," see the article by Romano Prodi, *Stampa Sera*, September 13, 1976, pp. 1, 2.

[18] See *L'Unità* and other major newspapers like *Corriere della Sera* and *La Stampa*, October 20-21, 1976.

[19] Ibid.

[20] Basic changes were made in the PCI Secretariat at this meeting. Several critics of Berlinguer's strategy were removed; key Berlinguer supporters Gerardo Chiaro-monte, Paolo Bufalini, and Gianni Cervetti were promoted. See the interesting analysis by Antonio Padellaro, "Terramato al vertice delle Botteghe Oscure?" [Earthquake at PCI's summit?], *Corriere della Sera*, October 22, 1976, p. 2.

members and the unions, on the other. Berlinguer's position, many times repeated by himself and other leaders like Napolitano and Luciano Barca, is that the PCI will not accept austerity measures that are little more than the application of neoclassical economic theories. In response to La Malfa's strictures, he noted that one must be open to the expectations and hopes of the masses; one must give them not just admonitions but a positive program that not only fights inflation but also promises to bring about structural changes in Italy's economy and social fabric. "Consensus," he warned, "cannot arise only from the knowledge of dangers; it must be sought in the confidence that one is really moving toward something new, and that a policy of austerity is not made to return things to the way they were earlier."[21]

To placate the unions (no mean assignment in the best of circumstances), Berlinguer had little choice except the one he pursued. Key union leaders lost no time in expressing their skepticism and hostility toward policies of austerity, particularly when the escalator clause seemed to be the item on which so many critics of the unions had trained their guns. Articulate key figures like Bruno Trentin (Italian General Confederation of Workers, CGIL), Pierre Carniti (Italian Confederation of Workers Unions, CISL), and Giorgio Benvenuto (Italian Union of Labor, UIL) demanded not only an equitable distribution of the sacrifices that austerity implied, but also a careful specification of how savings and new investments would be used to benefit the working class.[22]

The PCI faced particularly complex problems in its efforts to sell austerity to the CGIL, the confederation with which it is most intimately associated. Three points should be noted.

1. Historically, the CGIL had been viewed (outside as well as within the PCI) as an organization dominated by the party. The confederation had extricated itself from the Leninist image of the unions as a "transmission belt" for the PCI only very slowly, and not without acrimony between itself and the PCI. In the years following the

---

[21] See L'Unità, December 21, 1976, p. 1.

[22] See, for example, the interview with Bruno Trentin, one of CGIL's most prominent leaders and trade union theoreticians, in Corriere della Sera, October 22, 1976, p. 2. Trentin has long been an advocate of a trade union movement that espouses specific transformations of the capitalist system, translates these goals into concrete policy recommendations, and forces the policies on the political parties. Unlike some other trade unionists, Trentin is not an advocate of a new "corporativism" in which organized labor and business are the only valid interlocutors, hammering out political and economic policies in conjunction with the state. See his contribution in Istituto Gramsci, Tendenze del capitalismo italiano [Tendencies of Italian capitalism] (Rome: Editori Riuniti, 1962), pp. 97-144.

"hot autumn" of 1969, the Italian unions came into their own, achieving not only considerable autonomy but undeniable influence over public policy. Understandably, the unions were and remain reluctant to relinquish control to the parties—any party. More important, given its past, the CGIL was particularly sensitive to any accusation from the Christian Democratic (CISL) or Socialist-Republican-Social Democratic (UIL) union leaders that it might be retrogressing to "transmission belt" status.[23]

2. The PCI, on the other hand, has been markedly concerned about excessive trade union autonomy. One reason for this—the most often stated—is the fear of trade union sectarianism, or the danger of "corporativist" tendencies manifested by organized labor (as well as organized employers) in Italy. A second, less often publicly stated reason is the fear that patterns of industrial democracy that emerged in Italy after 1969 threaten not only the traditional trade union structure but (partly because of this) the PCI's plant-level influence over the workers as well. Industrial relations conducted by assemblies on the shop floor represent a form of populism that eludes the control of both the trade unions and the political parties. A third and related fear is that the PCI will not be able to deliver on its political economy commitments at the national level unless it remains reasonably confident that it can extract predictable, compliant behavior from the workers. The party's recent decision to reactivate factory-level party sections reflects its determination to do just that.

3. If the PCI has increasingly felt a pressing need to reassert some party hegemony over the trade union movement, it must proceed with the greatest caution. Steps in this direction will be resisted not only by CGIL leaders but also by others within the party (especially younger leaders) who are strongly opposed to tight control from the party center. A party under internal pressure to ease the tight reins of "democratic centralism" cannot openly pretend to reassert an older Leninist conception of the relationship between party and union.

[23] On the occasion of his election as UIL's secretary general, Benvenuto made a special point of insisting that all unions reaffirm their autonomy from parties and not return to earlier types of party-dictated conformism. See *Corriere della Sera*, October 1, 1976, p. 2. Similar admonitions, more or less veiled, have been directed to the CGIL by CISL leaders. It is one of the ironies of recent Italian trade union history that the very trade unions—and their leaders—brought forward through American assistance in the 1950s and 1960s should now turn out to be the most intransigent and radical in their demands. The best English-language discussion of the transformations the CGIL has undergone since the 1960s is Peter Weitz, "The CGIL and PCI: From Subordination to Independent Political Force," in Blackmer and Tarrow, eds., *Communism*, pp. 541-557. Cf. Gino Giugni, *Il sindacato fra contratti e riforme* [The trade union between contracts and reforms] (Bari: DeDonato, 1973).

Furthermore, the PCI itself has for some years now openly eschewed the transmission-belt concept, in recognition perhaps that it could not have it and a united trade union movement too.

Equally important, any such effort would be picked up by all those, in Italy and abroad, who have serious doubts about the PCI's commitment to "democratic pluralism." If some of these doubts are politically or opportunistically motivated, if some of them come (as is certain) from those who are incapable of accepting any evidence of the PCI's commitment to democracy, it nevertheless remains true that the phrases "democratic centralism" as regards the party and "transmission belt" as regards the party's relationship to the unions have negative connotations. One irony in all this is that many of these same persons would want the PCI to be able to keep the trade unions and their members in line in support of "responsible" policies.

In any event, the PCI leadership, under Berlinguer, has tried to steer the difficult middle way. Thus, one party spokesman bravely says that austerity policies are not to be understood as posing the alternatives of "Franciscan poverty and neocapitalism." If austerity requires, as it should and must, that the workers fight waste and certain forms of consumerism, it must also provide the basis for "a new enrichment of the individual in the collectivity." Austerity must mean careful, vigorous decisions regarding alternative uses of limited resources; new and different organization of the process of production, not just in the workplace but elsewhere as well; greater decentralization of governmental responsibilities; and less dependence on a model of society that rewards "exacerbated individualism." In short, austerity measures should be accepted not as something passive but, rather, as opportunities to be seized and channeled toward the creation of more socialist elements in society.[24]

If views such as these (however abstract) were designed to placate the workers and their leaders, others were designed to urge them to pull up their socks and step into line. Thus Luciano Lama, CGIL's secretary general, bluntly told them that a policy of austerity was *not* compatible with a policy of substantial wage increases. He severely chastized others who, writing in *Rinascita* in October-November 1976, failed to recognize and acknowledge this reality. He said:

[24] These views are derived from Achille Occhetto, "Austerity, New Needs and Development of Democracy," *The Italian Communists*, no. 2 (April-June 1977), pp. 98-110, esp. pp. 100-105. The article itself is a synthesis of three reports (by Occhetto, Eduardo Perna, and Salvatore d'Albergo) presented at a public meeting held in May 1977. As a member of the PCI Central Committee, Occhetto may be presumed to be writing for the party. For a similar statement by Berlinguer, see *The Italian Communists*, no. 1 (January-March 1977), pp. 35-48.

The fact is that unless we convince ourselves that the trade union works in a political reality together with others and that society is not a no man's land where only the good seed of the trade union can take root, we are fooling ourselves and abandoning a role which is essential and which only the union can play.[25]

Lama went on to say that something like the escalator clause could be defended only if the trade unions and the workers showed a willingness to come to grips with such fundamental problems as low productivity and high absenteeism. Moreover, he warned against any artificial division between the party and the trade unions; he suggested that such a course would invite disaster and that what he, and, indeed, the PCI wanted was *responsible* unions.[26]

Gianni Cervetti, in his important speech to the Central Committee in December 1976, was even more explicit regarding the party's relationship with the unions. While the party continued to acknowledge trade union autonomy, the party itself must bring a new presence—namely, its own—into the factories. According to Cervetti, "the Communists must become the active protagonists of a decisive move to extend democracy to the factory." Thus, whereas the party would continue to accept the idea of trade union autonomy, this could not be understood to imply party neutrality, or lack of concern, regarding the relationship of trade unions to workers, to workers' councils, to modes of worker participation in trade policy choices. Above all, Cervetti's speech suggested that the PCI must take action "to overcome the practice of a plebiscitary-type democracy."[27]

In his post-1979 reflections on the period between the two elections, Giorgio Napolitano provides an interesting insight into how Berlinguer's middle strategy worked out in practice. He finds the PCI remiss in letting the trade unions carry too much of the burden of reacting not only to the austerity program but also to many other policies proposed by the Government. Nor did the PCI take enough initiative of its own, either in setting the objectives of public policy or in ensuring policy implementation.[28] This failure was one of many reasons for the unhappy turn that the PCI's electoral fortunes were to take in 1979.

[25] Luciano Lama, "Talking Straight to the Workers," *Rinascita*, November 17, 1976. Reproduced in translation in *The Italian Communists*, no. 6 (November-December 1976), pp. 34-39, esp. p. 35.
[26] Ibid., pp. 36-37.
[27] *L'Unità*, December 14, 1976, p. 9. Translated in *The Italian Communists*, no. 6 (November-December 1976), pp. 25-27. Quoted material at pp. 25-26.
[28] Napolitano, *Guado*, p. xx.

The Apex and the Base. The PCI has had long experience in "preparing the base" for major changes in the party's doctrines, organization, and policies. Its typical approach is to authorize meetings at the regional and local-party levels; to organize party congresses to address specifically designated issues; and to send leading members of the apparatus to appear before such meetings to explain changes and to listen to reactions. Meetings of party women, youth, trade unionists, intellectuals, and so on are also encouraged, with nonparty members often invited to participate in the exchanges and debates.

This was the pattern followed regarding the changes in the PCI's posture and policies that were launched after June 1976. During the first three months of 1977, federation, regional, and section congresses were held throughout the country. According to party reports, over 11,000 such meetings took place and brought together several hundred thousand participants. The party's effort to implement political ecumenism was rewarded by Socialist participation in 2,500 section congresses and Christian Democratic participation in 1,200.[29]

What kinds of signals did the central leadership pick up in these encounters? Certainly they were abundantly alerted to the existence of considerable disorientation, dissatisfaction with the party's place in national politics, and even open hostility to the line of responsible collaboration with a *monocolore* Christian Democratic Government that the party was pursuing. To be sure, some of these feelings could readily be ascribed to the newness of the PCI's approach. Regarding many dissenters, therefore, it might be assumed that recapturing their loyalty and assent was simply a matter of time and education.

But the meetings, especially those at the local, section level, also revealed the growing sensitivity of party rank and file to the jibes and attacks of those outside the party, particularly on its left, who condemned it for selling its Marxist revolutionary heritage—for only half a bowl of Christian Democratic pottage at that! Beyond this, one party report on the congresses suggested that an internal clash of generations was under way. What Cervetti described as "youthism"[30] may actually reflect a more profound malaise, a lack of confi-

[29] For a public—and therefore not exhaustive—report on the temper and tenor of these meetings, see Gianni Cervetti, "A Mass Debate on the Party, the Movement and the Political Picture," *The Italian Communists*, no. 2 (April-June 1977), pp. 119-128. Nevertheless, the remarkable candor of this report reveals considerable internal party unrest, and even open hostility to the PCI strategy.

[30] Ibid., pp. 126-127. For an important, well-documented analysis of tensions between the PCI's center and periphery, between its leaders and followers, over the party's strategy, especially after 1976, see Marzio Barbagli and Piergiorgio Corbetta, "Una tattica e due strategie: Inchiesta sulla base del PCI" [One tactic and two strategies: an investigation of the PCI base], *Il Mulino*, vol. 27 (November 1978), pp. 922-967.

dence of younger leaders and activists in an older generation of leaders who led the party to support a DC Government that was not inclined to give the PCI and its working-class members something in return.

If the central leaders did not know it beforehand, these meetings no doubt taught them that they have (or had!) immensely more faith in the Christian Democrats than do the PCI rank and file. Referring to such faith, Hellman says, "It certainly does not exist among the PCI rank and file, who have seen the Christian Democrats vilified as *the* enemy for thirty years." Hellman adds that his own discussions with regional and provincial party leaders after 1976 "revealed much greater uncertainty than one might have expected in so single-minded a party."[31]

Although problems of membership had taxed the PCI's central leadership for some time, the matter became much more acute following the party's electoral surges of 1975 and 1976. As one observer noted, the PCI's problems on the left emanated not just from the small extremist groups but from its party and trade union adherents as well. If the regional and local congresses resulted in general support for the Berlinguer line, they also revealed that the secretary general was in considerable difficulty. PCI central leaders were queried about restlessness among their members; they went to great lengths to deny that the party was in fact becoming more "conservative."[32] The membership problem involves not just global statistics but also disquieting demographic and geographic patterns. In global terms, PCI membership between 1947 and the late 1970s averaged approximately 1.8 million members. The high points of 2 million or more members were registered in the late 1940s; the nadir occurred between 1969 and 1972, when the average dropped to about 1.5 million members. Events of the late 1960s caught the party somewhat flat-footed; transformations in Italian society were crystallizing so rapidly that the party found itself running after groups of Italians whose political views and demands were in many ways more specific and more radical than those that the PCI had been articulating. Youth, university students, trade union members, women, and residents in major urban centers spearheaded these changes. Their disenchantment with the PCI was inevitably registered in membership turnover and the party's failure to replace its losses with new recruits.

Historically the PCI had worried less about membership turnover than about success in its annual membership campaigns and overall membership levels. Continual dropouts were not only expected as

[31] Hellman, "The Longest Campaign," p. 180.
[32] See Paolo Berti, "Il PCI è diventato conservatore?" [Has the PCI become conservative?], *L'Europeo*, May 13, 1977.

inevitable; some of these party "alumni" were expected to retain a certain sympathy for the PCI and its mission in society. But a general and continuing drop in membership, of the kind that began in 1969, signaled that members lost through "natural attrition" were not being adequately replaced by new—and presumably younger—recruits. Trends of this kind created prima facie evidence that the party was not renewing itself and supplying a base for a later generation of leadership.

After 1972, PCI membership began to creep up again, but not evenly across the country, and not steadily from year to year.[33] Thus, in 1978, after four years during which global figures gradually rose from 1.65 to 1.81 million members, the number declined to 1.74 million.[34] Central leaders lamented this decline, but reassured themselves that the losses were less than might be expected, given the changes in the party's strategy and the perplexities, disorientations, and criticisms that these changes evoked at the party's base.[35]

If we turn from global figures to membership data in party auxiliaries like the Italian Communist Youth Federation (FGCI), a much more striking image is presented of the party's travail. Fedele, for example, shows that whereas, between 1948 and 1976 total PCI membership had declined by just over 14 percent, membership in FGCI had dropped by more than one-half! Furthermore, in the more industrialized North, the FGCI membership had fallen by more than two-thirds. The relative figures are shown in table 4–1.

Table 4–1 shows not merely the PCI and FGCI membership decline following the high points of the late 1940s, but also the gradual recovery of both organizations in the 1970s. It also reflects the party's organizational efforts in the South and the greater volatility of membership in that part of the country and highlights what appears to be the PCI's and FGCI's permanent decline in the industrial North —the region where the public disorder of recent years has been concentrated and where the parties on the PCI's left have registered their most impressive development.

[33] For annual membership figures from 1947 to 1977, see Marcello Fedele, *Classi e partiti negli anni '70* [Classes and parties in the 1970s] (Rome: Editori Riuniti, 1979), p. 180.

[34] The magnitude of the decline between 1977 and 1978 is somewhat unclear. If Fedele's figures for 1977 are accurate, the decline in 1978 would be in the neighborhood of 74,000. Berlinguer, however, in his speech to the PCI's fifteenth congress (March 1979), cited a 1978 loss of only 23,740 compared with a year earlier. See Enrico Berlinguer, "Report to the Fifteenth National Congress of the PCI" in *The Italian Communists*, nos. 1-2 (January-June 1979), p. 105.

[35] See Berlinguer's discussion of this matter in the "Report to the Fifteenth National Congress," pp. 106 ff. Cf. Cervetti, "A Mass Debate," pp. 125-127.

TABLE 4–1

VARIATION IN PCI AND FGCI MEMBERSHIP, IN ITALY AND BY REGION,
1948–1976
(index numbers; 1948=100)

	1948	1953	1958	1963	1972	1976
Italy						
PCI	100.0	100.9	86.0	71.0	74.9	85.8
FGCI	100.0	154.7	80.2	43.8	39.0	49.7
North						
PCI	100.0	93.2	68.7	64.7	67.5	77.2
FGCI	100.0	130.6	48.7	31.7	24.8	32.6
Center						
PCI	100.0	104.9	84.4	78.6	82.6	91.7
FGCI	100.0	166.6	67.7	50.0	44.4	51.8
South						
PCI	100.0	122.1	91.9	80.7	86.9	102.4
FGCI	100.0	214.9	89.3	73.9	76.5	100.0

SOURCE: Marcello Fedele, *Classi e partiti negli anni '70* [Classes and parties in the 1970s] (Rome: Editori Riuniti, 1979), p. 184. Reconstituted data.

In a careful study of the membership variations of the PCI and some of its most important auxiliary organizations, Barbagli and Corbetta point out that, without doubt, Italy's youth are the social category most violently affected by the "movement" of the late 1960s. If events of this era adversely affected global PCI membership, their impact on younger members was close to catastrophic. In 1969 alone, for example, the FGCI in one fell swoop lost almost half of its membership. It was this shock that led the party to concentrate its attention on reinvigorating that organization, an effort that continued unabated as the 1980s began.[36]

In recent years, the PCI has made major efforts to reinvigorate not only the FGCI, the organization that has traditionally been the training ground for its most important leaders, it has also been at pains to provide workers and women greater opportunities to secure representation on the party's directive organs. Berlinguer made a major

[36] Marzio Barbagli and Piergiogio Corbetta, "Base sociale del PCI e movimenti collettivi" [The social base of the PCI and collective movements], in Alberto Martinelli and Gianfranco Pasquino, eds., *La Politica nell'Italia che cambia* [Politics in a changing Italy] (Milan: Feltrinelli, 1978), p. 153.

TABLE 4–2
CHANGE IN PCI MEMBERSHIP IN SELECTED CITIES, 1949–1972
(index numbers; 1949=100)

City	PCI Membership, 1972
Bologna	134.2
Palermo	131.9
Catania	99.0
Venice	87.9
Rome	76.8
Florence	71.0
Bari	60.7
Genoa	54.8
Naples	50.9
Milan	34.9
Turin	34.7

SOURCE: Fedele, *Classi e partiti*, p. 187.

point of this in his March 1979 speech to the party congress, acknowledging as well that there remained much work to do in this area.[37]

Global membership figures also tend to obscure important variations found among the country's major cities. As recent electoral data suggest, the party has declined disproportionately in many of the industrial centers that, along with regions like Emilia-Romagna, Tuscany, and Umbria, constituted its membership and electoral mainstays. Only in the South, and not consistently there, can it be shown that the PCI's membership appeal is greater in large cities and provincial capitals than it is outside.[38]

Changes in PCI membership since 1949 in eleven of Italy's major cities are shown in table 4–2. Among these eleven cities, only the first four have indexes significantly above those for total PCI membership in 1972 relative to 1949. Since global membership has remained relatively close to the overall average of 1.8 million, the information in table 4–2 also points to the gradual spread of PCI membership from major urban centers to other parts of the country. Above all, how-

[37] Berlinguer, "Report to the Fifteenth National Congress," pp. 105-107. For an excellent depiction of the magnitude of the party's problems regarding the place of youth, workers, women, and other social categories in leadership positions, see Fedele, *Classi e partiti*, pp. 195-204.

[38] For a depiction of PCI membership by region, and by urban-rural areas, see Barbagli and Corbetta, "Base sociale del PCI movimenti colletivi," pp. 147-153.

ever, the table underscores the membership deterioration in the industrial triangle constituted by Milan, Turin, and Genoa. The losses registered in these places—once PCI strongholds, and the leading edges of a modern, industrialized Italy—cannot be a matter of indifference to the party.

In any event, as the electoral gains of the first half of the last decade saddled the PCI with more governmental responsibilities at the local and regional levels, and as the party confronted the task of integrating unprecedented numbers of new voters who flocked to its electoral ranks between 1972 and 1976, it had available smaller membership pools from which to derive the manpower needed for these tasks. By 1976, whereas the PCI vote had almost tripled over 1946, the party's membership had fallen by about one-seventh.[39] Moreover, members were less willing to be uncritically compliant, and much less willing to accept central direction, than ever in the past.

Modified and Accelerated Party Strategy

Restive party members, uncooperative trade unions, drumfire criticisms from younger leaders and members at the party "base" no longer happy to be muzzled by "democratic centralism," and the widespread accusation from outside that the PCI was selling out to the Christian Democratic establishment required that the party modify its strategy. This modification occurred in 1977 and involved (1) greater and insistent demands that the DC unequivocally commit itself to a series of policies demanded by the PCI, (2) insistence that it made little sense for the DC to govern all by itself, without the participation of parties from the democratic "constitutional arc," and (3) a stepped-up campaign to show that internal problems confronting the country were of such variety and magnitude as to require a Government of "national emergency" that would include the PCI.

In the spring of 1977 the PCI, along with other parties of the constitutional arc, began a complex, sometimes Byzantine, series of discussions with the DC, aimed at compelling the latter to make explicit commitments.[40] As Tarrow notes in the first chapter of this volume, these discussions were engendered by an accumulation of social, economic, and political crises and represented a gradual coming together of the parties committed to preserving the Italian republic. Andreotti's—and Moro's—skillful handling of these negotiations not

---

[39] See the table in Fedele, *Classi e partiti*, p. 191.
[40] See *La Repubblica*, April 22, 1977, for Luigi Covatta's comments on the DC method of negotiating.

only succeeded in keeping the DC right wing in check, it seemed to provide the PCI with some concrete gains, on the basis of which the leadership could respond to their internal and external critics.

At midyear, *L'Unità* published Berlinguer's reflections on the first twelve months of the party's support of the Government. His tone toward the DC was both critical and conciliatory. He noted that the PCI had faced limited choices: it could either have pressed for unity, or moved—as many in the DC would have preferred—toward a head-on collision with the Christian Democrats. Berlinguer pointed out that many in the DC had come around to accepting the necessity of cooperating with the Communists; that the 1977 programmatic agreement initiated by the coalition parties promised some genuine reforms; and that in confronting the monetary crisis of 1976 and maintaining a united front regarding the need to fight public disorder, Italy had been kept from going over the political precipice. He added that if it was true, as some newspapers claimed, that the PCI was like an army only halfway across the ford in the stream, the PCI would certainly not lose its nerve. In his view, it was the country, not the PCI, that was in transition, and the PCI was committed to make that transition, however tense and laborious, a democratic one.[41]

The Andreotti formula of keeping the Communists out of the Government majority while locking them into de facto support endured until January 1978, when the prime minister resigned under stepped-up PCI pressure on the DC to make the next move toward bringing them formally into the Government. In the protracted negotiations that ensued, there emerged a willingness on the part of the DC to accept the PCI in the governmental majority (as opposed to asking its abstention, as in 1976) on the vote of confidence regarding investiture of the second Andreotti Government.

A month following the onset of the cabinet crisis, Andreotti made public his basic approach, including three major points. First, the coalition parties would have to agree on the basic policies to be enacted *before* a new Government was formed. Second, the Government would consult the parties regarding the specific ministerial (cabinet) assignments designed to translate these commitments into legislation and implementation. Third, the Government would ask a vote of confidence from *all* of the parties involved in this agreement, including the PCI.[42]

Andreotti's formula did not have the enthusiastic endorsement

---

[41] *L'Unità*, June 19, 1977. Reproduced and translated as "One year after June 20th," *The Italian Communists*, no. 2 (April-June 1977), pp. 84-97.
[42] See *La Stampa*, February 16, 1978, p. 1.

of certain factions within his own party; and it also created perplexities regarding the relationship between Parliament and the executive.[43] Nevertheless, it clearly represented a positive response to Berlinguer and the PCI, resulting as it eventually did in March 1978 in the PCI's actually joining the parliamentary majority that brought the second Andreotti Government into existence. In exchange, Andreotti secured the support of the left, however reluctant, for an even more severe program of austerity than had existed earlier. Once again, the PCI found itself caught between its governmental vocation, on one side, and its need to insist on a policy of fair and equitable austerity, on the other. The pointed criticisms of both the PCI and the PSI regarding the lack of precision in Andreotti's proposals,[44] and the insistence of both parties that more attention be paid the demands of the hostile trade unions, did not keep them, in the final analysis, from risking once more the possibility of additional DC *trasformismo*.[45]

In accepting the Andreotti formula, Berlinguer also signaled that the second Andreotti Government would be only a stop-gap measure and that the PCI would continue to insist on a Government of national emergency of which it would be a formal part. Even if such insistence were not entirely dictated by internal party considerations, it would have been forced on Berlinguer by abundant evidence that all of the trade unions, including the CGIL, were fundamentally unsatisfied with the policy directions proposed by Andreotti.

The second Andreotti Government began under the most menacing of omens. Aldo Moro, the principal architect of the DC's softer

---

[43] For reactions to the Andreotti program, see *Corriere della Sera*, February 17, 1978, pp. 1, 2. Perplexities about executive-legislative relationships turned on what Tarrow in this volume describes as "rigorous recourse to the heads of parties of the 'constitutional spectrum' each time a new policy initiative was discussed." The point is that this pattern seemed to many to be as threatening to representative institutions as were the trade unions' demands that they and organized business be the major negotiators of political-economic policies. Andreotti's moves also created consternation in Washington, D.C., and elicited the now-famous U.S. statement of January 12 expressing an essentially negative response to the PCI's formal participation in Italy's Government.

Three things should be said about the U.S. declaration of January 12, 1978. First, contrary to many statements made by Carter officials to the effect that the January 12 statement was entirely consistent with what the administration had said before, the new language did represent a "hardening" toward the PCI. Second, whatever the words may have meant, before or after January 12, the Carter administration was never very happy about the prospect of the PCI in a national government coalition. Third, while U.S. governmental statements do not dictate Italian policy on this issue, they no doubt influence it. No one in Italy understands this better than do the Communists and the Christian Democrats.

[44] See *La Repubblica*, February 17, 1977, pp. 1, 2, 3.

[45] See Vittorio Siva, "E i sindacati non sono certo teneri," [And the trade unions certainly are not tender], *La Repubblica*, February 17, 1978, p. 3.

line toward the PCI, was kidnapped by the Red Brigades as he left his home for Parliament, where he intended to speak in favor of accepting the PCI in the parliamentary governmental majority. This act, and Moro's subsequent murder, ushered in one of the most turbulent periods in the republic's history. Whatever elation the PCI may have felt over its hard-won struggle for more legitimacy was greatly dampened by the knowledge that Moro's tragic death would sooner or later lead to internal DC shifts that would make any further progress highly problematical. Moreover, escalated violence and terror would serve to limit the PCI's freedom of action. At every turn it would be faced with a vicious dilemma: support policies that were unpalatable to its own members, many of its leaders, and the trade unions, or go into opposition, and thereby run the risk of being accused of pursuing narrow interests at the expense of the common good.

As Peter Lange points out, the dilemma was somewhat of the party's own making, in that it resulted in part from the vagueness of the PCI's recent strategy. For a while, the PCI had been able to pursue its campaign to become less a party of Leninism and more a party of gradual, democratic transformation in a socialist direction, without being too precise about the exact nature of the socialist society it sought or the policies and legislation that its creation would require.[46] But in the end events forced the party to abandon the ambiguity that had become one of its hallmarks. Escalated violence would force it to be explicit on the issue of public order. What would be the party's position on the organization of intelligence services? What precisely did the party want when it spoke of reforming the police force in a more democratic direction? As to other major problems, how exactly would the party reform the bureaucracy or the school system? How would it bring about improvement in the delivery of health care and other public services? If the program of austerity pursued by the Government were unacceptable because of its unfairness or its failure to anticipate a "restructuring" of the economy and society in a more "socialist" direction, how, precisely were these goals to be achieved?[47]

[46] Peter Lange, "Crisis and Consent, Change and Compromise: Dilemmas of Italian Communism in the 1970's," West European Politics, vol. 1 (October 1979), pp. 110-132.

[47] There were also pressures on the PCI to be more explicit in the area of foreign policy. Its responses revealed considerable willingness to accept the Atlantic Alliance, the European Community, and NATO, but even here there was a certain vagueness to many of the PCI's pronouncements. See, for example, Berlinguer's speech to the Central Committee and Control Commission of

To be fair to the PCI, we should note that it did make a number of specific policy proposals and, indeed, collaborated with the Andreotti Governments in bringing into existence several important laws. These included improvements in the public budgeting system that gave Parliament new budgetary oversight; a law designed to alleviate the very serious problem of unemployment among Italy's youth; a general plan to attack the food and agriculture problem; the establishment of new, more objective criteria for the appointment of managers to public sector agencies and enterprises; a general law on industrial reconversion; a highly controversial law on "fair rents"; and a much-desired law on decentralization, delegating more and specific governmental authority to regional and local bodies.

The PCI's leaders gradually discovered, however, that it is one thing to pass legislation and quite another to bring about its administrative implementation. Early sanguine expectations[48] about new jobs for the young and the delegation of power to regional and local governments turned into bitter frustration as the party came to recognize how great might be the abyss between legislative promise and bureaucratic performance. Later, Communist leaders were to admit that they had grossly underestimated what an albatross the Italian bureaucracy really is, how difficult it is to transform, and how the normal, routine processes of administration can be exploited by political forces bent on impeding or preventing change.

Economic Policies. In addition to frustrations of this kind, a number of factors led the PCI to lean toward opposition and to trigger the governmental crisis that led to the fall of the second Andreotti Government in the spring of 1979. For example, contrary to the party's dire predictions, the Italian economy simply did not continue to degenerate. Exports rose, the balance of payments improved, and Italy's "second economy" provided an astonishing degree of dynamism —as well as a good reason for believing that Italy's unemployment situation was not as desperate as the PCI claimed.[49] It may very well

January 1978, reproduced in *The Italian Communists*, no. 1 (January-March 1978), pp. 16-23. Cf. Gerardo Chiaromonte, "Communists and Social Democrats in Western Europe," *The Italian Communists*, no. 4 (October-December 1977), pp. 106-113.

[48] See, for example, Berlinguer's comments at the 1977 *"Unità* Festival," in *L'Unità*, September 19, 1977, p. 1. Berlinguer warned the critics of his policies not to make extremist demands, not to work to cut off the working class from its natural allies in the other parties.

[49] Italy's "second economy" and the "black labor" (i.e., hidden, exploited) it is supposed to encourage are still only imperfectly understood. The second economy consists largely of all of those activities, in the manufacturing and

be, as Giorgio Napolitano insists, that the PCI has not been crying wolf and that the economic crisis is real. But his, and the party's, argument is too complex and sophisticated to be easily understood by the average elector and translated into electoral support for the PCI.[50]

The PCI's response to the need to be specific in its policy pronouncements produced a number of recommendations of questionable utility as far as the average voter was concerned. It committed itself to the reform of agriculture; to the direction of additional investments to the South, in order to enlarge and transform that hapless region's productive base; to full employment and better working conditions; to antiprotectionism in foreign trade; and to a New International Economic Order that would rationalize the use of the world's resources and provide assistance to the third world.[51] The new buzzword for the party was "economic planning," which would be characterized by "planning agreements" within single industrial enterprises and groups of them. Planning also implied that the state would assume much more direction and control of total investment, not only in the public sector but also in the Italian and multinational private sectors. The mechanism of planning would presumably serve to introduce in Italy modifications in the market economy and those "socialist elements" of society that the party espoused.[52]

As many in Italy pointed out, not only were the PCI's proposals still somewhat vague, but its central focus on economic planning as the key to creating more socialism was not unlike the Socialist party's commitment to *programmazione economica* when the center-left was constituted in the early 1960s.[53] To the accusation that the party was fifteen years late in its economic planning proposals, Napolitano replied disdainfully, noting that his party had advocated planning for years and *also* that its recent proposals were aimed at a broad-gauged "renewal" of society. Indeed, Napolitano stressed that his party

---

services sector, that are unreported in Italy's national accounts. Some Communist leaders treated it in sterile, Marxist terms, underscoring its "exploitative" nature. Some economists stressed that upwards of 25 percent of Italy's actual GDP was produced by that sector. No clear picture has yet emerged about whether, and how, that sector should be treated by public regulation. For a fascinating collection of essays on this phenomenon, see Istituto di Sociologia, *Lavorare due volte* [Work two times] (Turin: Book Store, 1979).

[50] See Napolitano, *Il Guado*, p. xxv ff.

[51] Ibid., p. xxxiv ff. Cf. PCI, *Proposta di/projetto a medio termine* [A medium-term project proposal] (Rome: Editori Riuniti, 1977).

[52] See in particular Section 8 of Napolitano, *Il Guado*, pp. xlix-lxiii.

[53] For a recent expression of this view, see *La Repubblica*, March 25, 1980, p. 9.

TABLE 4–3

PCI, PSI, AND DC ELECTORAL RESULTS IN PR COMMUNES, 1978,
COMPARED WITH PREVIOUS LOCAL AND NATIONAL RESULTS
(percent)

Party	1978 Local Elections	Previous Local Elections	1976 National Elections
PCI	26.5	25.8	35.6
PSI	13.3	13.5	9.2
DC	42.5	37.5	38.9

NOTE: The PR communes—communes using proportional representation in local elections—are those with populations of at least 5,000.
SOURCE: *Corriere della Sera*, May 17, 1978, p. 2.

would use as a reference point the center-left's failures with economic planning.[54]

Interim Electoral Results. A second, equally important, factor that impelled the PCI toward opposition was the outcome of referendums and regional and local elections in 1978. In May of that year, virtually on the heels of Moro's murder, scattered communal elections sent a shock wave through the party. In the midst of intensified terroristic acts and recriminations among the parties as to the Government's handling of the Moro kidnapping,[55] the voters gave the PCI a devastating setback from the heights it had reached two years earlier. And, as if in recognition of the DC's judicious and courageous handling of the Moro crisis, the DC appeared to be electorally rewarded in almost direct proportion to the PCI's losses (see table 4–3).

[54] Giorgio Napolitano, "A Government Party," *The Italian Communists*, no. 6. (November-December 1976), pp. 13-18. On the failures of the center-left in economic planning see Joseph LaPalombara, *Italy: The Politics of Planning* (Syracuse: Syracuse University Press, 1966), esp. chaps. 6, 8. See also Berlinguer's "Report to the Central Committee" of October 18, 1976, *The Italian Communists*, no. 4-5 (August-October 1976), pp. 37-77.

[55] A source of particular anguish to the PCI was Bettino Craxi's breaking ranks on the question of negotiating with the Red Brigades for Moro's release. In reply to criticisms from the PCI, and from elements within his own fragmented party, Craxi replied, "Socialists cannot associate themselves with the triumphalism of the 'saviors' of the Republic." *Corriere della Sera*, May 8, 1978, p. 1. See also the major party newspapers for the first two weeks of May 1978.

In the May 15 elections, the PCI fell, on average, 9.1 percentage points from its 1976 showing. This represented a loss of over one-quarter of its electoral adherents. Although (as an omen of the 1979 debacle to come) the losses were much greater in the South (in regions like Abruzzi and Campania), they were apparent in northern provinces like Pavia and Novarra as well.

The PCI's initial reaction was understandably to minimize the implications of these scattered electoral contests. But there was immediate self-criticism too, some of it public. Gerardo Chiaromonte, for example, may well have given a laconic resumé of the PCI's operational (as opposed to strategic) dilemma. In accounting for the party's electoral setback, he cited three factors: First, many of Italy's problems defy short-term resolution. Second, the PCI had had to concentrate its energies on defending public order against violence and subversion. Third, the party itself had sometimes not been equal to the challenges thrown up by Italy's manifold crises.[56]

In June 1978, the voters went twice to the polls, once to express their views on two national referendums, once to participate in regional elections. The referendums were highly volatile "single issues" placed on the ballot by the Radical party and other groups on the left. One asked the voters whether they wished to abrogate the law authorizing the public financing of political parties; the other asked whether they wished to abrogate the Reale law on public order. Those who brought these issues to a referendum were opposed to both laws and were therefore looking for a "yes" answer to each question. Those who favored retaining the laws, and therefore campaigned for a "no" vote, included not only the PCI but all of the other parties of the constitutional arc.

Although the "no" vote prevailed in both cases, the level of support for abrogation (particularly on the issue of party finance) suggested a considerable lack of electorate confidence in the coalition parties. In view of the all-out effort that the PCI had made in favor of a "yes" vote, the results were felt to be particularly ominous for that party. Indeed, in the major cities of Italy, places where since

---

[56] *Corriere della Sera*, May 17, 1978, pp. 1-2. Leo Valiani, a respected journalist and historian, picked up Chiaromonte's theme and extended it. He noted that in response to protracted crisis and governmental temporizing, the voters had punished the DC in 1976 and the PCI in 1978. Furthermore, by 1978 the DC had made a number of explicit proposals for dealing with the economic and public order problems, and the PCI often appeared to be opposing, delaying, or carping about these measures. Above all, Valiani believed the PCI may have suffered from its ambiguous posture regarding whether Italy should remain integrated with the Western liberal, market-oriented democracies. *Corriere della Sera*, May 22, 1978, p. 1.

1975 the PCI had been a major partner in government coalitions, a majority of voters voted "yes" to abolish the public financing of parties. In Turin, Milan, and Rome, the "yes" majorities ranged from 52 to 55 percent; but in southern cities like Naples, Bari, Palermo, and Cagliari, the majorities ranged from 60 to 68 percent. These latter were the cities where, in 1979, the PCI would experience its heaviest losses.[57]

Later in June, regional elections in Friuli-Venezia Giulia and the Val d'Aosta brought arresting results not only for the PCI but for the DC as well. The PCI suffered severe losses in both areas over its 1976 showing, but also the DC declined, as *local* and *regional* parties gained unexpected followings. In the city of Trieste, the List for Trieste with 27.4 percent of the vote, actually emerged the strongest party in that community.[58] For the PCI, an additionally jarring signal from the Val d'Aosta was the 11.7 percent of the votes obtained by Proletarian Democracy (DP), one of the most vociferous critics of the PCI's participation in the Government.

Back to Opposition and Struggle. The PCI's decision to step up its demand for formal inclusion in the Government was compelled not by its growing electoral prowess but by its accelerating internal deterioration and manifest electoral weakness. When the latter became apparent in the summer of 1978, there was little reason to hope that a DC that had remained intransigent earlier would suddenly show a change of heart. The prospect of having the Communists on the ropes, the thought that 1979 might well produce the first *national* electoral reversal in PCI postwar history, was instinctively appealing— not just to diehard Christian Democrats but to Socialists and the other minor parties as well.

Although PCI leaders accuse the DC of having broken the coalition of national unity, it was the Communists, no doubt responding to the conditions we have explored, who withdrew from the majority at the turn of the year. In his report to the PCI's fifteenth party congress, Enrico Berlinguer told the delegates that he would not detail why the party leadership had concluded "that the situation had become unlivable" and had decided "to withdraw from the majority and demand

---

[57] The vote on the Reale law on public order was 23.3 percent for abrogation and 76.7 percent for retention; the outcome on the party finance issue was 43.7 percent for abolishing the law, 56.3 percent for maintaining it. See *Corriere della Sera*, June 13, 1978, p. 1.

[58] See *Corriere della Sera*, June 27, 1978, pp. 1, 6; June 28, 1978, p. 1; *L'Unità*, June 27, p. 1. The autonomists in the Val d'Aosta received 24.7 percent of the regional vote.

a thorough clarification of the political situation."[59] He reflected that differences between the PCI and the DC had appeared from the very beginning of the post-1976 experiment in collaboration. These differences had intensified over the Moro affair and its handling, over the strategy to be followed in the referendum on the Reale law on public order, over the appointment of managers to public agencies, and over Italy's membership in the European Monetary System.[60]

Beyond these issues, Berlinguer referred to a resurgence of anti-communism, and particularly to Christian Democrats' going to the United States to assure Washington that the DC was hard at work to weaken the PCI. Regarding one such episode, he said:

> This too counted, because no policy of collaboration can work when the traditions, reality, prestige, and pride of a great party like ours are continuously and gratuitously denigrated. You cannot ask the PCI to support a Government of Christian Democrats and then every day offend the Communists' deepest feelings and those of the millions of Italians who have faith in us.[61]

The "theses" that preceded the March 1979 PCI congress, as well as Berlinguer's report to that group, represent an extensive commentary on the party's recent history, its interpretation of the nature of Italy's crisis, its orientation to Western Europe and to major blocs in international politics, and its need for internal organizational changes.[62] Berlinguer reasserted the "correctness" of the party strategy pursued under his leadership and ascribed its shortcomings and failures not just to "terrorist violence" or the "duplicity of parties" but also to the "shortcomings of our own mass action."[63] Whereas he reiterated the concept of trade union autonomy, he lamented the "degeneration" of the trade union movement and warned that the unions could not replace the political parties in their relations with local, regional, and national governments.[64]

[59] Berlinguer, "Report to the Fifteenth National Congress," p. 75.

[60] Ibid., p. 75 ff. In this extremely important document, Berlinguer candidly explores many of the reasons why the party elected to withdraw to a posture of "responsible opposition." Of particular significance are his references to "the malaise of our base" (p. 78) and to the danger that further collaboration "could dim or impair certain essential features of the characteristics and function of the Italian Communist party" (p. 79).

[61] Ibid., p. 76. For another example, see the interesting article by Rodolfo Brancoli in *La Repubblica*, October 8, 1978, p. 9.

[62] See "Draft Theses for the Fifteenth National Congress of the PCI," in *The Italian Communists* (Special Issue, 1978).

[63] See Thesis 70, in "Draft Theses," pp. 88-89.

[64] Thesis 76, in "Draft Theses," pp. 99-100.

Regarding the electoral losses of 1978, Berlinguer acknowledged that the PCI had failed to strengthen the party's links to various social strata and institutions. Collaboration with the DC was said to have blurred what was distinctive about the PCI. Berlinguer called for redoubled efforts to increase party membership, bring the party more forcefully into the factories, strengthen and streamline party organization, and better adapt it to changes in Italian society.[65] In effect, the party in opposition would have to regroup, redefine its own nature, and prepare a new strategic approach to its long search for legitimacy.[66]

Berlinguer managed to "carry" his congress at an extraordinarily tense and difficult moment in the party's history. Although his victory was a tribute to the secretary general's supple leadership, the congress itself did not produce a clear strategic line. Nor did it put to rest internal differences over the kind of political party—whether "of struggle" or "of Government"—the PCI should be and the kind of leader-follower relationships it should cultivate.

The Campaign, the Electoral Outcome, and the Future

The fifteenth party congress and the debates that preceded it laid the groundwork for the PCI's 1979 electoral campaign. On the critical issue of public order, the party maintained a hard line, but it was not entirely convinced that additional, more Draconian, legislation was needed to deal with terrorism. It reminded the country that the police, intelligence, and judicial systems were badly in need of revamping. On the whole, it reaffirmed its well-established commitment to the republic. In the midst of the frightening escalation of terrorist acts that accompanied the electoral campaign,[67] party leaders from all points in the constitutional arc made different, controversial demands about the organization of the police, the use of the military to maintain public order, the revision of the penal laws, and so on. In this Tower of Babel, the PCI's was only one voice—and one against which the voices of all other parties, on the left, center, and right, were shouting in criticism or opposition. The Christian Democrats, of course, had a field day charging that the PCI's decision to break up

[65] See Theses 75-81 on mass organizations, and Theses 91-92 on party organization, in "Draft Theses," pp. 109-124.

[66] For an extremely interesting analysis of the party's options, see Peter Lange, "Il PCI e i possibili esiti."

[67] *Corriere della Sera*, May 6, 1979, p. 1, reported that during the first quarter of 1979 terroristic acts had been committed in sixty-nine provinces representing three-quarters of the national territory.

131

the parliamentary majority had served to weaken Italy when it most needed to maintain democratic solidarity.[68]

In the economic sphere, the party echoed the major themes it had pursued in preceding months: support for austerity and disciplined labor and trade union behavior, but only in exchange for clear evidence that the necessary sacrifices were being evenly distributed among the classes and sectors of society; a demand that the requests of the working class be accorded a fair and sympathetic hearing; [69] a commitment to alleviating unemployment, especially among youth; the development of agriculture; increased allocations of capital for the transformation of the South; and, above all, insistence on a form of democratic economic planning, centralized at Rome, to be sure, but in which regional, local, and plant-level groups would participate.

As the campaign unfolded, the Liberals and others expressed fears that the Communists and Christian Democrats might be secretly in collusion—even while the Christian Democrats, in the teeth of PCI criticism and disbelief, reiterated a "solemn pledge" that they would not form a Government with the PCI.[70] From the PCI's standpoint, the most disquieting development of the campaign was the DC's clear invitation to the Socialists to recreate the discredited center-left if the electoral arithmetic should turn out to make that retrograde step possible. At this prospect, Berlinguer and his colleagues warned that the PCI would oppose and vote against *any* Government that excluded the PCI.[71]

Bettino Craxi worked to place distance between the PSI and the PCI. He argued that a Government of national unity could not be easily reconstituted; he refused to discuss the PCI's surprising resurrection of the idea of the "Socialist alternative," deriding it as a "frontist alternative, not even useful as propaganda;" and he added

---

[68] See Zaccagnini's remarks to a group of Milanese industrialists, reported in *Corriere della Sera*, May 6, 1979, pp. 1, 2. The PCI understandably insisted that the real cause of the break-up of the parliamentary majority was resurgent anticommunism in the DC and the latter's flat rejection of the idea that the PCI should be formally included in the Government. See, for example, Enrico Berlinguer, "The D.C.'s Anti-Communist Veto Is the Cause of the Breakup of the Majority," *The Italian Communists*, no. 4 (October-December 1978), pp. 76-88.

[69] See the articles by Luciano Lama, *L'Unità*, May 1, 1979, p. 1; and Bruno Trentin, *L'Unità*, May 8, 1979, pp. 1, 2.

[70] See *Corriere della Sera*, May 7, 1979, p. 1.

[71] This issue ran throughout the campaign and produced predictable dissent among Socialist party leaders. The flavor of the exchanges between and among parties and protagonists can be gleaned from: *Corriere della Sera*, May 8, 1979, p. 1; *L'Unità*, May 9, 1979, p. 1; May 11, 1979, pp. 1, 2; May 12, 1979, p. 1.

that the PSI would not run after the PCI and "retreat to the woods to de-petal Leninist daisies."[72]

Openly assaulted from virtually all sides of the political spectrum, the PCI replied with some stinging attacks of its own. Paolo Spriano, for example, was disdainful toward those, like Craxi, who, while sounding the alarm over a possible DC-PCI "regime," were actually themselves leaning toward collaboration with the DC.[73] Giancarlo Pajetta warned about the resurgent conservatism of the DC and sought to undercut the overtures to the Socialists emanating from the same Amintore Fanfani who had promoted the center-left in the early 1960s.[74]

In effect, as the campaign unfolded and the PCI found itself surrounded by hostility, the Communists were pushed even farther from the conciliatory, collaborative posture that had characterized the party during the first two years following the 1976 elections. Those within the PCI who favored a more hard-line, intransigent campaign could argue that the DC had fallen under the control of a right-wing cabal and that there was therefore little reason to believe that the party would be willing to continue a dialogue with the PCI. On the contrary, the center of gravity within the DC had clearly shifted toward those who were outspokenly insistent that a coalition Government that included the PCI was, for an indefinite period of time, simply unthinkable.

Relations with the Socialists were, if anything, even worse. The Craxi strategy described earlier was clearly having some effect—if nothing else at least in terms of forcing larger numbers of PCI leaders to express their irritation and anger with the PSI's electoral tactics. Indeed, the PCI found itself under severe attack not only from the Socialists but also from the Radicals who single-mindedly questioned the PCI's democratic credentials. The Radical party's needling eventually produced from the PCI the questionable public response that the Radicals were not reasonably to be considered a part of Italy's left.

In effect, the PCI during the campaign came more and more to understand, to regret, and to react to the fact that its earlier strategy had been a failure. Not in substantive policy terms, in that the PCI's moderate, conciliatory posture was a major factor in the economic successes registered by Andreotti, but certainly in political terms, in that the Aldo Moro approach, continued by Andreotti, produced a

---

[72] See *Corriere della Sera*, May 13, 1979, p. 1; May 26, 1979, p. 1.

[73] *L'Unità*, June 1, 1979, pp. 1, 17.

[74] Ibid.

very wide spectrum of opposition to the idea that the PCI might be on the verge of becoming a formal part of a government coalition.

Public opinion polls suggested there was little the PCI could do to stop the electoral deterioration it had experienced in 1978.[75] From their own pulse-reading around the country, PCI leaders anticipated that they would be lucky to keep the party's fortunes at or above the 30 percent level. Given how much fire, domestic and international, was concentrated on the PCI and its governmental operations, the PCI leadership was probably correct in noting that the electoral outcome was better than it might have expected. Nevertheless, certain aspects of the vote turned out to be extremely disquieting. Among these, the following deserve passing reference:

1. *Loss of PCI appeal to the younger voters.* Although evidence for this slippage cannot be unequivocally derived from a mere comparison of electoral results for the Chamber of Deputies and the Senate (where the seven age cohorts between eighteen and twenty-four years do not vote), PCI leaders are convinced that the party suffered a disproportionate decline among younger voters. If, as Sani nicely shows in this volume, the overall electoral support for the left did not change very much in 1979 as compared with earlier elections, it appears that parties like the PR, the PDUP, and the NSU that have strong appeal for younger voters made a significant contribution to the PCI's decline.[76]

2. *Urban, working-class decline.* Not only did the PCI experience disproportionate losses in major industrial cities, but within such cities it appeared to be losing its hold on the poorest working-class districts. If, as more than one PCI leader observed, the Radical party's gains in places like Rome came primarily from middle-class districts where the younger voters may have opted for that party, the PCI should worry all the more about where the working-class gains it made in 1976 disappeared to in 1979. In other words, in larger cities, as well as in the South generally, discontent with the PCI may well have benefited parties like the DC.[77]

3. *Left abstentionism and invalid and blank ballots.* Unprecedented levels of voter abstention and record numbers of blank and

[75] See, for example, the polling results published by *La Repubblica*, May 29, 1979, p. 1. Public opinion trends are nicely summarized and examined by Giacomo Sani in his chapter in this volume.

[76] See Sani's chapter in this volume for an extensive, insightful treatment of this and other points summarized here. See also *Corriere della Sera*, June 6, 1979, pp. 1, 2.

[77] See, for example, the argument of Giorgio Botta in *L'Unità*, June 7, 1979, p. 2.

invalid ballots suggested to the PCI that it may have been disproportionately affected by these phenomena. Evidently, the spoiled ballots
contained striking numbers of insults, four-letter words, endorsements
of terrorism, and denunciations of the parties of the constitutional arc
or the establishment.[78] Given the controversy, even within its own
ranks, that accompanied the PCI's decision to support the Christian
Democrats, party leaders were appropriately concerned that these
manifestations of voter alienation may have hurt it more than other
parties.

It is of great concern to the PCI to sort out the relative impact on
its electoral fortunes of absentions as opposed to defections to other
parties. Not only do the latter count twice as much as the former in
the party's electoral reckoning; but party abstainers are presumably
more readily recaptured if the party can remove whatever caused them
to sit out 1979. Furthermore if, as some have shown, younger voters
abstained in larger proportions than older ones, the PCI might well
expect to benefit more if future participation rates from this category
of the "normal left constituency" improve.

4. *Single issues and demographic variations.* Perhaps the most
arresting discovery for the PCI was that a wide range of factors, and
not necessarily the same factors in different areas, were associated
with its decline. For example, the party appears to have suffered more
where unemployment was high and where opportunities to find work
in the "second economy" were lower. Then too, whereas the erosion
of the PCI seems to have been strongly associated with the strength
of the Radical party in some geographic areas, this was not true, for
instance, in the South, where the party suffered some of its most
spectacular losses. Furthermore, if the referendum votes can be taken
as measures of the importance of single-issues over broader ideological
identifications with political parties, then it is significant that the PCI's
losses were highest in places where the votes to abolish the public
financing of parties were highest.[79]

[78] See *Corriere della Sera*, June 8, 1979, p. 1. Luigi Barzini's lead editorial in
this same issue is an interesting commentary on the meaning of the abstentions and blank and spoiled ballots, which in 1979 represented an "invisible
party" numbering well over 5 million voters.

[79] For a highly sophisticated analysis of the correlates of the PCI's 1979 losses
over 1976, see Renato Mannheimer, "Un' analisi territoriale del calo comunista"
[A territorial analysis of the communist fall], *Il Mulino*, vol. 28 (September-
October 1979), pp. 694-714. On the important question whether the 1979
elections constitute a basic change in voter orientation and/or a party realignment in elector support, see the study of Genoa, Verona, and Bologna executed
by Piergiorgio Corbetta, "Novità e incertezze nel voto del 3 giugno: analisi dei
flussi elettorali" [Novelties and uncertainties in the vote of June 3: analyses of
electoral fluctuations], *Il Mulino*, vol. 28 (September-October 1979), pp. 715-748.

It may very well be that the results of the 1979 elections, as well as the rise in importance of single-issue voting of the kind suggested by the referendums of the mid and late-1970s, mark profound changes in the nature of Italy's political culture. If that is true, the PCI will be pushed to engage in much more serious reflections than those associated with the question whether its 1976–1979 flirtation with the Christian Democrats was necessary (that is, required by the nature of the Italian "crises") or productive (that is, successful in moving the party closer to full political legitimacy).

If, for example, the number of "floating voters" remains in the future much higher than in the past,[80] and if these voters are shopping around more than ever before for a party they can support on the basis of their position on single issues considered of overriding importance, such a change should have momentous implications for a party like the PCI, burdened as it still is with Marxist-Leninist assumptions about the dynamics of liberal democratic political systems. To be more specific, the PCI will have to appraise the extent to which the "New Party," as its leaders have called the PCI, is optimally positioned to integrate changes that characterize not only Italian voters in general, not only those voters who might support the PCI at the polls, but also those members of society who might become members of the PCI or its related and auxiliary organizations. For the voters as a whole, the one basic question is raised by Arturo Parisi and Gianfranco Pasquino:[81] Is it in fact the case that the incidence of strong party identification has declined and that more voters now make their electoral choices less on the basis of party label, more on the basis of single issues or other highly particularistic considerations?

These authors make a strong case that the "vote of belonging" (that is, the vote of strong party identification) was traditionally based on deeply imbedded subcultures that have been eroding. As the boundaries of these encapsulated, sometimes mutually exclusive, subcultures become more permeable, the basis for voting choice shifts in either or both of two directions. The first is the "vote of opinion," or what in American voting studies is denominated "issue voting." The second is the "vote of exchange," where the voter seeks short-term or immediate gratification of a particularistic interest. Voters who choose the latter seek an immediate trade-off of their vote for a par-

[80] For a sober and arresting commentary on this important question, see Arturo Parisi, "Mobilità non significa movimento" [Mobility does not mean movement], *Il Mulino*, vol. 28 (September-October 1979), pp. 643-668.

[81] See Arturo Parisi and Gianfranco Pasquino, "Changes in Italian Electoral Behavior: The Relationship Between Parties and Voters," *West European Politics*, vol. 2 (October 1979), pp. 6-30.

ticular gain. Where the benefit is not quickly forthcoming, these voters will shift allegiances to other parties. This is presumably what happened to the PCI in the South (that hotbed of clientelism) and in other places where the sharp rises in the PCI vote in 1975 and 1976 were not followed by the expected performance on the part of the PCI.

The explication offered by Parisi and Pasquino is much more nuanced and sophisticated than my summary treatment may suggest. The point is that if this kind of transformation is actually at work, the PCI will be frustrated if it uses shop-worn strategies designed to bring new voters into a party subculture that may itself be vanishing. Indeed, holding on to new voters of either the "opinion" or the "exchange" type will require that the party's basic approach to the electorate—the symbols it uses, the degree of specificity its proposals will have to contain, and the time frame within which it can reward its electorate—will have to change.

As for party members and the relationships among them, their local leaders, and those at the PCI center, no one has posed the dilemma better than Marcello Fedele. Is it not necessary, he asks, that the PCI make some "not secondary changes in its own internal life, its relationship to society"? It is Fedele's view that the PCI has not fully worked through the implications of its own transformation from a party of struggle to a party of Government. Because of this, the party slipped somewhat haphazardly into the role of a "state party," with all of the disaffection on the left that this brought about in recent years. Conversely, the retreat to opposition that preceded the 1979 elections was accompanied by symptoms of the tight internal control that is typical of a party of revolutionary struggle.[82]

Unless the contradictions are resolved, the PCI clearly risks losing the battle on *both* the governmental and the oppositional front. When it gets cozy with the DC but fails to articulate a clear posture regarding the role of trade unions, the ways of dealing with public order, the nature of the Italian economy, and the policies that are required

---

[82] Marxist intellectuals, as Bobbio has pointedly stressed, have not been very helpful to the PCI in the matter of working through the practical implications of what it means to be a Marxist "party of Government" in a pluralistic liberal democratic society. To paraphrase Bobbio, the intellectuals will have to come down from the ivory tower some day to show what are the practical implications for a party like the PCI of demonstrating that Marx was a structuralist rather than a historicist. As opposed to another exegesis of the Marxian sacred texts, they might try their hand at an *institutional* analysis of the bourgeois and the Marxist state. See N. Bobbio, "Esiste una dottrina Marxista della stato?" [Does there exist a Marxist theory of the state?], *Mondo Operaio* (August-September 1975), pp. 25-26.

and possible in a basically market-oriented configuration, it undermines the new basis for its potential electoral appeal. When it retreats to opposition and tries to keep its own restive troops in line through the instrumentality of democratic centralism, it risks eroding its own membership and leadership base. Indeed, the two facets of the party's problem are deeply connected. It may very well be that neither its operational code nor its organizational format is well suited to either a contemporary mass party with a genuine governmental vocation or a mass party devoted to "responsible opposition."[83]

On the critical issue of democratic centralism, the leadership's refusal to discard it in 1979 should not be superficially ascribed to Stalinist nostalgia or Leninist residues. Italy's political parties constitute a Byzantine maze of shifting party factions and subfactions. The PCI's fear of the fragmentation that party factions, or *correnti* as they are called, bring is roughly analogous to the Germans' feeling about inflation. And yet this fear will have to be overcome if the party's leadership is to succeed in responding creatively to internal pressures, on the one hand, and to its long-term search for legitimacy and governmental participation, on the other.[84]

Debates over the recent past and the party's future orientation continue unabated within the PCI. In the wake of the 1979 electoral defeat, leaders like Cossutta and Napolitano underscored that the PCI in opposition would not mean intransigent hostility or obstructionist politics. As Adalberto Minucci, who would be elected to the PCI Secretariat in July 1979, put it, the party would evaluate what has to be done and would critique policy proposals with the interests of the working class and the nation central to its thinking. Both he, and later Berlinguer, reiterated a defense of the PCI's commitment to austerity and of its willingness to make compromises with the DC and other parties without selling out too cheaply.[85]

[83] See Fedele, *Classi e partiti*, pp. 177 ff. Fedele makes the telling argument that the PCI's leaders are narrow technicians, more adept at keeping the party apparatus stable and resolving internal conflict than at managing a modern mass party. He adds (pp. 212-213) that, in its governmental vocation and in its recognition that the trade unions should play a new role in the political system, the PCI failed to come up with an operational code adapted to the new situation.

[84] The issues I am raising here are brilliantly treated by Salvatore Secchi in two articles: "L'austero fascino del centralismo democratico," [The austere attractiveness of democratic centralism], *Il Mulino*, vol. 27 (May-June 1978), pp. 408-453; and "Il nuovo statuto del PCI: Tra rinnovamento e continuità" [The new PCI constitution: between renewal and continuity], *Il Mulino*, vol. 28 (July-August 1979), pp. 585-613.

[85] See *L'Unità*, June 7, 1979, p. 1; A. Minucci, "Le permesse della ripresa comunista" [The premises for the Communist revival], *Rinascita*, July 6, 1979, pp. 1-2. See Berlinguer's statement in *Rinascita*, July 1-2, 1979, pp. 1-2.

Giorgio Napolitano's recent volume is an excellent example of such reflections, although it represents only one of several party viewpoints.[86] Those who opposed the historic compromise and Berlinguer's post-1976 strategy, those who retained the deepest reservations about the flirtation with the DC, those who warned that the party leadership's plunge toward its governmental vocation far outdistanced the point local leaders and members had reached (or wished to reach) were no doubt considerably vindicated.

If the fifteenth party congress did not produce a full-blown crisis of Berlinguer's leadership, it certainly toned down the historic compromise. Moreover, the events of late 1979 brought into public view the party's raging debate over the issue of austerity and what this might imply regarding the party's posture toward workers and their unions.

In November, Giorgio Amendola directed a stinging attack at the unions, accusing workers and their leaders of making unjustified wage demands, distorting the nature of the unemployment problem, overusing the strike, and protecting the escalator clause against any governmental tampering. Although Amendola appeared once again isolated—a lonesome voice with the wind against him—the responses of other members of the Central Committee revealed that his views have more support than appears at first blush. But the reactions also reveal that the party is far from resolving a key dilemma regarding its continuing commitment to being a party of struggle and of Government.[87]

In recent months, exactly that return to the old center-left that the PCI (and many others in Italy) feared has come to pass. It looks more sterile than the earlier version in that, on this most recent occasion, the PSI has made little pretense of extracting from the DC a policy quid pro quo. The present center-left seems as unworkable as its predecessor and so can be expected to do little to alleviate the state of recurrent and accelerating crisis into which the governance of Italy has fallen.

Those within Italy, as well as on the outside, who see the present Government and/or the internal realignment of DC forces that occurred at the DC's 1980 congress as a real solution to "the problem of the Communists" are leaning on a very weak reed indeed.[88] It may well be the case—indeed the forces of history and the norms of Italian politics may dictate—that the present shift to the right within the DC

[86] Napolitano, *Il Guado*, especially sections 4 and 9 of the introductory essay, and the essays beginning at pp. 225, 246, 272.

[87] See the pages of *Rinascita* and *L'Unità* for November and December 1979.

[88] On U.S. expectations, see Rodolfo Brancoli, "Aspettando il Centro-Sinistra" [Waiting for the center-left], *La Repubblica*, April 13, 1979, p. 11.

will represent in the longer run a bridge to some form of the historic compromise, under whatever name. Just as it was Amintore Fanfani who engineered an older "opening to the left," so it may be the DC center and right that engineers the PCI's entry under the governmental umbrella.[89]

In the last analysis, it will be the Italians (not those abroad) who decide, as they should, when and under what conditions the PCI will be accorded full legitimacy. As the first *real* public referendum on that issue, the voters' decision in 1979 seems to have been an unequivocal "not now." Whether that verdict turns into a "yes" will depend not a little on how the PCI itself deals with the dilemmas we have surveyed.

[89] One no more imagines that Moro could have brought in the PCI than that Hubert Humphrey, as opposed to the more conservative Richard Nixon, could have ended the Vietnam War.

5

The Italian Socialist Party: Electoral Stagnation and Political Indispensability

Gianfranco Pasquino

The results of the third parliamentary elections of the 1970s were not to the complete satisfaction of the Italian Socialist party (PSI). Indeed, they were another relative disappointment. The party scored limited percentage gains ranging from 9.6 to 9.8 points in the Chamber of Deputies and from 10.2 to 10.4 points in the Senate and more substantial gains in seats: five additional deputies and two additional senators. However, the PSI did not break through the 10 percent barrier in the Chamber of Deputies, as some surveys had timidly suggested it might, and, more important, it was unable to take advantage of the large erosion of the Communist electorate. Other leftist parties collected the votes of dissatisfied 1976 Communist supporters. Perhaps this is an indication that Socialist attacks on the PCI had been misguided and misdirected or that the PSI was still not considered a credible and viable alternative by many disgruntled Communist voters, or, finally, that moderately progressive voters still perceived a discrepancy between Socialist statements and Socialist behavior.

The outcome of all this was that the PSI remained by far the smallest Southern European Socialist party, and the PCI the largest Southern European Communist party (see table 5–1). At the same time, the area to the left of the PCI had grown, while the PSI had remained substantially stable. More specifically, table 5–2 shows that the position of the PSI barely improved in 1979, while the area at the left of the PCI had grown gradually and considerably (from 2.6 to 5.6 percent of the vote and from ten to twenty-four deputies). The elusive concept of a "socialist area" can no longer be meaningfully

This chapter was written for the most part while the author was a fellow of the Woodrow Wilson International Center for Scholars, Washington, D.C., in 1978-1979.

TABLE 5–1

ELECTORAL STRENGTH OF SOUTHERN EUROPEAN SOCIALIST AND
COMMUNIST PARTIES AT THE END OF THE 1970s
(percent)

Party	Italy 1979	Spain 1979	France 1978	Greece 1977	Portugal 1980
Socialists	9.8	30.8	22.6	25.3	28.7
Communists	30.4	10.9	20.6	12.0[a]	17.3

[a] Communist party of Greece, 9.36 percent; Communist party of Greece-Interior, 2.72 percent.

SOURCE: Italy, *La Stampa*, June 6, 1979, p. 1; France, Frank L. Wilson, "The French CP's Dilemma," *Problems of Communism*, vol. 17 (July-August 1978), p. 6; Greece, and Spain, José Maravall, "Political Cleavages in Spain and the 1979 General Election," *Government and Opposition*, vol. 14 (Summer 1979), p. 309; Portugal, official returns.

TABLE 5–2

EVOLUTION OF THE LEFT, CHAMBER OF DEPUTIES ELECTIONS, 1972–1979
(percent)

Party	1972	1976	1979
PCI	27.2	34.4	30.4
PSI	9.6	9.6	9.8
PSIUP	1.9	—	—
New Left[a]	}	}	0.8[c]
PDUP	} 1.1	} 1.5[b]	1.4
PR	—	1.1	3.4
PCI share of the left vote	68.3	70.1	65.9
PSI share of the left vote	24.1	20.1	21.1

Dash (—): not applicable.

[a] Il Manifesto, 0.7; Movimento Politico dei Lavoratori, 0.4.

[b] Democrazia Proletaria.

[c] Nuova Sinistra Unita.

SOURCE: For 1972 and 1976, Gianfranco Pasquino, "The Italian Socialist Party: An Irreversible Decline?" in Howard R. Penniman, ed., *Italy at the Polls: The Parliamentary Elections of 1976* (Washington, D.C.: American Enterprise Institute, 1977), p. 184; for 1979, *La Stampa*, June 6, 1979, p. 1.

applied to misguided potential PSI voters. If the concept retains any meaning at all, it must refer to a large pool of leftist voters few of whom are inclined to support the PSI consistently—the truly floating or opinion voters of the left.[1] The consequence is that the party cannot count on its ability to establish close ties with a large group of voters. The likely availability of a greater pool of voters unattached to a specific party, but floating within the area of the left has not produced, and might not produce in the future, sizable gains for the PSI. If the 1979 elections contain a lesson for the leaders of the PSI it is that for some time to come the future will be no brighter than the past.

The Background: Renewal of the Party and Its Doctrine

The disappointing results of June 1976 precipitated an agonizing reappraisal of the state of the party. Three major items were put on the agenda in the aftermath of the elections: turnover of the leadership, renewal of the organization, and updating of the doctrine. The defeat was fundamentally attributed to the inability of Secretary General Francesco De Martino to carry out convincingly and unwaveringly the political strategy of the leftist alternative as well as to his overall lack of attention to organizational problems. While certainly not an outspoken advocate of the leftist alternative, the new secretary general, Bettino Craxi (belonging to the right-wing faction of the party but elected through a generational alliance with the young "colonels" of the center and of the left wing, in particular Claudio Signorile) had been for a long time secretary of the large and powerful Socialist federation of Milan and was therefore considered a capable organizer.

The timing of the new leadership's efforts to strengthen the party and their position within it was important. The deadline the Socialists set themselves was the election of the European Parliament. They expected to do well in the European contest and hoped for a substantial domestic spillover: realizing that the Socialists had an

[1] For background material and a tentative definition of the "socialist area," see my chapter, "The Italian Socialist Party: An Irreversible Decline?" in Howard R. Penniman, ed., *Italy at the Polls: The Parliamentary Elections of 1976* (Washington, D.C.: American Enterprise Institute, 1977), pp. 183-186. The notion of opinion voters and floating voters of the left is dealt with in Arturo Parisi and Gianfranco Pasquino, "Relazioni partiti-elettori e tipi di voto" [Party-voter relationships and types of vote], in Arturo Parisi and Gianfranco Pasquino, eds., *Continuità e mutamento elettorale in Italia* [Electoral continuity and change in Italy] (Bologna: Il Mulino, 1977), especially pp. 221-223, 236-237, and 244-249.

absolute or relative majority at the European level, Italian voters, they seemed to reason, would jump on the Socialist bandwagon. It is difficult to say how well grounded this reasoning was. In any event, and much to the Socialists' disappointment and anger, the Italian elections were scheduled before the European elections. Thus, it became impossible either to test the hypothesis or to reap the benefits of the spillover. As it turned out, the PSI did better in the European than the Italian elections, but the European Socialists did not do well as a whole.[2]

While proceeding to the party's internal renewal, the PSI gave its "critical" support to the two Governments formed by the Christian Democrat Giulio Andreotti; abstaining in 1976 and formally entering the majority in 1978, it kept its preelectoral promise to join only governmental coalitions which did not exclude the PCI. The purpose was twofold. First and above all, the PSI did not want to allow the Communists to appear to the electorate as monopolizing the opposition while the Socialists were trapped in renewed subordination to the Christian Democrats. Second, the Socialists wanted to pave the way for the full legitimation of the PCI as a governmental partner. This decision grew out of a global concern to improve the functioning of the Italian political system, but it also reflected the fact that a fully legitimate PCI was a basic precondition for the implementation of the leftist alternative. The Socialists face a thorny dilemma in pursuing this strategy. Only through a large and more acceptable PCI could the Italian left achieve power. Yet, "a larger and more acceptable PCI represents a threat for the Socialists, pressing upon them the problem of finding an identity of their own, that is, principles, issues, and strategies substantially different from those of the PCI"[3] and potentially reducing their political space. Moreover, the PCI would use its electoral strength to pursue the "historic compromise" with the DC, not a Government exclusively of the left. Thus, the Socialists must steer a course that compels the PCI to modernize

---

[2] The Italian Socialists polled 11 percent overall in the European elections and improved their percentage in each of the five constituencies over their results in the Italian elections held the week before. The regional results, according to *Corriere della Sera*, June 12, 1979, p. 5, were:

	Northwest	Northeast	Center	South	Islands	Total
Italian elections	11.1	8.8	9.1	10.0	9.8	9.8
European elections	12.4	10.6	10.4	10.4	10.3	11.0

[3] I am slightly reformulating a point made by Giacomo Sani. The quotation is from his "Amici-Nemici; Parenti-Serpenti: Communists and Socialists in Italy," in Bernard E. Brown, ed., *Eurocommunism and Eurosocialism: The Left Confronts Modernity* (New York: Cyrco Press, 1979), p. 112.

TABLE 5–3

STRENGTH OF PSI FACTIONS AT NATIONAL CONVENTIONS, 1976 AND 1978
(percent of delegates)

Factions	1976	1978
Autonomists (Nenni-Craxi)	13	65
Left (Lombardi-Signorile)	18	
New Left (Achilli)		4
Demartiniani (De Martino-Manca)	40	24
Bertoldiani (Bertoldi)	9	
Manciniani (Mancini)	20	7

SOURCE: *Corriere della Sera*, March 29, 1978, p. 2.

its structure and ideology while the PSI keeps one step ahead. So far the Socialists have failed on both counts—and the Communists have been able to retain their electoral advantage without stepping up the pace of their modernization.

Aware of their need for time in which to accomplish the desired changes in the structure and ideology of the party, the Socialists decided not to prematurely rock the boat of the Governments of "national solidarity." Of course, many hurdles had to be overcome in the process: a governmental agreement on a better defined program was reached in June 1977, and a major governmental crisis was solved in March 1978 with the entry of the PCI into the parliamentary majority the same day as Aldo Moro, artificer of the complex agreement, was kidnapped. A few days later the PSI held its forty-first congress in Turin.

The leadership found its position fundamentally strengthened (see table 5–3), having acquired substantial majorities in many provincial conferences, especially in northern and central Italy. It is important to stress that regional variations remained conspicuous, as can be seen from figure 5–1. Craxi's and Signorile's factions had not made great inroads in the territories of the two major opponents of their strategy, former Secretaries Giacomo Mancini and Francesco De Martino. Nonetheless, the majority factions succeeded in achieving secure control over the Central Committee as well as over the Executive Committee. Moreover, the activism of the secretary and the vice-secretary coupled with the ascent of loyal followers to power in a majority of provincial federations, especially the most important ones (Turin, Milan, Bologna, and Florence), created an almost unprecedented situation. For the first time in many years, a factional alliance

FIGURE 5–1
Strength of PSI Factions at Regional Conventions, 1978

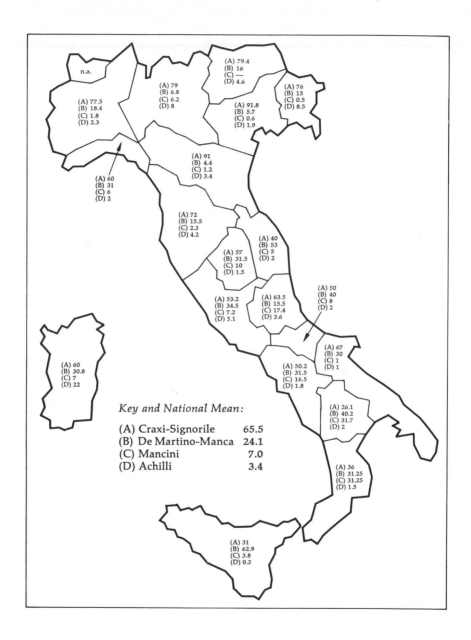

Note: n.a. indicates not available.
Source: L'Espresso, March 26, 1978, pp. 26-27.

146

had asked for and obtained a solid majority at a party congress, was in charge of party affairs, and could effectively implement its policies.

Thus, by the beginning of April 1978, one of the major goals of the secretary general had been basically achieved. The membership remained stable at approximately 435,000; but a renewal of cadres had been fostered, particularly at the level of the provincial executive committees, and active members and elected administrators at the local level seemed galvanized by what one might call the Socialist New Deal. Five new members were elected to the Executive Committee (Direzione), four of them on the Craxi-Signorile ticket so that the leadership of the majority seemed almost unchallengeable. Most of the challenges were launched by the extreme left of the party, specifically by the faction leader Michele Achilli and by the economist Paolo Leon. But what the majority feared most was the weakening or even breaking of the uneasy alliance between Craxi and the ambitious Signorile (a break that would eventually take place at the beginning of 1980) as well as the frequently dissenting positions taken by the influential old leader of the left Riccardo Lombardi.

In addition to a renewal of the cadres, the second objective pursued by Craxi and Signorile was a thorough reformulation of Socialist ideas and ideals. Traditionally, the PSI has suffered from, as much as it has been enlivened by, its ties with three different cultures and sets of political beliefs. The classic Marxist non-Leninist philosophy was embodied above all by Lelio Basso, who left the party with the split of the PSIUP in 1964; in the late 1970s its spokesmen were De Martino and the left-wing faction of Achilli. The other two strands both derive from the progressive liberal democratic tradition: social reformism is widely shared by Socialist deputies and goes back to the father of the party, Filippo Turati, while a more aggressive stance is combined with some elements of bourgeois radicalism. Lombardi is the political spokesman for this culture, which had its origins in the left wing of the Partito d'Azione (Action party), a short-lived party of intellectuals who participated in the resistance and then dispersed among various parties, from the Republicans to the Socialists and Communists.

The creation of a modern cohesive Socialist culture was felt by party leaders and intellectuals to be important and politically relevant. The Socialist monthly *Mondo Operaio* pursued this enterprise with essays and debates addressing aspects of the management of a modern industrial society and its transformation in a Socialist direction. Then the Secretariat itself decided to build upon these contributions and launched a major effort with the help of numerous Socialist intellectuals.

Patterned on the French Socialist party's blueprint *Changer la vie,* the Italian *Progetto Socialista per l'Alternativa* (Socialist project for the alternative) was meant to achieve several different objectives. It would be difficult to rank them by priority, but probably the most important was the doctrinal revision of the traditional charter of Italian socialism. The only previous case of a major revision was the ill-fated "Letter to the Comrades" by the long-time party leader Pietro Nenni in October 1966. This had been intended to supply the basis for a unification with the Social Democrats (PSDI) and at the same time to provide a better understanding of the role of the state in democratic systems. Nenni's had been an individual effort, while the second major objective of the Socialist Project was the mobilization of intellectual energies within and especially outside the party, to give more exposure to Socialist intellectuals, to stress the importance and originality of their thinking, to emphasize their contributions in terms not only of theoretical formulations but of policy-oriented proposals —and to show the PSI's responsiveness (a far cry from the Communists' attitude toward their "organic" intellectuals, who are summoned to provide justifications for the leaders' decisions). It was hoped that a new Socialist culture would emerge from this process which might unify the different threads present within the party and create a cohesive leadership group.

Two spillover effects of this activity, carefully orchestrated and organized, were expected. On the one hand, the production, publication, diffusion, and discussion of an original and innovative party document was intended to galvanize party members. Their *esprit de parti* was to be bolstered, their identification with the party strengthened. At the same time, the PSI and its ideas were to acquire greater exposure in the mass media.[4] The Socialist Project contained a lot that was and is relevant to an analysis of the international and domestic crisis of capitalism. In particular, the Socialists tried to do better than the Communists, who had put forward less than a year before a much less ambitious and inspiring "Plano a Medio Termine" (Middle-range plan) generally considered disappointing and quietly shelved. On the other hand, and very controversially, the Socialist Project served as the inspiration for the Craxi-Signorile motion at the congress, automatically antagonizing all the other groups. Neverthe-

---

[4] The target groups were specifically identified as the educated, politicized urban strata (unionized workers, technicians, professionals) inclined to shift their vote among different parties of the left according to political circumstances and type of electoral consultation. One might surmise that the recent mobility of the Italian electorate, especially in the North, is due to a quantitative growth in the pool of these voters.

less, it was adopted as a majority resolution by the Turin congress and thereafter became the official charter of the PSI.

While the entire document is devoted to spelling out why the leftist or Socialist alternative should come into being, its major planks are contained in chapter 4, which discusses ways to pull the country out of the crisis and build a new reforming alliance. This chapter stresses both the creation of renewed mobility for labor and the need to protect the position of temporarily unemployed workers and allow them to retrain without putting a burden on companies trying to modernize their equipment and production methods. The workers themselves through the trade unions would manage and control the workings of a new institution, the Agency of Labor. In this regard, the PSI's purpose is transparent: to forge new ties with the labor movement. This effort culminated in the election of Socialist Giorgio Benvenuto to the position of secretary of the Italian Union of Labor (Unione Italiana del Lavoro, UIL), an office rarely given to a Socialist trade unionist in a federation grouping Republican, Social Democratic and Socialist workers. As to the second component, a project for democracy, the starting point was an awareness of the perhaps irreversible crisis of the welfare state and the need to find new solutions. Building upon the Socialist Project, Craxi clarified the position of the PSI at the congress of the Socialist International held in Vancouver:

> Facing an economic crisis which erodes, day after day, the margins of traditional reformism, it is obvious that we cannot propose any longer a conception of socialism completely focused on the distributive phase and on the pattern of the welfare state. The resources necessary to such an operation do not exist any more and I believe that even the Social Democratic parties more attached to this vision are aware of this. The new socialist order can be founded only upon a gradual shift of political power in favor of the working classes, increasing their governing responsibilities.[5]

In order to accomplish this shift and, at the same time, to reform the state, the PSI called for two major democratic transformations: political decentralization (participatory democracy) and self-management (autogestion). On top of it all, the Project stressed not only the relevance but the indispensability of a Planning Agency capable of acquiring adequate information through widespread consultation and

[5] Quoted in "Dopo il Congresso dell'IS/Parla Craxi: Caro Breznev, apri le porte" [After the congress of the Socialist International/Craxi speaks: dear Brezhnev, open the doors], *L'Espresso*, November 12, 1978, p. 19.

participation to constantly review the consequences of its policies in order to proceed to further adjustments.

The overall context in which these transformations should be accomplished is of course a democratic form of government. In the working system outlined by the Socialist Project, it would be possible to create and sustain the conditions for the emergence of a leftist Government (the *alternativa*), while, through a healthy competition of ideas, programs, and solutions, it would always remain possible for different political coalitions to rotate in power *(alternanza)*. That is, the left accepted the principle of electoral accountability, which it considered a major component of the workings of democratic institutions. Starting from this premise, the Project attacked both the DC for having imposed a conservative hegemony on Italian society through its unscrupulous exploitation of the state machinery and patronage resources, and the PCI for proposing a consociational democracy, that is, an arrangement agreed upon by the political leaders of the three subcultures—Communist, Socialist, and Catholic—which would limit competition and safeguard their respective positions of strength. According to the Socialists, the lack of rotation in power had produced degeneration in the Italian political system—and the Christian Democrats were partly to blame. The establishment of a consociational democracy by means of the historic compromise would eventually stifle dissent, competition of ideas, and innovation. Not only would its implementation postpone indefinitely the transition to socialism, but it would jeopardize the growth and expansion of democratic forces in the Italian political system, depriving them of the fresh starts that grow out of conflict. Therefore, the Socialists opposed to the Communists' consociational democracy their ideal of a "conflictual democracy."[6]

This is not the place to further analyze the Socialist Project or pass a comprehensive judgment on it. Suffice it to say that the Project amounts to a major, much needed, and, on the whole, significant effort to revitalize culturally, and to a lesser extent politically, the Italian Socialist party. Its translation into organizational modifications has so far been rather slow and only partly effective. The Socialists have fluctuated between the ideal of encouraging flexibility and autonomy inside organizations that have political and cultural ties with the PCI and PSI as well as many of the same leaders and members—and the reality of competing for influence

[6] The most important Socialist and Communist contributions to this debate have been collected in *Quale riforma dello Stato?* [Which reform of the state?] (Rome: Quaderni di "Mondoperaio," 1978), vol. 9.

within such organizations. The second strategy has been pursued with some success in the trade unions and the League of the Cooperatives and through a merger of Socialist and Communist peasants and farmers into the Italian Farmers' Confederation (Confederazione dei Coltivatori Italiani, CCI). However, one should not lose sight of the fact that the most important goal of the Project, as its subsequent utilization showed, was to accomplish Craxi's dream: the restabilization of the Italian left.[7]

Restabilization of the Left

There are two ways of interpreting the goal of restabilizing the Italian left: increasing the strength of the Socialist party or decreasing the strength of the Communist party. Theoretically, of course, the first aim can be achieved without producing the decline of the Communist party. On the other hand, the decline of the Communist party does not automatically produce gains for the Socialist party. Briefly, there is no simple way to remedy a situation of imbalance within the Italian left that is the product of thirty years of struggles, transformations, and mistakes.

Craxi and his collaborators firmly believed that the electoral strength of the PCI was excessive, inflated by the Socialists' inability to exploit events to their advantage. It is difficult to assess how sincerely they could believe that the PSI might improve its position without eroding that of the PCI. A coherent leftist strategy, of course, should have taken into account the consequences of different courses of action for the combined size of the left. Partisan motivations instead, were paramount in the minds of Craxi and his friends. In view of the well-known difficulties encountered by parties of the left in Western Europe in their attempts to obtain simultaneous gains and thus enlarge the leftist area as a whole, there is little doubt that Craxi's strategy has to be analyzed along the pattern set by François Mitterrand when the French Socialist leader openly acknowledged that his party's goal was to win back 3 million votes from the French Communist party.[8]

[7] For an overall view, generally unsympathetic to Craxi and his strategy, mostly for sound reasons, see David Hine, "The Italian Socialist Party under Craxi: Surviving but not Reviving," *West European Politics*, vol. 2 (October 1979), pp. 133-148.

[8] A survey of the delegates to Socialist regional conventions taken in March 1978 revealed, however, a great deal of "closeness" to the PCI (see Gianfranco Pasquino, "Partito, formule di governo e modelli politici secondo i militanti socialisti" [Party governmental formulas, and political models according to

If this were the objective—and it was openly emphasized during the 1979 campaign—the Communists' reaction was understandable enough. They were all the more annoyed in that, while they were the central target of Socialist attacks, the Christian Democrats remained unscathed. Moreover, in their attempt to dissociate themselves from the PCI and to acquire visibility and room for maneuver within the coalition of national solidarity, the Socialists exploited the two major events that took place in 1978 after their national congress: Moro's kidnapping and the two referendums in June.

As to the former, a balanced account of the various parties' positions on whether and why to negotiate with the Red Brigades is not available. It seems fair to recall that the Socialists never dissociated themselves from the official position taken (perhaps too hastily) by the Government and the parliamentary majority not to negotiate under any circumstances. Still, they pursued the possibility of a clemency act on the part of the Italian Government that might save Moro's life. In all likelihood, the chances of a positive outcome were very slim from the beginning. Nevertheless, it would be too harsh a judgment to claim that the Socialists were purely opportunistic. It would also be unfair to attribute to them electoral motivations. After all, even if the Socialists interpreted the results of local elections held a few days after Moro's killing as a vindication of their more humane posture, their showings were mixed—as were, incidentally, the Socialist results at all subsequent elections in 1978. The PSI regained some of the ground lost since the 1976 elections but not very much of that lost since the previous local elections.

The campaign and results of the two referendums of June 1978 offered the PSI additional opportunities to differentiate its positions from those of the DC and the PCI and to acquire a new image. Once more, however, the Socialist position was not without contradictions and liabilities.[9] The party decided to leave its voters freedom of conscience insofar as the law on public order (the Legge Reale) was concerned. In 1975, in spite of the protests of Socialist trade unionists

---

Socialist activists] (Paper presented to the Annual Meeting of the Italian Section of Political Science, Bologna, September 29 30, 1978). It is, therefore, difficult to mobilize Socialist cadres against the PCI.

[9] For analyses of the results and evaluations of their implications, see Arturo Parisi and Maurizio Rossi, "Le relazioni elettori-partiti: quale lezione?" [Voter-party relationships: What can be learned?]; Gianfranco Pasquino, "Con i partiti, oltre i partiti" [With the parties, beyond the parties]; and Angelo Panebianco, "L'ultimo referendum?" [The last referendum?], all in Il Mulino, vol. 27 (July-August 1978), respectively pp. 503-547, 548-565, and 566-573.

and intellectuals, the PSI had voted in favor of this law. As to the law on public financing of political parties, the PSI went on the record supporting the law, while some of its leaders campaigned without official blessing against it—and often for repeal of both laws.

In any event, the Socialists seized the opportunity offered by the surprising outcome. The referendums revealed a high level of disagreement between the parties and the electorate. In commentaries on the referendum results, the Socialists emphasized three major themes. First, they claimed to have correctly assessed the mood of the voters as one of growing dissatisfaction with the parties, a crisis of political representation. Second, they attributed this climate, as well as the large increase in abstention, to the creeping alliance between the Christian Democrats and the Communists (both of whom campaigned against repeal of the laws), which left no room for dissent. Dissatisfied voters were forced to use any open channel to manifest their opposition to an all-encompassing DC-PCI alliance. Finally, they attacked the PCI for its patronizing attitude toward the voters, whom it pretended to instruct and guide and organize in all circumstances.

The lesson the Socialists drew from the results of the two referendums was, basically, that there existed a conspicuous pool of voters within the centrist as well as within the leftist area who were dissatisfied with their parties and inclined to rely more on their own judgment than on the commands of the PCI and the DC. These voters were available for a closer relation with a modern, open, flexible party, willing to listen to their demands and accommodate their preferences. While the PSI would have liked to think of itself as this type of party, it is fair to recall that the Radical party was much more coherent in its support for repeal of both laws, its opposition to the stifling alliance between the DC and the PCI, and its openness to social forces. Thus, even if the PSI were this type of new party, it lacked the means of communicating effectively with the new pool of opinion voters and had failed to live up to the image it wanted to project. Last but not least, it would face competition from the Radical party, which was much more closely identified with a coherent stand on the referendums and criticism of the bureaucratic parties.

In pursuing his strategy of restabilization within the left and trying to change the image of the Socialist party, Craxi relied on three basic elements. First of all, overemphasizing some strands already present in the Socialist Project, he wrote a widely publicized article in which he pitted Proudhon not simply against Lenin, but against

Marx as well.[10] The ostensible purpose was to resurrect an autonomous Socialist tradition antedating Marx and Lenin. Above all, the intent was clearly to highlight the exaggerated and outdated orthodoxy of the PCI—or, as Socialist spokesmen would put it, to press the PCI into making long-awaited and much-needed ideological revisions. The second element was a constant attack on the PCI for its positions on international issues and, more practically, for its alleged lukewarm support for Soviet and East European dissidents. The Socialist president of the Biennale of Venice organized an international conference on dissent which offered plenty of opportunity for criticizing the PCI and denouncing its excessively cautious and sometimes ambiguous statements on the issue. In the Socialists' view, the PCI maintained a double standard, with its daily, *L'Unità*, observing a pro-Soviet line and *Rinascita*, the theoretical weekly, taking more open and more critical positions. The Socialists claimed to be the real advocates and supporters of "socialism with a human face," while the PCI had retrenched somewhat since its condemnation of the invasion of Czechoslovakia by the troops of the Warsaw Pact.[11]

Finally, the Socialists tried to counterbalance Eurocommunism with Eurosocialism. Two components of Eurosocialism seemed particularly important to Italian Socialist leaders: solidarity of purpose and attitude among West European Socialist leaders and the mutual support they could give each other. Examples of Eurosocialist solidarity include the decisive support given by the West Germans to Portuguese Socialist leader Mario Soares during the 1975 crisis; and the joint expressions of confidence in Spanish Socialist Secretary Felipe Gonzalez during the electoral campaign of 1977 by Mitterrand, Palme, Brandt, and Craxi himself. Needless to say, the PSI downplayed the differences of opinion between Mitterrand and Schmidt, between Soares and Palme, and, for that matter, between Craxi and another prominent European Socialist, Andreas Papandreou. Similarly downplayed was the fact that four of the most important Socialist parties (the Swedish, the Spanish, the Portuguese, and the Greek) were unlikely to play a significant role on the European scene for some time to come.

[10] "Il Vangelo socialista" [The Socialist gospel], *L'Espresso*, August 27, 1978, pp. 24-29 and 98.
[11] For a lucid exposition of the differences between Italian Socialists and Communists—indeed, one that probably attempts to impose too much clarity on blurred issues—see Massimo L. Salvadori, "Eurocommunism and Eurosocialism as an Alternative: Critique and Dialogue" (Paper presented to the International Conference on Eurocommunism, Monroe Community College, Rochester, New York, October 19-21, 1978). See also by the same author, *Eurocomunismo e socialismo sovietico* [Eurocommunism and Soviet socialism] (Turin: Einaudi, 1978).

The second component of the Eurosocialist strategy was support for and advocacy of the process of European integration. If not the entire PSI strategy, certainly a large portion of it was based on the expectation that the Socialist parties would do well in the June 1979 elections to the European Parliament. A majority of seats for the Socialist parties was, at the time, a possibility not to be ruled out, and the Italian Socialists, as we have seen, hoped to be able to use this success as a trump card to improve their domestic electoral chances. They complained loudly and bitterly when, after much maneuvering and politicking, the Italian parliamentary elections were finally scheduled one week before the European ones. The trump card, if it was one, had been taken away.

During the long period when the Socialists were stepping up their attacks on the PCI and relations between the two parties at all levels were tense, many observers and politicians believed that Craxi was in fact paving the way for a new center-left coalition with greater bargaining power for the PSI. Needless to say, especially after the beginning of the governmental crisis in late January 1979 and during the electoral campaign, the Socialist secretary was openly courted by many Christian Democrats who had always looked on the national solidarity coalition as the product of a "state of necessity," to be jettisoned as soon as possible. Of course, Craxi's intentions and his more anticommunist statements were questioned within the PSI both by Michele Achilli's left-wing faction and by Francesco De Martino. However, Craxi could count on the support of the "Lombardiani": while not sharing Craxi's overall outlook and often chastising him for his most extreme statements, Riccardo Lombardi never withdrew his support and thereby kept the majority united behind the secretary. Moreover, he went on to declare that the secretary was acting out of profound personal conviction, not instrumental ambition, and to express his expectation that political circumstances would make it impossible for Craxi to abandon the long-term strategy of a leftist Government. A showdown between Craxi and Lombardi finally took place in January 1980. By March, Craxi was in full control of the party and Lombardi, deprived of any influence, resigned as chairman of the party.

Of course, there was complete agreement among all Socialists that the party's autonomy was the most important condition for the successful implementation of the leftist alternative. "Autonomy and Alternative" is the motto of the PSI. Nevertheless, Lombardi clearly differentiated his position from Craxi's by stressing that the PSI could not claim to be equidistant from the DC and the PCI, as Craxi's supporters often put it. As Lombardi and others saw it, the PSI was a party of the left bent on overcoming the Christian Democrats' hegemony over the Italian political system in order to create a working, governing coalition with the PCI.[12]

The Themes of the Socialist Campaign

In 1976 the Socialists had overthrown Moro's cabinet and precipitated the dissolution of Parliament. In 1979 they fought bitterly to prevent (or at least to postpone) this unwelcome outcome. Once overruled, they could legitimately point to the two major parties' inability to create and sustain a stable governmental coalition and to their responsibility for the premature elections. From this point of departure, the Socialists developed two major themes in their campaign.

The first theme was repeatedly stressed. The excessive electoral and parliamentary strength obtained in 1976 jointly by the DC and the PCI—*bipolarismo*, the tendency toward a bipolar system—had produced a stalemate instead of an incentive for both parties to engage in incisive reform of the socioeconomic system while at the same time democratizing and making more effective their organizations.[13]

The second theme was the very real risk that the new Parliament would reflect an unchanged distribution of political preferences and seats. In the light of the Christian Democrats' rejection of any governmental coalition including the PCI[14] and of the Communists' promise to remain in opposition unless they were full partners in the Government, the prospect of renewed governmental instability loomed large. The Socialists counteracted with proposals for constitutional engineering to strengthen the powers of the executive and move the electoral system away from proportional representation. Both reforms were rejected by the PCI, but the Christian Democrats entertained them

---

[12] See for instance Riccardo Lombardi's interview with Giampaolo Pansa in *La Repubblica*, May 13-14, 1979, p. 3.

[13] In his speech to the Central Committee, Craxi stated: "It is necessary to remove the conditions which have provoked the withering in a few months of what was supposed to be a wide-ranging policy and an effective antidote against the evils of the crisis. To a large extent, [these conditions] can be attributed to the 'bipolar system' and to the equivocations and the paralyzing effects which derive from it." *Avanti!*, May 8, 1979, pp. 1-2.

[14] The official communiqué of the National Council was neatly summarized by Guido Bodrato, "In ogni caso dopo il 4 giugno non andremo al governo con il PCI" [In no way will we join a Government with the PCI after June 4], *Corriere della Sera*, April 15, 1979, p. 2.

with interest and sympathy.[15] More will be heard about them in the near future.

These reform proposals were fundamentally addressed to the "experts." But the Socialists also had a major proposal for the voters: a contract between the PSI and them. "Five years of stability and strong democratic commitment" would be their objective.[16] On the basis of this pledge, the PSI asked for more votes to strengthen a Socialist "third force."

> The bipolar system of the two great forces around which all other forces revolve, in collaboration or in opposition, can be modified only through the consolidation of a Socialist third force which represents at the same time the socialist pole of the left and the reference point for the lay and Catholic forces of renewal and progress.[17]

The Socialists had not abandoned their ultimate goal, the leftist alternative (though, once again, they failed to agree on its interpretation), but they added to it the precondition of "autonomy." They had paid a high price during the center-left period for their perceived subordination to the DC. Again in 1976 they had paid a price for not differentiating their positions adequately from those of the PCI. Thus, their major effort in 1979 was to establish clearly both their long-term differences with the Christian Democrats and their political autonomy from the PCI. At the same time, it remained important for many of the candidates to stress their leftist identity in view of the competition coming from the Radicals. This, however, was considered a secondary goal.

---

[15] In the past, proposals for politico-constitutional reforms had been put forward by the right wing. For an overall view, see: n.a., "Discussione a sinistra: dobbiamo cambiare la Repubblica?" [Discussion within the left: must we change the republic?], L'Espresso, April 22, 1979, pp. 76-92. Communist reactions are formulated by Luigi Berlinguer, "Un trucco istituzionale per governare meglio?" [An institutional trick to govern better?] and "La DC vuole in realtà il monopolio del potere?" [Does the DC actually want the monopoly of power?], L'Unità, respectively March 25 and April 17, 1979, p. 3 and p. 1; and Francesco Galgano, "Dove mirano gli ingegneri dell' 'alternanza' " [The goal of the engineers of "alternation"], L'Unità, April 27, 1979, p. 3. Other interesting and feasible proposals for reform can be found in Le ricette dei politologi [The recipes of the political scientists], Biblioteca della Libertà, no. 72 (January-March 1979). For an assessment of the likely effects of different types of electoral laws see my "Suggerimenti scettici agli ingegneri elettorali" [Skeptical suggestions to electoral engineers], Il Mulino, vol. 28 (September-October 1979), pp. 749-780.

[16] Avanti!, May 8, 1979, p. 1.

[17] The same point was reiterated to the Central Committee by PSI Vice-Secretary Claudio Signorile, who called upon the voters to pass a severe judgment on the "bipolar system" and its protagonists. Avanti!, May 9, 1979, p. 2.

The keynote appeal of the campaign was probably the one delivered by Claudio Martelli in an interview. The voters should cast their ballots for the PSI:

> Because they wanted a European-style Socialist party and now they have it. Because they wanted a Socialist party independent of the DC and the PCI and now they have it. Because they wanted a Socialist party strengthened within the trade union movement but willing to represent [the interests of] all those who live from their work and there are many—technicians, professionals, farmers, artisans—and now they have it. Because they wanted a Socialist party linked with its glorious traditions but also renewed in its men, ideas, styles of political work, and now they have it.[18]

It was again Martelli, given an unprecedented amount of space in the pages of *Corriere della Sera*, who clarified the difference "between a party such as the PSI which speaks of itself, but is also committed to ensuring the governability and the stability of the country, and a party such as the Radical party which only speaks of itself."[19] But, of course, skirmishes with the Radicals continued. While the Socialists were attempting to dissociate themselves from the implementation, though not the conception, of the formula of national solidarity, the Radicals could attack simultaneously the major parties, the Socialists, and the very idea of a grand coalition, convincingly pointing to their role as the only significant opposition on the left. The Socialists steered a difficult course between support for the Governments of national solidarity and criticism of their objectives and meager results. The Socialists spoke of three faces on national unity: "for the DC the purpose of national unity is to prolong the hegemony of its own party; the PCI wants national unity as the anteroom to the historic compromise; the Socialists conceived it as a necessity brought about by the [parliamentary] arithmetic and the predicament of the country."[20]

The issue of political coalitions for the postelectoral period was bound to be the dominant theme of the campaign. Precisely because the PSI had to steer a difficult course between the DC and the PCI, it could not give an exact answer to demands and pressures coming

[18] "Martelli: gli italiani volevano un PSI autonomo, ora ce l'hanno" [Martelli: the Italians wanted an autonomous PSI, now they have it], *Corriere della Sera*, June 2, 1979, p. 2.
[19] "Martelli: fedele anti-ideologo di Craxi" [Martelli: Craxi's loyal anti-ideologue], *Corriere della Sera*, May 22, 1979, p. 4.
[20] Ibid.

from different sectors (particularly from the Christian Democrats and *Corriere della Sera*). Stressing that they were available to ensure stability and governability for the country, the Socialists also made clear that they would exact a price for cooperation. "A governmental collaboration with the DC," Craxi said, "might be implemented only within the conditions of parity indicated by the Socialists."[21] Parity meant a cabinet no more than half Christian Democrat. In addition, Craxi's and Martelli's repeated attacks on Andreotti, whom they considered responsible for cheating the Socialists in scheduling the elections, and their openly declared opposition to his remaining prime minister seemed to point in the direction of a coalition with a non-DC premier, perhaps a Socialist.

Be that as it might, the Socialists were requesting a high price for their support—dependent, of course, on the outcome of the elections. Having learned from previous unfortunate experiences, they tried to keep their electoral expectations low, at a time when the polls were consistently forecasting only very limited gains for the PSI.[22] And this time, as far as the Socialists were concerned, the polls were right. Even so, the PSI's small increase was well below its expectations. The party failed to cross the 10 percent threshold.

The Results

The Socialists had correctly interpreted the mood of the Italian electorate. The voters did express their dissatisfaction with the performance of the two major parties. For the first time, the PCI and the DC lost votes concomitantly. Understandably, leftist voters were more dissatisfied than centrist voters. By no means had their expectations been fulfilled. The Socialists had a great opportunity to take advantage of this dissatisfaction and collect a sizable share of the voters who had supported the PCI in 1976, especially if, as the Socialists believed, they had been "stolen" from the PSI. But just as in the centrist area the party that gained most was the Liberal party, in the leftist area the party not involved in the Government of national solidarity and outside the boundaries of the parliamentary majority,

---

[21] Craxi's speech to the Central Committee, *Avanti!*, May 8, 1979, p. 3.

[22] Gaetano Scardocchia, "Le caute ambizioni elettorali del PSI" [PSI's cautious electoral ambitions], *Corriere della Sera*, May 5, 1979, pp. 1-2, conveys the climate of restraint and limited expectations. See also the four scenarios delineated by Francesco De Vito, "Garofani, bei garofani. Quanti garofani?" [Carnations, beautiful carnations. How many carnations?] *L'Espresso*, May 20, 1979, pp. 8-12. The carnation is the new symbol of the party, superimposed on the hammer, the sickle, and the book.

TABLE 5–4
OUTCOME OF THE PSI CENTRAL COMMITTEE ELECTION, BY FACTION,
APRIL 1978

Faction	Percent of Votes	Seats
Craxi-Signorile	63.05	141
De Martino-Manca	25.90	58
Mancini	7.10	17
Achilli	3.95	9
Total	100.00	225

SOURCE: *Avanti!*, April 5, 1978.

the Radical party, reaped most of the benefits of the Communists' losses.

There were grounds for predicting this outcome. Well before the elections Giacomo Sani had perceptively remarked: "As to the shift of votes away from the Communist party in favor of the Socialists, it can be observed that if the PCI is going to pay a price for the 'historic compromise,' its losses are likely to benefit the radical left rather than the PSI."[23] This very simple fact meant that the entire strategy of restabilization of the left, apart from its theoretical foundations and verbal exaggerations, insofar as it was based on an attempt to draw votes away from the PCI as a nondemocratic and Leninist party, was doomed to failure. A redistribution of votes within the leftist area was bound to profit parties not involved in the same policy as the PCI. A restabilization of the left, understood in terms of an increase in votes for the PSI, could occur only if the PSI had been capable of attracting votes basically from the centrist area. If that was the case, then the PSI should have leveled its criticisms at the Christian Democrats and their performance, their culture, their ability to manage and transform a modern industrial system. There were dissatisfied voters within the centrist area, but the Socialist campaign and the quarrel within the left were not likely to attract them.

It is interesting to note that in a Doxa survey taken after a year of Socialist attacks on the Leninist features and Soviet connections of the PCI, the respondents' evaluations of the PCI were more favorable, in absolute and relative terms, than their evaluations of the PSI (see table 5–5). Indeed, more respondents believed that the PCI had changed for the better than believed it had changed for the worse,

TABLE 5-5
Voters' Assessment of Change in the PSI and the PCI, April 1979
(percent)

Assessment	PSI	PCI
Party has changed for the better	15.2	26.4
Party has changed for the worse	17.7	20.8
Difference	(−2.5)	(+5.6)
Party has not changed	38.4	35.8
Don't know	28.6	17.0

Survey question: "In your opinion, has the . . . party changed recently? If so, has it changed for the better or for the worse?"
Source: Doxa survey, April 1979, published in *L'Espresso*, June 3, 1979, p. 23.

while the opposite was true for the PSI. More significantly, "the most bitter criticisms of the PCI [came] mostly from the left."[24]

Who, then, were the voters who responded to the Socialist appeals? In the light of the campaign conducted by the Socialist party, addressed fundamentally to voters dissatisfied with the PCI or tired of the stifling relationship between the two major parties, one would expect specific patterns of shifts. In terms both of geographical location and of social composition, the Socialist electorate in 1979 should have been larger in the North than in the South and in urban than in rural areas; within the limits of the very small increases enjoyed by the party, one would also expect shifts in the Red Belt where Communist supporters are particularly numerous. Overall, higher PCI losses should have coincided with higher than average gains for the PSI.

Elsewhere we have speculated on the reasons why, after the exceptional advance of 1976, some Communist voters might have been attracted by the Socialist party, especially in northern urban areas.[25] These voters—at best loosely connected with Communist organizations and militants, exposed to the mass media, and generally more critical of the PCI in 1979 than in 1976 though still inclined to support political change—might have been more responsive to Socialist propaganda in 1979. One of the reasons they might have found

[23] Sani, "Amici-Nemici," p. 131.

[24] As reported by Cristina Mariotti, "Vuoi vedere che votano cosi?" [Would you bet they'll vote this way?], *L'Espresso*, June 3, 1979, p. 20.

[25] Parisi and Pasquino, "Relazioni partiti-elettori e tipi di voto," See also Arturo Parisi and Gianfranco Pasquino, "Changes in Italian Electoral Behaviour: The Relationships Between Parties and Voters," *West European Politics*, vol. 2 (October 1979), pp. 6-30.

TABLE 5–6

CHANGE IN THE DISTRIBUTION OF VOTES FOR THE PARTIES OF THE LEFT,
BY REGION, CHAMBER ELECTIONS, 1976–1979
(percentage points)

Region	PCI	PSI	PR	PDUP-NSU
Piedmont	−4.88	+0.30	+3.01	+0.77
Lombardy	−3.17	−0.35	+2.63	+0.76
Trentino A.A.	−2.14	−1.24	+3.01	−0.02
Friuli V.G.	−2.92	−3.79	+3.53	+0.26
Venetia	−2.04	−0.93	+2.68	+0.53
Liguria	−3.06	+0.66	+3.30	+0.58
Emilia-Romagna	−1.17	−0.35	+1.73	+0.59
Tuscany	−1.69	−0.07	+1.65	+0.90
Umbria	−1.75	−0.08	+1.43	+0.71
Marches	−1.82	−0.36	+1.62	+0.94
Latium	−5.75	+1.00	+3.34	+0.57
Abruzzo	−3.81	−0.23	+1.69	+0.36
Molise	−4.44	+0.68	+1.44	+0.15
Campania	−7.42	+1.65	+2.33	+0.43
Basilicata	−4.41	+0.69	+1.24	+1.53
Apulia	−4.97	+1.06	+1.57	+0.51
Calabria	−6.32	+1.31	+1.46	+1.07
Sicily	−6.46	+1.03	+2.07	+0.68
Sardinia	−3.85	−0.39	+2.64	−0.16

SOURCE: *Rinascita*, June 8, 1979, p. 6.

to vote for the PSI was the compelling fact that the alternative was more likely to be implemented if there were less imbalance between the PSI and the PCI.

As we have seen, however, the Socialist party's refurbished image failed to inspire large numbers; and, above all, it faced competition from another new, open, flexible party advocating the leftist alternative—the Radical party. One should not forget that the Radical slogan was "From the Radical Antagonist to the Socialist Protagonist." All the reasons that had motivated potentially Socialist voters to cast their ballots for the Radical party in 1976 stood in 1979, and more had been added. No wonder then that the pattern of electoral results was consistent with the ambiguities of the PSI's position and the type of challenge launched by the Radicals.

Table 5–6 presents an overall picture of the variations in the distribution of votes for the parties of the left between 1976 and 1979, by region. What is striking is that the PSI made very small gains at the expense of the PCI in only two out of the six northern regions, while the two extreme left parties gained in five regions and the Radicals in all of them. Thus, where the PSI could have become stronger because of large Communist losses, its potential gains were eaten up by the other three parties of the left. This pattern is clearly replicated at the constituency level in the North (see table 5–7). Interestingly enough, in only three out of the twelve northern constituencies did the PSI gain in comparison with its 1972 percentages.

The regions of the Red Belt (Emilia-Romagna, Tuscany, Marches, and Umbria) presented a slightly different pattern. Thanks to its formidable organizational, cultural, political, and administrative implantation, the PCI succeeded here in containing its losses to less than half the national average—which in turn kept the Radical gains below their national average and adversely affected the Socialist results. The PSI lost votes, albeit few, in all four regions. The pattern in the constituencies located in these regions was only slightly different. There were very limited Socialist gains in two out of the seven constituencies, one of them exclusively the product of positive shifts in the city of Florence. However, in spite of these losses in 1979, the Socialists did considerably better in 1979 than in 1972 in all these constituencies but one, where they broke even.

The overall picture changes significantly when one looks at the nine southern regions. The Socialists gained in seven of them, in some cases conspicuously and everywhere more than their national average. It was, of course, in these regions that the Communist party suffered its heaviest loss, while the growth in the Radical vote seems to have affected the PSI negatively only in Sardinia. Moreover, all the southern constituencies, with the two noted exceptions (constituencies covering the entire regions of Molise and Sardinia) show gains for the PSI in 1979 as compared with 1972 as well as gains between 1976 and 1979.

As table 5–8 shows, backward Calabria reconquered its position as the leading Socialist region over Lombardy, where the PSI remained strong but seemed to be declining. As the two major opponents of Secretary General Craxi, Giacomo Mancini and Francesco De Martino, themselves former secretary generals, were quick to point out, the PSI gained where Mancini and De Martino headed the PSI list (+1.5 percentage points in the Naples-Caserta constituency, De Martino's home territory, and +1.3 points in the Catanzaro-Cosenza-Reggio Calabria constituency, Mancini's stronghold) and lost both in Milan-Pavia where Craxi was *capolista* (−0.7 points) and in Mantua-

TABLE 5-7
CHANGE IN THE PSI VOTE, BY ELECTORAL DISTRICT, 1976–1979
AND 1972–1979
(percent and percentage points)

Electoral District	1979	1976–79	1972–79
Torino-Novara-Vercelli	10.6	+0.4	−0.3
Cuneo-Alessandria-Asti	9.7	+0.2	−0.9
Genova-Imperia-La Spezia-Savona	11.6	+0.7	+0.4
Milano-Pavia	11.2	−0.7	−1.3
Como-Sondrio-Varese	12.5	+0.7	−0.2
Brescia-Bergamo	9.9	−0.3	+0.3
Mantova-Cremona	12.4	−1.1	−2.2
Trento-Bolzano	6.6	−1.3	−0.4
Verona-Padova-Vicenza-Rovigo	8.8	−0.8	+0.3
Venezia-Treviso	10.8	−0.8	−0.3
Udine-Belluno-Gorizia-Pordenone	9.0	−3.9	−3.7
Trieste	3.9	−3.0	−2.6
Bologna-Ferrara-Ravenna-Forlí	8.3	−0.6	+0.6
Parma-Modena-Piacenza-Reggio E.	9.0	—	+0.1
Firenze-Pistoia	9.0	+0.2	+0.6
Pisa-Livorno-Lucca-Massa Carrara	10.4	−0.3	+1.0
Siena-Arezzo-Grosseto	10.2	−0.1	+1.1
Ancona-Pesaro-Macerata-Ascoli	7.9	−0.4	—
Perugia-Terni-Rieti	11.2	+0.1	+1.5
Roma-Viterbo-Latina-Frosinone	8.6	+1.0	+1.0
L'Aquila-Pescara-Chieti-Teramo	7.5	−0.3	+0.6
Campobasso-Isernia	7.4	+0.7	+2.3
Napoli-Caserta	8.7	+1.5	+1.0
Benevento-Avellino-Salerno	10.9	+2.1	+1.9
Bari-Foggia	10.2	+1.2	—
Lecce-Brindisi-Taranto	10.2	+0.9	+0.4
Potenza-Matera	11.0	+0.7	+1.2
Catanzaro-Cosenza-Reggio C.	12.8	+1.3	+0.4
Catania-Messina-Siracusa-Ragusa-Enna	10.1	+1.7	+2.5
Palermo-Agrigento-Trapani-Caltanissetta	10.0	+0.3	+0.3
Cagliari-Sassari-Nuoro	8.9	−0.4	+0.8

SOURCE: Author's computations from figures supplied in the appendix to *Italy at the Polls, 1976,* and *La Stampa,* June 6, 1979, p. 4.

TABLE 5–8

EVOLUTION OF THE SOCIALIST VOTE
IN THE PSI's FIVE REGIONAL STRONGHOLDS
(percent)

Region	1972	1976	1979
Calabria	12.41	11.49	12.80
Liguria	11.22	10.94	11.60
Lombardy	12.00	11.66	11.31
Umbria	9.52	11.27	11.19
Piedmont	11.11	10.02	10.32

SOURCE: *Rinascita*, June 25, 1976, p. 6, and June 8, 1979, p. 6.

Cremona (−1.1 points) where the *capolista* was Craxi's lieutenant Claudio Martelli. Moreover, their followers contrasted Mancini's and De Martino's personal success in terms of preference votes (100,000 and 85,000, respectively) with Craxi's relatively poor showing—only 74,000 in Rome and 65,000 in Milan—not to mention Martelli's mere 14,500.[26]

The secretary general's position appeared only slightly strengthened by the renewal of his party's parliamentary personnel.[27] In conformity with a longstanding but not very productive custom known as parachuting, the 1979 elections saw again the candidates who were members of the Executive Committee take advantage of the internal regulation allowing them to request the first slot on the party's list. Thus, after the 1979 elections, nineteen of the twenty-five members

[26] See the article by Giorgio Rossi, "Ultimatum di Craxi a Zaccagnini" [Craxi's ultimatum to Zaccagnini], *La Repubblica*, June 9, 1979, p. 3. Of course, a more valid way of assessing the meaning of the preference votes would be to calculate the ratio of party votes to candidate preferences. The results for the five candidates under consideration would be the following: Craxi (Milan), 0.19; Martelli, 0.23; Craxi (Rome), 0.27; De Martino, 0.47; Mancini, 0.70. That is, approximately one out of four or five Socialist voters cast a preference vote for Craxi and Martelli, while almost one out of two did so for De Martino and seven out of ten for Mancini. To put these data in the right perspective, one should not forget that in the South the candidate is often more visible than the party and consequently preferential voting has traditionally been and is more widespread in the South than in the North. The strength of clientelism and Mancini's fame as party boss are also relevant.

[27] A tentative estimate can be found in *Corriere della Sera*, June 7, 1979, pp. 1–2: "Primi flash su uomini e correnti del nuovo Parlamento" [First flashes on men and factions in the new Parliament]. According to this article, sixteen senators and deputies would join Craxi's faction; six senators and twenty-two deputies would belong to Signorile's faction; while De Martino and Mancini would share the remaining ten senators and twenty deputies.

TABLE 5–9

OVERLAPPING BETWEEN PSI PARTY AND PARLIAMENTARY OFFICES,
1976, 1978, AND 1979

(percent; absolute numbers in parentheses)

	July 1976	April 1978	June 1979
Percentage of PSI deputies on Executive Committee	36.8 (20)	60.0 (15)	64.0 (16)
Percentage of PSI senators on Executive Committee	— (0)	— (0)	12.0 (3)
Percentage of PSI Executive Committee members in Parliament	64.5 (20)	57.3 (15)	76.0 (19)

NOTE: The Executive Committee had thirty-one members in July 1976. After the forty-first congress held in March 1978 twenty-five members were elected. There are seven de jure members not computed in my calculations (the president of the Central Committee, the president of the Commission of Central Control, the whips of the parliamentary groups in the House, the Senate, and the European Assembly, the editor of *Avanti!*, and the secretary of the Socialist Youth Federation, Federazione Giovanile Socialista Italiana, FGSI).

SOURCE: Author's computations from data published in *Corriere della Sera*, June 6 and 7, 1979, respectively pp. 5 and 4 for 1979; *Avanti!*, April 5, 1978 for 1978; and Pasquino, "Italian Socialist Party," p. 195 for 1976.

of the Executive Committee were also members of Parliament (see table 5–9).

The Results and Their Political Consequences

Somewhat mollified by the satisfactory outcome of the European election, the Socialists undertook a sober analysis of the entire electoral period. According to Craxi:

> the results are adequate if they are related to the context in which the party was constrained, to the difficulties of a confrontation with almost all [the other parties], to the tough competition coming from contiguous electoral sectors. The results are inadequate when compared with the expectations and electoral forecasts which placed the party at the level attained the following week for the European election. The results are far from the level of support we asked the electorate to give us since they are not much different from the results of three years ago. . . . As a whole, this has been a

strengthening and a consolidation achieved in difficult circumstances, the beginning of an upward trend that will be a sound foundation for our future work.[28]

Craxi's opponents stressed the ambiguity of the Socialist political proposal and emphasized the need for an improvement in relations with the PCI. All seemed to agree that no return to a center-left coalition was conceivable. Craxi himself had put some blame on the organizational weaknesses of the party (the traditional scapegoat for PSI electoral defeats); other members of the Executive Committee stressed that the party had not been consulted and put to work and that the Central Committee had not been convened according to the statutes. More specifically, Federico Coen criticized

> the inclination of the cadres to transfer themselves en masse into the electoral lists and to acquire offices at the local level, the inability to put women and intellectuals to better political use, the excessive concentration of power at the top of the party, the tendency to deprive other bodies, and in particular the Central Committee, of any authority.[29]

The most vigorous criticisms, however, were formulated by former Secretary Francesco De Martino. In his opinion, the results were disappointing. The causes were policy mistakes, hasty ideological revisions, a process of renewal that worked by replacing people rather than exacting a better performance from them, policy ambiguities and fluctuations, and the willingness to present the party as a third force outside the traditional socialist area. De Martino urged a sharp effort to improve relations within the left, a firm rejection of the center-left, and a resumption of internal debate. In addition, he announced the revival of his faction.[30] Soon, however, the internal debate, which continued in the pages of *Avanti!* with contributions from party cadres and intellectuals, had to give way to the more pressing and important problem of the formation of a new Government.

True to their electoral promises, the Socialists refused to give their support to Andreotti's attempt to enlarge his governmental coalition by including the PSI. It was not simply an ad hominem attack but the rejection of a governmental formula: the center-left. Then, surprisingly, the president of the republic, Sandro Pertini, entrusted Bettino Craxi himself with forming a new Government. The precedent for an attempt by a non-DC leader had been set by Pertini in March

[28] Report to the Executive Committee in *Avanti!*, June 15, 1979, p. 3.
[29] Ibid., June 16, 1979, p. 4.
[30] Ibid., pp. 3-4.

1979 when the late Republican leader Ugo La Malfa had tried unsuccessfully to put together a governmental coalition. In addition, there were two reasons why Craxi should take up the burden. First, his adamant opposition had prevented Andreotti from succeeding. And second, the PSI had long made known that it was willing to participate in a coalition to ensure the country's stability and governability. Given a prestigious office, the Socialists enjoyed the opportunity to create a governmental coalition similar to, but in one fundamental component different from, a revived center-left.

Needless to say, the Socialists as well as many progressive sectors greeted the president's move with cautious satisfaction.[31] The Communists neither welcomed nor opposed it, remaining lukewarm throughout the fortnight.[32] To the Christian Democrats, however, Craxi's attempt immediately looked ominous. Fundamentally, the loss of the office of prime minister was unacceptable to all DC factions. Nevertheless, some groups, notably those led by Antonio Bisaglia, Carlo Donat Cattin, and Arnaldo Forlani, were willing to pay this price in order to create a gulf between the Socialists and the Communists and presumably to buy time for a different solution. The groups supporting Secretary Zaccagnini, and most vehemently of all the secretary himself, opposed this attempt almost from the start. Ostensibly, they aimed at keeping open the channels of communication and collaboration with the PCI—at the same time rigorously ruling out any form of full Communist governmental participation. Paradoxically, by so doing they might have created the conditions for closer collaboration between the Socialists and Communists.

The contradictions in the strategy followed by the DC Secretariat were apparent in the three major conditions Zaccagnini set down for Christian Democratic support for a Craxi Government: (1) a public disavowal of the strategy of the Socialist alternative, (2) a clear delimitation of the majority, that is, a declaration rejecting the support of the PCI even when its votes could be decisive for the approval

[31] See the leading article "Un socialista, per la prima volta" [A Socialist, for the first time], *Avanti!*, July 10, 1979, pp. 1-2.

[32] See the editorial by Emanuele Macaluso, "Governo: una situazione nuova" [Government: a new situation], *Rinascita*, July 13, 1979, pp. 1-2. With perfect timing, the pro-Socialist weekly *L'Europeo*, July 19, 1979, pp. 6-8, published the results of a Doxa survey (data collected the first week of July) which showed 53.1 percent of the respondents in favor of a non-DC prime minister vs. 31.4 percent for a DC leader and 15.1 percent "don't know." The survey also indicated that Craxi was the most popular of non-DC candidates for the office and that the center-left remained the preferred governmental formula, with a small margin over a formula including the DC and the left (24.4 percent vs. 23.1); a Government of the left was the choice of only 13.7 percent of the respondents.

of particular bills, and (3) the breaking up of all left-wing local governments, at least in the major cities, and their replacement with center-left coalitions.[33] While Craxi was willing to recognize the DC's leading role, he was by no means prepared to act as a puppet or a hostage.[34]

The PSI moved with cautious vigor, surprisingly united behind its secretary. Not a single dissenting voice was heard throughout the two-week period of Craxi's negotiations, or even later, when the Central Committee met. This was not a minor achievement for a party usually fragmented between factions and leaders advocating competing policies. Yet it was to no avail. Zaccagnini and his supporters accused Craxi of intending to split the DC, push it to the right, and launch the leftist alternative. Finally, they sank Craxi's effort, rallying the support (differently motivated) of all factions.[35]

While it is true that the Socialists—but not only the Socialists—hailed Pertini's decision as allowing "the beginning of *alternanza*," that is the first concrete chance of initiating a rotation in power, Christian Democratic opposition to Craxi could not be explained in very simple terms. Admittedly, even that limited *alternanza* charac-

[33] It is interesting to note that the issue of the correspondence between the composition of the national Government and that of local governments is a recurrent one. It surfaced in 1964 when the DC and the PSDI pressed the Socialists to break with the PCI at the local level and create center-left governments—with very limited success. It reappeared in 1972 in what is known as "Forlani's preamble," a request to the Socialists to make all local coalitions conform to the pattern of national coalitions, that is to break their collaboration with the Communist party at the local level. The PSI's rejection of this opened the way to a center-right national Government. Following the left-wing landslide in the 1975 local elections, many new PCI-PSI local governments were created. In the wake of the DC-PCI collaboration after 1976, it became the turn of the PCI to press the DC as well as the PSI into accepting the formation of so-called open governments at the local level—that is, open to the DC where the left was in power and to the PCI where the DC governed with or without the support of the PSI—as a prerequisite for full collaboration at the national level. The PSI opposed this policy both on the ground of political accountability to the voters who had installed left-wing administrations and in order not to jeopardize its privileged position as the pivotal partner in left-wing as well as center-left governments.

[34] An influential Socialist intellectual, Giuliano Amato, speaking on behalf of or to Craxi, wrote in *La Repubblica*, July 15-16, 1979, p. 6: "Il centro-sinistra non vale una messa" [The center left is not worth a mass], clearly and sharply defining the limits not to be overstepped by the PSI in coming to terms with the DC.

[35] For details see *La Repubblica*, July 25, 1979, and for a scathing comment, the article by the editor, Eugenio Scalfari, "L'arroganza dell'onesto Zaccagnini" [Honest Zaccagnini's arrogance], in the same issue. For the cleavages within the DC ranks see "Non passa il 'no' di Zaccagnini" [Zaccagnini's "no" does not succeed], *La Repubblica*, July 21, 1979, pp. 1-3. A fascinating Socialist account is offered by Signorile's diary published in *L'Espresso*, August 5, 1979, pp. 14-18.

terized by the replacement of a Christian Democratic prime minister with a Socialist one might introduce momentous changes in a party that had been in power uninterruptedly for more than thirty years and in a blocked political system. Undoubtedly, the DC feared losing its political "centrality" and being relegated to the conservative pole, while the PSI became pivotal in dealing with the PCI. In any event, after Craxi's failure, Socialist Vice-Secretary Claudio Signorile declared: "Socialist participation in the Government is ruled out; Socialist participation in the majority is ruled out; Socialist participation in negotiations with the DC is ruled out. In substance, the PSI has gone into the opposition."[36]

But a Government had to be formed. Needless to say, the Socialists immediately announced that they would not support any prime minister proposed by the DC Secretariat. Therefore, when a widely respected DC deputy and former minister of finance unidentified with factional politics, Filippo Maria Pandolfi, was charged with the task and appeared close to success, the Socialists defeated him. The truth of the matter, as Socialist Giacomo Mancini candidly declared, is that Pandolfi's effort had produced not a transient, weak cabinet, but a governmental coalition capable of lasting.[37] Demonstrating once more his independence and political flair, Pertini then appointed another respected DC deputy, former Minister of Interior Francesco Cossiga, who succeeded in forming a coalition very similar in its structure and composition to the previous Pandolfi coalition. It included a couple of technicians close to the PSI. The DC, the PLI, and the PSDI voted for the Government, while the PRI and the PSI made possible its inauguration by abstaining.

Concluding Remarks. The long governmental crisis, which had lasted more than two full months after the June elections—or more than six months, if one keeps in mind that the last Government enjoying parliamentary support had resigned at the end of January 1979—highlighted some important changes. Three of these changes are particularly noteworthy: emerging, deep cleavages within the DC; the self-inflicted isolation of the PCI, now in a position of clear

---

[36] "Signorile: colpa loro andremo all 'opposizione' " [Their fault: we'll go into the opposition], La Repubblica, July 26, 1979, p. 1.

[37] Mancini was quoted as saying: "Do you believe that this might be a Government of truce and that in six months we will be able to dislodge it? The truth is that in six months we will be a blackmailed party and will be accused of wanting the dissolution of Parliament." "Il gran rifiuto socialista: Pandolfi non deve passare" [The great Socialist refusal: Pandolfi must not pass], La Repubblica, August 2, 1979, p. 3. See also Mancini's interview: "Il governo puó passare se non riproporrá i ministri di Pandolfi" [The Government may make it if it does not nominate Pandolfi's ministers], La Repubblica, August 3, 1979, p. 3.

political weakness; and the renewed political visibility of the PSI. Socialist spokesmen joyfully announced the appearance of a "Socialist question," by which they mean that, sooner or later, the issue of a Socialist prime minister would arise again. This may well be the case. For a while, during the governmental crisis, the Socialists seemed to have the political initiative. They certainly succeeded in showing the true face of Christian Democratic power, its ruthless hold on the office of prime minister and its perquisites. Moreover, they highlighted the Communists' lack of a viable strategy. Paradoxically, though, the Socialist strategy itself cannot succeed unless it receives some support from both the DC and the PCI.

Only if the pro-Socialist faction within the DC (to oversimplify a complex distribution of attitudes and power) gains the upper hand, can the Socialists hope to acquire the office of prime minister and launch a rotation in power. Only if the PCI is willing to collaborate with the PSI, can a leftist alternative come into being with the creation of a viable progressive pole on the left of the Italian political spectrum.

My chapter on the PSI in *Italy at the Polls, 1976* raised two fundamental questions: whether the decline of the PSI was irreversible and whether the Italian political system was governable without a strong Socialist party. In fact, I concluded my chapter stating that "without a strong Socialist party the solution of the Italian crisis will be all the more difficult and painful."[38] The results of the 1979 elections did not give an unequivocal answer to the first question. For the first time since 1963 the PSI increased its share of the votes by so little (0.2 percentage points) that one can rightly speak of stagnation. With no end in sight, electoral stagnation will leave the Socialists too weak to lead a process of transformation. The PSI continues to be numerically and politically indispensable for the formation of a viable cabinet, but its electoral strength prevents it from playing a leading role either in the Government or in the opposition. Thus, the Italian political system remains blocked, and recurrent governmental crises and instability are on the agenda.[39]

[38] Pasquino, "The Italian Socialist Party," p. 227.

[39] Indeed, Cossiga's first cabinet fell in March 1980. Allegedly to ensure the governability of the country, the Socialists returned to the Government in the second cabinet led by Cossiga, which lasted until the end of September 1980. The PSI also joined the Government formed by Christian Democrat Arnaldo Forlani in October. Called *quadripartito* because supported by four parties (DC, PRI, PSDI, PSI), this Government was distinguished from traditional center-left coalitions in that the Christian Democrats had the same number of ministers as the other three partners combined, despite the fact that at the last election the DC took 38.3 percent of the popular vote, to the three parties' total of 15.6 percent.

6

The Victors: The Smaller Parties in the 1979 Italian Elections

Robert Leonardi

The results of the 1979 Italian parliamentary elections surprised everyone concerned, especially the small parties. After the disaster of 1976 and the less than rosy forecasts for 1979, the outcome of the elections could be considered a minor miracle. If anyone won the 1979 elections, it would have to be the lay parties of the center—that is, the Liberals (PLI), Social Democrats (PSDI), and Republicans (PRI)—and, on the left, the Radicals (PR). Others could speak of moral or psychological victories, but only the minor parties experiènced an increase in their vote as well as in their representation in Parliament. As one Socialist official observed, the trend was solidly away from the large parties: "The smaller the party the more votes it attracted."[1] Small regionalist parties succeeded in getting candidates elected to Parliament at an unprecedented rate. The 1979 election results appeared to decree the end of the era of unquestioned large-party domination of the Italian political system.

In 1976 the large parties—Christian Democrats (DC), Communists (PCI), and Socialists (PSI)—received the lion's share of the votes and seats in the House and Senate. The other seven parties on the ballot had to divide among themselves a meager 17.2 percent of the popular vote and 13.0 percent of the seats in the Chamber of Deputies. Three years later their share rose to 21.5 percent, and they were able to increase their presence in the Chamber by twenty-four deputies (see table 6–1). The biggest winner was undoubtedly the Radical party, which tripled its electorate in three years. However, major increases were also registered by the Social Democrats and Liberals. Table 6–2 shows that, when the small political parties are grouped into five political tendencies, the lay parties of both the

[1] Gianni DeMichelis, quoted in *Panorama*, June 12, 1979, p. 50.

TABLE 6-1
SMALL PARTIES' VOTES AND SEATS, HOUSE AND SENATE ELECTIONS, 1976 AND 1979

Party	Chamber				Senate			
	% vote 1976	Seats	% vote 1979	Seats	% vote 1976	Seats	% vote 1979	Seats
MSI	6.1	35	5.3	31	6.6	15	5.7	13
DN	—	—	0.6	0	—	—	0.6	0
PSDI	3.4	15	3.8	21	3.1	6	4.2	9
PRI	3.1	14	3.0	15	2.7	6	3.4	6
PLI	1.3	5	1.9	9	1.4	2	2.2	2
PLI-PRI-PSDI	—	—	—	—	1.1	2[a]	—	—
PR	1.1	4	3.4	18	0.8	0	1.3	2
PR-NSU	—	—	—	—	—	—	1.2	0
SVP	0.5	3	0.6	4	0.5	2	0.5	3
UV	—	—	0.1	1	0.1	1	0.1	1
Trieste List	—	—	0.2	1	—	—	—	—
PDUP	—	—	1.4	6	—	—	—	—
NSU	—	—	0.8	0	—	—	0.1	0
DP	1.5	6	—	—	0.2	0	—	—
Other	0.2	0	0.4	0	0.3	0	0.5	0
Total	17.2	82	21.5	106	16.8	34	19.8	36

Dash (—): Not applicable (party did not run).

[a] Of the two senators elected on the combined lay-centrist party ticket, Sergio Fenoaltea joined the Social Democratic party group and Cesare Cappulli identified with the Republican contingent.

SOURCE: *Corriere della Sera*, June 6, 1979 and *I Deputati e Senatori dell'Ottavo Parlamento* [The deputies and senators of the Eighth Parliament] (Rome: La Navicella, 1979).

TABLE 6–2

SMALL- PARTY VOTE, BY POLITICAL TENDENCY, CHAMBER ELECTIONS, 1976 AND 1979

(percent and percentage points)

Tendency	1976	1979	Change 1976–79
Right	6.1	5.9	−0.2
Lay center	7.8	8.7	+0.9
Lay left	1.1	3.4	+2.3
Regional	0.5	1.0	+0.5
Marxist left	1.5	2.2	+0.7

NOTE: Right = MSI-DN and DN; lay center = PLI, PRI, and PSDI; lay left = PR; regional = SVP, UV, Trieste List, and Sardinian Action party; Marxist left = PDUP and NSU in 1979 and DP in 1976.

SOURCE: Calculated by the author from data in *Corriere della Sera*, June 6, 1979.

center (PLI, PSDI, and PRI) and the left (PR) were the largest beneficiaries of increased voter support, while the regional parties—the South Tyrolian People's party (SVP), the Valdostian Union party (UV), and others—doubled the regionalist sentiment expressed in national elections. The minor Marxist parties also did well, but the party of Proletarian Unity (PDUP) was the only one that took enough votes to warrant representation in Parliament. The United New Left (NSU) failed in this regard, but it would succeed in reaching the quota for election to the European Parliament in the European parliamentary elections that took place a week later.[2]

In addition to quantifying the change in the public mood after 1976, the 1979 elections consolidated the new course in Italian politics that began in 1977. The new course could be described as the "revolt of the bourgeoisie" against the threat of structural reform and institutionalization of the Communist presence in national Government decision making. The resurgence of interest in the small lay parties can be attributed to what Sidney Tarrow has called the "dissolution of the crisis" of Italian politics. After the 1976 elections the third Andreotti Government (July 29, 1976–March 11, 1978), based on a six-party coalition of "national solidarity," pursued a number of reforms that were designed to rationalize the economic and administrative structure. Contemporaneously, the Communist party undertook

[2] See Giacomo Sani's chapter in Karl Cerny, ed., *The European Parliamentary Elections of 1979* (Washington, D.C.: American Enterprise Institute, forthcoming).

to pressure the trade union movement to accept a series of deflationary policies culminating in the EUR Accords.[3] The high point of the reformist thrust was reached in 1977 when a series of decentralization norms were passed transferring a number of national powers and significant financial resources to regional political bodies. The decentralization decrees were accompanied by a commitment of the six-party coalition to an ambitious schedule of reforms that if they had been completely implemented would have revolutionized the structure of Italian society.[4] However, 1977 was also the year that the Communist role in governmental affairs began to come under attack from the left and right. Emblematic of this rising tide of sentiment against the PCI were the March 1977 events in Bologna, which permitted the left to criticize the Communists for their alliance with the repressive DC dominated state and to revel in the "unmasking" of what the PCI had attempted to portray as a model Communist-dominated city.[5] The climax came with the kidnapping and murder of Aldo Moro, when the PCI and the Zaccagnini leadership group of the DC were identified (correctly) as the main bulwark of the policy not to negotiate with the Red Brigade terrorists.[6] With the killing of Aldo Moro, the far left began its descent in popularity and support.

The left emerged from the Moro affair and the two 1978 referendums in complete disarray.[7] In pursuing their "historic compromise" strategy the Communists had concentrated on protecting themselves from a Chilean scenario (that is, attack from the right), but in the process they left themselves ideologically exposed on the left. This error was to bring them a series of defeats culminating in the electoral disasters of the 1979 Italian and European parliamentary elections. The main beneficiary of the Communist decline in popularity was not the DC as most political commentators had predicted. Instead, it was to be the small lay parties. A tripartite coalition bringing together the

[3] See K. Robert Nilsson, "The EUR Accords and the Historic Compromise: Italian Labor and Eurocommunism," *Polity* (forthcoming). The EUR accords provided for an acceptance by the labor unions of wage restraints and labor mobility in exchange for a decrease in the levels of unemployment and adoption of national economic planning.

[4] For a discussion of the 1977 decrees, see Robert Leonardi, Raffaella Y. Nanetti, and Robert D. Putnam, "Devolution as a Political Process: The Case of Italy," *Publius*, vol. 11, no. 1 (1981).

[5] For a detailed account of the 1977 events in Bologna, see Gianfranco Pasquino and Angelo Panebianco, "Bologna," *Citta & Regione* (October-November 1977), pp. 172-192.

[6] Gustavo Selva and Eugenio Marcucci, *Il martirio di Aldo Moro* [The martyrdom of Aldo Moro] (Bologna: Cappelli, 1978).

[7] On the 1978 referendums see "I Quattro Referendum" [The four referendums] (Rome: Ufficio elettorale della Direzione del PCI, 1978).

DC, PSDI, and PRI took over in March 1979 after the collapse of the Andreotti Government, and another tripartite coalition (this time with the direct participation of the DC, PSDI, and PLI, and the parliamentary support of the PRI and PSI) was installed after the election. This Government, headed by Francesco Cossiga, was reminiscent of the coalitions that had predated the formation of the center-left in 1963. Those coalitions had prepared the terrain for a Socialist entry into the Government, while Cossiga's was designed to keep the Communists out.

How did the left succumb so quickly to the revolt against the coalition of national solidarity and attempts to implement structural reforms? This chapter will analyze the political developments that preceded the 1979 elections from the perspective of the minor parties. The discussion will focus on the four major political tendencies that characterized the minor parties. We will not look in detail at the two minor parties of the extreme left, which are the subject of the next chapter.

The Small Parties Between 1976 and 1979

Looking at the election results, one could argue that the large parties were the main protagonists as well as the main victims of the 1979 elections. After the elections the course of events slipped completely out of their control: the Communists were forced to return to the opposition after a clearly unsuccessful attempt to run the country in conjunction with the DC; the Christian Democrats did not experience the electoral surge that they and everyone else had expected; and the Socialists effectively boxed themselves into a political corner. In 1979 the only parties that had a clear vision of where they were going and what could be realistically accomplished in the country were the minor parties. Alberto Sensini, a leading Italian journalist, expressed the view on the eve of the election that "the clearest ideas are coming from the lay parties of the center that are asking for a vote for the return of the country to the center-left and to the Western bloc of nations."[8]

The Lay Center Parties: PLI, PSDI, PRI. The Liberals were the first of the six parties supporting the third Andreotti Government to bolt the coalition on the day of Aldo Moro's kidnapping. However, in 1976 the PLI decided to support the Government because the country was going through a difficult time, and it felt that the Government should

[8] Alberto Sensini, "L'impegno dei laici" [The commitment of the lay parties], *Il Resto del Carlino*, June 1, 1979.

be given the chance to prove itself. During the parliamentary debate on the vote of confidence for the Andreotti Government, Valerio Zanone, the PLI secretary, reminded the prime minister that a similar situation had existed immediately after the war. Once the crisis was over, Zanone reminded the Government, Alcide De Gasperi had broken off the alliance with the left and had formed a centrist Government. What particularly troubled the Liberals was the potential significance of the Communist party's de facto entrance into the governmental coalition. The PLI asked whether this represented the first step of an inexorable process through which the PCI would eventually come to dominate the national government.[9] Zanone wanted to make clear that the agreement among the six parties did not constitute "a political alliance, a parliamentary majority, or even a programmatic accord."[10] The ultimate goal of the Liberals remained the return to an organic alliance among the country's lay centrist, socialist, and Catholic forces.

When the PCI was also given de jure recognition as part of the coalition supporting the fourth Andreotti Government (March 11, 1978–March 20, 1979), the Liberals went into the opposition. Zanone stated that the grand coalition between the PCI and DC was a "cause of the crisis rather than a remedy for it."[11] From March 11, 1978, onward, the Liberal party joined the growing middle-class reaction against the institutionalization of the Communists in the Government majority. Government programs and reforms that had been passed after 1976 began to touch the interests of a stratum of the middle class that had for a long time benefited from Government inaction.[12]

At the beginning of the 1979 campaign the Liberals stressed their goal of creating a Government majority without the support of the PCI. In the lead editorial in the party newspaper's first edition during the electoral campaign, Zanone posed the problem facing the noncommunist forces in Italy: "The exit of the Communists from the majority presents the democratic parties with the challenge of demo-

[9] Valerio Zanone, *Diario Liberale* [Liberal Diary] (Rome: Edizioni *L'Opinione*, 1979), pp. 43-59.

[10] Ibid.

[11] Ibid., p. 138.

[12] The important reforms passed by Parliament were the *equo canone* which created a standardized method for calculating the rent for apartments; a scheme to rationalize pensions and weed out those who were not eligible; and the regional decentralization decrees. The Government made two attempts to battle the problem of youth unemployment, but both were gutted by unenthusiastic administrators. Initiatives were taken to reform the upper secondary and university systems though without ever getting to the stage of the formal passage of bills in Parliament.

cratically governing the country without the Communist party."[13] Pietro Bucalossi, who had switched to the PLI in 1979 after a long career in the PRI, argued that the brief experience of the Communists in the governmental majority had brought about a decline in the well-being of the country. In his televised press conference of May 22, Zanone blamed the Communists and Christian Democrats for all of Italy's ills:

> The warning that this grand coalition rather than resolving the crisis would make it worse is, after a year, evident to everyone. Terrorism bloodies our cities. It is increasingly difficult, especially for the young, to find a house or a job. Inflation steals from those on fixed salaries and with savings accounts. The legitimate rights of many retirees are placed into question by the disorganization of INPS [National Institute of State Pensions]. The economy is without guidance, while investments have stopped and inflation has once again started to get out of hand. If we want to get out of this situation, find a remedy, we have to look around us. We have to look toward the other parts of Europe where the public sector functions better than it does here.[14]

In an effective poster campaign the Liberals advanced the argument that in the rest of Europe governmental institutions, the economy, and public services functioned well because Liberal parties were strong, while in Italy the predominance of the historic compromise strategy had made inefficiency rampant.

While the Liberals expected to make major gains, the Social Democrats looked toward the election with great trepidation. PSDI leaders felt that if the campaign were managed exclusively by the DC through a one-party Government the small parties of the center would be squashed. One way of avoiding such an outcome was to join the Government coalition. With the creation of the fifth Andreotti Government (March 20, 1979–August 4, 1979) the DC became the object of bitter criticism for resorting to a minority coalition that had no autonomy from the other parties and offered no alternative to the government coalition represented by the national solidarity formula. From the PSDI point of view, however, the fifth Andreotti Government was exactly what the doctor ordered. The logic of the centrist,

---

[13] Valerio Zanone, "3 giugno: una svolta" [June 3: turning point], *L'Opinione*, May 8, 1979, p. 1.

[14] Valerio Zanone, "Conferenza Stampa del PLI" [PLI press conference], "Tribuna Elettorale, 1979" [1979 electoral forum], May 22, 1979, mimeo., RAI-TV, Rome, 1979, pp. 1-2.

minority coalition was that it would prevent the demise of the centrist parties (they could present themselves to the electorate as governing parties), and at the same time it would prevent the PCI from claiming to be the only alternative to the DC.[15]

As part of this strategy, the PSDI pursued two complementary goals. The first was the attempt to reestablish the credibility of the center-left formula. According to PSDI spokesmen, a new center-left Government would not be dominated by the DC. The lay centrist parties would not permit it. One way of guaranteeing that this did not come to pass was for the minor parties to work out a deal with the PSI that would enable them to meet the DC on an equal footing. Thus, the Socialists became the linchpin for the lay parties' hopes to return to the center-left. But the problem remained of how to woo the PSI away from its adamant advocacy of a leftist Government modeled after the Leftist Union in France. Pietro Longo, the PSDI secretary, was one of the first to hold out the bait of a Socialist prime minister. He stated flatly that "a non-Christian Democratic prime minister would be a major political happening."[16] Even if the Christian Democrats balked at such an eventuality, the tension created by the alternative of returning to the "opening to the left" formula would destroy any sense of cooperation that might emerge after the elections between the PSI and the PCI.

The second goal of the Social Democrats was to identify themselves in the eyes of the electorate with the European Social Democratic parties, especially the West German Social Democrats and British Labour party. The hope was that the association of the symbol and name of the PSDI with the likes of Willy Brandt, Bruno Kriesky, and James Callaghan would help people forget Mario Tanassi, the former head of the PSDI and minister of defense who had gone to jail because of his involvement in the Lockheed scandal.[17] The tactic worked very well. Support for the PSDI increased more than for all of the other lay centrist parties. The party did not disappear from the halls of Parliament as many polls had predicted. Instead, it returned stronger than before and took the driver's seat in the campaign to return to the center-left.

---

[15] Author's interview with Giuseppe Averardi (chief strategist for the PSDI's 1979 campaign), June 8, 1979.

[16] Pietro Longo, "Conferenza Stampa del PSDI" [PSDI press conference], "Tribuna Elettorale, 1979," May 24, 1979, mimeo., RAI-TV, Rome, p. 25. See also the interview with Longo in Il Resto del Carlino, May 26, 1979, p. 2.

[17] See Robert Leonardi, "The Smaller Parties in the 1976 Italian Elections" in Howard R. Penniman, ed., Italy at the Polls: The Parliamentary Elections of 1976 (Washington, D.C.: American Enterprise Institute, 1977), p. 244.

The one lay party that did not increase its percentage of the popular vote but which nevertheless saw its parliamentary contingent expand was the Republican party. Its electoral support went down from 3.1 percent to 3.0 percent while the number of representatives increased by one in both chambers of Parliament. The Republicans' relative success is quite remarkable given the loss of their leader, Ugo La Malfa, just before the beginning of the electoral campaign. La Malfa died soon after he made the last attempt to put together a cabinet that could rescue the national solidarity Government formula.

With La Malfa gone the Republicans drifted consistently rightward. During the campaign the party shifted from supporting the more progressive elements in Italy's bourgeoisie to championing the interests of the country's "silent majority"—"the sum of Italians who represent the general interest that doesn't scream in the piazzas."[18] The PRI explained in its platform that it was out to reverse the course of events that had caused a "proletarization" of wide sectors of the middle class through a "decline in the wage differential and the loss of the bourgeoisie's social function."[19] Spokesmen for the PRI pledged that the party would attempt to reverse these trends by limiting the increase of public expenditures, promoting private investments, reducing the economic power of salaried workers, increasing labor mobility in the workplace, and putting a halt to the expansion of the welfare state.[20] Such policies, of course, could not be pursued with the Communist party present in the Government or parliamentary majority. Doubts were even expressed whether the PSI could realistically be expected to vote for programs designed to dismantle the welfare state and give private enterprise some breathing room.[21]

The Republicans' forceful proposals found much support among other centrist party exponents and moderate public opinion. Part and parcel of the 1979 Republican program was also the prospect of restructuring Italian governmental institutions. Parliament, the administration of justice, and the schools were singled out for attention. The PRI felt that the parliamentary rules allowed minorities like the Radicals or the far left to block majority proposals. These rules had to be changed so that the majority designated by the voters and

[18] "I Repubblicani verso gli anni ottanta: Il programma" [The Republicans toward the eighties: the program], *La Voce Repubblicana*, May 20, 1979, p. 2.
[19] Ibid.
[20] See Bruno Visentini, "Conferenza Stampa del PRI" [PRI press conference], "Tribuna Elettorale, 1979," May 23, 1979, mimeo., RAI-TV, Rome, 1979.
[21] Giovanni Spadolini, "Ora e' in gioco il futuro della prima repubblica" [Now what is at stake is the future of the First Republic], *Il Resto del Carlino*, May 27, 1979, p. 2.

agreed to by the parties could have a chance to govern by itself without constantly having to obtain the prior approval of the opposition.[22] The Republicans also favored the transformation of the Senate into a "Chamber of Regions" along the lines of the Bundesrat in West Germany.

The Lay Left: PR. Another party which cast a critical eye on the functioning of Parliament was the Radicals. Like the Republicans, the PR does not believe that Parliament is the place for compromises, deals, or logrolling between the Government and the opposition for the purpose of getting bills through Parliament. Instead the representative arena should be a faithful reflection of the conflicts which characterize society at large. According to the Radicals, policies must be the product of a confrontation of principles and political power, and if the majority were wrong in its proposals, it would be the responsibility of the opposition to make public opinion aware of the mistakes rather than trying to correct them through negotiations. Each governmental bill must assume the nature of a referendum or vote of confidence in the Government. A byproduct of this classical approach to the role of representative institutions was the Radical party's opposition to the trend that had increasingly allocated decision-making powers and autonomy to standing committees, to the detriment of floor activities.[23]

The forerunners of the present Radical party leaders split off from the Liberal party in 1956 in opposition to the DC's laxity in implementing the constitution and the centrist coalition's inability to implement structural reforms. The party was "refounded" in 1962 and 1972 in an attempt to lay the foundation for a party that could tap the growing awareness of "postmaterialist" needs in the area of civil rights and personal freedoms.[24] The 1970s provided the Radicals with the appropriate socioeconomic conditions to launch their proselytizing for divorce, abortion, women's rights, homosexual rights,

[22] For a discussion of the 1971 changes in the rules of the Italian Parliament, see Robert Leonardi, Raffaella Nanetti, and Gianfranco Pasquino, "Institutionalization of Parliament and Parliamentarization of Parties in Italy," *Legislative Studies Quarterly*, vol. 3 (February 1978), pp. 167-169.

[23] See Massimio Teodori, Piero Ignazi, and Angelo Panebianco, *I Nuovi Radicali* [The new Radicals] (Milan: Mondadori, 1977), pp. 180-190.

[24] Postmaterialism refers to the set of civil rights and personal freedom issues that had been ignored for so long by the Italian left in favor of more pressing material needs of the population. For a discussion of postmaterialist values, see Ronald Englehart, "Value Priorities and Socioeconomic Change" in Samuel H. Barnes, Max Kasse, et al., *Political Action: Mass Participation in Five Western Democracies* (Beverly Hills: Sage, 1979), pp. 305-342.

safe energy, disarmament, and conscientious objection. After the "hot autumn" of 1968 labor had succeeded in obtaining many guarantees and wage boosts that placed the Italian labor force in the forefront of European labor.

It can be argued that in the 1970s Italy began its "neocapitalist" phase of development in which labor and capital were able to strike a bargain to keep social tensions as low as possible under the auspices of governmental fiscal policies. The role of government is now that of arbitrator and coordinator between capital and labor rather than the staunch ally of one part of the economy against the other. In this light, the problems of the centrist period between 1948 and 1963 were those of economic growth and capital accumulation; government intervened to promote the industrialization of the country. After 1963 under the political cover provided by the center-left coalition, government was slowly coaxed onto the side of labor and began to promote policies for the redistribution of resources and more even societal growth.

It is in this perspective that the Radicals can be conceived as a "neobourgeois" party. They are not a spokesman for the propertied interests versus the propertyless; rather the PR is a proponent of the cultural baggage of the middle classes that often was lost on the way toward the consolidation of power against the increased demands of the working class. One of the interesting aspects of the Radicals' approach to contemporary Italian society is their position that the social order is no longer dominated by traditional social cleavages such as those represented by social class, religious differences, or geographic identification. For the Radicals society is divided around specific issues that attract changing patterns of social alliances. Issue identification changes according to individual needs and experiences rather than a more collective orientation such as that provided by class consciousness.[25]

During the 1979 campaign the Radicals argued that the governing parties, from the Communists to the Christian Democrats, were insensitive to society's needs and as a result were destroying any semblance of social order and justice. Imagery used by Radical party leaders stressed the lack of any hope and the frustration with the government that were symptomatic of the impending collapse of the system. In his television press conference Marco Pannella, the charismatic leader of the Radicals, repeatedly talked about the sense of

[25] A very illuminating discussion of this point is contained in the debate between Angelo Panebianco and Gianfranco Pasquino which appears in *Argomenti Radicali* [Radical problems] (April-September 1979), pp. 116-126.

decay, nausea, loss of hope, resignation, and frustration that dominated the voters' reaction to government leaders and policies.[26] The
only recourse in this state of impending doom was to increase the
Radical vote so that the PCI would renounce its historic compromise
strategy and join the PR and other leftist forces in forging a leftist
alternative. The election results showed that the Radicals succeeded
in creating a mixture of radical chic and anticommunism that castigated the PCI for its adherence to Leninist doctrine while at the same
time attacking it for having dropped its revolutionary goals in its
head-long plunge to work out an agreement with the DC.

The Right: DN and MSI-DN. Out of the seven nonregionalist parties
that presented candidates in 1979 only two failed to meet the minimum requirement for representation in Parliament. One was the
extreme leftist NSU, the other the moderate rightist Constitution of
the Right-National Democracy (DN). DN was created in the winter
of 1976 to fill the void between the neo-Fascist MSI-DN and the
centrist parties. On December 22, 1976, seventeen deputies and nine
senators broke away from the MSI-DN parliamentary contingent. The
aim of the Demonationalists, as they called themselves, was to bring
to fruition the attempt to create an "acceptable right wing"—that is,
a right wing not tainted with Fascism or Nazism—that could organize
public opinion and electoral support to the right of the DC. Previous
attempts by the MSI-DN to achieve this goal through the absorption
of the Monarchists in 1972 and creation of the Constitution of the
Right in 1976 failed because the MSI-DN was never able to fully dissociate itself from the Fascist legacy. Despite the existence of a large
neo-Fascist right-wing constituency that floats between the DC and
the small centrist parties, DN was never able to attract much support
because of its severe organizational problems. First of all, National
Democracy suffered from a high turnover of leaders that saw three
different national secretaries in the span of two years. Second, the
party had only a makeshift organizational base. When the twenty-
six deputies and senators left the MSI-DN, they took with them their
personal machines but not entire party sections or provincial committees. At the time of the break with the MSI-DN, it was thought
that Giovanni Roberti's CISNAL (Italian Confederation of National
Trade Unions) trade union organization would provide DN with all
of the necessary structural support, but the former neo-Fascist trade
union movement proved to be practically moribund. A third incon-

[26] Marco Pannella, "Conferenza Stampa del PR" [PR press conference], "Tribuna
Elettorale, 1979," May 21, 1979, mimeo., RAI-TV, Rome, 1979, p. 2.

venience for DN was the lack of attention from the national media, which were transfixed by the dramas of the national solidarity coalition and terrorism. The final blow came in 1979 when DN was attacked from within its own ranks for appropriating public funds for personal use rather than to pay for party electoral campaign expenses.[27]

On the eve of the 1979 election DN party secretary Pietro Cerullo observed that the electoral prospects of National Democracy appeared quite dim, but unless voting patterns changed drastically the problem of forming a viable Government coalition without the Communists remained. The solution offered by the DN was to "thaw out" the right-wing votes that had previously gone to the MSI-DN and offer them in return for the creation of a Government without Communist support. Just as the lay centrist parties were pointing toward a return to the center-left of 1963, DN drew its inspiration from the aborted Tambroni experiment of 1960, which had failed because the MSI was perceived as the political heir of the Salò Republic. Cerullo and his supporters felt that the opportunity would present itself again if the centrist parties maintained their anticommunist resolve.[28]

The DN's hopes for a political affirmation in the 1979 elections were dashed to pieces by the electoral returns. The clear rightward swing in public opinion stopped at the shores of the Liberal party and did not spill over into the area occupied by the DN. One of the political reasons why the DN made a less than brilliant showing in the elections was that it was the subject of incessant attacks from the ranks of the MSI-DN, and it never achieved the positive response from the DC that it had expected. Leaders of the Italian Social Movement sarcastically referred to the DN as the "telephone area code party" in reference to its inability to get more than 1 percent of the vote in most of the local elections that took place between 1976 and 1979.[29] Christian Democracy did not come to the DN's rescue because the period between 1976 and 1979 was the least propitious possible for the DC to openly negotiate for right-wing support in Parliament. Thus, the DN was allowed to slip away from the political scene without a murmur.

Given the difficulties of DN and the coalition of national solidarity, the Italian Social Movement's campaign proved surprisingly

---

[27] Author's interview with Gastone Nencioni, June 9, 1979, and Cesare Pozzo, June 10, 1979.

[28] Pietro Cerullo, "Conferenza Stampa del DN" [DN press conference], "Tribuna Elettorale, 1979," May 26, 1979, mimeo., RAI-TV, Rome, 1979.

[29] In Italy the area codes begin with zero—06 for Rome, 02 for Milan, and so on.

quiet. It did not get off to the rousing start it had managed in previous campaigns. The MSI-DN focused on a defensive campaign aimed at minimizing the threatened erosion of votes by the DN or the quixotic campaign mounted by Pannella. In 1979 the MSI-DN did not try to present itself as a moderate right-wing party. It preferred to quietly cultivate its neo-Fascist appeal by solidifying its ties with other neo-Fascist forces in Europe such as Spain's Fuerza Nueva, Forces Nouvelles in France, and the Greek National Front.[30] The hope was that Italy's right-wing voter would recognize the genuine article rather than be deceived by the numerous imitations being offered in the 1979 campaign. The results showed that the MSI-DN leadership was basically correct in its approach. With 4.5 percent of the vote the MSI-DN remained the largest of the minor parties, and it was evident that this solid bloc of right-wing votes could not be dispersed by national cabals or anticommunist polemics managed by other parties.

The Regional Parties. The 1979 elections saw a fruition of local lists that siphoned off votes from the national parties. Regional sentiments are not new to Italian politics. Past elections show that regional parties have very uneven careers characterized by rapid growth and equally rapid contraction. The Valdostian Union party (UV) first appeared in the 1954 Val d'Aosta regional elections with 29.2 percent of the vote. Internal squabbles prevented it from running in the 1968 elections, and in 1973 its share of the electorate was only 6.7 percent, but it increased to 24.8 percent five years later.[31] In 1979 there were a total of eight regionalist parties: the South Tyrolean People's party, the Valdostian Union, the List for Trieste, the Friulian Movement, the Sardinian Action party, the Sicilian National Front, the Popular Calabrian party, and the Sicilian Justice Front. They accounted for 1 percent of the national vote and succeeded in electing six deputies and four senators.[32]

The most successful of the group was the SVP, which consistently attracts more than half of the popular vote in the province of Alto

30 *Eurodestra* [European right], April 21, 1979.

31Electoral Office of the PCI Directorate, *Elezioni regionali del 1978: Valle d'Aosta, Friuli-Venezia Giulia, Trentino-Alto Adige* [1978 regional elections: Valle d'Aostra, Friuli-Venezia Giulia, Trentino-Alto Adige] (Rome: Direzione del PCI, 1979), pp. 8-10.

32 A total of seventeen parties failed to get any candidates elected to Parliament: six were regional parties and the rest expressed a variety of ideological points of view. For the entire list and the number of votes that they received, see *I Deputati e Senatori dell'Ottavo Parlamento Repubblicano* [The deputies and senators of the eighth republican Parliament] (Rome: La Navicella, 1979), pp. 851-852.

Adige (or South Tyrol, as it is called by the German-speaking residents). Aside from its ethnic and linguistic orientation, the SVP is very much a centrist party in the mold of the more conservative factions in the DC. In the 1960s numerous acts of terrorism were committed by extremists proposing Alto Adige's secession from Italy and union with Austria, but since then a *modus vivendi* has been reached giving the province greater autonomy from the national government.[33] Secessionist threats were again made in 1975 on the heels of the Communists' impressive gains. The head of the SVP, Peter Brugger, stated that if the PCI ever entered the Government his province would join Austria.[34] That threat was not carried out after 1976 when the Communists entered the majority coalition, though the SVP remained outside the six-party national solidarity alliance.

Local lists organized around the defense of ethnic and linguistic minorities have been concentrated in Italy's five "special" regions—Sicily, Sardinia, Val d'Aosta, Friuli-Venezia Giulia, and Trentino-Alto Adige. All five were given special recognition by the 1947 constitution. The five were granted powers of autonomy that were not awarded to the other fifteen regions until the 1970s.[35] One of the innovations of the 1979 campaign was the creation of a subregional electoral list that was oriented toward the grievances of one city, Trieste. The main bone of contention for the Trieste List (or "Watermelon party," in reference to the symbol on the city's coat of arms) was the recent Osimo Treaty between Italy and Yugoslavia which ratified the existing boundaries and put to rest Italian irredentist pretensions to Yugoslav territory close to Trieste. Though the treaty represented a major diplomatic achievement by the Andreotti Government, it sowed a tremendous amount of discontent among parts of the local electorate. In the communal elections of 1978 the List for Trieste attracted 27 percent of the vote and made major inroads into the electoral bases of all the parties. The localist surge continued through the 1979 elections, with the Watermelon increasing its support to 30.3 percent. Those who suffered most this time were the DC, which fell fourteen percentage points from its 1976 result, and the MSI-DN, which was cut in half.[36]

It is still too early to tell whether the 1979 results were the beginning or the end of a trend that increased the popularity of local

[33] For a discussion of the Alto Adige-South Tyrol issue, see Anthony E. Alcock, *The History of the South Tyrol Question* (London: Joseph, 1970).

[34] "Per Chi Votiamo?" [For whom do we vote?], *Epoca*, May 14, 1979, special insert, p. XXII.

[35] See Leonardi, Nanetti, and Putnam, "Devolution."

[36] *Corriere della Sera*, June 6, 1979.

TABLE 6–3

SMALL-PARTY VOTE IN THE NORTH, CENTER, AND SOUTH, 1976 AND 1979
(percent)

Geographic Division	MSI-DN	DN	PLI	PRI	PSDI	PR
1976						
North	3.7	—	1.6	3.6	3.8	1.2
Center	6.4	—	0.8	3.6	2.8	1.2
South	9.6	—	1.2	2.4	3.1	0.7
1979						
North	3.3	0.5	2.6	3.3	4.2	3.9
Center	5.6	0.4	1.3	3.1	2.9	3.6
South	7.9	0.9	1.3	2.6	3.9	2.7

Dash (—): Not applicable (party did not run).
SOURCE: Robert Leonardi, "The Smaller Parties in the 1976 Italian Elections," in Howard R. Penniman, ed., *Italy at the Polls: The Parliamentary Elections of 1976* (Washington, D.C.: American Enterprise Institute, 1977), p. 253, and author's calculations from *L'Unità*, June 6, 1979.

parties representing particularistic interests. In the regional and local elections of 1980, local lists in the northeastern part of the country held their own against the national parties. However, they have not been able to do away with the major parties, which suggests that the tide in favor of local lists has reached its crest and is bound to ebb in the coming years.

A Geographical Analysis of the 1979 Results

The 1979 increase in the small party vote was characteristic of the entire country. Table 6–3 shows that the PR, for example, expanded its support everywhere. The party tripled its votes in all three sections of the country: in the South it went from 0.7 to 2.7 percent while in the North it reached 3.9 percent. Other parties, however, did not demonstrate such uniformity. The Liberals did well in the North, moving from 1.6 to 2.6 percent, but they hardly budged from their 1976 vote in other regions. In contrast, the PSDI and PRI made significant gains in the South though not in the Center or North. The PRI lost much of the increase that it had made in the northern part of the country in 1976. One explanation for the drop in the PRI's vote is the PLI's gain and the Republicans' share of responsibility in the later stages of the Government of national solidarity.

FIGURE 6–1

SMALL-PARTY URBAN VOTE, BY CITY SIZE, 1976

Percentage of Vote

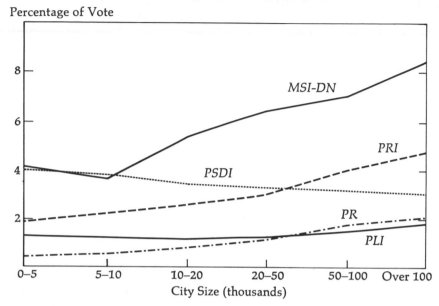

City Size (thousands)

SOURCE: Calculated by the author from data in *Elezioni Politiche 20 giugno 1976, camera dei deputati: Risultati per classi demografiche dei comuni* [Political elections, June 20, 1976, chamber of deputies: results based on demographic size of cities], vol. 1 (Rome: Ufficio Elettorale e di Statistica del P.C.I., 1977).

Voter support for the MSI-DN declined nationwide. Most of the decrease can be directly attributed to the DN vote. One exception to the rule was the southern vote where the combined DN and MSI-DN vote in 1979 is still almost one full percentage point below the neo-Fascist vote in 1976. Some speculate that the drop in the right-wing vote favored the growth of the DC in the South. Another possibility is that MSI-DN losses went to the PR, but this hypothesis finds little confirmation in the analysis of the southern large city vote, which suggests that the PR siphoned off votes from the left rather than from the right.[37]

In 1979 as in 1976 the small parties did much better in the large cities than in small ones. We can see from figure 6–1 that in 1976 the MSI-DN increased its share of the vote in cities in proportion to city size. The only exception is the PSDI, which did better on average

[37] See the articles by Luigi Petroselli, Giuseppe Vacca, and others in *Rinascita*, June 8, 1979.

FIGURE 6–2
SMALL-PARTY VOTE IN MAJOR CITIES, 1972–1979

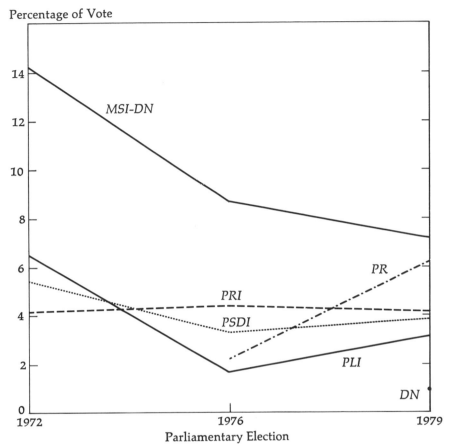

Percentage of Vote

NOTE: Major cities are defined as those with populations over 300,000. Eleven cities fall into this category.
SOURCE: Calculated from data in *Rinascita*, June 18, 1979.

in towns with less than 5,000 inhabitants than in cities with populations over 100,000. Data are still not available allowing a full comparison of the 1979 result according to city size, but the indications
are that the trend has been only slightly muted. Figure 6–2 presents
data comparing the last three national elections for Italy's eleven
largest cities. The data show that during the last seven years the
extreme right has fallen from a high of 14 percent in 1972 to 7.5 percent in 1979. The Radicals continued to advance in the cities but at
a rate similar to that in other parts of the country. In 1979 the PSDI

189

and PLI were able to reverse the 1972–1976 trend and increase their support in large metropolitan areas.

There has been a lot of discussion in the Italian press of who are the new voters that flocked to the small parties in 1979. Preliminary analyses show that the Radicals made significant inroads into the youth, unemployed, and tertiary sector vote.[38] Piero Ignazi has hypothesized that the increase in Radical support in large cities is due in part to an urbanized population's generally higher level of education, access to the electronic and printed media, and neocapitalist needs. He reports that after the 1978 elections the Radicals made a conscious decision to concentrate their efforts on the media as the privileged route for communicating with sympathetic voters. A lot of money was spent on programs and spots on the burgeoning system of private television and radio stations.[39] Between June 1 and 4 Marco Pannella and other Radical party spokesmen made live around-the-clock broadcasts from twenty-nine different stations covering almost the entire national territory. In 1979 many Italian voters abandoned the piazzas to turn on their TVs and radios for information on the electoral campaign, and what they heard or saw were mostly messages from the smaller parties. The large parties preferred to concentrate their attention on the national networks (two television and three radio) and more traditional appearances in the city squares.

The greater sensitivity of the small parties to new ways of communicating with the voters allowed them to attract voters away from the larger parties. However, not all of the small parties attributed their increases to campaign innovations. Social Democratic leaders explained their gains in the South as a product of their decision to nominate local public officials or *notabili* who had at their disposal local clientelistic networks. It was felt that the 1976 drop in support was in part due to the national focus on policies and to central-party domination of the candidate selection process. Three years later a lot more emphasis was placed on recruiting local leaders.[40]

The Lessons of 1979

The 1979 elections hammered home the message that the small parties were far from a dying phenomenon on the Italian political scene. They rebounded in terms of both electoral support and political in-

[38] Piero Ignazi, "Una analisi del voto radicale" [An analysis of the Radical vote], *Agromenti Radicali* [Radical problems], III (April-September 1979), pp. 130-158.
[39] Ibid., p. 134.
[40] Interview with Averardi.

fluence. The real loser of the election was the PCI, which saw its historic compromise strategy firmly rejected. However, the problem remained of determining what kind of political strategy or alliance could replace the defunct national coalition with a coalition to effectively govern the country. Even more fundamentally, Giuseppe DiPalma and others have asked whether Italy has ever had a government in the common meaning of the word[41] and whether it would tolerate strong leadership from a national Government. Strong central direction might upset the delicate balance that has been created between the state, the economy, and society. If this is the case, then the 1979 elections reconfirmed the status quo. The elections did not seem to point in any other direction. Looking at various other aggregates of the party vote, we find that the center-left was strengthened in comparison with the 1976 result, though it was still far short of its 1972 strength. The left had remained stable, and the right was only slightly weaker.

Recent events showed that the Social Democrats were correct in their view that the Socialists had become the determining factor in the creation of *any* coalition, but the PSI characteristically responded to increased opportunity with increased inability to decide on anything. As a consequence, the small parties remained in the driver's seat. The aftermath of the 1979 election served to reconfirm the rule that the small parties are effective when the large parties cannot agree among themselves on a proper course of action. Pietro Longo of the PSDI was the most aggressive in trying to maintain the minor parties' political momentum and influence over the coalition, while the PRI and PLI concentrated their attention on ways of overcoming Italy's current economic difficulties.

The 1979 elections also showed that the Italian Social Movement was immune to the threat of splinter groups. The parties of the center could not hope to compensate for eventual losses to the left by attracting disoriented voters from the right. What remained to the MSI-DN after the 1976 elections was a solid right-wing voting bloc that could not be fooled by the anticommunism of the Radicals or the more moderate message of National Democracy.

The future prospects of the PR were less clear. It seemed unlikely that the Radicals would grow beyond their 1979 ceiling in the 1980 administrative elections. The post-1979 Government coalition did not provide the same kind of grist for the Radical mill the Andreotti

---

[41] See Giuseppe DiPalma, *Surviving Without Governing: The Italian Parties in Parliament* (Berkeley: University of California Press, 1977), and Percy A. Allum, *Italy: Republic Without Government?* (New York: Norton, 1973).

national alliance Governments had. In addition, the novel quality of the PR attacks against the majority coalition had worn off. The Radicals got less attention from the printed media than was the case before the election, and their advantage in the electronic media was offset by parallel initiatives on behalf of the other parties. The future would prove difficult for the PR (as for the other small parties) unless it could consolidate its 1979 gains in the context of a clear program of national alliances and policies. Otherwise, in the next election the same floating voters who had benefited it in 1979 would once more abandon the PR.

7

The Parliamentary and Nonparliamentary Parties of the Far Left

Patrick McCarthy

The 1979 Italian elections seem at first sight to have been a success for the two parties of the far left—the party of Proletarian Unity (PDUP) and Proletarian Democracy (DP). In 1976 the PDUP-DP list had taken 1.5 percent of the vote; this time the two parties, presenting separate lists, won 2.2 percent. Yet this was a limited success by comparison with the Radicals (PR), who started off lower and rose higher, moving from 1.1 percent to 3.4 percent. Whether the Radicals were a New Left party is a question that was much discussed during the election and that cannot be decided here. But certainly they and the New Left were competing for some of the same voters, as the campaign polemics showed. Moreover one segment of Continuous Struggle (LC) joined with the Radicals and provided them with two members of Parliament. The 1979 elections, then, were also a defeat for the New Left parties, which failed to dominate the enlarged space to the left of the PCI.

The two parties entered the campaign with very different strategies and histories, and they emerged with very different results. The PDUP took 1.4 percent and elected six members of Parliament; running as the United New Left (NSU), the DP and its allies won only 0.8 percent, thus failing to reach the quota and electing no members. Each strategy represented a response to the 1976 defeat and to the mass demonstrations of 1977. Both strategies had to take into account the nonparliamentary groups like Continuous Struggle and Workers Autonomy. Terrorism, too, was an integral part of the elections since the Red Brigades ran their own campaign with guns and bombs.

This chapter has two parts. The first analyzes the election results and attempts to explain the New Left's limited success. The second and longer part places the elections in the context of the previous three years.

TABLE 7–1
Far Left Gains and PCI Losses in Selected Provinces, 1979 Chamber Election
(percentage points)

Province	Far Left Gains	PCI Losses
Emilia-Romagna	0.59	1.17
Tuscany	0.90	1.69
Umbria	0.71	1.75
Campania	0.43	7.42
Calabria	1.05	6.32
Sicily	0.68	6.46

Source: *Rinascita*, June 8, 1979.

The Shifting Fortunes of the PCI and Far Left

In 1979 the New Left gained votes in every Italian province except one. Trentino-Alto Adige is doubly an exception, because the New Left's vote fell (though only by 0.02 points) and because the NSU did better than the PDUP. Both phenomena stem from the PDUP's weakness in these heavily Catholic, partly German-speaking provinces. Elsewhere the New Left's gains were roughly proportional to its existing strength; there were few dramatic shifts.

Yet the pattern of New Left advance and Communist retreat is not a simple one. Where the PCI succeeded in limiting its losses, the New Left was still able to make gains. In the Red Belt the Communist losses were below the national average, but the New Left's increase was higher than its national average. In Campania and in Sicily the New Left profited less than it might have from the massive Communist slump (see table 7–1, which compares the three provinces of the Red Belt with three southern provinces where the Communists did especially badly). Clearly the New Left could appeal more to convinced but disillusioned left-wingers than to the voters who had been first drawn to the PCI in 1976. In Emilia-Romagna, where the PCI's slump was smaller than in any other province, the ratio of New Left gains to Communist losses was one to two, whereas in Sicily it was almost one to ten.

The New Left was drawing on voters who were disappointed because the PCI's policy of the "historic compromise" had failed to bring about social and economic change. As will be shown, the PDUP's entire strategy was aimed at such voters. Indeed, the party

TABLE 7–2

RADICAL AND FAR LEFT GAINS IN SELECTED CITIES,
1979 CHAMBER ELECTION
(percentage points)

City	Radical Gains	Far Left Gains
Turin	4.29	0.91
Milan	4.48	0.45
Genoa	4.20	0.65
Venice	4.60	0.70
Bologna	2.96	0.68
Florence	2.85	1.31
Rome	5.00	0.31
Naples	4.70	0.27
Bari	4.20	0.41
Palermo	4.60	0.46

SOURCE: *Rinascita*, June 8, 1979.

probably lost support among middle-class people, but it gained votes among working-class, former Communist supporters.[1] The 1979 elections reversed the position of 1976. Then the left's share of the vote had grown, the PCI's share had grown still more, and the parties on the far left had declined; this time the left declined, the PCI declined much more, and the New Left grew.

Yet the New Left was badly beaten by the Radicals, as is shown by the voting patterns in the big cities where the New Left was strongest (see table 7–2). The Radicals drew votes from parties other than the PCI, but they were also more successful than the New Left in wooing Communist votes. PR leader Marco Pannella's strategy appealed to a broad swath of voters who were disappointed because the Communist-Christian Democrat alliance had not produced strong government or economic improvement. The Radicals also picked up a strain of dissent from which the New Left—especially the NSU—had hoped to profit. Distrust of Parliament, an antinuclear stance, and the defense of soldiers', prisoners', and women's rights all were themes which the New Left stressed. But the Radicals also exploited them, and their success prevented the New Left from growing as much as it might have.

[1] According to PDUP poll-watchers in Bologna the party did less well among middle-class voters in the Colli area and better among working-class voters in the San Donato area.

If Pannella was one victor, the PDUP was the other. For two years it had been following the line which it reiterated during the campaign. The PDUP argued that there could be no transformation of society without the support of the historic working class and its political expression, the PCI; the task was to woo the Communists away from the historic compromise and toward a left Government. Clearly this line appealed to Communist working-class voters who were dissatisfied with Berlinguer's policies. The PCI itself seemed to indicate that the PDUP was at least partly correct because it left the Andreotti Government and took the tougher position at its fifteenth congress. The PDUP did well throughout Italy in a homogeneous vote that reflected its clear policies.

Meanwhile the DP was attempting to pull together the remnants of the 1977 Movement and to build on the strikes that had taken place in the autumn of 1978. Its organization was poor, it had no precise policies, and it began the campaign with a dispute about whether to run as a party (DP) or as part of the United New Left (NSU). Not surprisingly, the NSU gained only half as many votes as the PDUP and failed to reach the quota in the Milan-Pavia constituency.

A comparison of the results shows that the NSU ran ahead of the PDUP in only two provinces, Trentino-Alto Adige and Lazio. In the first it had done fairly well in the regional elections of November 1978, and it was helped by its connection with Continuous Struggle, which was still strong in Trentino. Moreover, if the PDUP was handicapped in this province because it was close to the PCI, the NSU was helped by its Catholic component. In most northern provinces the NSU ran well behind the PDUP: in Piedmont it won 0.94 percent as opposed to PDUP's 1.6 percent. In the South, where it had even less organization and where its newspaper, *Quotidiano dei Lavoratori*, had no circulation, the NSU often obtained less than half the PDUP's vote. In Campania the figures were 0.61 percent to 1.30 percent and in Puglia 0.52 percent to 1.14 percent. In the Red Belt it was far less successful in attracting disgruntled Communists: in Emilia-Romagna it obtained 0.53 percent to the PDUP's 1.04 percent.

If the NSU failed to attract Communist deserters, this was because its strategy was aimed at a different political and cultural group. The Lazio result reflected the NSU's strong performance in Rome, which was sufficient to counterbalance the province. Usually this was not the case, but the NSU ran ahead of the PDUP in most northern cities (see table 7–3). Even where it ran behind, as in Bologna and Venice, the difference was smaller than in the province as a whole. South of Rome the balance shifts even in the cities, which suggests

TABLE 7–3

THE PDUP AND NSU VOTE, SELECTED CITIES, 1979 CHAMBER ELECTION
(percent)

City	PDUP	NSU
Turin	1.38	1.43
Milan	1.79	1.83
Genoa	0.80	0.86
Venice	1.53	1.33
Bologna	0.95	0.93
Florence	1.31	1.41
Rome	0.88	1.03
Naples	1.29	0.82
Bari	1.17	0.68
Palermo	1.23	0.68

SOURCE: *Rinascita*, June 8, 1979.

that the NSU was the stronger political force only where the New Left's potential electorate was more sophisticated and more critical of the Communists and the trade unions. There are signs that the NSU often did better among young people than the PDUP. In Turin it took 4.5 percent of the eighteen to twenty-five year-old vote as opposed to the PDUP's 4 percent. (Once more the Radicals fared much better, with 22.6 percent.)

In general the NSU did best in cities like Milan and Rome where the 1977 Movement had flourished. Its campaign was aimed at the Movement's supporters, and it worked; concomitantly, it failed where the Movement had failed. The PDUP and the NSU were quite different parties, as they had been for the past three years and more.

Dilemmas of the New Left, 1976–1979

Reactions to the 1976 Elections. "The elections of June 1976 must surely be one of the most depressing moments in the history of the New Left." "The results of June 20 were immediately perceived by the Lotta Continua militants as the end of an era."[2] These statements were typical of New Left reactions to the outcome. The PDUP-DP coalition had hoped for 3 percent and had taken 1.5 percent. Still

[2] Daniele Protti, *Cronache di Nuova Sinistra* [New Left chronicles] (Milan: Gammalibri, 1979), p. 79, and Luigi Bobbio, *Lotta Continua* (Rome: Savelli, 1979), p. 171.

more important, the left had no overall majority and the Christian Democrats did not collapse. Disappointment was all the greater because optimism had risen so high. Moreover the New Left was eight years old and its militants had little to show for their years of effort. Within the groups that made up the PDUP-DP alliance—Manifesto, PDUP, Workers Vanguard (AO), and Continuous Struggle—there were three different responses to the defeat.[3]

Lucio Magri and the leaders of the old Manifesto group were hardheaded. The DC had held the line, and it remained the main enemy. It could not be combatted without the PCI, which had to be lured away from the historic compromise. The Communists could not be written off. Since the attempt to construct a large New Left party had failed, the New Left had to return to the traditional working-class organizations—the PCI and the unions. Continuous Struggle took the opposite course, and at its Rimini congress in December 1976 it dissolved, or rather became a patchwork of protest groups. Between the two stood the group that would become DP: it was both a party and a movement, parliamentary and nonparliamentary.

In the autumn of 1976 the Manifesto-PDUP alliance broke up. If disappointment was the catalyst, it was not the real reason, for the split had appeared at the congress of February 1976, and indeed the unity had never been real. Profound differences, political and cultural, separated the two groups. Manifesto bore the traces of its Communist background: it believed in clear theoretical analysis and party unity; PDUP, socialist and trade unionist, was more pragmatic and favored a looser party structure. Manifesto was more intellectual and PDUP more activist. In 1974 Manifesto comprised 36 percent students and teachers and only 20 percent workers, while PDUP was 60 percent workers and 16 percent students.[4] The two had different views of the state and of the left in power. At the February congress Magri argued that the main task was political: the creation of a left Government. The PDUP leader, Vittorio Foa, maintained that the real issue was worker control: left-wing power must be rooted in the struggles in the factories.

This in turn led to different views of the PCI. The key tactical

---

[3] For the earlier history of these groups see Mino Monicelli, *L'Ultrasinistra in Italia* [The far left in Italy] (Rome: Laterza, 1978). Manifesto was made up of a group of PCI intellectuals—Lucio Magri, Rossana Rossanda, and others—who were close to Pietro Ingrao's position. They were expelled from the Communist party in 1969. PDUP was made up of old PSIUP (Partito Socialista Italiana de Unità Proletaria) members who had not moved to the PCI or the PSI after the 1972 election defeat.

[4] Monicelli, *L'Ultrasinistra in Italia*, p. 44.

question that has plagued the Italian New Left is how to analyze the PCI. Is it a revolutionary party, needing only to be spurred on from without, or is it an irremediably reformist party that must be broken up? Dissident as they might be, the Manifesto group held the first view, while PDUP held the second. The concomitant question was the relationship with the rest of the New Left. Manifesto was suspicious of the nonparliamentary groups, especially Continuous Struggle, while the PDUP was more conciliatory. These differences ran through the 1970s. They undermined the spurious unity of 1976, and they explain why no common list was formed in 1979.

Meanwhile Workers Vanguard was also splitting. This organization, based in Milan, had its strength in the Comitati Unitari di Base, the shopfloor organizations formed after 1968 outside of and in opposition to the unions. However, unlike Potere Operaia (Potop), another far left group, Workers Vanguard believed in a strong, centralized party. Its mixture of shopfloor militancy and discipline enabled it to survive where Potop could not, but, as worker activism died down in the mid-1970s, Workers Vanguard was forced to become ever more of a party and even an electoral party. In 1972 it had ignored the elections, but it campaigned in the divorce referendum of 1974 and in the regional elections of 1975. It was following a general trend, for the attempt to build parties was the hallmark of the Italian far left in the mid-1970s.

But the strategy failed; after the June 20, 1976, elections, Workers Vanguard lost members and disputes broke out. One group moved with Aurelio Campi to Manifesto which kept the name PDUP. This was the political segment of Workers Vanguard, which interpreted the electoral defeat not as a rejection of parties but as a spur toward a clearer and more moderate line. The second group, which believed in the primacy of social and factory-based activism, joined with most of the old PDUP to form DP.[5]

PDUP. Surprised by the 1977 Movement, the PDUP quickly criticized it and condemned Workers Autonomy as a new barbarian horde. In September 1977 it called on its militants not to attend the Bologna demonstration organized by the nonparliamentary groups. The Move-

[5] The figures are a matter of dispute. Workers Vanguard had approximately 10,000 members in the mid-1970s, but many of them drifted away and did not join either PDUP or DP. Protti says that only 10 percent went to PDUP, but his account is colored by his anti-Magri prejudice. The best guess is that about 1,000 went to PDUP and 3,000 or 4,000 to DP. A more objective account of the 1976 events is given by Rocco Pellegrini and Guglielmo Pepe, *Unire è difficile, breve storia del PDUP per il communismo* [The difficulty of uniting: a short history of PDUP] (Rome: Savelli, 1977).

ment was hostile to the PCI and the unions and it was tinged with violence; in keeping its distance from the Movement, the PDUP indicated clearly that it intended to look for its support among the organized working class and on the fringes of the PCI. The party itself changed, for it began to attract workers and lose intellectuals; it became less theoretical and more practical.[6]

Yet the PDUP was plagued by splits within the ruling group. In April 1978 the paper *Manifesto* broke away. Its importance in intellectual circles came partly from its independent slant, and it did not wish to become the organ of a party, especially of an ever more unified one. In the early 1970s the paper had been the focus of the group; now it was being subordinated to the party. Then too, the editors felt that Magri was tying the PDUP too closely to the PCI.

The dispute came to a head at the PDUP's Viareggio congress in November 1978. Six hundred delegates elected by the 3,000 members assembled to take stock. According to Magri, the left had lost ground, as had the far left; the impetus of 1968 had petered out and violence was a menace; the left as a whole must be relaunched. Magri reiterated the importance of politics and the need for the left to take power. The PDUP was to be the driving force of a unified, revitalized left. Clearly this meant a special relationship with the PCI, and equally clearly the PDUP was turning its back on the other New Left parties.

Another of PDUP's "historic leaders," Rossana Rossanda, disagreed. The PCI was blocked by its false vision of the historic compromise and the PDUP would be unable to influence it. Instead it should rebuild among the young and give political expression to the discontent in the country. Rossanda admitted that the PDUP had been too quick to dismiss the Movement. The flaw in her analysis was that it meant reversing the line the party had taken in the previous two years, which Rossanda herself had expounded. It also meant running the risk of alienating potential ex-PCI voters.

Rossanda's real disagreement had to do with the party. Implicit in Magri's project was a tougher, more obedient party, whereas Rossanda's proposal for a PDUP that would serve primarily to focus discontent not only left a greater role to the newspaper but also implied less obedience within the party. These ex-Communists' ambivalence about authority was reflected in Rossanda's reaction to Magri's project: "I will not accept the discipline involved."[7]

---

[6] Recent estimates issued by the Bologna Federation of the PDUP are that the party has 35 percent workers and only 25 percent students and teachers. There has been an influx of skilled workers and middle-echelon trade unionists.

[7] *Manifesto*, November 12, 1978, p. 2.

No satisfactory solution was found to the dispute between paper and party. During the election campaign *Manifesto* called on its readers to vote for the left, but, although Rossanda said she was voting PDUP, that party received no special treatment.[8] Meanwhile Magri, who had won a comfortable victory at the PDUP congress,[9] was well received at the PCI's fifteenth congress. His strategy seemed to be working.

The PDUP ran a quiet campaign, for it remained an elitist party. Its organization had improved, but it was still weak at the grass roots. Its leaders reiterated their appeal to the segment of the voters that lay between the Communists and the Movement. Even as the PDUP attacked the historic compromise, it criticized the far left's decline into barbarity, and it was firm in its denunciations of terrorism. It also understood the Radical challenge, for it kept asserting that the Radicals were incoherent, that they had nothing positive to offer. The PDUP had an ally: the Workers Movement for Socialism (MLS), which had grown out of the Milan student movement of 1968, was a tough, disciplined group. It had long stood aloof from electoral politics, but now it was in decline and needed fresh impetus. It was also under pressure from Workers Autonomy, so an alliance with PDUP was logical, if unexpected. The advantage for the PDUP lay in the quest for the Milan quota: about one-third of the PDUP's Milan votes came from the MLS.

The PDUP's success has brought perils of its own: since its new votes come from dissatisfied Communists, it runs the risk of becoming a satellite of the PCI. Since the election Magri has called for a united left. When Craxi was asked to form a Government, the PDUP was sympathetic but warned that there must be no repetition of the center-left coalitions of the 1960s. If it is to keep its new support, the PDUP needs to show that the united left can offer an *alternativa*—a left Government without the DC.

DP-NSU. When part of AO, most of PDUP, and a small Tuscany-based group called the Communist League (Lega dei Communisti) fused to form the DP, they had officially 15,000 members. The real

---

[8] *Manifesto* gave space on successive days to each of the four parties of the left; they were allowed, without paying, to describe their programs. It did not offer the same treatment to the Radicals.

[9] Magri's motion obtained 58 percent of the votes, Rossanda won 24 percent, and 13 percent went to a motion from the Turin branch which, like Rossanda, stressed social opposition.

number was much lower, perhaps 6,000, with AO in the majority.[10] Clearly the unity of such a party would be difficult to sustain, and it is no coincidence that during the campaign a split developed between the Milan branch, dominated by AO, and the rest. The DP was the antithesis of Magri's PDUP: it was stronger in the factories but even less well organized; it was more activist and less theoretical, more local and less national. And it had to face the problem of the 1977 Movement, which must be discussed here, if only very briefly.

The 1977 Movement. The emergence of the Movement was the most important event in the last three years of the far left's history and it influenced the elections, if only in a negative way. For foreigners it is a difficult phenomenon to understand because, whereas the disturbances of 1968 were Europe-wide, the 1977 Movement was limited to Italy.

Its underlying social causes must be sought in the state of Italy's universities and in the level of youth unemployment. In 1968 there had been 500,000 students in Italy; in 1977 there were over 1 million. Of these only about 10 percent attended classes and only about 5 percent obtained degrees. If students remained at the university, it is probably because they needed the tiny government stipends and because they had no other outlets. By late 1976, unemployment for the age group sixteen to twenty-five was running at 14.4 percent (compared with 7.6 percent in France and 5 percent in Germany). By early 1978, 800,000 young people were looking for jobs, and twice as many would have, had there been any jobs.[11] The universities were full of youths without prospects. The Movement was merely one small, oblique expression of this general problem.

Its protagonists were not the factory workers but the students and the unemployed or underemployed. Indeed the organized working class and its political expressions, the PCI and the unions, were perceived as enemies, indifferent to the new subproletariat of the 1970s. The Movement's greatest battles were fought against the PCI and the unions, not against the DC. In February 1977 the Communist union leader Luciano Lama was expelled from the precincts of Rome university, and in March the Movement tried to take over the PCI's showcase city of Bologna.

---

[10] Once more the exact figures are hard to obtain, but the old PDUP contingent had probably dwindled to about 2,000 and AO adherents were not more than 4,000.

[11] The university figures are given by Monicelli in *L'Ultrasinistra*, p. 67. For the unemployment figures see *Le Monde*, July 3, 1979, p. 19 and *Paese Sera*, October 19, 1978, p. 5.

The sense of being a special, isolated group is perhaps the key trait of the 1977 Movement, which was thoroughly disillusioned with the previous nine years of revolutionary politics.[12] It is no coincidence that, just before the Movement exploded, both the PDUP and AO had been losing militants and Continuous Struggle had dissolved. The Movement was less interested in world issues or proletarian revolution than in its own situation. Politics was to become "the politics of our own needs," and the Movement busied itself with occupying empty houses and forcing cinemas and restaurants to reduce their prices. Its goal was to create "free spaces" where the capitalist ethic of work and profit would no longer prevail.

Clearly a movement as skeptical and as defensive as this one, a movement with such a narrow social base, could not become a national political force. Its high point came in September when 50,000 militants again marched through Bologna, this time peaceably.[13] But no clear political line emerged from the three-day congress which accompanied the demonstration, and afterward the Movement declined. By 1978 it was fragmented, many of its members had drifted away, and the only group which seemed to be growing stronger was the aggressive Workers Autonomy.

The DP and the Movement. The problem the Movement posed for DP was difficult. It was an opportunity because it promoted issues like youth unemployment, university reform, and the need for dissent in the face of the seeming PCI-DC alliance; it also offered thousands of potential recruits. But it was chaotic, absorbed in the personal, and prone to violence. The DP's decision to embrace the Movement was not consciously made at the top, as was the PDUP's decision to reject it. The DP members found themselves in the mass demonstrations of Rome or Bologna, so they participated and they evolved a strategy. The Movement might see itself as creating a "politics of our own needs," but the DP militants knew that all protest movements are class based. According to the DP, the Movement was the expression of the new subproletariat—students without prospects and young, unemployed workers—which had been created by the crisis of Italian capitalism. The DP's task was to explain the Movement to itself and turn it into a new revolutionary party.

[12] This skepticism shows itself in the slogans with which the Movement decorated the walls of Bologna: "Groucho Marx lives" and "After Marx, April."

[13] Part of the credit for the peaceful occupation should go to the PCI, for, although Berlinguer denounced the Movement in September 1977, the Bologna Communists met Movement leaders and worked out an agreement. This truce did not, however, lead to better relations between the PCI and the Movement.

This was not easy, and the DP encountered two problems. The first was organization. The DP was reluctant to build up its organization because this would divorce it from the Movement, which distrusted parties. The DP deliberately moved slowly throughout 1977, trying to be both a party and a part of the Movement. Its other internal tensions were compounded by the division between those of its members who were in the Movement and those who were not. Meanwhile its first national congress was not held until April 1978 so that DP was quite unprepared for the 1979 election.[14]

The second difficulty concerned politics. DP was trying to woo the Movement away from "our own needs" and violence and toward a more political protest. This led to clashes with Workers Autonomy; within the Movement DP stood on the right. Yet the Movement's antiunion slant troubled DP, which had many trade union supporters. Its old PSIUP-PDUP component included Vittorio Foa, who had influenced a generation of trade union left-wingers, and it had the backing of men like Antonio Lettieri of the metalworkers union. But in its rank and file it counted many young workers and unemployed to whom all unionists, even those to the left of the PCI, were hopelessly "establishment." This dispute grew worse in the autumn of 1978 during the hospital workers' strike and the renegotiation of the metalworkers' contracts.[15] The DP could find no secure ground between PDUP and Workers Autonomy.

The DP-NSU and the elections. At the start of the 1979 election campaign the DP fell into further confusion. A group of trade unionists and intellectuals suggested that PDUP and DP agree on a joint New Left list. At first DP was hostile because it needed to establish itself as a party; then it agreed, only to have PDUP withdraw. The mutual reluctance was, one feels, correct, especially after the 1976 fiasco. PDUP and DP had always been very different parties, and the differences had grown larger over the last three years. After PDUP's withdrawal the DP decided to retain the name United New Left and to draw on allied groups. It accepted candidates from Continuous Struggle, from professional organizations like Magistrates for Democ-

---

[14] The best indication of this is the pessimistic ending of Protti's book, which was published after the election but completed before it. Protti anticipated a DP defeat.

[15] Protti feels that the split between the *sinistra sindacale* (unionist left) and the *opposizione operaia* (workers opposition) was the most important split of all. It may also explain why exponents of the *sinistra sindacale* like Lettieri and Serafino suggested the joint New Left list: they wished to counterbalance the *opposizione operaia* component in DP.

racy or Psychiatrists for Democracy, and from left-wing Catholics. The effect, however, was to blur the DP's image.

The NSU's campaign illustrated the difference between itself and the PDUP. It argued that capitalism was still strong and that there was no chance of a left Government. PDUP's concept of *alternativa* was nonsense; the task of the far left was to give political expression to the social opposition in the country. PDUP's attempt to influence the PCI was also nonsense; instead the far left must establish itself as a rival force. The DP defended the Movement and refused to excommunicate Workers Autonomy. It affirmed that terrorism could not be understood except as a reaction, albeit unacceptable, to the authoritarianism of the state. The DP realized, too, that its most dangerous rivals were the Radicals, so, although it was allied with them in the Senate elections, it denounced them as an interclass party which defended civil rights but took no interest in the working-class struggle.

The DP-NSU was too divided and too extreme to be electorally successful. Yet the DP militants' disappointment with the results was intense. And they received a further blow after the elections when their daily, *Il Quotidiano dei Lavoratori,* had to close for lack of funds. Meanwhile the debate has started all over again: should the DP be a political party or a focus for social protest? Either way its future is doubtful and its failure both reflects the inability of the 1977 Movement to transform itself into a political organization and leaves an empty space to the left of the PDUP.

Continuous Struggle. Some of the same considerations emerge from the recent history of Continuous Struggle, which also embraced the Movement. The decision taken at the Rimini congress in December 1976 ended LC's attempt to become a party, but it continued as an "area": some of its local offices remained open, its newspaper was still important, and many of its militants continued to organize demonstrations and strikes. Indeed Rimini provides an illustration of LC's peculiar talent for picking up what was new in Italian society. Continuous Struggle had never been as organized as AO, and it had never had theoreticians like the Manifesto group, but it had always been able to give shape to new forms of protest. For example, the prison movement grew, in part, out of the prison committees which LC formed in the early 1970s. Now it foresaw the end of the little New Left parties and the rise of the 1977 Movement.[16] It also antici-

---

[16] Luigi Bobbio offers a different interpretation of the 1976 decision and sees LC's earlier attempt to organize itself into a party as the sensible course. Not surprisingly Bobbio supported the NSU list in the election.

pated the new brand of politics. LC's decision to dissolve was not caused merely by disappointment at the 1976 election. It was prompted by feminist and worker groups who were weary of working for the revolution and wanted a political activism based on their "own needs."[17]

Most of LC's some 30,000 militants were absorbed into the Movement, where they worked to reconcile DP and Autonomia. At the Bologna congress of September 1977 they argued successfully against violence. As long as the Movement flourished, the "area" LC had occupied could flourish too, but by the end of the year it was in difficulty. In December the Movement split over the decision whether or not to demonstrate with the metalworkers. The DP said yes, while Workers Autonomy organized its own demonstration. The LC split too, a miniature version of the Movement.

By 1978 LC had no organization and seemed to exist only as a newspaper, which had, however, assumed great importance as the cultural focus of the Movement. As militants turned more to their private lives, *Lotta Continua* published articles about drug addiction and ecology, about the new philosophers and radical psychologists, about the Rolling Stones and Walt Whitman. The letter page offered debates about sexual problems, protests by soldiers, and a weekly series of letters from prisoners.

Yet some LC militants were dissatisfied with this personal and cultural debate, and they called for political action. In February 1979 a group occupied the paper's offices in Milan and demanded that LC reenter politics. In April a meeting was held in Rome but it broke up in disorder. Significantly one segment insisted that the paper tone down its denunciations of terrorism. LC seemed likely to make little impact on the election; indeed, once the campaign began, it split into three currents favoring support for the Radicals, support for NSU, and abstention.

The first group was strongest among the leaders and within the newspaper. After the breakdown of the PDUP-DP negotiations Marco Boato and Mimmo Pinto stood as Radicals and took part of the "area" with them. Cooperation between LC and the Radicals was not new, for the two had come together during the Trentino regional elections of November 1978. A New Left list, supported by both, had gained 4.4 percent, a significant result. Boato's view was that in a period of left-wing decline it was useless to form new parties; the far left

---

[17] Lotta Continua militants, fresh from the Rimini congress, helped launch the Bologna Movement in January 1977 with the first wave of *autoriduzioni:* forcing cinemas and restaurants to reduce their prices.

should cultivate the distrust of parliamentary politics that ran through the Movement and which was surfacing in Italy as a whole. Clearly this led Boato to favor the Radicals, who were the voice of this distrust.[18]

The largest part of LC supported the NSU, and the Turin militants protested against the newspaper's pro-Radical stance.[19] NSU's loose structure and its theme of social opposition suited LC just as much as the Radicals' libertarianism. In Alto Adige, where LC leader Mario Cossali was on the list, and in Rome the LC contribution was significant.

The third group called for abstention and took roughly the same position as Autonomia Operaia. "Struggle is more Important than Voting," was its slogan. It despised the newspaper, with its letter page and its preoccupation with personal life. It wished to renew the revolutionary struggle. This group found intellectual expression in the review *Lotta Continua per il Communismo* and was organized into factory and neighborhood collectives.

How influential any of these groups was is hard to assess. Boato and Pinto were both elected and clearly helped the Radicals. Disgusted NSU supporters feel that, if the Milan LC had not been heavily abstentionist, the quota might have been reached in Milan. As for the future, the newspaper itself is in difficulty and LC seems finished as a national force, although its militants are active locally.

Workers Autonomy. By contrast Workers Autonomy—known simply as Autonomia—seemed, until recently, to be growing, even as the other New Left movements declined. It was founded in 1973 after the dissolution of Potere Operaio, and some of its leaders—Toni Negri, Oreste Scalzone, and Franco Piperno—came from Potop.[20] Because of its "autonomous" character and its reluctance to publish statistics on itself, Autonomia is the most difficult of these groups to analyze. But it grew up in the mid-1970s and at the end of the decade remained strong in the big cities: in Genoa, where it has a group in the Ansaldo factory, in Milan, in Rome, where its via dei Volsci commune is hardline, and in Padua, where its theoreticians are well represented on the

---

[18] Marco Boato, "Uno Spettro si aggira sulle Dolomiti" [A ghost stalks the Dolomites], in *Cerchio di gesso* (February 1979), pp. 14-17.

[19] The paper opened its columns to PDUP, NSU, the Radicals, and Autonomia on an equal basis but its own articles tended to favor the Radicals.

[20] Potere Operaio, formed in 1967, held to the belief in a worker uprising. It dissolved in 1973 both because worker militancy was declining and because some members believed that worker militancy could only be fostered by violence. They helped form Autonomia Operaia.

political science faculty. Autonomia draws on the poorer students and young workers; it has no more than several thousand supporters and a broader swath of sympathizers.[21]

Autonomia was helped by the Movement and may even be seen as an extreme version of certain trends within the Movement. Its theoreticians took up the theme of "our own needs" and of "free spaces" and turned them into a new anticapitalist ethic. To counter the alienation generated by a profit-based industrial society, Autonomia proposed a system based on human needs for leisure and freedom as well as material prosperity. This was the new "rationality" that would replace an irrational exploitation. Naturally enough, such thinking appealed to young people who distrusted the notion that austerity was necessary to overcome the economic crisis and who were, in any case, faced with unemployment. The new ethic was to be applied in "autonomous" communities that would be independent of capitalist society.[22]

Autonomia had a creative side which emerged from its theme of pleasure, but it also had a tough, militaristic wing. Free space must be defended and extended, if necessary, by violence. Autonomia's concept of violence was different from the Red Brigades' terrorism, which it condemned. The Red Brigades had isolated themselves from the masses, and their spectacular assassinations awoke no response except increased repression. The dissent of the Italian working class must be sharpened by a more diffuse violence that was more clearly related to everyday life: as one of Autonomia's spokesmen put it, "The growth of mass illegality is necessary and foreseeable."[23]

Clearly this had a certain appeal for a Movement that was discovering the limits of its political influence. Autonomia's themes of the self-contained group and of diffuse violence seemed the only solution. By the end of 1977 Autonomia seemed dominant.[24] Yet it was probably always weaker than it appeared, because the tactic of violence led only to increased violence. After battling the police, the militants offered nothing but further battles. And after the killing of

[21] See Monicelli, L'Ultrasinistra, p. 114, ff.

[22] For a recent restatement of Autonomia's creed see Pier Aldo Rovalti, "Dai bisogni alla nuova razionalità" [Needs and the new rationality], Aut-Aut (Milan) (May-June 1979), pp. 2-12.

[23] Antonio Negri in Terrorismo et stato della crisi [Terrorism and the crisis of the state] (Bologna: Il Mulino, 1979), p. 92. For an NSU view of terrorism see Federico Stame's contribution to the same volume, pp. 108-113.

[24] Monicelli, whose book was finished in early 1978, clearly thought that Autonomia was on the rise.

Aldo Moro distrust of violence increased within the far left.

Just before the election campaign Autonomia received a fresh blow when Negri, Scalzone, and others were arrested on various charges of masterminding the Moro kidnapping, being the leaders of the Red Brigades, and inciting rebellion against the state. At the time of writing these accusations have still not been clearly formulated, specific charges have not been made, and Negri and the others are still in prison. The arrests isolated Autonomia even more and damaged its few remaining allies and apologists in LC and NSU. At the election Autonomia reacted defiantly. Piperno, who was then on the run, had a kind word for the Radicals as champions of dissent,[25] but in general Autonomia called for abstention. It probably had some effect, for poll-watchers in Milan and Turin reported that abstention among young people was unusually high, and in Liguria about two-thirds of the total number of abstentions came from under twenty-five-year-olds.[26] The Autonomia radio stations claimed credit for these abstentions, although apathy may have been an even greater influence.

The Red Brigades. The theme of terrorism was much discussed during the election, for the Red Brigades were conducting their own campaign. On May 3, they attacked the DC office at the Piazza Nicosia in Rome, killing a policeman and causing much damage. The Government replied by sending soldiers to guard public buildings, and a group of policemen attacked the *Lotta Continua* office. In Genoa there was a spurt of terrorist assaults and of arrests, while in Rome the Red Brigades handed out leaflets openly. Meanwhile the trial of Maria Pia Vianale and the remnants of the Nuclei Armati Proletari stirred up memories of earlier terrorism, and the arrest of Valerio Morucci and Adriana Faranda brought hints of dissent within the Red Brigades.

The influence of terrorism on the elections cannot be separated from the role it had played during the previous three years. Left-wingers, whether of the PCI or the NSU, argue that the Red Brigades helped the right. Certainly the NSU's "soft" stand on terrorism cost it votes. Its leaders lamented that "terrorism, whether concentrated or diffuse, made it more difficult to create a consensus on the far left."[27]

---

[25] *Lotta Continua*, April 25, 1979.

[26] This figure is based on the difference in abstention between the lower and upper house elections. For the Senate, where the voting age is twenty-five, abstentions ran at 2.9 percent whereas for the House they were 8.6 percent.

[27] *Relazione del Comitato Direttivo sul risultato ellettorale et sulla situazione e i compiti di DP* [Report of the Committee of Direction in the election results and on the position and the responsibilities of DP], June 16, 1979, p. 23.

Moreover the PCI stressed that, by kidnapping Moro, the Red Brigades had pushed the DC toward the right and blocked the Communist advance. Certainly the Red Brigades have harmed the right less than they have harmed the left. But they have done some damage to all parliamentary parties and to parliamentary government itself. If dissatisfaction with the major parties was so prominent an issue in the elections, it is partly because they had failed to solve the problem of terrorism. The attack at Piazza Nicosia was striking proof of the government's weakness.

Meanwhile the Red Brigades themselves had changed. A document composed by the dissenting group, which included Morucci and Faranda, stated that since 1976 the Red Brigades had pulled their militants out of protest movements and had set up a tighter, more centralized chain of command. This had brought greater efficiency, as the Moro kidnapping revealed, but it had isolated the terrorists from the masses and prevented them from making political gains.[28] Certainly the brutal execution of Moro and his guards diminished the tolerance or comprehension which some New Left members felt for the Red Brigades. At the Bologna congress of September 1977, the terrorists were referred to as "comrades who have erred"; since then opinion has hardened against them.

The dissenting group, while stressing the need for armed struggle, proposed to undertake actions that could win support among factory and neighborhood organizations. Industrial sabotage or reprisals against unpopular landlords were supposed to help the Red Brigades to emerge from their isolation. Links should be reestablished between the clandestine fighters and sympathizers who worked in legal movements. This seemed to be a return to the strategy which the terrorists had tried unsuccessfully in the early 1970s. But nothing came of the Faranda-Morucci line. The dissenters fell silent and the Red Brigades have remained isolated and brutally efficient. In 1980 the revelations of "repentent" terrorists like Patrizio Peci helped the police to destroy some of the Red Brigades cells in Northern Italy. But the Red Brigades are still far from beaten.[29]

---

28 "Brigatisti dissenzienti" [Dissenters of the Red Brigades], Lotta Continua, July 25, 1979, pp. 7-12.

29 In Western European terrorist movements failure to gain popular support goes along with ever more efficient violence. The Red Brigades grew more efficient in the mid-1970s precisely as they lost the sympathy which had surrounded Curcio and Franceschini. The Provisional IRA in Ireland seems to have undergone a similar evolution since 1976.

Conclusion

The history of the Italian far left may be divided, very roughly, into three phases: 1968–1972 saw the rise of student and worker protest, which was influential but failed to create a mass revolutionary movement; 1972–1976 was the period of miniparties, the attempt at organized, electoral politics; the last three years of the decade saw the rise of the Movement and a swing to the extreme positions of Workers Autonomy. Yet, as mass militancy ebbed and as distrust of violence grew, the New Left changed again, and the unlikely victors of the 1969 elections were the "moderates"—the PDUP and the Radicals.

Yet this "moderation" may be short-lived. The Radicals have been changed by their electoral success, and as they cease to be a vehicle of pure protest they may lose their New Left sympathizers. PDUP's new voters come from the PCI and may return to it. Moreover, although NSU, LC, and Autonomia are all in crisis, they have a potential electorate which can probably not be reconquered by the PCI. Italy's economic and social difficulties have created a mass of students, young workers, and unemployed who provide the social base for the New Left. Throughout the 1970s this social force has been too disorganized and too divided to become a political force. It can exert influence neither within nor without the PCI; it can give birth to protest movements but not to lasting organizations. Still, as long as it exists, it provides a breeding ground for future New Left experiments.

8

The Italian Parliament
in the 1979 Elections

Robert Leonardi

The 1979 Italian elections had a profound impact on the composition and distribution of power in Parliament. As has been stressed in other chapters, the election witnessed a shift in voter support away from the Communists, who lost 4 full percentage points in the vote for the Chamber of Deputies and 2.6 points for the Senate. The only other parties to suffer declines in voter support in comparison with the 1976 election were the Christian Democrats (0.4 points in the Chamber and 0.6 in the Senate) and the right-wing Italian Social Movement-National Right, which lost approximately 300,000 votes in both houses of Parliament. All of the other parties experienced increases, which were duly translated into more parliamentary seats. Those who benefited most from the 1979 election were the Radicals, the Social Democrats, the Liberals, and three of the small regional parties (South Tyrolean People's party, Valdostian Union, and List for Trieste).

In 1979 a total of twelve political parties succeeded in getting their representatives elected to Parliament. Two others failed: the United New Left was 13,530 votes shy of the quota in the Milan constituency, and the moderate National Democracy fell a full 23,782 short in the twenty-second electoral district, Naples-Caserta. Table 8–1 provides a rundown of the changes in the parliamentary strength of the various parties between 1976 and 1979. The Communists lost a total of thirty-five members in 1979, seven in the Senate and twenty-eight in the Chamber. Despite its decline in electoral support, the DC did not experience a parallel loss of seats. In fact, Christian Democracy was able to translate its status as the relative majority party in the system into three extra Senate seats, which more than compensated for its loss of one deputy. The d'Hondt highest-average proportional-

TABLE 8–1

Change in the Distribution of Seats in Parliament, 1976–1979

Party	Chamber			Senate			Total		
	1976	1979	Change	1976	1979	Change	1976	1979	Change
DC	262	261	−1	135	138	+3	397	399	+2
PCI	229[a]	201	−28	116	109	−7	345	310	−35
PSI	57	62	+5	30	32	+2	87	94	+7
MSI-DN	35	31	−4	15	13	−2	50	44	−6
PSDI	15	21	+6	7	9	+2	22	30	+8
PR	4	18	+14	0	2	+2	4	20	+16
PRI	14	15	+1	7	6	−1	21	21	0
PLI	5	9	+4	2	2	0	7	11	+4
PDUP	—	6	+6	—	0	—	0	6	+6
DP	6	—	−6	0	—	—	6	0	−6
SVP	3	4	+1	2	3	+1	5	7	+2
UV	—	1	+1	1	1	0	1	2	+1
List for Trieste	—	1	+1	—	—	—	0	1	+1
Total	630	630	—	315	315	—	945	945	—

Dash (—): Not applicable.

[a] This figure includes one seat won in Valle d'Aosta by a coalition that included the PCI and the PSI. The official election returns for 1976 give the PCI 228 seats.

Note: The total number of senators is 322. The seven senators omitted from this table are those who have been named to the Senate for life. They are: Amintore Fanfani, Giuseppe Leone, Cesare Merzagora, Eugenio Montale, Ferruccio Parri, Giuseppe Saragat, and Leo Valiani.

Source: Calculated from data in *Corriere della Sera*, June 6, 1979, and *I Deputati e Senatori dell' Ottavo Parlamento Republicano* [The deputies and senators of the Eighth Parliament] (Rome: La Navicella, 1979).

representation formula used in selecting senators tends to favor the larger parties.[1] Accordingly, the DC was able to raise its share of Senate seats by 1 point from 43 percent in 1976 despite a 0.6 point loss in votes. By contrast, the Liberals with 2.2 percent of the vote were allocated only 0.6 percent of the seats in the Senate in 1979.

One of the truly great surprises in the distribution of representation in the Eighth Parliament was that the Socialist party managed to translate a minuscule 0.2 percentage point increase in its vote for each branch of Parliament into a sizable expansion of its parliamentary contingent: from eighty-seven senators and deputies in 1976 to ninety-four in 1979. The vagaries of the election process gave them five additional deputies and two senators. The Social Democrats registered a similar increase in members, but they had nearly four times the increase in votes obtained by the Socialists.

These examples suggest that the Italian system of proportional representation does not produce a perfect fit between popular vote and parliamentary representation, though it does better in this regard than systems based on simple-majority, winner-take-all, or modified proportional representation rules. After the 1979 election there was some debate among political commentators over the desirability of a change in the electoral process. What concerned them was the nagging problem, once the voters have spoken, of putting together a stable Government. The Italian electoral system does a very good job of guaranteeing that even the tiniest party will secure representation in the national legislature, but it is less predisposed toward producing a clear majority.[2]

Enthusiasm for a change in electoral rules, however, quickly subsided after Fulco Lanchester, a student of Italian constitutional law, showed that if Italy were to adopt another electoral system (he took the examples of England, West Germany, and Sweden) the distribution of seats in Parliament would be quite different from what it actually was. Taking the 1979 Senate results as a base, he showed that Christian Democracy would have been able to translate its 38.4

---

[1] See the discussion of the d'Hondt formula in Douglas Wertman, "The Italian Electoral Process: The Elections of June 1976," in Howard R. Penniman, ed., *Italy at the Polls: The Parliamentary Elections of 1976* (Washington, D.C.: American Enterprise Institute, 1977), pp. 44-51.

[2] There is considerable debate among students of Italian politics over whether the difficulty in governing the country is due to the nature of the political parties, whose strong ideological orientations make compromises difficult to achieve, or to the electoral system. For an expression of the former view, see Giuseppe DiPalma, *Surviving without Governing: The Italian Parties in Parliament* (Berkeley: University of California Press, 1977).

TABLE 8–2

SEAT DISTRIBUTION IN THE ITALIAN SENATE: ACTUAL RESULT AND
RESULTS PROJECTED UNDER WEST GERMAN
AND SWEDISH ELECTORAL SYSTEMS
(percent)

Party	1979 Senate Vote	Distribution of Seats Under:			
		Actual Italian system	British system	West German system	Swedish system
DC	38.4	44.0	72.2	46.0	46.5
PCI	31.5	34.6	27.4	35.4	35.3
PSI	10.4	10.2	0	11.7	11.6
MSI-DN	5.7	4.1	0	6.3	5.7
PSDI	4.2	2.9	0	0	0
PRI	3.4	1.9	0	0	0
PR-NSU	2.6	0.6	0	0	0
PLI	2.6	0.6	0	0	0
DN	0.6	0	0	0	0
SVP	0.6	1.0	0	0.6	0.6
List for Trieste	0.2	0	0.4	0	0.3
Other	0.1	0	0	0	0

SOURCE: *Panorama*, October 15, 1979, p. 50.

percent of the vote into an overwhelming 72.2 percent of the seats
under the British system, while the PCI would have won almost all
of the remaining constituencies. The German and Swedish methods
of seat distribution would not have significantly changed the allocation of seats to the DC, PCI, PSI, MSI-DN, and small regional parties,
but all of the small national parties like the Radicals, Social Democrats,
Republicans, and Liberals would have been eliminated. This is a price
that few Italians are willing to pay for increased efficiency in the
formation of majority cabinets.

Parliamentary Turnover

Despite the shifts in the parties' strength, the membership in Parliament changed much less in 1979 than it had three years before (see
table 8–3). In 1976 more than one-third of the seats were occupied by
representatives who had not sat in the previous Parliament (1972–

TABLE 8–3
Turnover in Italian Parliamentary Party Groups, 1976–1979

	New Members in Chamber		New Members in Senate	
Party	Number	% of party group	Number	% of party group
1979				
DC	54	(21)	24	(17)
PCI	49	(24)	23	(21)
PSI	29	(47)	13	(41)
MSI-DN	15	(48)	7	(54)
PSDI	9	(43)	4	(44)
PRI	4	(27)	2	(33)
PLI	5	(55)	0	—
PR	11	(61)	2	(100)
SVP, other	4	(67)	1	(25)
PDUP	3	(50)	0	—
Total	183	(29)	76	(24)
1976				
DC	101	(38)	50	(37)
PCI	103	(45)	49	(42)
PSI	15	(26)	14	(47)
MSI-DN	5	(14)	3	(23)
PSDI	3	(20)	3	(43)
PRI	2	(14)	1	(17)
PLI	2	(40)	1	(50)
PR	4	(100)	0	—
SVP, other	1	(33)	3	(75)
DP	6	(100)	0	—
Total	242	(38)	124	(39)

Dash (—): Not applicable.

NOTE: Former senators elected to the Chamber and former deputies elected to the Senate are not counted as new members.

SOURCE: Calculated from *I Deputati e Senatori* for the Seventh and Eighth Parliaments.

1976). There was only a slight difference between the rate of turnover for the Chamber and the Senate, but there were dramatic differences in turnover from one party to another. In 1976 the Communists led all of the parties except the fledgling Radicals and Demoproletarians in electing new faces to Parliament. Worst of all in this regard were the MSI-DN and PLI. The Christian Democrats and Socialists were close to the average rate of turnover for the entire Parliament, though the Socialists did change almost half of their Senate members. In the Chamber only one-quarter of the PSI representatives were new.

Things were quite different in 1979. Among the mass parties the Socialist contingent changed considerably while the Communists' and Christian Democrats' turnover rate dropped by almost half. In 1979 only 19 percent of the DC and 23 percent of the Communist members had not been present in the previous Parliament. The Communists were undoubtedly affected by their less than brilliant showing, which left many aspirants to parliamentary seats out in the cold. This was a reversal of the 1976 result when a number of PCI candidates had been surprised to find themselves elected. In 1979 the surprise victories went to PSI candidates. The increase in Socialist M.P.s permitted the new leadership group under Bettino Craxi to elect some of its principal spokesmen such as Claudio Martelli, Valdo Spini, Giorgio LaGanga, and Giorgio Gangi, but the older generation of leaders represented by former party secretaries Francesco De Martino and Giacomo Mancini (both from the South) also succeeded in getting their followers elected: Mario Casalinuovo in Calabria, Antonio Landolfi and Francesco Spinelli in Lazio, and Rino Formica in Milan.[3]

In contrast to 1976, 1979 saw a major renewal of the MSI-DN contingent. Half of its parliamentary group were people new to the parliamentary scene. This shift was not a product of the party decision-making process, which in the past had heavily favored incumbents; instead, the change was caused by the defection in December 1976 of over half of the MSI-DN parliamentary group to the new National Democratic party (DN). Seventeen out of thirty-five deputies and nine out of fifteen senators joined the nascent party. Of the twenty-four members who remained with the parent MSI-DN organization, all but one were reelected. Giuseppe Abbadessa failed to retain his Senate seat by a mere 0.049 percentage points. The impact of the DN defection was to force the Italian Social Movement to undertake a circulation of elites, which it would ordinarily not have done. Even under these circumstances the turnover was not complete because one-third of the "new" members had already served in Parliament prior to 1976. These candidates had received a new lease on their political life after the 1976 defections to DN.

Similarly, though the turnover among Liberal representatives was 55 percent, three of the five new PLI seats were filled by former

---

[3] *Il Messaggero*, June 6, 1979, p. 5.

deputies. But the other small parties could claim more newcomers. The PDUP filled three of its six seats with people who had never been in Parliament; and thirteen out of the PR's sixteen new seats were allocated to freshmen M.P.s. Even here, however, there is a hitch. At the tail end of the Seventh Parliament the four Radicals elected to the Chamber in 1976 had resigned en masse and been replaced by the runner-up candidates. The new representatives of the Radical party remained at their posts for less than three months, and in 1979 all eight "former" members were reelected.[4]

The parties with the lowest turnover rates were the Christian Democrats and the Communists. The figures do not substantially differ from one branch of Parliament to the other, though in both cases there was a greater circulation of deputies than senators. These low rates of turnover, however, did not prevent both major parties from bringing new personalities into the parliamentary arena. The Christian Democrats brought in prominent admirals, prefects, journalists, and magistrates to add prestige to their parliamentary groups.[5] There was some support in the DC for proposing the candidacy of Aldo Moro's brother, Alfredo Carlo Moro. Alfredo Moro had been a leader of Catholic Action and would have been willing to run for the Senate in his brother's former constituency, but the plan was vetoed by Aldo Moro's wife who threatened to run her son, Giovanni, as a Socialist candidate if the DC insisted on presenting Alfredo. Aldo Moro's family was still bitter about the DC's unwillingness to deal with the Red Brigades in an attempt to save his life. This clash also prevented the DC from running Romano Prodi, an academician who was minister of industry in the third Andreotti Government, and Pietro Scoppola, a highly respected Catholic intellectual, both of whom refused to run unless the DC leadership guaranteed the candidacy of Moro's brother.

Of particular interest on the Communist side of Parliament was the election of two magistrates, Liberato Riccardelli and Luciano Violante, who had become well known as a result of their investigations of the Red Brigades and neo-Fascist violence. In 1979 the Communists attempted to project themselves as a bulwark against terrorism and guarantor of the democratic system.

[4] For the purpose of calculating the party turnover rate, only the original four PR deputies were counted as having been active in the previous Parliament. Their substitutes served only a small fraction of their parliamentary mandate, and during that period Parliament went through its process of dissolution in preparation for the June 3 elections.

[5] As we will see below, all of the prestige candidates for the DC were presented in Senate races.

TABLE 8–4

BACKGROUND CHARACTERISTICS OF FRESHMAN M.P.S,
BY PARTY GROUP, 1979

Party	Mean Age	% National Party Leaders	% Held Local Office	% Participated in World War II	N
Chamber of Deputies					
DC	45	17	72	2	(54)
PCI	45	18	59	10	(49)
PSI	42	28	52	3	(29)
MSI-DN	47	53	60	20	(15)
PSDI	51	44	50	75	(9)
PRI	44	50	75	0	(4)
PLI	48	75	50	0	(5)
PR	43	55	18	9	(11)
PDUP	37	100	0	0	(3)
SVP, other	53	—	17	0	(4)
All freshman deputies	44	27	48	8	(183)
Senate					
DC	52	25	29	21	(24)
PCI	52	26	48	48	(23)
PSI	51	15	31	15	(13)
MSI-DN	57	57	71	57	(7)
PSDI	53	25	75	50	(4)
PRI	56	50	50	0	(2)
PR	50	100	0	0	(2)
SVP, other	49	—	0	0	(1)
All freshman senators	53	28	39	30	(76)

Dash (—): Not applicable.
SOURCE: Calculated from *I Deputati e Senatori* for the Eighth Parliament.

Background Characteristics of the New Members. Taking the 259 new members and separating them by branch, we see in table 8–4 that the mean age of the 1979 freshmen in the Chamber is forty-four while for the Senate it is fifty-three. The oldest groups in the Chamber are the "mixed" contingent representing the SVP and other regionalist parties, followed by the PSDI. The youngest members are to be found in the PDUP—and in the PSI, which suggests that Bettino Craxi's "new course" strategy may have had the effect of bringing in new

TABLE 8–5

MEAN AGE OF PARTY GROUPS IN THE ITALIAN CHAMBER OF DEPUTIES, 1958 AND 1979, AND OF FRESHMAN DEPUTIES IN 1979

| Party | 1979 | | 1958 |
	All deputies	Freshmen	
DC	48	45	50
PCI	47	45	45
PSI	47	42	47
MSI-DN	53	47	45
PSDI	53	51	49
PRI	50	44	54
PLI	43	48	52
PR	44	43	57
PDUP	46	37	—
SVP-Others	48	56	40
PNM[a]	—	—	51
PMN[a]	—	—	56
Chamber	48	44	47

Dash (—): Not applicable.

[a] In 1958 there were two monarchist parties: the National Monarchist party (PNM) and the Popular Monarchist party (PMN).

SOURCE: Calculated from *I Deputati e Senatori* for the Third and Eighth Parliaments.

blood. The PSI's freshman senators are also younger than their colleagues in other parties. Table 8–5 permits us to compare the mean age for freshman deputies and for the entire membership of the Chamber. On the average the new deputies are four years younger than their colleagues. The largest gap between the two sets of figures is found among the "Pdupinni," followed by the Republicans and neo-Fascists. The table also demonstrates that there has been little substantial change in the age distribution of members when one compares the 1958 with the 1979 Parliament. The average age for the mass parties has remained substantially the same, while the PSDI and MSI-DN deputies have on the average become older. It is surprising to find the Republicans and Liberals quite a bit younger than their counterparts in 1958.

Returning to table 8–4, we can see that many of the new deputies elected to the 1979 Parliament are experienced politicians. Almost half have held local public office, and 27 percent were members of their party's national leadership. Other interesting patterns also emerge from the data. Many of the freshman deputies from the minor parties are members of national party organs (central committees and directorates), while fewer than one-quarter and even one-fifth of the mass party deputies have achieved similar levels of power in their own parties. In fact, there is almost a perfect inverse relationship in this regard. A similar trend characterizes the new senators.

The figures for previous election to local office point in the opposite direction. Deputies from the largest parties are more likely to have had local office experience than their counterparts in smaller parties. The exceptions are the MSI-DN and PRI M.P.s, who report considerable familiarity with political office at the local level. One interesting statistic is the relatively low number of Social Democrats who held local positions prior to election to the national legislature. This contradicts one of the possible reasons given by the PSDI leadership for the party's success in the 1979 elections—that many of its candidates were local politicians who could bring in their wake a large number of votes.[6] The strategy may have served to convince local politicians to run on the PSDI lists, but very few of them were elected to the House. The Senate candidates did slightly better.

Another notable discrepancy shows up for Christian Democrats in the Chamber and Senate. Local representative experience is very high for new deputies (72 percent) but very low for freshman senators (29 percent). The imbalance between the new arrivals in the two houses of Parliament is attributable to the DC's penchant for placing local notables or men of prestige who do not have an extensive political background on its senatorial lists, while the candidacies for the Chamber are more frequently allocated to seasoned politicians adept at waging the struggle for the all-important preference vote. Thus two admirals, Giuseppe Oriana and Severino Falluchi, as well as a former prefect of Milan, Libero Mazza, and a former head of IRI, Giuseppe Petrilli, ran for Senate seats.

The Communists do not have to make such drastic choices between the Chamber and the Senate because the party has stronger control over the preference votes of its supporters. Before an election, the local provincial party organization decides who will be elected and the order in which preference votes should be cast. A similar procedure is followed by the Christian Democratic party organizations, but in the case of the DC surprises in the final tally of preference votes are much more common. One reason is that the mobilization of

---

[6] See the discussion of the PSDI campaign in chapter 6 in this volume.

preference votes is managed by the factions, which may or may not adhere to prearranged party agreements.[7]

The Communists' ability to control the casting of preference votes has permitted them since 1963 to create an Independent Left contingent in the Chamber of Deputies to parallel the long-standing and sizable Sinistra Independente group in the Senate. The role of such groups in Parliament is to permit prominent left-wingers who are not members of the party to get elected to office. The PCI gains prestige in the eyes of the public by associating its electoral symbol with well-known personalities, and these individuals do have a chance of expressing their views on the vital issues discussed in Parliament. Other parties have tried to copy the Communist strategy, but none has succeeded so well in both houses of Parliament. In 1979 the PCI elected ten deputies and fifteen senators as independent leftists.

That the Independent Left group is larger in the Senate than the Chamber suggests the greater honorific value of membership in the Senate, though the two chambers of Parliament are perfectly equal in power. Another indication of the Senate's greater prestige is the higher incidence among newly elected senators of Second World War service in either the resistance, the Italian army, or the forces of the Salò Republic: 30 percent among freshman senators and only 8 percent for deputies. The percentages for the Communist, Social Democratic, and Italian Social Movement senators are particularly noteworthy.

Geographic Distribution of Parliamentary Seats

The geographic distribution of seats in the Italian Parliament is linked to the size of the population. In 1979, 47 percent of the seats in the House were found in the northern constituencies, 19 percent in the Center, and 34 percent in the South and Islands. Since 1948 there has been a gradual shift of population from the southern to the northern parts of the country. Table 8–6 shows that in 1979 the North had forty-one more seats than it did thirty-one years earlier, and the South has barely kept its 1948 seat allotment despite an overall fifty-six-seat expansion of the Chamber. This change would be occurring much faster if Italian electoral laws required citizens to vote in the commune where they live. Instead they must vote in the commune where they maintain their legal residence; there are no provisions for postal voting, but citizens returning to their home commune to vote are charged greatly reduced train fares, and as a

---

[7] The competition among factions for preference votes is quite fierce. Intrigues and double-crosses are very common.

TABLE 8–6

GEOGRAPHIC DISTRIBUTION OF SEATS IN THE CHAMBER OF DEPUTIES,
1948–1979

Election	North	Center	South	Total
1979	297	118	215	630
1968	282	117	231	630
1958	263	108	225	596
1948	256	105	213	574

NOTE: The three geographic areas are defined as follows: North, electoral districts 1 through 13 plus 31 and 32; Center, districts 14 through 19; and South, districts 20 through 30. See appendix C for the names of the constituencies.
SOURCE: Calculated from *I Deputati e Senatori* for the First, Third, Fifth, and Eighth Parliaments.

result many people, in order to take advantage of a free trip home, maintain their legal residence in their place of birth even after they have moved away.

Aside from the regionalist parties that get all of their votes from clearly designated constituencies in the northern part of the country, the parties demonstrate a surprising degree of national homogeneity. The political parties whose strength varies most according to geographic area are the Liberals, strong in the North, and the MSI-DN, which does quite well in the South. In table 8–7 we can see that the MSI-DN receives 58 percent of its seats from the South, though the area accounts for only one-third of all deputies. From a comparison of the last two elections it is clear that in 1979 the PSDI and PLI increased their strength in the North and that the PR became a more national party. In 1979 28 percent of the PR M.P.s came from the South, versus none in 1976.

The pattern in the Senate is similar, though slightly accentuated (see table 8–8). The Liberals were awarded representation only in the North, and the MSI-DN southern contingent made up almost three-quarters of the party's total. Comparisons of the 1976 and 1979 results show that in the last election the PCI returned to the allocation of seats it had in the South before 1976. In fact, the seven-seat differential between its 1976 and 1979 allocations was entirely the result of losses in the South. The distribution of representation in the North and Center matched exactly the 1976 result.

Communist losses in the South were matched by Christian Democratic and Socialist party gains. The PSI went from ten to

TABLE 8–7

SEAT DISTRIBUTION IN THE CHAMBER OF DEPUTIES, BY PARTY
AND GEOGRAPHIC AREA, 1976 AND 1979

Party	North No.	%	Center No.	%	South No.	%	Total No.	%
1979								
DC	117	45	44	17	100	38	261	100
PCI	94	47	48	24	59	29	201	100
PSI	29	47	11	18	22	35	62	100
MSI-DN	8	26	5	16	18	58	31	100
PSDI	13	62	2	9	6	29	21	100
PR	10	55	3	17	5	28	18	100
PRI	9	60	3	20	3	20	15	100
PLI	8	89	1	11	0	—	9	100
PDUP	3	50	1	17	2	33	6	100
SVP, other	6	100	0	—	0	—	6	100
Total	297	47	118	19	215	34	630	100
1976								
DC	121	46	44	17	97	37	262	100
PCI	103	45	54	24	72	31	229[a]	100
PSI	30	53	9	16	18	31	57	100
MSI-DN	8	23	7	20	20	57	35	100
PSDI	8	53	2	14	5	33	15	100
PR	3	75	1	25	0	—	4	100
PRI	9	64	2	14	3	22	14	100
PLI	3	60	1	20	1	20	5	100
DP	4	66	1	17	1	17	6	100
SVP, other	3	100	0	—	0	—	3	100
Total	292	46	121	19	217	35	630	100

Dash (—): Not applicable.
[a] This figure includes the seat won in Valle d'Aosta by a coalition that included the PCI and the PSI. The official election returns for 1976 give the PCI 228 seats.
SOURCE: Calculated from *I Deputati e Senatori* for the Seventh and Eighth Parliaments.

twelve seats and the DC from forty-eight to fifty-three. Among the smaller parties, the only change was the Social Democrats' gain of one Senate seat.

TABLE 8–8

Seat Distribution in the Senate, by Party
and Geographic Area, 1976 and 1979

	North		Center		South		Total	
Party	No.	%	No.	%	No.	%	No.	%
1979								
DC	61	44	24	17	53	39	138	100
PCI	50	50	28	24	31	26	109	100
PSI	15	45	5	16	12	39	32	100
MSI-DN	2	15	2	15	9	70	13	100
PSDI	5	56	1	11	3	33	9	100
PR	1	50	1	50	0	—	2	100
PRI	3	50	1	17	2	33	6	100
PLI	2	100	0	—	0	—	2	100
SVP, other	4	100	0	—	0	—	4	100
Total	143	47	62	19	110	34	315	100
1976								
DC	64	47	23	17	48	36	135	100
PCI	50	43	28	24	38	33	116	100
PSI	15	50	5	17	10	33	30	100
MSI-DN	3	20	3	20	9	60	15	100
PSDI	3	42	2	29	2	29	7	100
PRI	4	57	1	14	2	29	7	100
PLI	2	100	0	—	0	—	2	100
SVP, other	3	100	0	—	0	—	3	100
Total	144	46	62	20	109	34	315	100

Dash (—): Not applicable.
Source: Calculated from *I Deputati e Senatori* for the Seventh and Eighth Parliaments.

The Distribution of Power in Parliament

The distribution of power in the Italian Parliament is intimately tied to the nature of the governing coalition. Aside from the strength derived from numbers, parliamentary power is the product of positions that permit party representatives to manage the course of legislation. In the U.S. Congress committee chairmen, the speaker of the House, and the president of the Senate are looked upon as men possessing considerable influence in the formulation of public policy. Their counterparts in Italy do not enjoy the same amount of power, but their influence is still important. Parliamentary party group leaders, on the other hand, have a lot more influence than their counterparts (minority or majority party whips) in the U.S. Congress. It can be argued that in the Italian Parliament there are three important points of reference for the management of power: the parliamentary group leaders, the presidents of the two houses of Parliament, and the chairmen of the standing committees.

The most important of the three is the group leader (*capogruppo*), who is the chief coordinator for the activities of members elected on a particular party ticket. He is the point of contact between the extra-parliamentary party organization and the M.P.s. The task of the *capogruppo* is to see to it that the party's program is translated into legislative proposals and that the party's parliamentary contingent operates in accordance with party dictates. On the whole, the sense of commitment to party dictates is stronger among members of the traditional opposition parties like the PCI and the MSI-DN than it is among governmental parties (the DC, PSI, PSDI, and PRI).

In 1971 substantial changes were made in the parliamentary rules and procedures; the new rules allocated a significant amount of power in deciding on the schedule of parliamentary activities to the caucus of parliamentary group leaders.[8] Before 1971 this task was left up to the presidents of the two legislative branches. The new rules specify that the caucus is convened by the presidents of the legislature, and a representative of the Government is invited to sit in on the meeting. Decisions in the caucus are taken by unanimous vote. Disagreements among the leaders are settled by a majority vote in an open session of each house of Parliament. The Chamber of Deputies decides on three-month agendas, while the Senate agrees to six-month schedules. These schedules are subsequently broken down into fifteen-day "executive calendars" that set out the issue to be discussed the initiation and termination of the discussion, and the body (or sequence of bodies) that will consider the matter. It is in this context that the Government coalition must be sustained by a solid majority in Parliament. Otherwise, Parliament has the power to short-circuit the Government's power of initiative in proposing legislation. One of the reasons why the Communists were so quickly accepted into the parliamentary majority sustaining the Andreotti Government was the feeling that with their increased strength and prestige the Communists could bring Parliament to a halt if they

[8] For a discussion of the new parliamentary rules, see Robert Leonardi, Raffaella Nanetti, and Gianfranco Pasquino, "Institutionalization of Parliament and Parliamentarization of Parties in Italy," *Legislative Studies Quarterly III* (February 1978), pp. 163-169.

remained in opposition. It can be argued that the first Cossiga Government formed after the 1979 election suffered from the disease that Andreotti had been able to avoid. Cossiga had enough support in Parliament when it came to votes of confidence, but he did not have the "working parliamentary majority" that would have permitted him to get his legislative proposals introduced into or passed by Parliament.

Despite the changes instituted in 1971, the presidents of the two legislative branches still exercise considerable power. For instance, it is the presidents' prerogative to decide whether a bill should be assigned directly to a standing committee with primary responsibility for the subject matter under discussion (for example, housing) or whether to send it to another committee for a consultative opinion (possibly, the Budgetary Committee for a preliminary analysis of the financial impact of a new housing program on the national budget). In addition, the presidents manage the provision of parliamentary services such as library facilities, research staff, commissaries, and eating facilities that are made available to individual M.P.s as well as to party groups.

The task of the committee chairmen is to manage the discussion and votes on bills in accordance with the executive calendar. One important point that has to be remembered with regard to Italian parliamentary committees is that they can pass legislation on their own without subsequent referral of bills to the floor. The decision to allow them to do so is made by the party group leaders' caucus, but the final result is still very much in the hands of the committee chairman unless there is a solid, preconstituted majority that can impose its will on the committee. What happens most often, however, is that bargaining and compromise between the parties take place before legislation is formally proposed for the final vote. Giuseppe DiPalma reports that between 1948 and 1968 the PCI voted in favor of 71 percent of all Government and majority party (DC) bills that were eventually passed. When one considers the amount of legislation produced annually in the Italian Parliament (approximately 400 laws), one is led to conclude that the process of compromise is well institutionalized.[9]

In 1976 the Communist party, for the first time since 1947, participated in the distribution of key positions in Parliament. Pietro Ingrao became president of the Chamber of Deputies, and PCI M.P.s were awarded the chairmanships of four committees in the Chamber and three in the Senate (see table 8–9). The accession of Communists to leadership roles in Parliament was concrete proof that the PCI "had

[9] DiPalma, *Surviving without Governing*, pp. 48–57.

TABLE 8–9

PARTY DISTRIBUTION OF THE PRESIDENCIES OF STANDING COMMITTEES
IN PARLIAMENT, 1976 AND 1979

Party	1979		1976	
	Chamber	Senate	Chamber	Senate
DC	7	8	5	5
PCI	0	0	4	3
PSI	0	0	3	2
PSDI	3	2	1	1
PRI	3	2	1	1
PLI	0	0	0	0
MSI-DN	0	0	0	0
PR	0	0	0	0
PDUP-DP	0	0	0	0
SVP, other	1	0	0	0
Total	14	12	14	12

SOURCE: Calculated from *I Deputati e Senatori* for the Seventh and Eighth Parliaments.

finally arrived" and been accepted as an open participant in the determination of the nation's policies. By the same token, when the Communists were denied committee chairmanships in 1979, this signaled the end of the coalition of national solidarity that had ruled between 1976 and 1978. However, the party did maintain control of the presidency of the Chamber and one special committee in Parliament dealing with the regions. After the 1979 elections Ingrao made clear that he did not want to return to his post because he wanted to dedicate himself to the task of rebuilding the party, and the PCI turned to Leonilde Iotti, a former vice-president of the Chamber. Iotti was accepted by all of the other major parties, which signified that the new coalition was not willing to completely break with the Communists.

The rearrangement of the presidencies of standing committees in the 1979 Parliament, however, did represent the first sign of a growing commitment among the minor centrist parties, the Christian Democrats, and the Socialists to experiment once again with a center-left coalition majority in Parliament as well as in the Government. After speculation that Bettino Craxi would be called upon to form the first Socialist-led cabinet in the postwar period, the task of putting together a new Government fell on Arnaldo Forlani. The creation of the

Forlani Government in October 1980 left intact the distribution of posts in Parliament. It is unlikely that there will be any further changes in the ruling coalition until after the next elections which will take place no later than 1984, and if change does come it will be first manifested in the composition of or relationships among the parties in Parliament.

9

Women and Parliamentary Politics in Italy, 1946-1979

Karen Beckwith

In any society, the degree of female emancipation is the natural measure of the general emancipation.

Charles Fourier

Political Parties and Women as a Social Force

Women's full political citizenship began in Italy on February 1, 1945, when Italian women were enfranchised. This enfranchisement was the result of women's participation in the fight against Fascism at the end of World War II, rather than the fruit of a long struggle by an organized women's movement. The original women's suffrage movement in Italy had been cut short by the advent of Fascism just at the time women in other Western nations were receiving the vote.[1]

The two major political parties in Italy, the Christian Democrats (DC) and the Communist party (PCI), are grounded in political subcultures and ideologies which have always recognized women as a specific group to which political appeals could be made. The two major parties have never ignored women as a social force. Both gave strong support to women's enfranchisement. It was widely expected that Italian women would overwhelmingly give their votes to the DC and that female suffrage would have an important impact upon the constitution of postwar government and politics.[2] The DC was

[1] For accounts of the women's suffrage movement in Italy see: Sandra Puccini, "Condizione della donna e questione femminile (1892-1922)" [Woman's condition and the woman question (1892-1922)] and Enzo Santarelli, "Il fascismo e le ideologie antifemministe" [Fascism and antifeminist ideologies], in *Problemi del Socialismo*, vol. 18, no. 4 (1976); and Mary Cornelia Porter and Corey Venning, "Catholicism and Women's Role in Italy and Ireland," in Lynne B. Iglitzin and Ruth Ross, eds., *Women in the World* (Santa Barbara, Calif.: Clio Books, 1976).

[2] This argument is made by Giorgio Galli and Alfonso Prandi in *Patterns of Political Participation in Italy* (New Haven: Yale University Press, 1970), pp. 18, 26, and 57; and by Mattei Dogan in "Le donne italiane tra cattolicesimo e marxismo" [Italian women between catholicism and Marxism] in Alberto Spreafico and Joseph LaPalombara, eds., *Elezioni e comportamento politico in Italia* [Elections and political behavior in Italy] (Milan: Edizione di Comunità, 1963), pp. 475-494.

confident of attracting the majority of female voters, in part because of the successful organizing of women by Catholic Action (AC)[3] and in part because of Italian women's traditional support for the Catholic church and its organizations.[4] The PCI, expecting to attract fewer female voters, supported enfranchisement nonetheless as part of its long-term strategy of building an indigenous Italian communism. In explaining the PCI strategy—which put the party at an electoral disadvantage in 1945—Nadia Spano and Fiamma Camarlinghi write: "That the Communists have posed the problem of women's right to vote assumes a significance beyond the issue itself: there has been throughout the country a process of renewal which, as Togliatti said, has needed the participation and democratic maturation of women."[5]

At the time that the PCI and the DC were examining the effect women's suffrage might have on each party's electoral strength, they were also directing women who had been partisans during the war in forming their own voluntary associations, which were formally autonomous but financially dependent upon the parties. In 1945, the Unione Donne Italiane (Union of Italian Women, UDI) was established as an organization concerned with women's issues, especially women's new political rights, and representative of all women, regardless of ideology. UDI's initial membership was predominantly Communist and Socialist, and with the establishment of the Centro Italiano Femminile (Center of Italian Women, CIF), also in 1945, UDI's membership continued to consist equally and primarily of Socialist and Communist women. UDI receives encouragement from the PCI and the PSI, draws most of its financial support from them, and remains tied to both, particularly the former. UDI's semiautonomous status and financial dependence upon the PCI and PSI were issues of considerable debate within the organization in the late 1970s.

CIF proposed "regrouping and coordinating openly and actively Catholic women's organizations 'in view of the serious moral, social and civic responsibilities' that a democratic order imposes upon women."[6] Its membership consists not only of Catholic women, but also of women who vote for the DC, the party from which CIF draws its major financial support.[7]

---

[3] For a description of Catholic Action, see Galli and Prandi, *Patterns of Political Participation*, pp. 174-177.

[4] See Maria Weber, *Il voto della donna* [Woman's vote] (Turin: Biblioteca della libertà, 1977), pp. 13-20.

[5] Nadia Spano and Fiamma Camarlinghi, *La questione femminile nella politica del PCI* [The woman question in PCI politics] (Rome: Edizione Donne e Politica, 1972), p. 126.

[6] Galli and Prandi, *Patterns of Political Participation*, p. 193.

[7] For a description of CIF, see Galli and Prandi, *Patterns of Political Participa-*

The CIF, the DC, and the DC's affiliated voluntary associations, such as Catholic Action, have consistently treated women as a group distinct from but no less valuable than men. In their view, women's specific difference and strength is their role as wives and mothers, especially in the recent past, in response to the feminist challenge, the DC and CIF have addressed women's issues from a perspective that assumes that women are not permitted to fulfill the roles from which they derive their strength and contribute most to the nation. For example, while they strongly oppose liberalizing the abortion laws, CIF and the DC assert that women face severe economic obstacles to raising healthy children and that women cannot function as good mothers when the economy forces them to work. The CIF and the DC are part of the "women's movement" (*movimento femminile*), which seeks to confirm and maintain woman's traditional roles —in contrast to the "feminist movement" (*movimento femminista*) which challenges those roles.

The DC's position on *la questione femminile* is based on respect for woman's role as wife and mother; the focus is on the home and the family. The family is no longer presented as the mainstay of patriarchy and social authority, but rather as "an organization [for providing] services, the satisfaction of needs, a place of consumption, and a compensatory refuge from the outside world."[8] The woman is seen as the focal point of the connection between personal life and the public sphere.[9] Maura Vagli argues that the DC has *two* positions on the question of Italian women, revealed in its legislative behavior. One derives from the DC's attempt to renew itself as a party and to appeal to more progressive sources of support; this position is more liberal and emphasizes concrete issues and generally noncontroversial measures, such as reforms designed to improve the lot of Italian

tion, pp. 192-195; Weber, *Il voto della donna*, pp. 13-20; and Yasmine Ergas, "1968-69, Feminism and the Italian Party System," pp. 7-10 (Paper presented at the American Political Science Association meetings, Washington, D.C., 1979). For a discussion of UDI, see Galli and Prandi, *Patterns of Political Participation*, pp. 196-199; Weber, *Il voto della donna*, pp. 20-25; Ergas, "1968-69, Feminism," pp. 7-10; Giulietta Ascoli, "L'UDI tra emancipazione e liberazione (1943-1964)" [UDI between emancipation and liberation, 1943-1964], in *Problemi del Socialismo*, vol. 18, no. 4 (1976), pp. 109-159; and Karen Beckwith, "Female Communist Deputies to the Italian Parliament: A Thirty-Year Retrospective" (Paper presented at the Conference for Europeanists, Washington, D.C., 1979), pp. 14-16.

[8] Maura Vagli, "La DC tra tradizione e novità [The DC between tradition and innovation], *Donne e politica*, vol. 8, nos. 39-40 (1977), p. 37.

[9] See Flaminio Piccoli, "La famiglia per una società personalistica" [The family, for a more human society] (Speech given at the Conference "Una politica per la famiglia," organized by the DC Women's Movement, Rome, July 2-4, 1967).

women at work.[10] The second position is part of the DC's attempt to maintain its support among more conservative Catholics. It surfaces in response to issues of sexuality and reproduction—in the DC's stands on contraception, divorce, and abortion. Both these positions see the Italian woman pressed by the demands and needs of the family, on the one hand, and those of society on the other.

This attempt to divide women's issues into two realms is a response to the pressures upon the DC to maintain a conservative Catholic support base while attracting the more liberal support group that has become increasingly necessary for electoral success. Gioia Longo di Cristofaro argues that despite its new approaches to women's issues, the DC has always seen the question of women in Italian society only in the context of the family and only as a part of that larger issue. As a result, women's unique political and social status becomes "diluted" and obscured by the DC's more "general" discussion of family and society.[11]

The DC does not call for equal participation of men and women in political life; rather it recognizes the joint humanity of women and men and speaks of an "equality" which benefits society and makes women able to deal with their own special problems. It has criticized other parties for speaking of "emancipation for women only, suggesting a break with human values which are also Christian values."[12] In addition, the DC is concerned that women retain the active social roles that give them strength: motherhood and the education of young children.

Through CIF, the DC stresses the "importance of women but [also] a renewal of the family." With its Catholic orientation, the organization opposes the feminist position on issues like abortion.

---

10 See Grazia Leonardi, "Democristiane al convegno" [Christian Democratic women in convention], *Donne e politica*, vol. 8, no. 41 (July-August 1977), p. 44, for a discussion of the women's issues emphasized by the DC.

11 Gioia Longo di Cristofaro, "Associazionismo cattolico" [Catholic associationism], *Donne e politica*, vol. 8, nos. 39-40 (March-June 1977), p. 32. For an analysis of the DC's position on women, see the issue of *Donne e politica*, "Chiesa, mondo cattolico, DC" [The Church, the Catholic world, and the DC], vol. 8, nos. 39-40 (March-June, 1977).

12 "I punti d'approdo delle donne democristiane" [Connection points for Christian Democratic women], interview with Maria Eletta Martini, DC deputy to Parliament, *Rinascita*, no. 47, December 2, 1977, p. 23. See M. Teresa Paggi, interview with Umberto Betti of the Christian Association of Italian Workers (ACLI), "Il mondo cattolico e i problemi della famiglia, il referendum, il divorzio, la condizione della donna, il movimento operaio come alternative culturale" [The Catholic world and problems of the family, the referendum, divorce, the condition of women, the workers' movement as cultural alternatives], *Rosa*, no. 1 [1973], pp. 55-60.

Mainly it underlines the equal dignity of housework and work done outside the home.[13] The other women's organization associated with the DC is the Women's Movement of the Christian Democrats (Il Movimento Femminile della DC). While CIF is formally autonomous, the DC Women's Movement is an internal party organization,

> a specialized movement within the party, which is integrated into all [the party's] parts, with fixed responsibilities . . . in particular, the specific assignment of explaining [in terms that do not challenge the party's unity or principles], the exigencies and problems of the woman's world, contributing in this way to the elaboration of the party's political line. The democratic articulation of the Movimento Femminile is organically connected with all party structures. . . .[14]

The Movimento Femminile was established in 1946 at the DC's first national convention. Its responsibilities included dealing with "ideological problems, the historical rapport between the Catholic world and Italian society, and finally, problems of women's emancipation."[15] The creation of separate women's groups within the party was fought by some party members, such as Elisabetta Conci, later a DC deputy to the Chamber, who believed that women should participate in the party through the same channels as men. The Movimento Femminile has been less than successful in addressing women's issues; since its founding, it has suffered from low membership, organizational problems, and the limitations placed upon it by its role as a party organization.[16]

Neither the DC nor the PCI allies itself with feminism or the feminist movement. Both major parties see the issue of woman's role as part of a larger vision of society and social change. Nevertheless, the PCI has always been more responsive than the DC to the feminist movement, and in periods when the latter has been strong, the PCI has addressed itself to issues like economic parity, political representation, divorce, and abortion. This was the case during the

[13] See Costanza Fanelli, "In coda al partito-papà" [In line with the father-party], *Noi donne*, no. 21, May 23, 1976, p. 19.

[14] *Regolamento del Movimento Femminile: Democrazia Cristiana* [Regulations of the Women's Movement: Christian Democracy], n.p., n.d., Title I. These rules were approved by the National Convention of Provincial Delegates of the DC Women's Movement in Rome, September 22-24, 1972, and ratified by the DC National Council on February 9, 1973.

[15] "Il movimento femminile della DC" [The Women's Movement of the DC], in Gianfranco Poggi, ed., *L'Organizzazione partitica del PCI e della DC* [The party organization of the PCI and the DC] (Bologna: Il Mulino, 1968), p. 418.

[16] See "Il movimento femminile della DC," pp. 417-424.

immediate postwar period (roughly 1945–1950), when the influence of female partisans was strong within the PCI, especially in its parliamentary representation, and it has been so again during the last five to ten years, with the advent of an autonomous radical feminist movement. The PCI's parliamentary representation both in 1976 and 1979 shows the electoral response of the party to feminist demands for representation. The PCI's "theses" published before the fifteenth party congress deal specifically with the party's need to develop female leadership within the party organization and the party in Parliament.

Between 1950 and 1972 the PCI was not particularly concerned with the issue of women as a progressive social force outside their traditional roles. Despite its Marxist analysis of society, the PCI viewed women as the DC did: as a source of comfort to workers at home, and as a source of inspiration for the rising generations who would fill the Communist ranks—that is, as wives and mothers. According to Spano and Camarlinghi, Italian women were to play a role in the "Italian road to socialism" after 1945: "Togliatti strongly encouraged Communist women to consider the questions of the family, of childhood, and other such issues, in a spirit of national and social solidarity, including . . . women with strong religious beliefs."[17]

During this period, there was no strong autonomous feminist movement in Italy forcing the PCI to respond to women as a non-traditional social force; moreover, the PCI was embroiled in other issues which engaged its energies, especially those arising from Soviet involvement in Hungary and Czechoslovakia.[18]

The PCI's position on women shifted slightly in the early 1970s, when the current phase of the Italian feminist movement was in its initial stages of development. In 1972 in discussions preceding the thirteenth party congress, the question of how to build a popular democratic front to solve the problems of Italian society opened up an opportunity to include women as a social force. Women could be integrated into the "historic compromise." Aida Tiso, analyzing the relationship between the PCI and the feminist movement in the 1970s, argues that the PCI saw women as a cross-class group that could be mobilized in support of the party. "It is part of the strategy of the historic compromise," she wrote,

> to recognize . . . the strongly unifying nature of the woman
> question: unifying because it interests women of all social

[17] Spano and Camarlinghi, *La questione femminile*, pp. 139-140.
[18] See Beckwith, "Female Communist Deputies," pp. 16-17; and Galli and Prandi, *Patterns of Political Participation*, pp. 85-90.

classes, unifying because the solution depends upon large movements of emancipation and liberation, unifying finally because only with the agreement of the democratic parties is it possible to arrive at a solution, aspects of which concern the condition of women.[19]

The PCI began to promote itself as the party best equipped to deal with women's issues, such as family rights, day care provision, and equality in employment, particularly equal pay.

At the fourteenth party congress, Berlinguer publicly acknowledged that the PCI had been inattentive to feminist issues and recognized the role of women within the party in bringing their importance to the fore. "A correction is being made in our work," he said.

Progress you have undoubtedly made, thanks to the commitment, the spirit of initiative, of our female comrades. But we are still far from having organically incorporated the woman question in the daily activities of the whole party, in our work programs, and in our issues for study.[20]

At the fifteenth party congress, held in March 1979, the PCI gave greater evidence of its attention to women's issues, including more radical or explicitly feminist issues, such as increased representation of women in leadership positions in the party and in party parliamentary delegations,[21] increased efforts at strengthening party ties with social movements such as the autonomous feminist movement,[22] and issues of sexuality and male-female relationships.[23]

In an interview with Carla Ravaioli, Ugo Pecchioli, a member of the PCI Central Committee and Directorate and a senator since 1972, admitted that the feminist movement had been responsible for persuading the PCI to adopt some feminist positions and show concern for the status of women within the party. He argued that the party should encourage and help sustain social movements like feminism. "The party itself," he said, "assumes the responsibility of constructing or contributing to the construction of a movement, an organization, even when the conditions for doing so are only partially present. Communist women are not separate; they are a component of the

---

[19] Aida Tiso, *I comunisti e la questione femminile* [The Communists and the woman question] (Rome: Editori Riuniti, 1976), p. 134.

[20] Tiso, *I comunisti*, p. 140.

[21] "La discussione al congresso" [The discussion at the (party) congress], *Rinascita*, no. 17, May 4, 1979, p. 53.

[22] See Yasmine Ergas, "Movimento femminista e 'terza via'" [The feminist movement and the "third way"], *Rinascita*, March 3, 1979.

[23] "La discussione al congresso," p. 53.

party. . . ."[24] Pecchioli noted, however, that the PCI had been most active on women's issues *in response* to feminist pressure—when women had initiated the political debate.

That the feminist movement has had an impact upon the PCI cannot be disputed. The 1979 theses give ample evidence of the increase in the party's concern with women's roles in the party, in Italian society, and in personal and social life.[25] The theses mention sexuality and personal relations between men and women as a point of party concern: "The workers' movement must grow in its capacity to struggle for a rapport between men and women, founded on respect and equality; for a family based on common responsibility; for a society which, in its diverse manifestations, confronts the major problems of the masses of women."[26] Thesis 81 concerns the women's movement as a necessary partner in a mass movement built with the PCI's help: "It is evident that in order to win the liberation of women [who] are in a state of subjection and inferiority, a democratic movement is necessary, one which has the strength to bring not only economic and social change, but civil, cultural, and behavioral change as well."[27] The PCI now affirmed the

> commitment of the workers' movement to a family which confronts, within the family and in society, the issues of housework and "the refusal of women to be considered sex objects"; signaling our own political action, [which is] gathering strength from the new subjectivity of the masses of women, and the transformation of the relationship, accepted as given until now, between family and society and between male and female roles.[28]

Finally, the party admitted that the woman question was not "automatically resolvable by overcoming class conflict."[29]

Women have also won some attention from the minor political parties in Italy, notably the recently revived Radical Party (PR), whose

[24] Carla Ravaioli, "Esser donna nel PCI" [To be a woman in the PCI], interview with Ugo Pecchioli in *La questione femminile: intervista col PCI* [The woman question: Interview with the PCI] (Milan: Bompiani, 1977), p. 157.

[25] See Magda Negri, "La rivoluzione più lunga e la 'terza via'" [The longest revolution and the "third way"], pp. 48-49; Angela Bottari, "Le donne e il partito: una riflessione" [Women and the party: A reflection], p. 51; "La discussione al congresso," p. 53; and Maura Vagli, "La questione femminile non è più un capitolo a parte" [The woman question is no longer a separate chapter], pp. 50-51, all in a special edition on women of *Rinascita*, no. 17, May 4, 1979.

[26] "La discussione al congresso," p. 53.

[27] Ibid.

[28] Negri, "La rivoluzione più lunga," p. 50.

[29] Bottari, "Le donne e il partito," p. 51.

alliance with the Women's Liberation Movement in forming electoral party lists has been but one sign of the party's dedication to feminism.[30] The Socialist party, despite its struggle for civil legitimation of divorce and its support for a liberalized abortion law, has been less successful in attracting feminist support and more ambivalent about the role of women in Italian society. This lack of receptivity to feminism on the part of a minor political party whose strength comes from a predominantly socialist subculture may be part of a more general failure to incorporate social movements into the party's ideology, programs, and electoral support.[31]

The party of Proletarian Democracy (DP) is as explicitly committed to a feminist party line as the Radicals, although each party approaches the issue from its own political perspective. The DP is a Marxist coalition of the Manifesto group, the Democratic party of Proletarian Unity (PDUP), and Workers Vanguard (AO), all of which have a history of involvement in a variety of social movements, particularly those of the late 1960s.[32] DP's perspective accommodates many of the feminists' criticisms of the traditional Marxist analysis of the woman question, which ignores the economic value of housework and assumes that a socialist revolution will resolve oppression stemming from patriarchy.[33] The DP integrates feminist issues more fundamentally into its party line than any other political party, and it is the only political party with a feminist commitment which has seemingly resolved the problem of double militancy.[34] Like many

[30] For a history of the Radical party, see Massimo Teodori, Piero Ignazi, and Angelo Panebianco, I nuovi radicali [The new radicals] (Milan: Mondadori, 1977), especially pp. 106-111 for a discussion of the party's alliance with the "movimento di liberazione della donna."

[31] See Gianfranco Pasquino, "The Italian Socialist Party: An Irreversible Decline?" in Howard R. Penniman, ed., Italy at the Polls: The Parliamentary Elections of 1976 (Washington, D.C.: American Enterprise Institute, 1977), pp. 196-200.

[32] The PDUP ran candidates in the 1976 elections with Workers Vanguard under the DP label, but ran their own candidates on PDUP lists in the 1979 elections, where they were less successful. It is worth noting that Maria Macciochi, a PCI member since the 1940s who split with the party to join the Manifesto group, was elected in 1979 as a Radical party deputy. See Robert Leonardi, "The Smaller Parties in the 1976 Italian Elections," in Penniman, ed., Italy at the Polls, 1976, pp. 248-249.

[33] For a summary of this criticism, see Mariarosa dalla Costa, Women and the Subversion of the Community (London: Falling Wall Press, 1972).

[34] "Double militancy" (doppio militanza) refers to political activism in more than one organization—for example, a political party and an independent feminist organization. The requirements and ideologies of such organizations sometimes conflict, producing problems of conscience and loyalty for those who are militant in more than one. The joint memberships in the PSI and PR (before the PR ran electoral lists of its own in 1976) are another example of double militancy. For a discussion of the PSI and PR joint memberships, see Leonardi, "The Smaller Parties," p. 232.

other parties, it accommodates women's sections; unlike the others, the DP actually encourages them, as enabling the party to reach a firm understanding of issues important to women. These sections give women a private setting in which to come to grips with the issues that concern them; later, they can present the results of their discussion to the larger membership. The DP's relationship with the Women's Liberation Movement-Autonomous (Movimento per la Liberazione della Donna-Autonoma), which is independent of the party, gives it strong ties to the nonparty feminist movement—of a kind the PSI tried and failed to develop, to its electoral detriment. In response to a question concerning the usefulness of the DP's relationship with the autonomous feminist movement, Luciana Castellina, a member of the National Directorate and spokesperson for the majority of feminists associated with the party, replied: "The sisters within our party are integrated into all the work collectives and they reject the women's committee ghetto. But they have also necessarily retained some indispensable autonomy—the coordination of feminist comrades—in a period in which, within the party, a clear battle to impose feminist demands is still necessary."[35] The DP's commitment to feminism stems in part from the influence of the strongly feminist PDUP, which claims as one of its major objectives

> the transcendence or explosion of the male-female contra-
> diction (above all, through the work of small consciousness-
> raising groups), the solution of the problem of sexuality and
> the reappropriation of one's own body, . . . the creation of
> women's maternity clinics, and the free choice to abort, at
> public expense, in safe public facilities controlled by
> women.[36]

At the PDUP's first national congress, two motions concerning women were discussed: (1) the establishment of complete autonomy for feminists within the party (which was approved by a large majority) and (2) the necessity of an organizational structure that would permit the most extensive possible internal debate, first among women and then throughout the party.[37]

The Liberal party (PLI) as a "lay" or "anticlerical" party, may allow women some influence upon its policies.[38] By virtue of its

---

[35] "PDUP: una linea delle donne" [PDUP: a women's line], Noi donne, no. 7, November 15, 1976, p. 14.

[36] Ibid., pp. 13-14.

[37] Ibid., p. 13. The DP and the PR explicitly refer to feminism and the feminist movement, while the PCI prefers discussing "issues of concern to women" (la questione femminile) and avoids the term "feminist."

[38] For a description of the PLI, see Leonardi, "The Smaller Parties," pp. 238-241, and chapter 6 in this volume.

position on the separation of church and state, the PLI supported the liberalized divorce legislation of 1970 and opposed its repeal by referendum in 1974. Among the issues discussed at the PLI National Council's meetings in Rome in 1976 were family rights, abortion, and contraception legislation. The PLI Women's Advisory Board (Consulta Femminile) has worked in support of feminist positions within the party; like the comparable bodies in other parties, it stepped up its activity with the advent of the Italian feminist movement. One of its achievements was to insist that the PLI parliamentary group amend the pending abortion legislation to include provisions for contraception and sex education.[39] The Women's Advisory Board also called for the establishment of a cabinet-level ministry to deal with the serious problems of women, youth, the elderly, family rights and family law, children's rights, and economic recognition and security for housewives.

At the 1976 PLI national congress in Naples, the party membership undertook (with what measure of seriousness is unclear) an effort at self-criticism on the issue of women in Italian society. The discussion focused on internal party behavior, such as the custom within the women's advisory boards of men's being the primary initiators of policy. The limited attention given to women's issues was, as in other parties, a response to the Italian feminist movement and to changed attitudes among the mass of Italian women in regard to their role in Italian society.

Luciana Sensini, a member of the PLI National Council, summarized the position of the Women's Advisory Board and the National Council: "Today reality is changed—women are maturing. . . . It is true that the woman question must be addressed."[40] Beyond a recognition of changes in the role of Italian women, however, there seems to be little change within the party, although the new activism of the Women's Advisory Board may presage some future confrontation with the PLI.

The Social Democrats (PSDI), in their changing and confusing political strategies of the past decade,[41] have given little attention to, and have no particular party perspective on, women's issues and the women's movement, especially by comparison with the other minor parties in Italy (the MSI excepted). The issues that have plagued

[39] "PLI: le richieste della Consulta Femminile" [PLI: Demands of the Women's Advisory Board], *Noi donne*, November 15, 1976, p. 14.

[40] "Alle donne solo baciamani" [For women, nothing but handkissing], *Noi donne*, no. 17, April 25, 1976, p. 13.

[41] For a discussion of recent PSDI history, see Leonardi, "The Smaller Parties," pp. 243–246.

other political parties, causing considerable internal debate, if not policy change, have been given short shrift by the PSDI. The response of the PSDI to demands from its women's committees in recent years has been to ridicule its "feminist" membership and to respond negatively to proposals for change within the party. For example, the party leadership refused to consider requests for a change in the status of the party's women's committees from their consulting role to a voting role. This was described by one observer as "a modest enough claim in substance, but not understood by the men in the party."[42] Pietro Longo, a PSDI deputy, argued that the party's failure to respond was the result of the proposal's apparent lack of support among the party's female membership. Franca Orsello, meanwhile, has suggested that, in essence, feminists haven't wasted their time in the PSDI because other parties of similar political perspective are more open to a consideration of women's issues.[43]

Women's Elite Political Participation

While the PCI, DC, and PR are clearly the parties that draw mass support from women, more complex patterns of participation emerge at the elite level, particularly in the various parties' delegations to Parliament.[44] Maurice Duverger has argued that parties of the left are more likely to support women as parliamentary candidates than are conservative or confessional parties;[45] while this is true of the two major political parties in Italy, it is not consistently true across the minor parties.

The variation or lack of variation in the treatment of women as a specific group by the PCI and the DC has been reflected in their delegations to the Chamber of Deputies (see table 9–1). The DC has always had women representing it in the Chamber; the number has been more or less constant and seems to be independent of the success of the party as a whole (see table 9–2). Despite the fact that the DC has had some well-known women deputies, it still has a considerable number of female deputies serving for the first time (see table 9–3). An examination of the complete party lists for the 1976 and 1979 elections reveals that the DC does not place women randomly on

[42] "Le donne: le scegliamo noi" [Women: we choose them ourselves], *Noi donne*, no. 13, March 28, 1976, p. 20.

[43] Ibid., p. 20.

[44] Because of the differences in electoral laws regulating the Chamber of Deputies and the Senate, this chapter is concerned with the election to the Chamber only.

[45] Maurice Duverger, *The Political Role of Women* (Paris: UNESCO, 1956), p. 82.

TABLE 9-1

Female Deputies, by Party, 1946–1979

Party	Constituent Assembly, 1946		1948		1953		1958		1963		1968		1972		1976		1979	
	No.	%	No.	%	No.	%	No.	%	No.	%	No.	%	No.	%	No.	%	No.	%
PCI	9	8.7	19	14.5	16	11.2	10	7.1	13	7.8	8	4.7	16	9.1	37	16.7	36	18.8
DC	9	4.3	16	5.2	11	4.2	10	3.7	11	4.2	8	3.0	7	2.6	9	3.4	9	3.4
PSI	2	1.7	2	3.8	4	5.3	2	2.4	2	2.3	1[a]	1.1	1	1.6	1	1.8	1	1.6
PR	—	—	—	—	—	—	—	—	—	—	—	—	—	—	2	50.0	5	27.8
PDUP	—	—	—	—	—	—	—	—	—	—	—	—	—	—	1[b]	16.7	1	16.7
PRI	0	—	0	—	0	—	0	—	0	—	0	—	0	—	1	7.1	1	6.7
MSI	1[c]	3.1	0	—	0	—	0	—	1	3.7	0	—	0	—	1	2.9	0[d]	—
Chamber	21	3.8	39[e]	6.8	33[f]	5.6	22	3.7	27	4.3	17	2.7	24	3.8	52	8.3	54[g]	8.6

Dash (—): Not applicable.

[a] In 1968 the PSI and PSDI presented joint lists.

[b] PDUP and Avanguardia Operaia presented joint lists as Democrazia Proletaria in 1976.

[c] One woman elected on a Uomo Qualunque (Everyman) party list. Uomo Qualunque was the first postwar neo-Fascist political party, a precursor of the MSI.

[d] Includes Democrazia Nazionale-Costituente di Destra, which ran candidates for the first time in 1979.

[e] Includes two women elected on minor party lists who were part of the "mixed" parliamentary group.

[f] Includes two women elected on Monarchist party lists.

[g] Includes Aurelia Benco Gruber, elected from Trieste on the Associazione per la zona franca integrale a Trieste e nella sua provincia (Association for a free zone in Trieste and its province).

SOURCE: Calculated from I Deputati e Senatori del Parlamento Repubblicano [Deputies and senators of the republican Parliament], 1948-1979, and I 556 Deputati alla Costituente [The 556 delegates to the Constituent Assembly], both published in Rome by La Navicella, 1946-1979; and "Il PCI ha elettato più donne" [The PCI has elected more women], L'Unità, June 24, 1979.

TABLE 9–2

STRENGTH OF WOMEN IN PARTY GROUPS AND OF PARTY GROUPS IN CHAMBER, 1946–1979
(percent)

Party	Constituent Assembly, 1946	1948	1953	1958	1963	1968	1972	1976	1979
PCI									
Women in party group	8.7	14.5	11.2	7.1	7.8	4.7	9.1	16.7	18.8
Party group in Chamber	18.7	22.8	24.2	23.5	26.3	28.1	27.8	35.2	30.4
DC									
Women in party group	4.3	5.2	4.2	3.7	4.2	3.0	2.6	3.4	3.4
Party group in Chamber	37.2	53.3	44.4	45.8	41.3	42.1	42.3	41.6	38.3
PSI									
Women in party group	1.7	3.8	5.3	2.4	2.3	1.1[a]	1.6	1.8	1.6
Party group in Chamber	20.7	9.1	12.7	14.1	13.9	14.4	9.7	9.0	9.8
PR									
Women in party group	—	—	—	—	—	—	—	50.0	27.8
Party group in Chamber	—	—	—	—	—	—	—	1.1	3.4

Dash (—): Not applicable.

[a] In 1968, the PSI and PSDI presented joint lists.

SOURCE: Calculated from *I Deputati e Senatori, 1949–1976; I 556 Deputati alla Costituente;* and *L'Unità,* June 24, 1979.

TABLE 9–3
Newly Elected Female Deputies, by Party, 1948–1979

Party	1948 No.	%	1953 No.	%	1958 No.	%	1963 No.	%	1968 No.	%	1972 No.	%	1976 No.	%	1979 No.	%
PCI	13	68	3	19	0	—	7	54	1	13	13	81	27	73	8	25
DC	7	44	4	36	1	10	3	27	2	25	2	29	5	56	4	44
PSI	2	67	3	75	1	50	1	50	0	—	1	100	0	—	0	—
PR	0	—	0	—	0	—	0	—	0	—	0	—	0	—	3	60

Dash (—): Not applicable.

NOTE: The percentage base is the party's total female contingent. Thus, 68 percent of the PCI's women deputies elected in 1948 were serving in the Chamber for the first time.

SOURCE: Calculated from *I Deputati e Senatori, 1948-1976; I 556 Deputati alla Costituente*; and *L'Unità*, June 24, 1979, p. 2.

TABLE 9–4

NUMBER OF WOMEN CANDIDATES AND PERCENT ELECTED,
BY PARTY, 1976–1979

Party	Number of Districts where Women Nominated		Number of Women Candidates[a]		Percent of Women Candidates Elected	
	1976	1979[b]	1976	1979	1976	1979
DC	22	27	39	46	23.1	19.6
PCI	29	31	155	115	23.9	31.3
PSI	27	28	69	87	1.4	1.1
PR	31[c]	30	309	204	0.6	2.5
PDUP[d]	29	26	86	96	1.2	1.0
MSI	23	25[e]	43	48	2.3	0

[a] Women nominated on more than one list are counted more than once.

[b] No women were nominated by any party in the thirty-first electoral district, where only the DC, PRI and MSI presented lists.

[c] The PR ran lists in only thirty-one districts. All of the other parties mentioned ran lists in all thirty-two districts.

[d] PDUP and Avanguardia Operaia presented joint lists as Democrazia Proletaria in 1976.

[e] The Democrazia Nazionale-Costituente di Destra nominated women in twenty-seven districts, none of whom were elected.

SOURCE: *I Deputati e Senatori*, 1976 and 1979.

these lists, but rather places those it wants to win in advantageous positions[46] and the remainder in positions where clearly they cannot win seats. The distribution, therefore, of women candidates on DC lists is bimodal—a very few near the top of the lists and the remainder at the bottom. It should be noted that the DC has always nominated and elected female candidates to Parliament, although it has tended to run more all-male lists than the other major parties. In 1976, there were no women on the DC lists in ten of the thirty-two districts where the party ran (see table 9–4).

The PCI has the best record for electing female deputies; it has always elected more women to the Chamber than any other party and in the last three elections—1972, 1976, and 1979—has succeeded in electing more women to Parliament than all the other parties combined. In 1979, the PCI nominated women in all of the thirty-one districts where it ran lists. However, the fate of female PCI deputies in

[46] For example, Tina Anselmi headed her party list in 1976.

Parliament has not been as consistent over the years as the fate of their DC counterparts. The numbers and percentages of female PCI deputies declined considerably throughout the late 1950s and the 1960s, concurrently with the PCI's waning attention to women as a social force. In addition, the PCI's female deputies in the past have consisted of well-known party members, the most dramatic example of whom is Leonilde Iotti, the first woman elected president of the Chamber of Deputies (in 1979).[47] It was not until 1976 that a large number of relatively unknown women were elected to represent the PCI in the Chamber; in 1976 female candidates were distributed more evenly throughout the PCI party lists than they were on DC lists, although there were still fewer women candidates on PCI lists, and therefore fewer women clustered at the top than there were men.

The Radical party has the best percentage representation of women serving in the Chamber in the history of the republic. When the PR first ran, in 1976, it drew up its lists in coordination with the autonomous feminist organization, the "movimento di liberazione della donna," with the purpose of providing perfect sex equality on the party's lists.[48] In 1976, the PR nominated women in all of the electoral districts in which it nominated candidates; for the uninominal seat in the thirty-first district (Aosta), the PR was the only party to nominate a woman. A woman was *capolista* (first on the list) in every district in which the PR competed. The average female percentage on PR lists in 1976 was 50 percent, and the share of women elected was a perfect 50 percent as well.

In 1979, the PR dramatically increased its representation in Parliament, from four to eighteen seats in the Chamber of Deputies and from zero to two seats in the Senate, but the percentage representation of women deputies was cut almost in half. Of the eighteen deputies elected to the Chamber from PR lists, only five were women, two of whom were first elected in 1976.

Duverger's thesis holds when we examine the two major political parties, but only for recent years. The DC, it is worth noting, appointed the first female cabinet minister in the history of the republic,

---

[47] Iotti is an outstanding and influential force in the PCI, the only woman who has served in the Chamber of every republican Government and who, as a member of the Constituent Assembly, was one of the "Seventy-Five" who drafted the constitution. For more on Iotti (sometimes spelled Jotti), see *I Deputati e Senatori del Settimo Parlamento Repubblicano* [The deputies and senators of the seventh republican Parliament] (Rome: La Navicella, 1976); and "Nilde Jotti Presidente," *L'Unità*, June 21, 1979, pp. 1-2.

[48] *Noi donne*, no. 25, June 20, 1976, p. 30. Using the lower case acronym mld is apparently part of the movement's political statement.

when in 1976 Tina Anselmi was named minister of labor—though, of course, the DC has been the only party in a position to appoint cabinet ministers; we may speculate that this might have occurred earlier had a party of the left been able to appoint cabinet ministers. In the Government headed by Francesco Cossiga, formed in August 1979, there were no female ministers, although Anselmi had been included on a list submitted by Filippo Pandolfi when he was attempting to form a Government.[49]

The PR's behavior, if a little uneven, lends credence to Duverger's thesis, since the PR identifies itself as a party of the left. However, when we examine the pattern among the other minor parties, we are presented with some problems. The PSI, as we note in table 9–1, has a poor record of electing female deputies, a record which is independent of its overall electoral success. For example, in 1946 the Socialists elected 115 deputies to the Constituent Assembly, six more than the Communists, the other major party of the left; but only two members of the entire PSI delegation were women. The PSI has never elected more than four female deputies (in 1953) and has generally had a very low level of female representation to the Chamber despite its appeals to feminists and its support for civil divorce legislation and progressive abortion legislation. The PSI has elected only one female deputy to each Parliament since 1968 even though its representation increased in 1979. The PSI clearly does not fit Duverger's hypothesis about leftist parties.

The other confounding political party is the Italian Social Movement-National Right (MSI-DN), which—though explicitly anti-feminist and without the benevolent concern for women that the DC has expressed over the years—has been successful in the past in electing female representatives to Parliament. Its record is embarrassingly close, in this regard, to those of the Socialists and the Republicans and is clearly better than that of the Liberal party, which has never been represented in Parliament by a woman. In 1976, the MSI nominated forty-three women in twenty-three of the thirty-two seats for which it nominated candidates, one of whom was elected. Most of these women were at the bottom of the party lists, but nonetheless they were there.

The Republican party (PRI) has had little success in electing female deputies and little apparent interest in doing so. Its nomination and election of Susanna Agnelli, mayor of Monte Argentario since 1974, are evidence less of its devotion to the cause of women and to increasing its female representation in Parliament than of its success

---

[49] *La Stampa*, July 31, 1979, pp. 1-2.

in attracting a well-known and popular individual to stand for Parliament on a PRI list. Of the fifty-five women nominated by the PRI in 1979, only Susanna Agnelli was listed so that her election was ensured; she was *capolista* in the first electoral district. All other female PRI nominees were placed so far down on party lists that defeat was a foregone conclusion. The PRI nominated women in only twenty-three of the thirty-two districts in which they nominated candidates.

Proletarian Democracy (DP), a minor party to the left of the PCI, offers support for Duverger's assertion. The DP nominated women for eighty-six seats in twenty-nine of the thirty-two districts where it presented lists in 1976. Of the six seats the party won in the Chamber, one was held by a woman, giving the DP a record of electing women second only to the RP and the PCI.

Duverger's thesis is consistent with the record of the major Italian political parties in this decade but not with that of parties like the PSI and the MSI.[50] The two major political parties have always exhibited, to a greater or lesser degree, an interest in women as a specific social force—both parties responding to the initiatives from an autonomous feminist movement, and the DC responding, in addition, to its own social and political doctrines regarding woman's place. To Duverger, we must suggest that support for women candidates, at least, is less related to socialist or conservative ideologies than it is to the pressure an autonomous women's movement can bring to bear upon mass political parties.[51]

[50] The MSI and the DN presented separate lists in 1979.

[51] Jorgen Rasmussen, in a study of women's nomination chances in Great Britain, found that the women's liberation movement had had little impact, writing "The conclusion seems inescapable that Women's Liberation has not penetrated either the British political process in general or individual parties, at least in the sense of expanding opportunity to enter a significant segment of the political elite. Insofar as some gains have been made since the time when women were shut out from the elite entirely, these gains appear to have been made prior to the time that the Women's Movement had attained any prominence." Rasmussen, "Women in British Elections," *Journal of Politics*, vol. 39, no. 3 (November 1977), p. 1052. Rasmussen discovered that women were more likely to be nominated for Parliament by minor parties expected to lose, in part confirming Susan and Martin Tolchin's claim that "women's chances for nomination have increased in what are known as 'throwaway districts,' districts in which the candidate is expected to lose, either because of a strong incumbent, a strong machine, or a combination of both in the opposition." Tolchin and Tolchin, *Clout: Womanpower and Politics* (New York: Capricorn, 1976), p. 68. In contrast, the Italian feminist movement has been responsible for the increase in the number of female deputies nominated and elected by the PCI, the PR, and the DP in 1976 and 1979. It is worth noting that, in terms of women's participation as national legislators, Italy is doing well compared with the United States. Twenty-one women serve in the U.S. House of Representatives (5 percent) and two women serve in the Senate (2 percent). In contrast, in Italy, fifty-four women serve in the Chamber

The Backgrounds of Women Legislators. It has been suggested that frequently women are nominated for and elected to legislative seats not as women, but as representatives of an established political family, usually as wives or widows of powerful party leaders. While it has been more than commonplace for the women elected to the U.S. Congress to begin their careers "over the dead bodies of their husbands,"[52] this seems not to be the case in Italian politics. This does not mean that there are not female deputies with strong connections to important political figures; rather, those women who do have family connections, by and large, appear to have their own independent political strengths. Examples from the left of the political spectrum are Rita Montagnana, Leonilde Iotti, Teresa Noce, and Giuliana Nenni.

Rita Montagnana, a deputy for the PCI to the Constituent Assembly, was the first wife of Palmiro Togliatti, former secretary of the PCI. Before her marriage in 1924, Montagnana was involved in the Socialist women's group The Defense, which she joined in 1914 at the age of nineteen; she joined the PCI in its founding year (1921) and later the same year was a party delegate to the Communist International in Moscow. After her marriage, Montagnana's political life was linked to that of Togliatti, with whom she spent much of the Fascist period in the Soviet Union. Upon her return to Italy in 1944, she was one of the founding members of UDI.

Montagnana's political career follows a pattern typical of many female deputies on the left: (1) initial political involvement through women's organizations or women's sections of a political party, followed by (2) a period of partisan activity under Fascism, either as an organizer, secret supporter, or combatant (for example, Gina Borel-

---

of Deputies (8.6 percent) and eleven women serve in the Senate (3.4 percent). This evidence disputes the popular assumption that "an anti-feminist attitude remains stronger in the Latin than in the Anglo-Saxon and Nordic countries." Duverger, *The Political Role of Women*, p. 9.

52 The first woman elected to the United States Senate who did not fill the vacant seat of her husband was Nancy Landon Kassebaum, a Republican who became the junior senator from Kansas in 1978. Kassebaum's political career was not hurt, however, by the attention given to the fact that she is the daughter of Alfred Landon, 1936 Republican presidential nominee. Kassebaum campaigned using her maiden as well as her married name (she is divorced), making the political connection to her father clear. The first woman elected to the U.S. Senate without benefit of association with a male relative's previous political experience was Republican Paula Hawkins of Florida, in 1980. Diane Kincaid argues that the women who fill the vacant legislative seats of their husbands are not politically inexperienced, but this still leaves to be explained the fact that only one woman has succeeded in being elected to her first Senate term without such family ties. Kincaid, "Over His Dead Body: Positive Perspectives on Widows in the U.S. Congress," *Western Political Quarterly*, vol. 31, no. 1 (March 1978), pp. 96-104.

lini), followed by (3) activism in founding UDI, and culminating in (4) a seat in Parliament. Montagnana's political involvement preceded her marriage, and her election to the Constituent Assembly, while probably unhindered by her connection to Togliatti, can hardly be interpreted as a favor given by the PCI to a political novice.[53]

Teresa Noce, wife of the former secretary of the PCI Luigi Longo, is another example of a deputy whose political connection to a prominent politician was preceded by an independent political career. Noce is unusual in two respects: (1) almost all of her political activity concerned trade unions and the workers' movement, and (2) her political activities began at the age of eleven, when she participated in her first strike; she had already been working as a seamstress and laundress for a year.

Noce's political record reads like a history of the PCI itself: active in the workers' occupations of the factories in Turin in 1920, a founding member of the PCI in 1921, an editor of L'Unità and La Risaia, and a contributor to Grido del Popolo and Ordine Nuovo. During the Fascist period, she participated in the anti-Fascist struggles in Spain, was arrested numerous times, and was twice incarcerated in concentration camps. In 1941, she escaped from the second camp and returned to Italy and active involvement in the resistance. She was long a member of the Central Committee and the Directorate of the PCI and served in the Italian Parliament from 1946 to 1953.[54] This activity and success were independent of Noce's marital status. One of her hardest political struggles was for her nomination as national

[53] Montagnana ran in the thirteenth electoral district in 1946 as "Rita Montagnana." See I 556 Deputati alla Costituente [The 556 delegates to the Constituent (Assembly)] (Rome: La Navicella, 1946), p. 600. In his 1968 study of Italian deputies, Samuel Barnes finds that those on the left joined a political party by age twenty-one and were influenced by "their reaction to fascism, the resistance, and the promise of a bright future." Barnes, Representation in Italy (Chicago: University of Chicago Press, 1977), p. 137. Barnes also suggests that "none of the parties had impressive numbers of deputies with experience in women's organizations" (p. 141). However, none of the parties have impressive numbers of female deputies to begin with (we might expect female deputies to be more interested and active in women's organizations); within the female elite, especially among female deputies of the left, background experience with a women's organization is the norm.

[54] Noce was reelected to Parliament as a deputy in 1948, with 73,286 preference votes. She ran in the Parma-Modena district and was second on the party list. She ran as "Teresa Noce Longo." Gina Borellini was third on the same list; Leonilde Iotti was seventh. See I Deputati e Senatori del Primo Parlamento Repubblicano [Deputies and senators of the first republican Parliament] (Rome: La Navicella, 1948), and "Protagoniste femminili del primo novecento" [Heroines of the early twentieth century], Problemi del Socialismo, vol. 17, no. 4 (1976), pp. 254-255.

secretary of the Textile Workers' Union (FIOT); Noce claimed that the opposition to her (eventually successful) nomination was the result of the PCI's policy of returning *tutte a casa* (all women to the home) after World War II.[55]

Leonilde Iotti, like Montagnana, had a political record that preceded her involvement with Togliatti. She was a member of the Constituent Assembly and one of the "Seventy-Five" who drafted the Italian constitution. The only female member of the Chamber who has served in every Parliament, she has been *capolista* for the PCI in the Parma-Modena district since 1968.[56] Since 1953, she has been a member of the Secretariat of UDI; she has been a member of the PCI Central Committee since 1956 and a member of the PCI Directorate since 1962,[57] as well as director of the PCI Central Women's Section since 1961. In 1972, Iotti was elected vice-president of the Chamber of Deputies, and in 1979 she became the first woman to serve as president of the Chamber. Like many other female deputies on the left, she has participated in primarily female organizations such as UDI.

Giuliana Nenni comes closest to fitting the image many have of female representatives in the United States. She is the daughter of Pietro Nenni, former secretary of the PSI. Giuliana Nenni was elected as a Socialist deputy to the first republican Parliament in 1948[58] and

---

[55] See Ravaioli, "Esser donna nel PCI," p. 155.

[56] Iotti's electoral success is remarkable for a woman and for a PCI deputy, since the PCI's informal policy is to maintain a one-third turnover of its deputies in every Parliament. See Douglas Wertman, "The Italian Electoral Process: The Elections of June 1976," in Penniman, ed., *Italy at the Polls, 1976*, p. 65. However, Iotti's victories have not been of constant magnitude. Elected to the Constituent Assembly from the Parma-Modena district with 15,936 preference votes, she won increasing numbers of preference votes as her name was moved up on subsequent party lists. She was listed seventh in 1948, when she won 51,340 preference votes; fourth in 1953, when she won 33,480 preference votes; and second in 1958 when she won 49,937. In 1963, Iotti was ranked eleventh on the party list in the Bologna district and was the last elected before total party votes were used to assign the remaining seats; she received 19,969 preference votes. In 1968, she was returned to the top of the list in the Parma district, winning 47,406 preference votes. She has headed the list since then, winning 51,203 preference votes in 1972 and 55,282 in 1976. Iotti's drop in party ranking and in preference votes occurred at a time when women's issues were not a PCI priority. See *I Deputati e Senatori del Parlamento Repubblicano, 1948-1976* (Rome: La Navicella).

[57] Iotti was one of three women in the thirty-two-member PCI Directorate chosen in 1979. The other two were Adriana Seroni and Miliana Marzoli. "I nuovi organismi dirigenti del PCI" [The new directive organs of the PCI], *L'Unità*, July 12, 1979, p. 1.

[58] Nenni ran on a joint PSI-PCI list, the Popular Democratic Front for Freedom, Peace, and Work, in the Bologna district. She was ranked ninth and won

reelected from the Bologna district in 1953 with 13,086 preference votes. She was second on the party list. By the time of her first election, Nenni had a credible political record, although her experiences were influenced by her father's activities as head of the PSI. The Nenni family was exiled in France during most of the Fascist period, when Giuliana Nenni became politically active,[59] joining the PSI in 1934. In 1945, after her return to Italy, Nenni was active in UDI and, at the time of her first election, was a member of the Central Committee and Secretariat of UDI.

The other female PCI deputy with an outstanding political background who must be mentioned is Camilla Ravera, long held in esteem by feminists and PCI party members. Ravera joined the PSI in 1918 in response to "the spectacle of the workers' struggle, . . . the 1913 metalworkers strike, 'Red Week,' and the Turinese revolt of August 1917."[60] She was part of the Turin Communist faction within the PSI and was one of the original members of the PCI. Ravera was condemned to fifteen years in prison by the Special Tribune for the Defense of the State in 1930 for her political activities. A member of the Central Committee from 1922 to 1930, she was nominated to the Directorate in 1945. Ravera had been active in the partisan movement in Italy and was one of the founders of UDI. Her political background is congruent with the predominant pattern for leftist female deputies.

Changes Between 1976 and 1979: a Footnote. In general, the 1979 elections to the Chamber show little change in women's representation (see table 9–1). The change for the PCI is related to the slight electoral loss the party experienced overall;[61] nonetheless, the numbers and percentages remained almost constant. The DC likewise remained true to its pattern of electing some women—a few. The real change occurred within the PR. First, the PR more than doubled the number of women representing it in the Chamber; in this sense, the feminists won an important victory, since the PR's female candidates come out of the women's liberation movement. The DC's female deputies are not feminists, although they tend to have a history of activism within

---

40,871 preference votes. She was nominated for the Senate in 1958 and ran second on the PSI list in the Emilia-Romagna district, winning 27,426 preference votes. In 1963, she was returned to the Senate from Emilia-Romagna with 25,195 preference votes, again listed second.

[59] See *I Deputati e Senatori*, 1948-1963.

[60] E. S., "Camilla Ravera: Protagoniste femminili," *Problemi del Socialismo*, vol. 17, no. 4 (1976), pp. 254-255.

[61] *L'Unità*, June 24, 1979, p. 2.

women's organizations and the *movimento femminile*. And PCI female deputies are not uniformly feminists: the "double militancy" issue discourages some feminists from entering Parliament as PCI delegates; and some women, in 1976, were nominated not as women, but as independents who might attract those outside normal party support groups—for example, Catholics.[62] Second, the PR cut the female percentage of its representation in the Chamber by almost half, indicating a retreat from its original commitment to intraparty sex parity.[63] The PR nominated fewer women, in fewer districts in 1979 than in 1976; women were more likely to be placed near the bottom of party lists, and were *capolista* in only fourteen districts, in fewer than half the districts in which the PR ran lists. In 1976, women were *capolista* in every district in which the PR nominated candidates. Had the PR constructed its lists in 1979 the way it did in 1976, there would be more women representing it in the Chamber.

Overall, the 1979 elections seem to have confirmed the positions of the two major political parties in regard to women. At a time when the Italian feminist movement is becoming increasingly institutionalized and perhaps "mainstream,"[64] the PCI stood firm in its commitments to women, and, moreover, declared the intention to initiate a discussion of women's issues at the fifteenth party congress. The DC, likewise, confirmed its previous attitude to electing women to Parliament by continuing to nominate some, to elect fewer, and to regard them as party notables rather than as people representing a uniquely female constituency.

---

[62] Christina Conchiglia Calasso, mayor of Copertino, is an example of a PCI candidate who was not a PCI member; she received an unusually large number of preference votes in 1976.

[63] However, the Radical party did elect one woman to the Senate, maintaining a perfect 50 percent representation of women there.

[64] See Ergas, "1968-69, Feminism," passim.

10

The Mass Media in the Italian Elections of 1979

William E. Porter

In its last issue before election day in 1976, the Italian newsmagazine *Panorama* carried a brutal caricature of Amintore Fanfani, the leader of the conservative wing of the Christian Democrats. He was wearing a Fascist uniform with death's-heads on the epaulets. On the cover of its last issue before election day three years later, *Panorama* carried a photograph of Pope John Paul II superimposed on a feminine face; the cover headline read "Exclusive: The True Story of the Youthful Love of the Pope/Karol and Halina."

On election morning 1976, the front page of the Roman daily *Il Messaggero* shouted in black type "Vote for Change!" with a subhead reading "We must save the nation!" On election morning three years later it read "A Vote for National Unity"; its front-page editorial was a low-key discussion suggesting that the Christian Democrats clearly were going to maintain their plurality, and that this was not altogether bad, but that changes were needed. The editor suggested that a vote for the left might be a good way to go about it.

During the electoral campaign of 1979, the Italian mass media were less partisan, less impassioned, and more "responsible" than during any other campaign in the First Republic's history. They also, of course, were less colorful and interesting; it was a campaign frequently described by journalists as *noioso*, which means "tedious." Most of those making that complaint did not realize that they themselves had made it tedious, whether deliberately or not, in response to a combination of changes, both in their profession and in Italian life, which appeared gravely threatening. The analysis which follows begins with some discussion of those changes and goes on to examine the content of the media during the campaign.

The author would like to thank the Howard R. Marsh Fund of the department of communication, University of Michigan, for its assistance.

The Italian Journalist

Chapter 8 of an earlier volume of this series describes the special circumstances of the practice of journalism in Italy and sets out something of its recent history.[1] In brief, journalism is one of twelve professions given special status under Italian law; admission to it comes through a carefully controlled apprenticeship, and its daily exercise is governed in detail by a national contract which has the force of law. Since the early 1960s Italian journalists have been among the best paid in the world; they also have been among the least read (fewer than one Italian in ten reads a daily newspaper) and the least trusted. Toward the end of the 1960s a reform movement developed within the profession. Essentially it was based upon the premise that ownership, and therefore control, of Italian newspapers and magazines was almost entirely in the hands of industrialists whose pro-Christian Democrat views had not only dominated but also corrupted Italian journalism for many years. This belief was reinforced in the early 1970s (justifiably or not) by a widespread attempt—on the part of Eugenio Cefis, then head of the vast Montedison conglomerate, and, after his failure, of Angelo Rizzoli—to acquire the country's leading newspapers. The reformers, who had assumed the leadership of the journalists' trade union, felt it critical that a greater share of the policy-making role in all media (including the government-controlled broadcasting system) rest in the hands of working journalists, with the *comitato di redazione* (Journalists Committee) as the key organization in each newsroom.

At the time of the 1976 election these committees probably were at the height of their power; certainly the confusion and restlessness in Italian journalism, both as business and as profession, was at its height. Many of the country's most important journalists in 1976 felt that a lessening of the Christian Democrats' dominance was essential. Most of the formal leadership (though not necessarily the majority) of the profession was Socialist. Journalists Committees devoted themselves to exerting the maximum influence in that election.

Predictably, this varied from newsroom to newsroom. In the major media there was a tendency to overplay the Socialists (judging by the party's performance at the polls since the regional elections of 1972). Journalists Committees in the major papers pressed for,

[1] William R. Porter, in *Italy at the Polls: The Parliamentary Elections of 1976*, Howard E. Penniman, ed. (Washington, D.C.: American Enterprise Institute, 1977), pp. 259-286.

and obtained, a rule forbidding the selling of advertising to the neo-Fascist MSI and National Right bloc; newsroom staffs extended the prohibition to include news columns, and there was almost no reporting of far-right activities. During the electoral campaign of 1976, most of the mass publications, both newspapers and magazines, were vigorously committed to the left and anti-Christian Democrat. Their Journalists Committees were active in the anti-Government cause, and their product demonstrated it.

What elements combined to produce, over a period of three years, the more circumspect Italian media of the spring of 1979?

Paolo Murialdi, president of FNSI, the journalists' trade union, feels that the explanation is economic.[2] Most Italian newspapers always have been money-losers; only *Corriere della Sera* (Milan), *La Stampa* (Turin), and *Il Messaggero* (Rome) traditionally had made a profit. During the decade of the 1970s these became heavy losers as well.[3] Almost everybody recognized that fact by the spring of 1979, despite much talk about Italy's "hidden economy." The evidence of nascent disaster was everywhere. The cost of newsprint was rising nearly 25 percent a year; each new contract with the printers and journalists represented new costs. Copy sales and advertising revenue were up only modestly, and increases in per copy costs (the price went from 200 to 250 lire—about twenty-six cents—during the electoral campaign) did not help; such increases, in whatever circumstances, also cut into sales for at least several months. In 1977 total losses for the industry were $154 million; publishers said they were losing almost fifteen cents per copy.

The gravity of the situation was very clear not only to the negotiators representing trade unions in their dealings with publishers, but to all the members of newspaper and magazine staffs. Individual journalists expressed their concern about the viability of their jobs; by the fall of 1979, a member of the Journalists Committee of *Il Giorno*, the national daily in the most severe financial trouble, was expressing to an interviewer his doubts that the Journalists Committee as an institution in Italian journalism would be able to survive at all; owners and publishers would simply wave off any staff initiatives on the grounds they had neither the time nor the money for such things, and staff members could only accept their judgment.

[2] Personal interview, October 24, 1979.
[3] Luigi Guastamacchia, "L'assurda industria dei giornali: più si venda e più si perde?" [The absurd newspaper industry: the more you sell, the more you lose?], *L'Editore*, no. 1 (1978).

Other factors also affected the decline of the aggressive spirit on the part of journalists seeking a larger role in the affairs of their organizations. There was a predictable increment during the 1970s of what might be called bureaucratic fatigue. Essentially the struggle for the right to make important decisions in Italian media has been a confrontation between bureaucracies, a slow process which inevitably erodes the enthusiasm of firebrands. Journalists Committees are, under the contract, elected by the staff; in the early 1970s, activists associated closely with the reform movement were elected in many newsrooms. Party affiliation was important (it was commonly alleged by management that most were Communists), campaigning was lively, and the dialectic energetic. By the end of the decade, few such people sought committee posts. For the most part they were replaced by journalists who were willing to play caretaker. Even political identity meant less.[4]

Some of this inertia probably was related to the fact that a sizable number of the original objectives of the reform movement—in terms of provisions of the contract negotiated biennially between FNSI and the Italian Federation of Newspaper Publishers (FIEG)—had been achieved by the late 1970s; not all, but most. Even more important may have been the rise of a different breed of editor. The *direttore responsabile* is a post comparable, although not entirely equivalent, to that of editor on an American newspaper. Some earlier *responsabili*, particularly on the country's great papers, did not see themselves primarily as professional journalists but as having a wider role. During the 1960s, for example, *Corriere della Sera* was under the direction of Giovanni Spadolini, an academic and historian who eventually went into the Italian Senate and is, at the time of this writing, very much a visible presence in the country's intellectual and cultural life.

Spadolini's replacement in 1972 was Piero Ottone, who had been editor of a paper in Genoa. Ottone was not essentially a political man, nor was he a certified intellectual; he was a highly competent professional who had demonstrated that he knew how to run newspapers. He also proved to be an expert in the management of restive journalists. When he came to the editorship of *Corriere* the mood of the staff was leftist. Ottone not only went with it, but

---

[4] In the fall of 1979, the Journalists Committee of *Il Giorno* of Milan was made up of one Craxi (main-line) Socialist, one member of the Radical party, and one conservative Christian Democrat. The committee they had replaced the previous spring was made up entirely of members of the Communist party. When an interviewer inquired about the significance of the change, one of the members replied "nothing to do with politics. It was purely coincidental—in both cases."

sometimes was ahead of it, speaking out for an even larger staff role in decision making than any the group had yet requested. After the election of 1976, when the reformist fires began to cool, *Corriere* began to move back toward the center—not only in its politics, but also in its tone and even its format. In the opinion of most interested outsiders, Ottone's talent for artful human relations was the most important factor in the change. Ottone resigned in late 1977 and became a high-level corporate officer in the Arnoldo Mondadori organization, a publisher of newspapers (including the influential *La Repubblica*), books, and magazines, and investor in private broadcasting. He was replaced by Franco Di Bella, a longtime second-level *Corriere* news executive with even less visibility outside the business than Ottone.

Alberto Ronchey was replaced as editor of *La Stampa* in May 1973, by Arrigo Levi. Levi had remarkable credentials as a journalist, but he was a political reporter rather than a commentator with strong partisan convictions. Levi insisted that the staff of *La Stampa* approve his nomination before he accepted the editor's post and throughout his tenure gave his primary attention to putting out a good newspaper. He resigned in 1978 and was replaced by Giorgio Fattori, a longtime professional little known outside journalistic circles.

Even the most controversial—and best-known, at least according to one survey—Italian journalist of the 1970s, Indro Montanelli, was much more professional than political.[5] He was not always perceived that way. Montanelli was a longtime star of *Corriere della Sera*; in September 1973, with the Journalists Committee at the peak of its influence and the paper well to the political left, he noisily broke away, taking with him some twenty other staff members, and established a new daily called *Il Giornale Nuovo*. Montanelli was unmistakably a conservative but without much party identification; in the election of 1976, he advised readers to "hold their nose and vote Christian Democrat," and when, in the spring of 1977, he was "kneecapped" by the Red Brigades, almost every daily in the country including the Communist *L'Unità* carried an affectionate editorial wishing him well. Like Ottone and Levi, in the eyes of his fellow professionals he was always first a journalist.

---

[5] Anon., "Come valuta i quotadiani e come giudica i giornalisti il lettore italiano" [How the Italian reader evaluates daily newspapers and judges journalists], *Prima Communicazione*, no. 42 (May 1977), p. 60. In this study a rather casual sample of newspaper readers were asked to volunteer the name of a journalist; 16.9 percent first mentioned Montanelli, about four times as many as the next most frequent. Ottone was mentioned by 2.6 percent and Levi by only 1 percent.

The increasing eminence in Italian journalism of administrators who were not ideologues, through either conviction or subsidy, seems to have been another of the factors that helped reduce the partisan passions of Italian journalism. It is this writer's conviction, however, that one shattering event had more effect than any other.

That event was the kidnapping and killing of Aldo Moro. The Moro affair brought to Italian journalism a spontaneous unity unlike any that had been seen since the departure of the troops of the German occupation. It was a unanimity that set the Red Brigades and similar organizations outside the limits of political discourse. Terrorism, despite all the rhetoric about revolution, became a crime, and terrorists criminals. That attitude appears to have been of great importance in the coverage of the 1979 election. In his book *Brigate Rosse-Stato* Alessandro Silj provides chronological documentation of the coalescing of opinion in major papers around two commitments: that the kidnapping was a criminal, not a political, act; and that the Italian Government should not participate in any way in negotiations suggested by the Red Brigades which might produce a trade of imprisoned terrorists for the DC leader.[6]

Moro was kidnapped on March 16, 1979; his body was found on May 9. At the time of his kidnapping he probably was the best-known and among the most respected of Italian politicians. All the country's political journalists knew him, and most of the editors; the first response in Italian newsrooms was personal shock. After that it was dancing to the macabre tune played by the Red Brigades.

Since they had first surfaced, the Red Brigades had always demanded cooperation from the press. If communiqués were not handled precisely as indicated or their text in any way altered, there were reprimanding, sometimes threatening, complaints. In pre-Moro days, the press generally complied, grousing occasionally in editorials, but hooked by the Italian journalist's passion for exotic political fauna. Now, with Moro's life hanging in the balance, they were reduced to helpless messengers who could only pass on what the terrorists chose to give them. What they got was increasingly harrowing and humiliating.

There were photographs of Moro, posed with a newspaper the headlines of which could be easily read, demonstrating that on that particular day he was still alive. There were announcements of his upcoming trial (to be conducted in secret by his kidnappers) on

---

[6] Alessandro Silj, *Brigate Rosse-Stato* [Condition: Red Brigades] (Florence: Vallecchi, 1978).

charges which seemed hopelessly rhetorical, followed by the announce-
ment of his guilt and condemnation to death. Most agonizing of all,
there were the holograph letters from Aldo Moro himself to his
colleagues in the Christian Democratic party—the first on March 29
to Francesco Cossiga, at that time minister of internal affairs[7] and
therefore director of the security forces which were searching for
him and his captors; after that, numerous others to other politicians
and his family. These pleaded, in ever more urgent tones, for the
Government to negotiate for his release. As time wore on, Moro's
pleas became increasingly desperate and the estrangement between
his family, which of course wanted negotiations, and the attitude of
the Government and the press more severe. Most newspapers treated
the later letters as the products of a man brainwashed, or drugged, or
for whatever other reason incompetent; it was the only possible way
of reconciling what seemed to the editors the only acceptable position
for the Government and the human agony of one individual.

For their part, the Red Brigades orchestrated the situation with
great skill, to the extent of an appeal to the secretary-general of the
United Nations for his intervention. A final bitter note was added by
the family when the executed leader's body was located—following
the instructions of the Red Brigades—near DC headquarters. Within
hours the family released a statement that, in accordance with Aldo
Moro's own request, there should be "no state funeral, no ceremonies
or medals."

The whole period was one of intense, bleak soul-searching for
the Italian press (and for Italians in many other fields as well, of
course). There was a sense of disgrace about serving the Red Brigades'
wishes. Typical were the reactions to the release of the first photograph of Moro in captivity, along with a statement from the Red
Brigades, on March 18. "Gritting our teeth, and after much doubt,
the editors of *Corriere della Sera* have decided to publish, as have
all the other mass media, the photograph. . .," said that newspaper in
its lead editorial. It also published the full text of the statement. The
Communist daily *L'Unità* commented, "We publish this photo with
the loathing of someone who touches a document handled by paid
killers"; it published only excerpts from the statement.[8]

Breast-beating expiated nothing, eased nothing. To go back into
those publications is to marvel again at how hard, as the old phrase
has it, the Italian press took the Moro affair. Something irreparable
cracked in Italian journalism with that event. In a sense, it was as if

[7] Cossiga became prime minister in July 1979.
[8] Both quoted in the *New York Times*, April 2, 1979.

all of them, politicians and journalists, had been like those hobbyists of military history who dress up in authentic costumes and, firing blanks, recreate great battles; and then on one occasion somebody brings real bullets, and somebody dies. The game can never be the same again. Italian political journalism has not been the same since Moro died, as the coverage of the campaign of 1979 makes clear.

The electoral campaign of 1979 was the first in Italy in which television was sufficiently developed to be the most important medium. Almost all the expenditures for advertising went to private broadcasting. The most popular magazines carried only a few pages; newspapers, at least judging by a quick inspection, had less than half the advertising of the 1976 campaign; and the once-spectacular field of poster art, already in decline in 1976, continued to fade away. The availability of television reduced the importance, and therefore the frequency and dimensions, of the traditional open air Italian *comizi*, political rallies. By the time the campaign was over, Italian politicians had learned a great deal about both the broadcast media and themselves, and most of the lessons were bitter. In this examination, therefore, we shall want to look at broadcasting in detail.

It nevertheless seems appropriate to begin with the newspaper press. Only this medium covered the campaign as a daily running story; Italy's several lively weekly newsmagazines concentrated on special topics, and the substantial political content of broadcasting, both by the government's Radiotelevisione Italiana (RAI) and by private broadcasters, was almost entirely under the control of the political parties.

The Press

The media chapter in the earlier *Italy at the Polls* volume describes certain differences in staff organization between Italian and American newspapers, in the professionalization of journalists; it also discusses the then-volatile ownership situation and the then-distant prospects for substantial government subsidies to help overcome spiraling deficits throughout the industry.[9] Some of the changes that came over the next three years already have been indicated. The *comitati di redazione* were much less restive in 1979 and made few attempts to affect the handling of political news. The most noticeable episode was in Turin at *La Stampa*, where the staff rebelled upon receiving the news not only that the paper was to cover a neo-Fascist MSI rally on March 17, but that MSI advertising was to be permitted as well.

9 Penniman, ed., *Italy at the Polls, 1976*, pp. 259-286.

Strikes closed down the paper for two different days, but the order was enforced. The question of who owned what and aspired to own what, which had so animated the scene in 1976, also had lost much of its interest. Angelo Rizzoli was no longer seeking to buy major papers, and most of the talk was about the company's financial affairs. Rizzoli owned *Corriere*, *Il Mattino* of Naples, and a number of smaller dailies. Agnelli and the Fiat organization still owned *La Stampa*; the giant government-underwritten conglomerate Montedison still was pumping money into *Il Messaggero*, and Montedison's sibling L'ENI still owned *Il Giorno* of Milan, although they wanted to sell it.

All were waiting for Parliament to pass the first comprehensive program of subsidization. The proposal was generous—more than $120 million over nine years—and there was no partisan opposition, nor even much grumbling by the owners about the restrictive provisions largely engineered by the FNSI. These included the mandatory publication of a yearly balance sheet which identified all owners and all sources of income, and an antitrust provision which regulated percentages of both circulation and advertising revenue.

Two major newspapers had changed editors since 1976. Piero Ottone had resigned from *Corriere della Sera*. His replacement, as we have seen, was a relative unknown outside of journalism who had been for many years one of *Corriere's* second-level news executives There were resignations from the staff upon his ascension, but largely on the grounds of his professional inadequacy. Arrigo Levi departed from *La Stampa* in 1978 and was replaced by Giorgio Fattori, who also was little known outside journalism. The founding editors of two important dailies begun during the 1970s, Indro Montanelli of *Il Giornale Nuovo* in Milan (1974) and Eugenio Scalfari of *La Repubblica* of Rome (1976), were still directing those publications.

Most observers would agree that by 1979 there had been changes in status and influence from the time of the earlier campaign. It is clear that *Corriere* remains the highest status paper in the country (this seems to be a given among educated Italians, much as the preeminence of the *New York Times* is among educated Americans, including those who seldom read it). *La Stampa* also has ranked high for the past three decades. The reputations of two other *giornali d'informazione* (general newspapers) of nationwide circulation, however, have been in decline. *Il Messaggero* has been the subject of much experimentation, in aspects ranging from front-page layout to political control by its Journalists Committee, and all of it seems to have hurt more than it helped. It remains, however, the chief newspaper of the capital, and the change in its political position between 1976 and 1979—while its staff remained substantially unchanged—is so striking that it deserves attention here. *Il Giorno's* national reputation declined during the late 1970s, largely, perhaps, because of unimaginative direction. Not only was its editor unremarkable, but the publisher assigned to it by L'ENI at the end of the decade was best known as the head of a chain of small variety stores. It was increasingly marked by pedestrian centrist politics, but it remains an important local paper in Milan.

Il Giornale Nuovo and *La Repubblica* were still new in 1976. *Il Giornale* (the adjective *Nuovo* has shrunken steadily in the logotype until it now is almost invisible) was barely two years old at that point but had already built a substantial and devoted clientele. Montanelli was producing a vigorous, highly professional paper of conservative stance but almost nonpartisan in the literal sense. In 1976 he endorsed forty candidates for Parliament, blithely admitting that he knew nothing about them but did know something about the people they ran against and that his candidates could only be an improvement. Thirty-seven of the forty were elected.

After 1976 matters became more difficult. An attempt to provide national distribution proved to be far more expensive than the results in circulation justified. Montanelli himself was shot through the legs by the Red Brigades, an event which at first seemed only to make him more buoyantly crusty, but he was no longer young; he turned seventy shortly before the beginning of the 1979 campaign.

Montanelli had left *Corriere* in anger and established a paper designed to seriously weaken that paper's hold on Milan and reduce its circulation. The "anti-*Corriere*," as it was sometimes called, simply never worked. Instead, after rapid growth in 1976, *Il Giornale* seems to have begun to slide. Certainly it stopped expanding, and *Corriere* showed no effects. Instead of capturing the elite Milanese audience, *Il Giornale* seems to have tapped, to a modest extent, the vast pool of educated Italians who simply had not been reading newspapers at all. By 1979 it was common talk that Montanelli wanted to sell *Il Giornale*.

La Repubblica of Rome began publication after considerable promotional ballyhoo by its parent company, the well-known publishing house of Arnoldo Mondadori. Prospective readers were promised revolutionary innovations, all of which sounded admirable. Most Italian *giornali d'informazione* at that point were—and are still—handicapped by a sometimes erudite, always in-group prose style which makes them difficult for the citizen with only a secondary education to read. Front pages have been heavy, with nine columns of packed type, a dismaying amount of it italic. Traditional political writing almost has been arcane; a well-known journalist named Enzo

Forcella once estimated that there were only 1,500 readers in the entire country who could understand it.[10] *La Repubblica*, the advance promotion promised, was going to change all that. It was going to be tabloid size, a format rarely seen in general newspapers in Italy. Its articles were going to be shorter, livelier, and easier to read.

Publication began shortly before the electoral campaign of 1976, and *La Repubblica* lived up to most of its promoters' promises. Despite its smaller size, the pages were airy and graceful; news stories were indeed shorter. But it clearly was not designed to be popular.[11] A first requirement to that end would have to be a deemphasis of politics. Instead it became, for the years between the elections of the late 1970s, the most important political journal in the country. That circumstance was directly related to its editor, Eugenio Scalfari.

There are interesting and curious resemblances between *La Repubblica* and Indro Montanelli's *Giornale Nuovo*. The politics are antithetical, but both are centered almost completely on not only the professional competence but the personality of one man. Both have demonstrated first-rate minds at work and a sense of style well above most Italian journalism.

Before the founding of *La Repubblica* Scalfari was an established figure in both politics and journalism. He had been elected to Parliament as an "independent" Socialist in 1968; he also had been editor of *L'Espresso*, one of Italy's lively news weeklies and the furthest left. More than anything else, the word "socialist" conveys skepticism about Establishments—free enterprise economics, the secular activities of the Catholic church, the tenets of orthodox Marxism and the actions of its disciples. In the case of Scalfari, it includes mistrust of the leadership of the Italian Socialist party. Perhaps we tend to think of the person who is suspicious of everything as more honest than the true believer in anything. In any case, *La Repubblica* became the platform and Scalfari the chosen interlocutor for some of the most important political exchanges of the decade. In February 1978, Aldo Moro called Scalfari and asked him to his office; in the interview that followed, he first opened the door for a rapprochement with the Communists: "I well know that Berlinguer thinks and says that at this time in Italian life it is impossible that one of the two major political

---

[10] Enzo Forcello, "Millecinquecento lettori" [Fifteen hundred readers], *Tempo Presente* (November 1959), pp. 452-458.

[11] A more heavy-handed attempt, a tabloid daily named *Occhio*, was begun by Rizzoli in October 1979. It not only featured sex and scandal on the front page, but a list of the 1,500 most commonly used Italian words was drawn up and handed to the staff with instructions to restrict themselves to it in their writing.

forces should be in opposition. On this point his thinking and mine are perfectly identical."[12]

In January 1978, Luciano Lama, secretary of the Communist-dominated confederation of Italian trade unions (CGIL), chose *La Repubblica* as his mouthpiece by which to renounce as "nonsense" a fundamental position held by his organization since 1969—that wage levels should be considered without reference to a firm's profit. In August the same year, Enrico Berlinguer chose Scalfari as questioner in an interview in which the head of Italian communism set out the relationship between his party and Leninism. *La Repubblica* has published many such interviews with the powers of Italian politics, almost invariably initiated by the politicians. In the process, it has gained a unique position in Italian journalism, and Scalfari himself, status among the most influential people in the country.

The Campaign in Print

Throughout the period of the electoral campaign the most important story in the Italian print media was not politics but terrorism. That fact is central, and it is reflected in many ways in the coverage.

On May 5 a group of fifteen to twenty people, armed with sophisticated automatic weapons, carried out a frontal assault on the headquarters of the Rome section of the Christian Democratic party in the Piazza Nicosia. In the gun battle two members of the security forces protecting the headquarters were killed; one was a brigadier of *carabinieri*. The terrorists took time to spray graffiti on the walls, including the initials BR (Brigate Rosse), and escaped. Several dramatic photographs came out of it. One which was particularly wrenching appeared all over the world. It showed the dead officer, not in uniform but in sweater and stocking cap, face down as he had fallen. It was not a grisly photograph; no blood showed, his eyes were closed. He simply looked tragically human.

There was a great deal of irony in what happened immediately within the Italian establishment. Amid all the rhetoric and sloganizing of the Red Brigades there always has been one fundamental premise: the first stage of the revolution is the "destabilization" of the current system; once the society is reduced to chaos, something better—although the destabilizers cannot specify its exact form—is certain to emerge. Far from spreading chaos in the Italian polity, the attack in the Piazza Nicosia served to reestablish what might be called the

---

[12] Quoted in *Panorama*, no. 685, June 5, 1979.

Moro syndrome. Literally within hours the secretaries of the major parties—Berlinguer of the PCI, Bettino Craxi of the PSI, and Benigno Zaccagnini of the DC—appeared together in the Piazza Nicosia to declare a united front against terrorism. *Il Manifesto,* most articulate and influential of the splinter-left newspapers, commented bitterly, "terrorism works in such a way that one forgets that the Christian Democrats are the party of Lockheed [a reference to the bribery scandals]; it quickly becomes a party of virgins and martyrs."[13] *Corriere della Sera's* headlines said "The BR Opens its Electoral Campaign," and the front-page editorial was entitled "The Fruits of Permissiveness." The funeral of the dead brigadier was elaborately covered; *Il Giorno's* photographs were in color, a complex and expensive process rarely used in the paper's news columns. Less than a week later was the first anniversary of the discovery of Aldo Moro's body. All major papers gave the occasion substantial attention. *Il Messaggero* carried a three-page memorial to Moro on May 8 and ran another major article on May 9.

Some of this commemorative journalism was sentimental enough that judgments seemed to become fuzzy; one of *Corriere's* anniversary pieces lamented the lack of other men of Moro's stature in Italian political life, a thought that would have seemed odd to many Italians before the kidnapping. Another article was headed "A Violent Italy is No Longer Folklore"—a reference to the bitterness Italians have felt for years about being stereotyped as gangsters and Mafiosi.

The terrorists took no further action comparable to the Piazza Nicosia attack during the remainder of the campaign, but they were sufficiently active to keep the war against them an almost constant presence in the news media. On May 19 they bombed party offices in Rome and Perugia, without casualties; on May 22, a bomb was found and defused in the offices of Rome's chief magistrate. The same day a group calling itself the Territorial Cells for Boycotting the Elections—previously unheard of—exploded a bomb at a Catholic institute. In a bizarre episode two days later, a group calling themselves Red Brigadists handcuffed a councilwoman in Genoa to a railing, poured glue over her head, hung a sign around her neck, and, after taking photographs, released her. On May 25 a right-wing group calling itself the Popular Revolutionary Movement who had blown up a section of Rome's city hall (designed by Michelangelo) in April reappeared with a bomb which damaged the offices of the Foreign Ministry. On May 30, people calling themselves members of the Red Brigades "kneecapped" a DC candidate for the European Parliament

13 *Il Manifesto,* May 4, 1979.

in Genoa; the next day, Brigadists invaded a classroom at the University of Genoa and shot a professor of political science through the legs.

Not all of these were Red Brigades enterprises, it will be noted; other groups claimed responsibility for some, and some attributed to the Brigades may have been the work of somebody who found that identity convenient (for example, the curious business of the councilwoman and the gluepot has a non-BR quality about it). But all of them were increasingly lumped together by the Italian press, with the Red Brigades the ultimate symbol, and the drum roll of events made terrorism a bigger story than anything the politicians were up to. Various corollary activities reinforced the attention-getting character of the acts of terrorism. Some members of NAP (Armed Proletarian Nucleus), a group which seemed to be attempting to prove itself even bloodier than the BR, were on trial in Genoa. On May 7 a group of Brigades members said to be connected with the Moro killing were arrested, an event given great amounts of newspaper space. And throughout the period there was recurrent attention to Antonio Negri's arrest and detention.

At the time of his arrest, Negri was a professor of sociology at the University of Padua. He was generally recognized by political thinkers of whatever persuasion as a leading theoretician of revolution; Italian authorities arrested him on the grounds that he was much more than a theoretician and was, in fact, an important tactical planner in far-left terrorist activities. His arrest was one of a wave preceding the electoral campaign through which Italian authorities felt they had finally reached the nerve centers of terrorism in the country. Negri contended that he had exercised his right of academic freedom along with the freedom of thought and personal expression guaranteed by the Italian constitution. Although the Negri case was the kind in which most major Italian dailies and magazines once would have automatically sympathized with the accused, the coverage at this point could best be described as nonsympathetic. In major newspapers and magazines there were no flat-out assumptions of Negri's guilt, but neither was there much support for him, even on abstract grounds. *La Repubblica*, the newspaper most predictably inclined to careful sophisticated analysis of the broad issues, did carry an article by the French Marxist philosopher Gilles Deleuze in support of Negri,[14] but followed it the next day with a rebuttal by Giorgio Bocca, who argued with Deleuze's "half-truths."

[14] *La Repubblica*, May 10, 1979.

The DC headquarters murders, on top of the still painful memory of the Moro case, put most publications tied to the political left, or even traditionally sympathetic to it, in a difficult position. The primary concern of most, of course, was to dissociate themselves as far as possible from any terrorist group which used traditional Marxist slogans or referred to themselves as the real Communists; no newspaper in Italy was more intensely anti-Brigades than the PCI daily, *L'Unità*. During the campaign period the respected and influential *Il Manifesto*, while continuing its asperity toward the PCI and the Government parties, handled the terrorist issue with great care. (During most of May—although the timing seems odd—*Il Manifesto* was caught up in major structural changes; two pages were added to the usual four, the official tie with the PSDUP was dropped, and the function of publisher was taken over by a committee.)

Despite this circumspection and the absence of substantial overt attacks equating terrorism and communism on the part of the center parties (whose leadership probably realized that the issue would work better for them if they stayed away from it officially), the linkage was commonly made in the popular mind. There were graffiti reading "BR=PCI," or a variant, on Italian walls, and the connection was constantly made in local-level campaigning.

One is tempted to see this concentration upon the problem of terrorism, and the concomitant emphasis upon national unity, as something more than a matter of news judgment; there seems to have been almost an eager embrace of something besides the standard fodder of Italian journalism, party politics. A rudimentary content analysis of the front page of the two papers generally considered the country's best, *Corriere* and *La Stampa*, during the 1976 and 1979 campaigns reinforces this suspicion. Table 10-1 covers issues of each paper for the periods May 22–June 22, 1976, and May 5–June 5, 1979. All items appearing on the front page were coded by subject matter, a process carried out by the author and a graduate student and not systematically checked for reliability because agreement was so obvious. The category headed "the election" included any story that made a reference to the upcoming balloting. "Terrorism" was even more self-evident, but it should be noted that it included more than straightforward news accounts of terrorist activities; particularly during the 1979 campaign, there were numerous background stories and front page editorials. Of particular importance is the category "all other." Even if diminished front page attention to the election could be explained on the basis of additional space given to terrorism —which is highly arguable—the increased attention given to other subjects seems to indicate a clear alteration in priorities. There was

TABLE 10-1

CONTENT ANALYSIS OF CORRIERE AND LA STAMPA FRONT PAGES,
1976 AND 1979 CAMPAIGNS

	Corriere		La Stampa	
Subject	1976	1979	1976	1979
The elections				
Number of stories	77	57	57	30
Percent	37.6	21.4	31.7	13.7
Terrotism				
Number of stories	17	46	14	32
Percent	8.3	17.2	7.8	14.6
All other				
Number of stories	111	164	109	157
Percent	54.1	61.4	60.5	71.7

SOURCE: Author's analysis of front pages of *Corriere della Sera* and *La Stampa* for the periods May 22-June 22, 1976, and May 5-June 5, 1979.

further evidence of this at the conclusion of the campaign. None of the major *giornali d'informazione* made specific endorsements in their final editorial comments before voting began on June 3. *Il Messaggero* of Rome supplemented the national unity theme sounded in its major headlines and quoted at the beginning of this chapter with an editorial signed by Italo Pietra, the old Socialist who was once its editor, rather diffidently criticizing the Christian Democrats but saying at the same time that they clearly were not going to be defeated; that the problem, therefore, was to shake them up, to signal impatience with corruption and business as usual. *La Repubblica's* last issue before the balloting carried nothing resembling a position statement; its major headline said "Italy at the Polls/Before the Voters, Difficult Choices and Uncertain Results." *Corriere della Sera* not only abjured any advice about voting, but—astonishingly for an Italian newspaper—expressed the hope that it had had no influence at all.

Such treatment seems to indicate not just a tendency to downplay the election, but an endemic skepticism about partisan politics. Others were more explicit. *Panorama* made much of audience surveys which indicated that television viewers turned off their sets when politicians came on, and bitter asides were common in its columns. The cover of its May 22 issue featured caricatures of Craxi, Berlinguer, and Andreotti addressing an inattentive television audience; an angled band across the upper right corner said "ORIANA FALLACI: Politicians, I Hate You!" Inside there was a long interview with Fallaci, a well-known journalist, ranging over many topics including her personal life. The letters-to-the-editor column in the next issue carried a letter from the writer who had conducted the interview complaining, "I wish . . . to make it clear that the cover line (Politicians, I hate you!) does not correspond to the opinion which the authoress very articulately expressed in the interview."[15]

Italy's satirical artists may not hate politicians, but they do mock and belittle them, and the years between the elections saw a rapid growth of jugular-oriented cartoons. By the end of the 1970s literally dozens were appearing regularly in print. Many appeared in new, frequently marginal, publications which are called in Italian *fumetti* (literally, little puffs of smoke—the balloons carrying the spoken words of cartoon characters). The most conspicuous of these was a cheaply printed and gloriously scruffy sheet called *Il Male*, which means "bad" or "evil." Article 21 of the Italian constitution prohibits "printed publications, performances and all other manifestations contrary to morality" and sets out the process for sequestration of publications. Forty of *Il Male's* first fifty-two issues were seized by the authorities, and the rate has continued high; between January 1978 and September 1979 it was 70 percent. *Il Male* is published on Thursday, and its buyers, of whom there are an estimated 120,000, know that Thursday is the only day to buy it; by Friday, the police usually have acted. Three editors have been arrested and given jail sentences.

Il Male is primarily concerned with politics, but not exclusively. It is baldly obscene, both in text and art work, as cruel as imagination can make it, and frequently very funny. The Vatican is a favorite target; the first *direttore* to be sentenced to jail went there for his parody of the papal election process. Furthermore, the magazine's young staff also indulge in street antics. They staged a mock papal coronation on the balcony outside its offices and have sold small jars of what was identified as water from the papal swimming pool. When it comes to politicians and party politics, *Il Male* does not comment; it slays.

The art of satirical political cartooning has not been restricted to those on the edge of respectability, however. Probably the best known satirist of all is Giorgio Forattini, a cartoonist from a somewhat earlier generation with an incomparable platform in *La Repubblica*. Forattini likes to draw politicians naked, sometimes with the symbol of their party serving as a fig leaf. He is a wickedly skillful caricaturist and

[15] *Panorama*, no. 684, May 29, 1979.

an excellent semiologist. His postelection cover for *Panorama*, for which he also occasionally draws, showed a naked Berlinguer bearing a cross marked *Libertas* (the cross, that is, from the Christian Democrats' emblem) and wearing a crown, not of thorns, but of roses (the rose is the symbol of the Radical party, which gained fourteen seats, largely at the cost of the PCI). It goes without saying that his naked politicians look strange indeed—frail, weak, and vulnerable. None inspires confidence.

Print coverage of the electoral campaign, thus diminished by an editorial consensus that the major continuing story was government versus terrorism, along with what appears to have been some distaste for politics generally under the circumstances, was direct, simple, and by Italian standards overwhelmingly dull. By U.S. standards, a good deal of it also was good journalism.

A major element in the 1979 coverage which was functionally new was the elaborate use of polls and surveys. There had been some use of these instruments in 1976, particularly for projecting results within a few hours after the balloting ceased, but this time they were used by the print media from the beginning of the campaign. Most were carried out under contract by commercial polling organizations. Most proved, not surprisingly, to be substantially accurate in their prediction of the results of the actual vote, although they overestimated the seat totals of both the Christian Democrats and the Radicals.

(The potential effects of opinion polls upon *parliamentary* systems of government obviously are enormous, although somewhat outside the scope of this chapter. It was a notable coincidence that as early as May 6, shortly after the first publication of survey findings, Berlinguer issued a statement which could be described as conciliatory, stressing the PCI's interest in new conversations with the Christian Democrats and "confirming that Italy does not need to leave NATO."[16] It seems unlikely that the Communists would have forced an election without some idea of their electoral prospects, but in any case, the dynamics of a parliamentary system clearly are altered when political party leaders think they have dependable information about how they will fare if they bring about an election.)

Corriere della Sera went far beyond the reporting of surveys of national party preference. During the course of the campaign it carried detailed examinations of each of the regions of Italy, including analysis of public opinion on election issues and voting trends, as well as discussions of regional economics, leadership, and traditions. These

[16] *Corriere della Sera*, May 6, 1979.

Corriere articles appeared on inside pages headed "The Elections." Beyond the front page, Italian dailies generally are sectioned under such rubrics as foreign news, economic affairs, and the like; along with *Corriere, La Repubblica, Il Messaggero, La Stampa,* and others added an election section during the campaign. *La Repubblica* used the heading "June 3–10," referring to the national elections on June 3 and those for the European Parliament on the following Sunday.

Many U.S. newspapers have used the same scheme. The chief characteristic of their "battle pages" is careful balance, the content a mixture of party statements, accounts of rallies, news of endorsements, and the like. Essentially they are service departments; since media research has indicated many times that their readers commonly are seeking reinforcement of the beliefs they already hold, it is a service for the already converted.

One of the staples of Italian journalism is the question-and-answer interview. During both the 1976 and 1979 campaigns the nationally circulated general newspapers carried the texts (edited and polished, to some extent) of extensive conversations with leaders from the three major parties. Since the resignation of the rather low-key Francesco De Martino as Socialist party secretary in 1976, that small but critical group has been led by a more contentious and visible leader, Bettino Craxi, and Craxi, as an American journalist might say, makes good copy. He was the most frequently interviewed of the party leaders in 1979; although he had enemies in his own party, including Scalfari, he was the only reasonable subject for a formal interview setting out the PSI's positions. Andreotti and Benigno Zaccagnini, the party secretary, were the most interviewed Christian Democrats, although *Corriere's* conversation was with Flaminio Piccoli; in addition to Berlinguer, Gerardo Chiaromonti sometimes appeared for the Communists.

The journalistic tradition for such interviews calls for playing it straight; hard questions are permissible, but bear-baiting is not, and the politician's answers, although generally edited down for length, are reproduced without comment. In effect, the interview pages are the equivalent of carefully balanced free air time in the broadcast media. They are interesting if read carefully, but never surprising.

The following factors, then, helped make for low-key campaign coverage in print: (1) the major attention given to terrorism and opposition to it, which, both directly and indirectly, served as a national unifying force and set radical rhetoric outside the limits of political discourse in the judgment of the media; (2) the conscious attempt, on the part of general newspapers, to provide balanced coverage through the use of special sections, elaborate use of polls and surveys, and formal interviews; and (3) the frequent expression, generally in undertones but sometimes explicit, of boredom, if not disdain, with and for politicians and political parties. Perhaps there was an unintended final comment on the campaign on the front page of La Repubblica the first day of voting, June 3. The only photograph in that most important space in the most important newspaper for political journalism in the country had nothing to do with politics at all. It showed Pope Wojtyla, as the Italian media almost invariably call him, arriving in Poland.

Broadcasting in the Campaign

Roberto Savasta, a lawyer from Milan, had been a Liberal party candidate for the Chamber of Deputies in 1976. He had averaged seven appearances a day at outdoor rallies, generally in semideserted piazzas under the sun of one of the hottest Junes in modern history. In 1979 he interviewed constituents with a tape recorder, had the results chopped into convenient lengths for advertising spots, dubbed in a couple of bars of Beethoven's Ninth, and spent most of the campaign indoors. Dozens of other candidates for the Chamber of Deputies, the Senate, and the European Parliament did the same. Enrico Berlinguer made only fourteen speeches at political rallies but participated in some thirty interviews, press conferences, and round tables on television—double the number for 1976.

Such intensive electronic campaigning was possible only because of the presence of private broadcasting. Radiotelevisione Italiana (RAI), the government-controlled one-time monopoly system, did not sell time in any form to political parties or candidates. In fact, RAI's professionals had the right to make few decisions. As in 1976, all broadcast campaign programming was under the direct control of a committee made up of Parliament members carefully chosen for political balance. The leadership of the political parties secured from this committee (1) the right to produce all RAI campaign programming and (2) protection from attractive competitive programming on the other of Italy's two channels.

RAI formats were generally the same as three years earlier[17]— "press conferences," interviews, discussions, and speeches. RAI broadcast an average of slightly more than one hour a day under the title "Tribuna Elettorale." There was a sharp difference in detail, however. In 1976 the press conferences provided a party leader to answer questions from about a dozen journalists. The journalists were

[17] Penniman, ed., Italy at the Polls, 1976, p. 274 ff.

chosen by the parliamentary committee and always included some who were of opposing persuasions. Even this arrangement produced largely rhetoric, but there were occasional flashes of conflict. In 1979 the outside questioners on all of the shows were screened by the parties. Clashes occurred only in the debates between functionaries of different parties—for example, the PCI's Gian Carlo Pajetta and Renato Zangheri of the Christian Democrats. Even these encounters produced no genuine sparks, however. They were largely exchanges of predictable cliches in *partitese,* as some have called the in-group language of Italian politics.

"Tribuna Elettorale" drove away listeners by the millions, to the open delight of the country's print media. Newspapers and magazines carried repeated accounts of the dullness and ineffectiveness of the broadcasts. Not all of this was rooted in high-minded, detached judgment, of course; advertising, and therefore the revenue from it, is allotted to Italian media by agencies which essentially are state-controlled, and bitter feelings have for years centered on the amount that goes to RAI.

Admittedly, "Tribuna Elettorale" began with a handicap; most broadcasts were between 10:00 and 11:00 P.M., an hour during which many members of the audience would have turned off their sets and retired, regardless of the program; at the same time, the Italian dinner hour is late, particularly in Rome and in cities to the south.[18] At a minimum, it is clear that "Tribuna" had no capacity for keeping them up. The published results of studies carried out by a market research firm indicate that during the first five "Tribuna" broadcasts the audience was highest at the beginning of the program (the familiar phenomenon of carry-over from the preceding program), projected at about 10.5 million viewers. After half an hour, about 5 million remained; at the end of the hour, about 2.4 million.[19] The others had either turned to another channel or gone to bed. There is no evidence that politicians did any better on private television, but their eagerness to spend money on it indicated an almost touching confidence.

For many years Italian broadcasting, like that of most European countries, was strictly a government monopoly, vaguely modeled on the BBC. Since the end of the Second World War there had been numerous "outlaw" radio stations, transmissions that would simply appear and continue to operate until the authorities tracked them

[18] RAI's research department has published several studies of audience composition and media use but none, to this writer's knowledge, of the total audience between 10 and 11 P.M.

[19] Lem-Graman TV-meter finding quoted in *Panorama,* no. 683, May 22, 1979.

down; the government monopoly would then request their suppression, citing the legislation which undergirds RAI. Television stations of the same sort appeared in due course, and the government's attempt to close one of them down brought about a series of unexpected court rulings in 1975. These set out the principle that RAI's monopoly was restricted to nationwide broadcasting and that nothing forbade local broadcasting. A wild and disordered growth of local TV and radio stations began even before the case reached the Constitutional Court, the country's highest, which upheld the earlier ruling. A few hundred radio stations and perhaps a few television outlets were on the air at the time of the 1976 campaign, but little use seems to have been made of them. The only campaign program of note was the call-in talk show conducted, at length and frequently, by Marco Pannella, head of the then-new Radical party.

Things were different in 1979. The lack of dependable data begins with the fact that it is impossible to determine how many transmitters were even on the air. In Italy, private broadcasting was, at the end of the decade, totally free of regulation (except when a signal interfered with a RAI transmission). Stations could start broadcasting wherever they liked, at whatever frequency and power they chose; there were no restrictions on who could own them or for what they could be used (late night stripteases and soft-core porno films are common). There has been general agreement in Italy for several years that some system of regulation must be developed, but it obviously will be long in coming, in part because of foot-dragging on the part of station owners. These include almost all the major print media corporations and, frequently on a partial and covert basis, political parties.

Agenzia Giornalistica Italiana, a specialized news agency particularly concerned with business affairs, estimated in April 1979, that there were about 600 television stations (the United States had at that point 727 commercial television stations). Other guesses range downward from that, some as low as 300. It is generally agreed that there are around 40 in the Rome market area and around 60 in Milan.

The range of disagreement about the total sum spent by candidates and parties on campaign broadcasting is somewhat narrower. A trade journal for private broadcasting called *Millecanali*, in a comprehensive summary article after the election, offered the figure 30 billion lire (about $36.5 million) but admitted there were some who felt that 40 billion (about $48 million) was more likely.[20] About

---

[20] *Millecanali*, no. 55/56 (July-August 1979), p. 68 ff.

half the spending was by individual candidates, the remainder by the parties. The PSDUP daily *Il Manifesto* reported that the Christian Democrats spent a "good part" of their budgeted total of 7 billion lire (about $7.5 million) for advertising; the Socialists spent about $950,000 on broadcast campaigning, something more than a third of their total budget; and the Radical party spent about $60,000 for advertising, almost all of it on private broadcasting.[21] The PCI spent little of their $3.5 million on broadcasting; *Millecanali* asks archly, "What price did they pay in terms of votes?"[22]

Most of this apparently was spent on spot announcements (the Italians have picked up the American phrase). Since rates were, by American commercial standards, quite modest, the density of saturation was striking. Prices varied from station to station and, of course, with the time of day. Spot prices seem to have averaged around $240 per minute in major cities, with the price for larger units—fifteen minutes for speeches or discussions, for example—ranging from around $400 to $1,200. Apparently the highest prices were charged by GBR, generally considered the dominant station in Rome; a half-hour of prime time on GBR cost $6,000. Most stations which were owned by, or tied to, a political party did not charge the party for time, casting further doubt upon any gross figures. But as a general practice stations sold time to all comers at their established rates. The one exception seems to have been the refusal of some owners (Rizzoli, for example) to carry advertising by the MSI.

Millecanali (a publication catering to the industry, it must be remembered) referred to the spots as being in an "American" style and identified some it thought particularly bad—for example, the commercial of a Liberal candidate which showed a Rube Goldberg machine, pedal-powered and bearing the symbols of parties of the left, which spewed out snakes, frogs, and other unattractive animals; when the Liberal symbol appeared on the machine, however, there emerged from it a unified Europe. In another, a gaggle of young females wearing thin and clinging sweaters bearing the DC's emblem dropped various *double entendres* on the way to identifying the candidate.

The longer formats were used for "round tables" centering on a personality such as Giovanni Spadolini or Marco Pannella; press conferences, in which the "journalists" frequently were actually campaign aides; and half-hour programs which featured celebrities, and were distributed to many stations in the hope that they would be used without charge.

[21] *Il Manifesto*, May 31, 1979.
[22] *Millecanali*, no. 55/56 (July-August 1979).

The first broadcast of the campaign on private television featured Giulio Andreotti accepting telephoned questions from the audience, the type of program most used on radio during the 1976 election. When such programs took unarranged and unscreened questions, the results were seldom newsworthy but often interesting—Andreotti, for example, was asked such things as "Why did you get yourself elected to the Rome city council and then never attend?" and "Why do you deputies talk about austerity and then vote yourselves raises?" The candidates' understandable wish to exercise more control over the message, however, made such programs infrequent.

Certainly the most visible personality on private television was Marco Pannella. Photogenic, with elegant long white hair, bright and acerbic, overwhelmingly articulate, and at war with practically every Italian institution imaginable, he put his party's total resources into the newest medium. Officially, the Radical party's expenditures amounted to a modest 500,000 lire, a little more than $60,000; but some professional sources contended that the figure was around 5 *billion* lire, a figure greater even than the Christian Democrats'.[23]

As in 1976, in this campaign conventional daily newspapers paid little attention to Pannella and his party, though they included the Radicals in their "battle pages." He received one extraordinary endorsement, however: on April 22, Montanelli blandly espoused him in *Il Giornale*, adding that he was a mountebank, a charlatan, and a man who would steal the corpse so he could be the central figure at a funeral—but he divided and confounded the left. Pannella and the Radicals received much better play in the magazines, but they saw the broadcast media as their chief hope for a greatly increased PR presence in Parliament. The featured format was a round table with Pannella presiding, talking with a set of leaders once primarily identified with other parties; the group regularly included such people as Marco Boato of Continuous Struggle and Alessandro Tessari of the PCI. Panels of this sort appeared on a network of twenty stations. Even with air time at bargain rates, a good deal of money had to be involved.

The Effects of the Broadcast Campaign

What effect did all this torrent of talk and graphics have?

Tracing and measuring the effects of mass media on political behavior has long been a major activity of social researchers, but the subject is still imperfectly understood. In the case of Pannella and the

---

23 Staff members of *Prima Communicazione*, a respected media trade journal.

Radicals, there is a quick, annihilating—but possibly misleading—answer. The surveys published at the beginning of May 1979, before campaign broadcasting began, projected an eventual 5 percent of the vote for the PR. The party actually received 3.5 percent, raising the mind-bending possibility that all the propagandizing actually hurt their cause. That probably was not the case; the survey agency, instead, probably made a sampling error. It should be noted that the Radical party nevertheless made remarkable gains in the number of seats held in the Chamber of Deputies—which is, after all, the name of the game. The actual increase in the vote from 1976 was almost 250 percent, but because of its geographical distribution it produced an increase in seats of 450 percent, from four to eighteen. Pannella may well have considered the results worth the money.

Edilio Rusconi, owner of a group of popular consumer magazines in Italy, was responsible for a more indirect but still striking measure of effect, or lack of it. Before the 1979 campaign got under way, he announced that his five television stations in the Rome area would accept no political advertising and, of course, carry no political news. The first reports on Italian audiences by the Nielsen agency, the dominant firm in national ratings in the United States, were about to begin, and it was generally assumed that Rusconi's decision was based upon his belief that Italians were bored by politics. If that was the case, his judgment seems to have been accurate; it was reported that his five stations averaged about 45 percent of the audience during the campaign, while the other thirty-five stations shared the rest.

It is a safe prediction that political candidates in Italy will never abjure broadcast advertising, now that it has arrived, even if its effectiveness remains undemonstrated and its costs unjustifiable in the cold terms of the balance sheet. Too many other satisfactions are involved, including the probability that there is nothing so gratifying to a politician's ego as seeing and hearing himself on videotape. Nevertheless the experience of the 1979 campaign had to be depressing for the typical Italian candidate. Not only was the evidence clear that the magic new medium did little for him, but the newspapers and magazines were contemptuous of politics and the people in it. Satirists drew savage cartoons and comic strips; the voter turnout was the lowest since the end of Fascism. Even the walls, the most ancient medium of all for political discourse, were turned to demeaning the people who wanted to govern. The most bizarre artifact of the Roman spring was a poster which appeared one morning in literally hundreds of locations all over the city, showing a gaunt young man with long blowing hair, a mouth set hard, and narrowed eyes. In giant script at the bottom was the legend "Craxi tried to kiss me." After a vast flurry of predictable rumors, the truth came out: the poster was the work of a photographer who did not know Craxi at all. He was simply seeking attention as a means of publicizing a show of his photographs in a local gallery. He told a reporter that he would also like to put some up in New York, substituting "Carter" for "Craxi," and in Moscow, substituting "Brezhnev," but feared that the latter would be risky. It was anything but risky in Rome: during the next few days, politicians all over the city put up their own posters as close as possible to his, hoping to get the passing viewers' leftover attention.

Summary. In summarizing my chapter in the first *Italy at the Polls* volume, I suggested that, despite the extraordinary politicization of the press and of journalists, the final phase of the 1976 campaign seemed to demonstrate a growing caution, almost fear, about the future of the state and a tendency to dampen some of the excesses of traditional partisanship. The implications of that attitude seemed to predict more sober journalism in the future. The self-examination brought about by the killing of Aldo Moro and the perceived need for a common front against terrorism greatly intensified the tendency.

Terrorism, both the acts of the Red Brigades and other groups and their arrests and trials, provided a major theme of newspapers and magazines throughout the campaign; the attack upon the Christian Democratic headquarters at its beginning established a pattern that never changed and that reinforced the tendency to dampen political partisanship. It would be preposterous to say that Italian journalism became depoliticized; all journalism, in however torpid a nation, is politicized, and more so than the citizenry. But the tendency *toward* depoliticization in Italy has been clear.

It has been further reinforced by other, less dramatic factors. The reform movement within the licensed profession of journalism which peaked not long before the 1976 election continued to diminish. Its essential thrust was the obtaining of a larger role in policy making for the professional staffs of newspapers, magazines, and broadcast news operations; to some extent this had been accomplished. Journalists also came to realize that newspapers, in particular, were in severe financial trouble and that jobs were at stake. This perception also contributed, indirectly, to the weakening of the old stereotype of ownership-management whose objectives were manipulatively political, with bottomless reserves of cash to achieve their dark purposes. It had become apparent that they were more interested in money instead, and were hurting for it. Much of the attention of the journalists' trade union was turned to shaping the legislation which would provide government subsidies.

The election of 1979 was the first "television election" in Italy, a condition which did nothing to improve examination of the issues or increase public interest or produce better candidates. The most charitable thing to be said for it, perhaps, was that it did give the average citizen a chance to see repeatedly and at close range the people who ran his government or wanted to run it. Judging by the ratings, it was not an experience that the average citizen found worth prolonging.

For the time being, then, political journalism (in contrast to political campaigning) will continue to be the function of the newspaper and magazine press. It is a press system moving steadily away from its old glories of dazzling eloquence, of fractionated and idiosyncratic partisanship, of covert subsidies and functioning as a mouthpiece, toward a press which is first of all a part of the economic order and whose essential product is information. The Italian press is not very far down that road as yet, but it seems to be on the way.

11

Elections and Italian Democracy: An Evaluation

Samuel H. Barnes

Elections function in the Italian political system as the moral equivalent of war. Those few political questions that have been resolved in the postwar period have been settled by voting. The choice between a republic and a monarchy and the issue of divorce were submitted to referendums. The question of whether Italy would "go communist" has been repeatedly put before the electorate and repeatedly settled by that body, with the results accepted by all. Electoral turnout hovered around 93 percent until 1979, and the high rate of voting, whatever the reasons for it, has served to legitimize outcomes. The deep divisions of the postwar years, the struggle between Christianity and communism, the ideological contest between Marxism and its opponents, the highly mobilized subcultures that softened the transition to a more secular, urban, and industrial society all remain among the perpetual issues that dominate Italian public life. Behind the forms, however, the reality has been changing. The intensity and passion have eroded; individuals have mellowed; subcultural networks have atrophied or been transformed. In its moment of triumph, when it has gained hegemony among Italian intellectuals, Marxism has lost its ability to unify and to guide political action: where all are Marxists, other criteria must differentiate individuals and courses of action. And the reforms of recent popes have weakened both the organizational and the ideological bases of Catholic integralism, that is, the movement for a specifically Catholic solution for social, economic, and political problems.

Italian society has been transformed since the Second World War. Economic growth has greatly expanded both the industrial proletariat and the middle class. The peasantry has been reduced to a fraction of its former size, and what is left is being converted into an independent farming class. Migration to urban areas throughout Italy, migration from South to North, and continuing migration to other countries are reducing, though not eliminating, external differences among regions and between town and country. The nationalization of the media and especially the dispersion of television are accelerating the creation of a single, more homogenized national mass culture.

The political system has done relatively little to guide this transformation. Some would say that it had a negative impact, that it has, through its inefficiency, merely made the inevitable more difficult. Certainly what has taken place in Italy is not a purely Italian national phenomenon. Italy has been integrated into Europe and the world economy; the transformation that we refer to has made Italy extremely vulnerable to the vicissitudes of that world economy, and especially to the high cost of energy and the availability of low-wage labor in developing countries. Nevertheless, the Italian society and economy have been impressively resilient. The standard of living for all categories of the population has increased rapidly. Balance of payment problems, while serious, have been successfully managed. The European commitment of Italy, shared by all major parties, seems irrevocable. And democracy seems firmly established.

The entrenchment of the democratic republic during a period of massive social transformation is not a historic accident.[1] Elections and the electoral system have played an important role in the system's adaptation to societal changes. The parties have had to change, to adapt. In the process they have undergone a transformation, clinging to the old labels and forms while altering behavior and policies. Elections have not only been the way to keep score: they have been goads to change, active agents of political transformation. The struggle for electoral survival has kept the parties in tune with changes in the society. In the process, old myths have been discarded (and replaced by new ones). Party clienteles have changed. Organizational survival and vitality have led to massive shifts in the political agenda, in the organization and fortunes of the parties, in their electoral strategies and behavior.

Parliamentary elections must be viewed as formal readings of the nation's pulse, punctuating a process that began with the establishment of the republic and that will only end with its demise. Among those elections, the 1979 "political" or parliamentary election is one

[1] The wide acceptance of the democratic ethos in Italy has been noted, among others, by Giacomo Sani in "The Political Culture of Italy: Continuity and Change," in Gabriel A. Almond and Sidney Verba, eds., *The Civic Culture Revisited* (Boston: Little, Brown, 1980), p. 281, and Robert Putnam, *The Beliefs of Politicians* (New Haven: Yale University Press, 1973), pp. 226-236.

of the least significant in terms of issues and consequences. It was called largely as a result of calculations in the game of coalition building. It did not result from the need to clarify the public's orientation toward any of the major items on the policy agenda, and it solved no problems arising from that agenda. Nevertheless, the 1979 election permits us to assess the current state of the Italian political system in its continuous adaptation to societal transformation.

The election revealed several important things about the Italian system. The capacity of the system to unite against terrorism, to resist "strong" solutions to problems of public order, and to engage in orderly debate even in times of fear and seeming chaos were impressively demonstrated. That this capacity is now widely taken for granted is itself testimony to the solidity of democracy in Italy. The election destroyed the myth of the relentless advance of the Italian Communist party and called into question the future of Eurocommunism and the "historic compromise." The election demonstrated the continuing capacity of the Christian Democratic party to adapt, to survive. It witnessed a revival of the minor parties, which had feared that the PCI-DC rapprochement, however fragile it might be, could relegate them to the periphery of the system. Finally, the election documented that secular changes in the behavior of the electorate were beginning to have weighty consequences for the outcome of elections. Each of these concerns merits detailed analysis.

The Solidity of Italian Democracy

Terrorism itself reflects the strength of the present Italian democratic system. Individuals and groups desirous of extensive modification in the system, whether they represent the left or the right, no longer expect this transformation to be possible through parliamentary means. The domestication of the PCI, the continued weakness and division on the right, and the splintering of the numerically weak parties on the extreme left result in a low potential for revolutionary change within the present system. Terrorism involves at most a few hundred activists and a few thousand supporters; their ability to disrupt, however, is impressive. It is unlikely that they can cause a breakdown in the functioning of any significant sector of the system through outrageous acts. The kidnapping and murder of Aldo Moro was a critical test of the political system and especially of elites, and it was a test that they successfully met. The solidarity of most party elites was impressive, as was the massive outpouring of public sympathy and indignation. The full story of the negotiations for Moro's release may never be known, but the obvious calm and reasoned response of most parliamentary leaders to an attack on the heart of the system seem to show a maturity of Italian democracy that merits emphasis. The Communist reaction was reassuring for Italian democracy. Faced with a no-win situation—the PCI seemed destined to suffer from backlash whatever it did—the party took the path of solidarity with the Christian Democrats. In turn, the latter party refused to exploit the passions of the moment to equip itself with special powers beyond the modest ones acceptable to the wider bloc of "constitutional" parties. That the republican system seems stronger with time, rather than weaker, and despite the assault of terrorism, is remarkable evidence for its institutionalization.

Whatever one thinks of the merits of the alternation in power of different parties as a model of democracy, the Italian way is a different one. Historically, Italy has been a dominant-party system.[2] Elections do not determine, at least in the short run, who will form the Government. They do set parameters within which a majority must be found, but the identity of the dominant partner is assumed before the election. Nor are the policies to be followed by the Government determined by the electoral results. Referendums may settle policy questions; parliamentary elections do not. Rather, it is the search of the dominant party—in Italy this has always been the Christian Democrats—for a long-range formula that will ensure its continued dominance that leads to shifts in policy.[3] The role of elections is to register the relative success and failure of the contemporary formula in continuing that dominance, and also to identify which parties are necessary and, sometimes, willing coalition partners. Elections, then, are soundings of opinion, snapshots of the electorate at a particular time, and not the occasion for deciding who will take charge of the country and what they will do with their power. From this perspective, both the "opening to the left" of the 1960s and the current historic compromise are long-range elite strategies designed to perpetuate the Italian pattern of changing Governments by accretion rather than alternation. The skill of the bargainers in both the PCI and the DC in negotiating a graduated approach to one another, a rapprochement, has been remarkable. However, the election called

---

[2] The concept of a dominant-party system is developed in Alan Arian and Samuel H. Barnes, "The Dominant Party System: A Neglected Model of Democratic Stability," *Journal of Politics*, vol. 36 (August 1974), pp. 592-614.

[3] A variation on the dominant-party model is described in Giuseppe Di Palma, *Political Syncretism in Italy: Historical Coalition Strategies and the Present Crisis* (Berkeley: University of California—Institute of International Studies, 1978).

into question the necessity of increased PCI involvement at the current time; the reasons for this merit examination.

Italian Communism in 1979. The 1979 election was the largest set-back the PCI has received in the postwar period. It demonstrated that it was, in at least some ways, a party like the others, that electoral fortunes could go down as well as up. We will discuss changes in the electorate in a later section; here we will examine the status of the PCI in 1979 from the viewpoint of its organization and long-range strategies.

No one should doubt that the Italian Communist party has a future. It is too deeply rooted in Italian social structure, too strong as an organization, and too well led for it to cease being a force in Italian politics. Yet the future of the historic compromise, like the future of Eurocommunism, is open to question. Put simply and without scholarly qualifications, the historic compromise was one proposed solution to the eternal problem of finding a majority. With the Communist party gaining votes in each election it seemed unlikely that a majority would long be possible without that party's support or acquiescence. That situation may not have changed fundamentally for the long run. In the meanwhile, however, the PCI is not as indispensable as it had seemed, though that condition could change with the calculations of the Socialists and the center-left parties.

The Communists themselves have reasons to question the historic compromise. They have benefited electorally from their moderation of the past few years, and accumulating evidence suggests that the party is widely viewed as a legitimate and democratic contender for power. On the other hand, the moderation it has practiced has cost it heavily in several ways. One is with those who want extensive change in the system. This group is not limited to terrorists and the extraparliamentary opposition. Many PCI militants undoubtedly find the policies of Berlinguer hard to accept. And the party is especially concerned with the impact of these policies on youth and on trade unionists. A *cure d'opposition* will be welcomed by many. Moreover, the PCI risks having little more to show for its cooperation than the Socialists did fifteen years ago. The Christian Democrats have weaknesses, but lack of bargaining skill is not one of them. Furthermore, the 1979 election weakened the bargaining position of the PCI, though not dramatically and certainly not permanently. The desire of the Socialists to occupy the presidency of the council of ministers and the limited but critical revival of the small secular parties increase the freedom of action of the DC.

More serious for the PCI than the current pause in the journey to the historic compromise is the future of Eurocommunism.[4] This very Italian invention seems to be in trouble. Despite the spate of scholarly and journalistic attention it has received in recent years, it has neither prospered nor withered. The Spanish Communist party continues to adhere to that line, despite resulting internal problems similar to those of the Italians. The French party, the third major example of the genre, has returned to being more orthodox than the Czar.

Problems of orientation both internal and external were never put to rest by the PCI.[5] The fear that the practice of democratic centralism is incompatible with democracy continues to bother many, and it is often pointed out that the implications of democratic centralism are much more serious in a governing party than in one in opposition. The charge that the party is not internally democratic and hence not to be trusted is a perennial albatross. PCI members do not seem disturbed by it; its wider electorate likewise ignores the problem. But the intellectual challenge will not go away, even though there are easily identified groups and opposing leaders within the PCI. It is not surprising that the party does not abandon its organizational structure: it is a source of cohesion, unity of purpose, and organizational effectiveness. But it is also an object of recurrent criticism.

The PCI possesses an additional weak spot in its close identification with the Soviet line in foreign affairs. In European matters it has generally taken an independent line; in non-European areas it often supports the Soviet position. Perhaps token adherence to the Soviet line in areas of little concern to Italy seems the least it can do for a former mentor and presently difficult but necessary comrade. The PCI undoubtedly realizes that few Italian voters care much about what happens far away, and there is virtually no disagreement among Italian parties on NATO, the European Community, and the orienta-

---

[4] Among the dozens of studies of Eurocommunism that approach the topic from diverse points of view are Carl Boggs and David Plotke, eds., *The Politics of Eurocommunism* (Montreal: Black Rose Books, 1980), Roy Godson and Stephen Haseler, eds., *Eurocommunism: Implications for East and West* (London: Macmillan, 1978), Ernest Mandel, *From Stalinism to Eurocommunism* (New York: Schocken Books, 1978), Keith Middlemas, *Power and the Party: Changing Faces of Communism in Western Europe* (London: Andre Deutsch, 1980), R. Neal Tannahill, *The Communist Parties of Western Europe* (Westport, Conn.: Greenwood Press, 1978), and Rudolf L. Tokes, ed., *Eurocommunism and Detente* (New York: New York University Press, 1978). As the titles indicate, there is widespread interest in the international implications of Eurocommunism.

[5] A penetrating analysis of these problems is Guiseppe Are, *Radiografia di un partito: il PCI negli anni '70: struttura ed evoluzione* [X-ray of a party: the PCI in the 1970s: structure and evolution] (Milan: Rizzoli, 1980).

tion toward the West rather than the East.[6] Nevertheless, its orientation in foreign policy is often a source of difficulties for the PCI: the international situation and historical circumstances make it unlikely that the Western powers from Bonn to Washington will ever welcome a PCI-governed Italy.[7] Various arrangements that would grant leverage to the PCI within a Christian-Democrat-dominated coalition would minimize the risk of negative international reactions, reassure Italian moderates, and free the PCI from assuming full responsibility for the domestic and international consequences of Communist participation.

The PCI is suffering internal strains from its courtship of participation in the national Government. Different points of view over strategy, always visible to careful observers, are more evident than ever. The need to succeed in the electoral game has led to the development of highly differentiated appeals to diverse groups. Almost every category of society is seen as a potential source of new voters, even including some elements of managerial and entrepreneurial strata. That the party is able to formulate, articulate, and promote such a complex electoral strategy is evidence of its intellectual and organizational vitality. But there are costs to absorb. In particular, the moderate image needed to attract the peripheral potential vote clashes with the concerns of the PCI's traditional working-class clientele as well as some revolutionary intellectuals. Party militants are indoctrinated with the need to recruit beyond the leftist subculture, but the resulting strains on understanding and enthusiasm are considerable. It is impossible to satisfy all groups completely; some must be disappointed in the party's search for the maximum number of votes.

The PCI's success in recent years has left it with vast governmental responsibilities at the communal, provincial, and regional levels. Indeed, the PCI is a governing party like the DC: they differ mainly in the levels at which they govern. And the need to staff the new governmental structures has taxed the organizational resources of the party. The renewal of the party cadres of the last few years has taken place at a time of unprecedented expansion of the PCI presence in government, especially in the "red" regions and in the city halls of large communes, most of which now involve the PCI in their administration. The tasks of managing a party in opposition and

[6] See Robert Putnam, "Italian Foreign Policy: the Emergent Consensus," in Howard R. Penniman, ed., *Italy at the Polls: The Parliamentary Elections of 1976* (Washington, D.C.: American Enterprise Institute, 1977), pp. 287-326.

[7] This issue is explored in the essays in Austin Ranney and Giovanni Sartori, eds., *Eurocommunism: the Italian Case* (Washington, D.C.: American Enterprise Institute, 1978).

running a government differ. While the PCI has exhibited as much competence as other parties, the vaunted superiority claimed for Bologna's long Communist administration—whether justified or not—has seldom been matched elsewhere. In short, the Communists have not been magicians in running local government.

The demands made on the party's organization by the need to staff governmental positions have been compounded by the need to absorb the new voters of the past decade. We will discuss changes in the electorate later in the chapter. Here we will merely note that the characteristics of many new voters, including the young, southerners, and those recruited from outside of the traditional leftist subculture, make them difficult to incorporate into the impressive organizational network that has been the pride of the party. One reason for the seemingly inexorable advance of the PCI was that it followed up on its electoral successes with organizational mobilization of new recruits, ensuring their loyalty and support in future elections. Whether because of the sheer magnitude of the tasks facing them or because of the characteristics of more recent new voters, the party has not been as successful as in the past in tying new voters securely to its traditions and organizations.

The party has also lost some of its appeal to youth and especially to those desiring revolutionary change. Not only terrorists despise it: the parliamentary and extraparliamentary parties on its left have recruited well among groups that were previously natural clienteles for the PCI. These parties suffer from fragmentation and impermanence, but their voters are numerous and undoubtedly would be attracted to a different kind of PCI, one that promised a thoroughgoing change, the romance of revolution. The PCI has lost the romantic cachet and other indefinable advantages it once received as *the* revolutionary party of the left.

A final source of difficulty for the PCI is the loss of its close organizational tie with the largest union in Italy. The long-range significance of the changing structure of the Italian labor movement is hard to estimate. At the end of the period of rapid economic expansion of the 1950s and early 1960s, Italian trade unions began to exhibit new levels of militancy and effectiveness.[8] The "hot autumn" of 1969 saw labor emerge as an independent force in Italian politics. The unions broke away from their close dependence on the political parties and demanded wage increases and a wide range of guarantees and reforms. In a few years Italy lost its status as a low wage country.

---

[8] A recent evaluation of Italian unions in politics is Walter Tobagi, *Che cosa contano i sindacati* [What do trade unions stand for?] (Milan: Rizzoli, 1980).

More directly relevant for domestic politics was the growth of cooperation among the three major labor federations in the pursuit of the interests of their members. In many ways, this movement reflected the desires of workers for a larger share of the economic pie that had grown so impressively. But in other ways, the militancy reflected a particularly trade-union radicalism, a revival of syndicalist tendencies long submerged in loyalties to party programs and societal concerns. The new union programs did not always fit with those of the parties, committed as they were to wider societal issues. This meant that the PCI could not count on the automatic support of its union allies; even if the union leaders were loyal Communists the need to compete with noncommunist trade unions and, especially, their often militant leaders altered the longstanding assumption of an identity of interests between party and union. Leaders had to choose between parliamentary and union careers; the unions could no longer be taken for granted by the party.

Changes in relations between unions and parties call into question the future ability of the PCI to govern effectively. The party has long cultivated the myth of organizational effectiveness. Alone among Italian institutions, the PCI possessed the capacity to make and enforce policy, to implement decisions in a rational and efficient manner. Its discipline and coherent leadership made it the last great hope for providing strong leadership for the modernizing of the Italian state and society. Now it can no longer ensure that policies it adopts will be accepted by the major trade union. It is ironic that this change in the nature of discipline within the party should be widely seen as a weakness, as democratic centralism was viewed as an impediment to its acceptance as a fully democratic organization. In truth, it is the structure of the trade union movement rather than the internal organization of the PCI that has changed. But, especially when combined with the other organizational problems referred to above, the independence of the unions makes the party appear less and less like a stern and perhaps threatening cure for the illnesses of the country and more and more a party like the others. From this perspective Communists are a progressive and modernizing force, but they are also Italian and, like all Italians (now that the pope is Polish), fallible. There is less discussion of what the party would be like in power. Would it be democratic? Would it give up power if it lost an election? Would it respect civil liberties? These questions have never been answered. Perhaps no answers are possible because of the contingent nature of all such political matters. Furthermore, while the election of 1979 by no means ensured that Italy could be governed without the PCI, it did seem to push further into the future the time when the PCI, alone or with left partners, could assume control of the Italian Government.

Christian Democracy in 1979. The Christian Democratic party seems to lose all the arguments and yet not lose elections. Its percentage of the vote has been remarkably constant over a thirty-year period of vast transformations and extensive changes in the composition of its electorate. It has been the dominant party of the Italian system and promises to remain so.[9] The reason is that its leaders have sought and achieved political power above all else, and in doing so they have followed rational strategies for maximizing votes. The future role of the PCI in the governance of Italy depends more than anything else on how well the DC leaders continue to place the desire for power ahead of other goals. In recent years, some DC leaders who were too young to serve in the first postwar cabinets have achieved top positions, including the presidency of the council of ministers. Most top leaders, however, have been at the top throughout the republican period. The succession of a new set of leaders has not taken place, but there are no clear indications that this will be a problem. The DC has thus far surmounted several potentially disastrous crises; its capacity for survival is perhaps its greatest strength.

In the transformation of Italian society the historic trend has been toward secularism. This trend has been reinforced by the policies of recent popes, who have sought to withdraw the church from the most exposed social and political positions. The prospects for a Catholic party in a period of secularization and church retrenchment would seem to be poor, but the DC has adapted by developing into a party of moderate conservatism and by refining its electoral techniques.

While the DC remains a Catholic party, it has not been dependent on the church organizationally for decades.[10] It automatically receives the votes of most practicing Catholics, though some support right-wing parties, hence it cannot take policy positions that deviate greatly from the official position of the church. This is evident in disputes over divorce and abortion, for example. Issues such as these create severe difficulties for the party, and of equal danger are potential revisions of the treaties between the Vatican

[9] Two recent general studies of the DC are Giorgio Galli, *Storia della D.C.* [History of the DC] (Rome: Laterza, 1978) and R. E. M. Irving, *The Christian Democratic Parties of Western Europe* (London: George Allen and Unwin, 1979), pp. 58-111.

[10] Irving emphasizes the vitality of the DC organization compared with that of Christian Democratic parties in other countries. Irving, *The Christian Democratic Parties*, p. 60.

and the Italian state. But the church influences DC policy largely in a negative sense, by establishing parameters that the party must treat with great caution. In the areas of social and economic policy, however, and of course excepting such key symbolic issues as divorce and abortion, the party is free to develop an independent line, or lines, and many points of view coexist within the party. The intellectual heritage of social Catholicism, which has played such an important role in other Christian Democratic parties, is but a minor strand within the DC. The party has been free to develop into a pragmatic governing party, oriented toward the interests of the status quo, but with little dogma or nostalgia, and with room for progressive Catholic elements. The religious connection is therefore often a strength and seldom a source of difficulty. Yet the DC is far more than a religious party. It has evolved into the conservative party of the system. The existence of the neo-Fascist MSI and Liberals today, and the Monarchists in the past, has enabled it to occupy the center in the ideological spectrum of Italian politics. It is indeed a center party in the Italian context, and that has been the key to its dominance.

Christian Democratic policies have been designed to preserve the DC's political power. Public expenditures are often used to pay off clients of the party; a massive patron-client network unites the DC electorate to the *sottogoverno*, the informal government of politicians, bureaucrats, clerics, and influence peddlers.

At the same time, the DC has adopted new electioneering techniques exploiting the mass media. Dominant parties do not require the massive organization an opposition party like the PCI must have; indeed, new techniques of campaigning plus a more sophisticated and differentiated electorate may cause a decline in the importance of organization for all parties. As a governing party as well as a conservative and religious party the DC has access to enormous resources relevant for electoral campaigns. On the negative side it is often noted that the DC electorate is aging, that the youth disproportionately support the left, that the party's strength is increasingly in backward areas and social strata while the PCI dominates cities and progressive strata.

The population-replacement model of social change suggests an impending leftist hegemony over the Italian political system. Indeed, the data are unambiguous on that point: if the model were precisely applicable, one could predict with confidence that Italy would gradually become more and more leftist as conservative voters leave the electorate through death, and new voters, disproportionately leftist in voting behavior and ideological sentiment, enter it. But, as Giacomo Sani, who has carefully examined the population-replacement model's applicability to Italy, has noted, the model may not describe Italy's future very well.[11]

Three closely related factors cause us to pause before accepting the model's postulates as predictions: the nature of conservatism as an ideology and as a political force, the nature of a dominant-party system, and the changing characteristics of the electorate. Unlike Marxism or liberalism, conservatism is a "positional" ideology, one that varies from time to time and place to place. It has few sacred texts and no Marx or Locke or Mill. Even more than other strands of thought, it is embodied in specifically national modes of expression, rests heavily on national traditions and myths, and is defined as much by what it is against as what it is for. It may take on a religious coloration or it may be completely secular. It may extol the church or the state or the gentry or the "people" or business. Unlike reactionaries, who want to stop or reverse change, conservatives want to slow it down, to control the pace. Viewed from this perspective, conservatism is never permanently out of date or out of style. A purely rational (in the economic sense) polity would hover around an equilibrium, with conservatives supported by those with less to gain from change. Many factors other than rationality enter, of course, so the rational model describes reality poorly. The point is that the content of conservatism changes through time.

As a center party, the Christian Democrats should receive a large portion of the Italian conservative vote. They can adapt to changing conditions. The role of the church may be extremely important in this regard, as it establishes parameters that may limit the "rational" adaptation of the DC. But economic and social evolution should continually provide it potential recruits, as today's youth age and tomorrow's youth, different in some of their attitudes, enter the electorate.

The second point is that the DC already plays the role of a dominant party in a dominant-party system. It can remain at the center, a weighty bloc without which no governmental majority is possible, if it continues the positional politics that it has so well employed in the past. The chief danger it faces at present seems to be the decline of the right; the DC very much needs the neo-Fascist MSI and Liberals if it is to remain near the center of Italian politics. That center role may also be challenged by the growth of other parties.

[11] This model is developed in Giacomo Sani, "Ricambio elettorale, mutamenti sociali e preferenze politiche" [Electoral change, social change, and political preferences] in Luigi Graziano and Sidney Tarrow, eds., La crisi italiana [The Italian crisis], vol. 1 (Turin: Giulio Einaudi, 1979), pp. 303-328.

The Other Parties.   In chapter 6 in this volume, Robert Leonardi says the new course that was consolidated in the 1979 election was "the revolt of the bourgeoisie against the threat of structural reform and institutionalization of the Communist presence in national Government decision making." Parties other than the three largest—the DC, PCI, and PSI—increased their share from 17.2 percent of the popular vote to 21.5 percent. While far from a landslide, this was a substantial percentage increase in the vote and an even greater gain in terms of seats in Parliament. But the greatest significance of the gain is that it' reassured those whose "cultural baggage" includes a concern for individual rights and a secular state. These sectors of the population had been badly frightened by the threat of the historic compromise, which they feared would result in a de facto division of public life between two parties more noted historically for their integralist traditions than for their defense of the individual. Parties on the extreme left improved their percentage of the vote slightly but not their parliamentary representation. The neo-Fascist MSI declined slightly; more significant was the failure of the National Right (DN) to gain any seats or to cut into the hard core of support that the MSI retains. This failure of the DN makes a center-right coalition strategy even less feasible than it was before the election. Thus the electoral results make the small parties the arbiters of the system. The Radicals (left rather than center), Republicans, Social Democrats, and Liberals—along with the Socialists, of course—provide the potential support necessary for any coalition that does not include the Communists.

The Socialists are in part a center party and in part a party of the left, in part a mass party and in part a party of notables. They are the crucial element in the revival of the center-left formula and are equally important for any coalition of left-wing parties. The latter solution is rendered unlikely by parliamentary arithmetic; the former has been tried in various permutations over almost two decades, and there is no other acceptable way to create a majority coalition not dependent on the tacit support of the PCI. Thus the election did little to alter the situation of the PSI.

It is the other parties, the Radicals, Republicans, Social Democrats, and Liberals, that benefited from the election. The Republicans actually lost slightly in the popular vote, but, given the sudden death of Ugo La Malfa, their dominant figure for decades, just before the campaign, their resilience is surprising. The Liberals and Social Democrats picked up votes and seats.

It was the Radical party that made the most impressive gains. The freshness of its approach to politics, a colorful leader, and its unequivocal policy stands seem responsible for its success. It is certainly a leftist party in its program and electoral appeal, yet it fits uneasily within the traditional left. Its voters are young and well educated, its leftism is nondoctrinaire, its organization meager. It is a very modern party in its creative use of the media in campaigning and in its orientation to issues and sets of issues rather than grand schemes of reform. It seems designed to siphon off much of the protest vote from those for whom the PCI and the PSI are too rigid and the extreme left too doctrinaire. The nature of its appeal and clientele, the substance of its policy stands, and the personal ties of its leaders make it an unlikely partner in the game of coalition politics. It may be a flash party, destined to fade in future elections. But its success was the surprise of the 1979 election.

These small parties are much more important than their numbers suggest. Their voters are well situated in the stratification system, and the parties themselves are well placed spatially to play an important role in the coalition game. They provide one ingredient the Italian system lacks—flexibility. Between the red and black giants, the small parties offer, if not alternatives, nuances badly needed in the governing process. They guarantee some degree of vigilance in a system never characterized by punctiliousness on the part of governmental authorities. The election demonstrated the capacity of these small parties to survive and even prosper. For many, this is a sign of the vitality of Italian democracy.

The Changing Electorate

The changing Italian electorate calls into question the utility of the population-replacement model in anticipating the nature of political change in Italy. Here we will point to several factors that will have an impact on the future voting habits of Italians, but without engaging in extensive analysis.

The most important single factor is likely to be an increased volatility of the electorate, which, in turn, is the product of several forces.[12] The years of the cold war, of the struggle between God and communism, are over. Individuals socialized in those years retain much of the intense partisanship of the era, but younger people,

[12] Presenting evidence from Bologna, Marzio Barbagli and his colleagues suggest a much higher volatility of the electorate throughout the postwar period than is generally assumed from the electoral results: M. Barbagli, P. Corbetta, A. Parisi, and H. M. A. Schadee, *Fluidità elettorale e classi sociali in Italia* [Electoral change and social classes in Italy] (Bologna: Il Mulino, 1979), pp. 111-154.

while ideologically sophisticated and opinionated, may lack both the emotional intensity and the organizational commitment characteristic of the old. Even the institutions that bred that intensity are in decline. On the right, Catholic Action is peripheral to politics, church attendance is down. On the left, changing leisure patterns and prosperity have reduced the intensity of subcultural identification and integration. A decade of moderation by the PCI, DC, church, and other organizations has taken its toll on passion in politics. This generalization does not apply to the extremes, where the savagery of terrorism reflects a rejection of moderation. But terrorism also reflects the realization that only extraordinary actions have any possibility of reversing the trend toward the center in Italian politics. The almost universal condemnation of terrorism suggests that extremists will not be successful in disrupting the Italian system.

A concomitant of this lack of intensity is the difficulty faced by parties in mobilizing new voters into the organizational networks of their subcultures. This is especially important for the PCI, which has been remarkably effective throughout the postwar period in consolidating its electoral gains by incorporating new adherents into the party's impressive communications networks. Until 1979 the party never retreated from one election to another in its march toward electoral dominance. But in 1979 the trend was reversed. The party suffered in the public mind from the Moro kidnapping and murder; indeed, the PCI's electoral setback may have been merely a reaction to that terrible affair, a public reflex not merited by the actual behavior of the PCI. But the pattern of 1976 gains and 1979 losses, as analyzed by Giacomo Sani in his chapter in this volume, suggests that the PCI has been far less successful in absorbing new voters in recent years than in the past. The number of new voters undoubtedly placed strains on a party organization already taxed by its efforts at personnel rejuvenation and faced with new responsibilities for regional and local governments. In addition, the characteristics of new voters complicate the task of absorption. Contemporary youth are more difficult to organize, while the expansion in the South includes large numbers of clientelistic voters who expected quick payoffs from Communist successes in recent elections. Without rewards, these votes go elsewhere.

Changes among young people are extremely difficult for the PCI to cope with. Many Italian youths, even the extremists, are heirs to the libertarian views of the past decades. They are well educated, extremely critical, and in revolt against the "consumer society" in which they have so much trouble finding a niche. An accumulating literature documents the changing expectations of youth in advanced industrial societies and their impatience with progress defined solely in material terms: these "postmaterialist" values are widespread among well-educated and affluent Italian youth. While they share many ideological assumptions with the Communists, they are likely to view the PCI as tainted by accommodation with the status quo and incapable of bringing about fundamental changes.

The political style of the young today fits uneasily with the organizational rigidity of the PCI. In truth, that party has been inventive in developing organizational forms more compatible with the preferences of a generation raised on ideas of direct participation. Such innovations as neighborhood councils have been established in several cities under PCI-leftist control. The Italian electorate in general, however, is likely to be less and less attracted to activity in traditional party organizations. The economic and emotional needs filled by this activity are likely to seem less pressing to a better educated population in a more affluent era. If Italy follows the pattern of other advanced industrial democracies, as it seems to be doing, increased participation is more likely to take place in single-interest organizations than in political parties themselves. Inventive parties, of course, will seek to establish these organizations as satellite bodies; much of the future of party organization depends on the extent to which such structures arise independent of the parties themselves. The success of the Radical party, which has made a special effort both to choose relevant issues for its agenda and to exploit relationships with special interest movements such as feminists and gays, suggests a possible future pattern. It is true, however, that other countries do not possess large parties with the strong organization of Italian parties. Single-interest organizations in Italy may run up against entrenched parties that limit their expansion. What is obvious is that the changing Italian electorate will cause problems for party organization in that country.

These problems will be compounded by the changing nature of campaigning. Italy retained the mass political rally and campaigning focused on parties rather than candidates or issues long after the electronic media and advertising professionals had become central in other comparable countries. As William Porter's chapter in this volume demonstrates, the situation is now changing in Italy. The media were very important in the 1979 campaign. In this environment, money is perhaps as vital as organization; the huge apparatus of the PCI may be of declining significance in getting out the vote.

The DC is not as handicapped organizationally as the conventional wisdom suggests. In the first place, it is organizationally stronger than its counterparts in other European countries. Its factional divisions are probably an electoral advantage rather than a handicap, as local organizations tend to be controlled by a single faction so that divisions seldom appear at that level. If media campaigns should lead to the nationalization of electioneering, the different faces of the DC in different parts of the country could become a problem. But the large parties already have highly differentiated electoral tactics in different areas, and there is no reason why that should not continue. Increased importance of regions and local government, which is advocated by the left, would accentuate that trend; the DC is at its best in adapting to local needs and local configurations of power.

Finally, change is affected by the limits set by population. The electorate is already highly mobilized. Social change, by encouraging massive geographical and social mobility, has broken down old ties and freed people for new ones. Even so, as John Low-Beer has demonstrated, partisan loyalties have survived vast social mobility.[13] The exodus from the countryside will be a trickle in the future. In the post industrial society, the middle class will grow faster than the working class. The PCI is running up against the limits of its clientele. It has sought in a very creative fashion to expand those limits by appealing to "progressive" forces in every class, but this creates strains within its working-class core. It is a strategy difficult to maintain over time if few rewards are evident. The PCI in power has to make policy decisions that favor some groups over others, and the PCI is now in power all over Italy. In short, it will be difficult to broaden the appeal of the party indefinitely.

It is not to be assumed that the DC will be the necessary beneficiary of the forces discussed above. The capacity of the PCI to innovate in policy and organization has historically been impressive; it may not suffer much. Another outcome could be the growth of the smaller parties. An increasingly sophisticated electorate makes that outcome feasible. Such a development would not solve the problems of authority and legitimacy. It would, however, provide flexibility and the possibility of reform. The historic compromise has, at least for the moment, receded from the stage. The problem of creating a viable coalition to govern the country seems eternal.

---

13 John Low-Beer, *Protest and Participation: The New Workingclass in Italy* (Cambridge: Cambridge University Press, 1978).

Appendix A

Government Formation in Italy

Douglas A. Wertman

The Process of Forming A Government. It is necessary to form a new Government after a parliamentary election or, between elections, when the incumbent Government loses a vote of confidence or resigns. The president of the republic consults with the leaders of the political parties as well as with ex-presidents and the presiding officers of both the Chamber of Deputies and the Senate. During these consultations the president will get an indication of the possible parliamentary majority and of the candidates for the prime ministership preferred by the leading party (the Christian Democrats so far) as well as some of the other parties. After these consultations, the president names a prime minister-designate.

This prime minister-designate then begins his own round (or two) of consultations with the leaders of many of the other political parties. His consultations as well as the negotiations among the parties will ultimately result either in a Government or in the prime minister-designate's going back to the president to report failure. If the consultations have succeeded, the parties of the new Government (or the new majority) will reach an agreement on the Government program as well as on the distribution of cabinet positions among them. Of course, if there is a one-party Government or if the program is not coordinated among the majority and any abstaining parties, there may be a much looser agreement on the program and/or on personnel.

If the prime minister-designate's consultations have failed, either the president will tell him to try again or, as happens more often, the president will consult again with party leaders and name a new prime minister-designate. If a new candidate is named, the process described earlier begins again. The president, of course, also has the option of dissolving the Parliament and calling new elections.

299

The prime minister-designate has succeeded when he (1) has reached solid agreement with enough parties to ensure his Government a majority in Parliament or (2) at least expects that his Government will get enough support in Parliament to win a vote of confidence. He then reports this to the president, takes office, and asks for a vote of confidence in each chamber of the Italian Parliament. To remain in office the Government must obtain at least a majority of those voting in each house separately. A failure on the vote of confidence in either chamber means resignation.

Some Important Terms. Being *in the Government* means voting for the Government on the vote of confidence as well as having ministers in the cabinet. Being *in the majority* means voting for the Government on the vote of confidence to help it exist but having no ministers in the cabinet. The Government program might or might not be coordinated among the parties in the majority. A party in the majority may on occasion, particularly in an uncoordinated majority, vote against specific legislative proposals of the Government. Thus, a Government with a *formal* or *numerical majority* (a majority of the votes cast in the vote of confidence) might or might not have a *working parliamentary majority* (enough support on individual measures to get them through Parliament).

During the 1976–1979 period, a distinction was frequently drawn between a *programmatic majority* and a *political majority*, the latter implying a closer relationship among the parties involved. The Christian Democrats tried to minimize the implications and political effects of the July 1977 "agreement among the six" and the Communists' entry into the majority in March 1978 by calling them both manifestations of a programmatic majority. The Christian Democrats said that this was not a political majority like the center-left, which had implied a more far-reaching agreement among the parties involved.

Abstaining on the vote of confidence means giving the Government indirect support by reducing the majority the Government needs on a vote of confidence. This practice reached its extreme with the Government of *non-no confidence* formed shortly after the 1976 election (only the DC and SVP supported the Government on the vote of confidence, while the PCI, PSI, PSDI, PRI, and PLI abstained). Abstentions might or might not be coordinated among the parties involved, and abstaining parties might or might not have a say in negotiating the program. A party abstaining on the vote of confidence may on occasion (particularly when its abstention has not been directly agreed upon among the parties involved) vote against specific legislative proposals of the Government.

Being *in the opposition* simply means voting against the Government on the vote of confidence. There is no constitutional "loyal opposition" like that of the largest opposition party in the United Kingdom.

A *monocolore* Government is one in which all the members of the cabinet come from only one party. The Governments formed in 1976 and 1978 were both *monocolore* DC Governments.

The *constitutional arc* refers to the political groupings which participated in the resistance movement during World War II and helped bring about the restoration of a democratic political system in Italy. It includes six parties today: the Communists (PCI), the Socialists (PSI), the Social Democrats (PSDI), the Christian Democrats (DC), the Republicans (PRI), and the Liberals (PLI).

ITALIAN GOVERNMENTS, 1976–1979

Governmental Negotiations	Government	Composition of Majority	Composition of Government
July-August 1976	Third Andreotti Government	DC, SVP (PCI,[a] PSI, PSDI, PRI, PLI abstain: Government of non-no confidence. March-July 1977, negotiations lead to "agreement among the six," under which DC, PCI, PSI, PSDI, PRI, and PLI support a joint program; no new vote of confidence is held)	DC *monocolore* (but PCI given some chairmanships of parliamentary committees and presidency of Chamber[b])
January-March 1978	Fourth Andreotti Government	DC, PCI,[c] PSI, PSDI, PRI (Liberals refuse to enter a majority including Communists)	DC *monocolore* (PCI retains committee chairmanships and presidency of Chamber)
January-March 1979, attempts to form Government by • Giulio Andreotti • Ugo La Malfa[d] • Giulio Andreotti	Fifth Andreotti Government	Defeated by 1 vote in Senate	DC, PSDI, PRI

April 2, 1979, President Pertini dissolves Parliament, calls new elections
June 3–4, 1979, parliamentary elections

June-August 1979, attempts to form Government by • Giulio Andreotti • Bettino Craxi • Filippo Maria Pandolfi • Francesco Cossiga	First Cossiga Government	DC, PSDI, PLI, SVP (PSI and PRI abstain)	DC, PSDI, PLI, and 2 "technicians from the PSI area"

NOTE: The first Andreotti Government lasted from February 17 to February 26, 1972, when it was defeated in a vote of confidence, precipitating early elections. The second Andreotti Government lasted from June 26, 1972, to June 12, 1973.

[a] First time since 1947 that the PCI is not in the opposition.

[b] First PCI parliamentary offices since 1947.

[c] First time since 1947 that the PCI is in the majority.

[d] First non-DC prime minister-designate since 1945.

SOURCE: Author.

Appendix B

Italian Ballots, 1979

Reproduced here are Chamber of Deputies and Senate ballots used in the Italian elections of June 3, 1979. The Chamber ballot shows only party symbols. The voter draws an X across the symbol of the party he has chosen. Then, if he wishes to cast preference votes, he writes the names of the candidates he supports, or their numbers, on the party list, in the spaces provided. (Voters may cast three or four preference votes depending on the size of the district.) The number of ballots cast for the party determines the number of seats it wins, while the preference votes determine which candidates will occupy them. The Senate ballot shows the name of each party's leader as well as its symbol. The voter folds both ballots before dropping them into the ballot box.

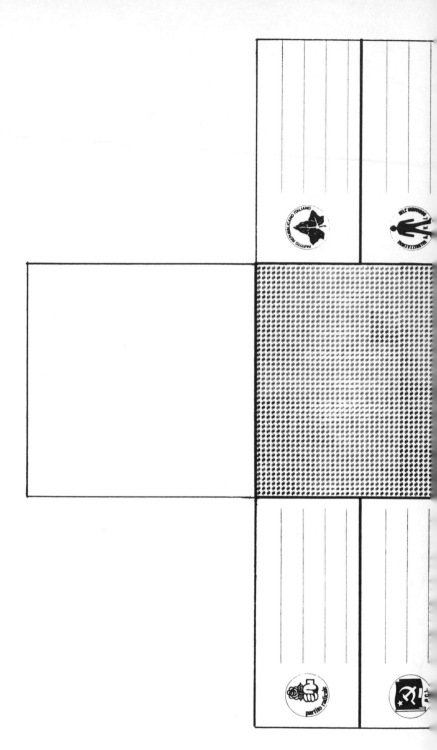

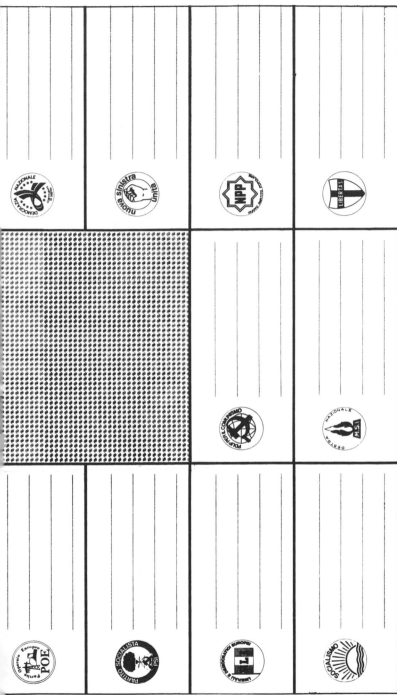

Chamber of Deputies ballot, unfolded (actual width 12¾ inches)

ELEZIONE DEL SENATO DELLA REPUBBLICA

3 giugno 1979

L A Z I O

Collegio di VITERBO

SCHEDA PER LA VOTAZIONE

Firma dello scrutatore

TIMBRO

Senate ballot, folded (actual size)

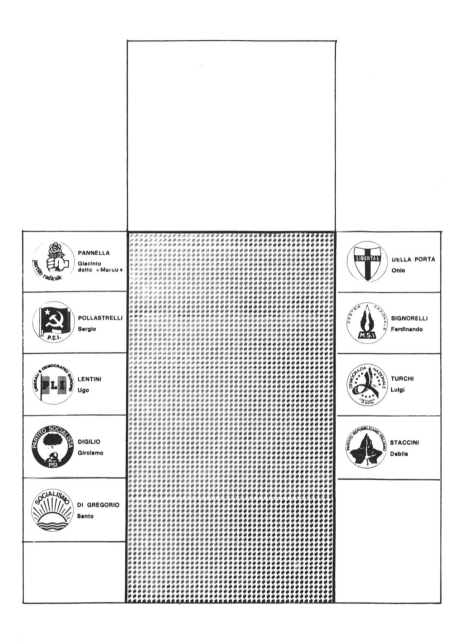

Senate ballot, unfolded

Appendix C

Italian Election Returns, 1979

Compiled by Richard M. Scammon

ITALY: CHAMBER OF DEPUTIES ELECTION RETURNS, 1979

Constituency	Total	DC	PCI	PSI	MSI-DN	PSDI	PR	PRI	PLI	PDUP	Joint Tickets and Other[a]
1. Torino-Novara-Vercelli											
Valid vote	2,219,777	687,440	729,210	234,037	87,066	107,829	111,839	94,780	89,986	39,315	38,275
% of vote		31.0	32.9	10.5	3.9	4.9	5.0	4.3	4.1	1.8	1.7
Seats	33	12	12	4	1	1	1	1	1	—	—
2. Cuneo-Alessandria-Asti											
Valid vote	864,394	357,466	213,214	83,836	23,720	48,034	29,969	33,513	50,461	12,125	12,056
% of vote		41.4	24.7	9.7	2.7	5.6	3.5	3.9	5.8	1.4	1.4
Seats	12	7	4	1	—	—	—	—	1	—	—
3. Genova-Imperia-LaSpezia-Savona											
Valid vote	1,303,447	419,195	462,943	150,260	48,794	43,144	63,092	44,821	43,647	11,346	16,205
% of vote		32.2	35.5	11.5	3.7	3.3	4.8	3.4	3.3	.9	1.2
Seats	18	7	8	2	—	—	1	—	—	—	—
4. Milano-Pavia											
Valid vote	3,101,127	1,034,717	994,768	348,495	124,661	125,090	147,531	108,355	94,834	60,428	62,248
% of vote		33.4	32.1	11.2	4.0	4.0	4.8	3.5	3.1	1.9	2.0
Seats	50	18	17	6	2	2	2	1	1	1	—
5. Como-Sondrio-Varese											
Valid vote	1,142,664	498,173	267,419	143,174	38,086	49,798	41,041	33,440	32,807	20,490	18,236
% of vote		43.6	23.4	12.5	3.3	4.4	3.6	2.9	2.9	1.8	1.6
Seats	15	9	4	2	—	—	—	—	—	—	—

	Total										
6. Brescia-Bergamo											
Valid vote	1,249,965	638,294	269,755	124,305	39,333	44,758	34,544	24,659	25,722	26,221	22,374
% of vote		51.1	21.6	9.9	3.1	3.6	2.8	2.0	2.1	2.1	1.8
Seats	17	11	4	2	—	—	—	—	—	—	—
7. Mantova-Cremona											
Valid vote	509,976	192,514	175,743	63,008	18,038	16,434	12,590	8,663	7,696	9,852	5,438
% of vote		37.7	34.5	12.4	3.5	3.2	2.5	1.7	1.5	1.9	1.1
Seats	7	3	3	1	—	—	—	—	—	—	—
8. Trento-Bolzano											
Valid vote	571,564	177,362	63,374	37,876	13,453	15,326	24,270	12,439	7,143	5,008	215,313
% of vote		31.0	11.1	6.6	2.4	2.7	4.2	2.2	1.2	.9	37.7
Seats	8	3	1	—	—	—	—	—	—	—	4
9. Verona-Padova-Vicenza-Rovigo											
Valid vote	1,718,150	926,990	336,693	150,745	57,057	65,084	60,717	45,107	33,273	20,356	22,128
% of vote		54.0	19.6	8.8	3.3	3.8	3.5	2.6	1.9	1.2	1.3
Seats	25	16	5	2	—	1	1	—	—	—	—
10. Venezia-Treviso											
Valid vote	1,039,742	464,157	263,046	111,713	29,474	47,155	41,300	33,180	18,519	17,415	13,783
% of vote		44.6	25.3	10.7	2.8	4.5	4.0	3.2	1.8	1.7	1.3
Seats	14	8	4	2	—	—	—	—	—	—	—
11. Udine-Belluno-Gorizia-Pordenone											
Valid vote	824,462	343,654	192,591	74,561	30,601	62,610	30,695	22,881	12,975	10,677	43,217
% of vote		41.7	23.4	9.0	3.7	7.6	3.7	2.8	1.6	1.3	5.2
Seats	11	6	3	1	—	1	—	—	—	—	—

(Table continues on next page)

ITALY: CHAMBER OF DEPUTIES ELECTION RETURNS, 1979 (continued)

Constituency	Total	DC	PCI	PSI	MSI-DN	PSDI	PR	PRI	PLI	PDUP	Joint Tickets and Other[a]
12. Bologna-Ferrara-Ravenna-Forli											
Valid vote	1,671,439	413,764	802,158	138,005	45,539	65,422	49,385	100,111	24,086	16,642	16,327
% of vote		24.8	48.0	8.3	2.7	3.9	3.0	6.0	1.4	1.0	1.0
Seats	23	6	13	2	—	1	—	1	—	—	—
13. Parma-Modena-Piacenza-Reggio Emilia											
Valid vote	1,225,630	376,092	569,457	110,261	31,276	46,597	29,594	22,908	16,121	13,612	9,712
% of vote		30.7	46.5	9.0	2.6	3.8	2.4	1.9	1.3	1.1	.8
Seats	16	6	9	1	—	—	—	—	—	—	—
14. Firenze-Pistoia											
Valid vote	1,046,446	304,654	506,156	93,607	28,222	23,290	28,382	25,649	10,040	14,582	11,864
% of vote		29.1	48.4	8.9	2.7	2.2	2.7	2.5	1.0	1.4	1.1
Seats	14	5	8	1	—	—	—	—	—	—	—
15. Pisa-Livorno-Lucca-Massa Carrara											
Valid vote	936,142	303,637	385,006	97,122	35,430	27,807	23,945	30,498	8,984	13,817	9,896
% of vote		32.4	41.1	10.4	3.8	3.0	2.6	3.3	1.0	1.5	1.1
Seats	12	5	6	1	—	—	—	—	—	—	—
16. Siena-Arezzo-Grosseto											
Valid vote	585,248	164,226	285,289	59,938	19,680	12,896	10,997	14,571	5,004	7,309	5,338
% of votes		28.1	48.7	10.2	3.4	2.2	1.9	2.5	.9	1.2	.9
Seats	9	3	5	1	—	—	—	—	—	—	—

17. Ancona-Pesaro-Macerata-Ascoli Piceno

Valid vote	979,497	371,036	373,016	77,604	38,757	27,494	22,829	34,627	9,772	15,212	9,150
% of vote		37.9	38.1	7.9	4.0	2.8	2.3	3.5	1.0	1.6	.9
Seats	13	6	6	1	—	—	—	—	—	—	—

18. Perugia-Terni-Rieti

Valid vote	673,146	209,524	289,598	75,187	34,447	12,792	13,671	17,736	5,115	8,526	6,550
% of vote		31.1	43.0	11.2	5.1	1.9	2.0	2.6	.8	1.3	1.0
Seats	10	4	5	1	—	—	—	—	—	—	—

19. Roma-Viterbo-Latina-Frosinone

Valid vote	3,192,292	1,164,944	965,403	274,332	257,877	109,405	166,628	106,133	61,262	29,135	57,173
% of vote		36.5	30.2	8.6	8.1	3.4	5.2	3.3	1.9	.9	1.8
Seats	49	20	16	4	4	1	2	1	1	—	—

20. L'Alquila-Pescara-Chieti-Teramo

Valid vote	791,653	361,367	246,080	59,751	46,195	20,536	18,316	14,123	6,829	8,372	10,084
% of votes		45.6	31.1	7.5	5.8	2.6	2.3	1.8	.9	1.1	1.3
Seats	12	7	4	1	—	—	—	—	—	—	—

21. Campobasso-Isernia

Valid vote	202,808	110,990	43,658	14,927	10,535	5,614	3,915	4,203	4,430	3,557	979
% of vote		54.7	21.5	7.4	5.2	2.8	1.9	2.1	2.2	1.8	.5
Seats	4	3	1	—	—	—	—	—	—	—	—

22. Napoli-Caserta

Valid vote	2,054,888	801,798	556,615	177,389	207,990	83,805	74,699	60,240	24,362	25,571	42,419
% of vote		39.0	27.1	8.6	10.1	4.1	3.6	2.9	1.2	1.2	2.1
Seats	36	15	11	3	4	1	1	1	—	—	—

(Table continued on next page)

ITALY: CHAMBER OF DEPUTIES ELECTION RETURNS, 1979 (continued)

Constituency	Total	DC	PCI	PSI	MSI-DN	PSDI	PR	PRI	PLI	PDUP	Joint Tickets and Other[a]
23. Benevento-Avellino-Salerno											
Valid vote	1,024,888	497,813	211,147	111,973	74,446	44,958	18,677	19,479	12,966	14,724	18,705
% of vote		48.6	20.6	10.9	7.3	4.4	1.8	1.9	1.3	1.4	1.8
Seats	17	10	4	2	1	—	—	—	—	—	—
24. Bari-Foggia											
Valid vote	1,237,302	521,409	335,671	126,313	102,668	51,469	31,407	23,712	18,874	12,131	13,648
% of vote		42.1	27.1	10.2	8.3	4.2	2.5	1.9	1.5	1.0	1.1
Seats	21	10	6	2	2	1	—	—	—	—	—
25. Lecce-Brindisi-Taranto											
Valid vote	1,027,344	448,165	269,743	104,474	92,580	36,067	18,748	20,431	11,178	13,643	12,315
% of vote		43.6	26.3	10.2	9.0	3.5	1.8	2.0	1.1	1.3	1.2
Seats	16	8	5	2	1	—	—	—	—	—	—
26. Potenza-Matera											
Valid vote	358,739	156,485	103,572	39,296	20,870	12,770	5,949	4,410	3,293	7,104	4,990
% of vote		43.6	28.9	11.0	5.8	3.6	1.7	1.2	.9	2.0	1.4
Seats	5	3	2	—	—	—	—	—	—	—	—
27. Catanzaro-Cosenza-Reggio di Calabria											
Valid vote	1,113,863	475,879	297,348	142,640	77,910	35,712	21,612	18,540	7,364	19,526	17,332
% of vote		42.7	26.7	12.8	7.0	3.2	1.9	1.7	.7	1.8	1.6
Seats	20	10	6	3	1	—	—	—	—	—	—

28. Catania-Messina-Siracusa-Ragusa-Enna

	Total										
Valid vote	1,431,262	606,836	309,154	144,528	135,534	70,754	39,526	46,902	26,883	15,942	35,203
% of vote		42.4	21.6	10.1	9.5	4.9	2.8	3.3	1.9	1.1	2.5
Seats	24	12	6	3	2	1	—	—	—	—	—

29. Palermo-Trapani-Agrigento-Caltanissetta

	Total										
Valid vote	1,314,811	594,800	267,999	131,539	83,924	57,089	42,724	60,212	25,567	16,025	34,932
% of vote		45.2	20.4	10.0	6.4	4.3	3.2	4.6	1.9	1.2	2.7
Seats	22	12	5	2	1	1	—	1	—	—	—

30. Cagliari-Sassari-Nuoro-Oristano

	Total										
Valid vote	925,419	352,689	293,535	82,345	57,860	30,142	31,918	17,703	12,100	12,236	34,891
% of vote		38.1	31.7	8.9	6.3	3.3	3.4	1.9	1.3	1.3	3.8
Seats	15	7	6	1	1	—	—	—	—	—	—

32. Trieste

	Total										
Valid vote	218,120	50,854	49,901	8,338	13,133	5,127	13,572	3,800	2,193	1,490	69,712
% of vote		23.3	22.9	3.8	6.0	2.4	6.2	1.7	1.0	.7	32.0
Seats	3	1	1	—	—	—	—	—	—	—	1

	Total										
TOTAL Valid Vote	36,556,205	14,026,924	11,129,262	3,591,579	1,925,156	1,405,008	1,264,082	1,107,826	713,486	502,389	890,493
% of vote		38.4	30.4	9.8	5.3	3.8	3.5	3.0	2.0	1.4	2.4
Seats	551	253	190	54	20	11	8	6	3	1	5
NATIONAL ASSIGNMENT	78	8	11	8	11	10	10	9	6	5	—
TOTAL SEATS	629	261	201	62	31	21	18	15	9	6	5

(Table continued on next page)

ITALY: CHAMBER OF DEPUTIES ELECTION RETURNS, 1979 (continued)

NOTE: This table does not include the vote in the single member constituency of Valle d'Aosta (number 31), which uses a plurality electoral system. The vote in that constituency was: Unione Valdostana-Unione Valdostana Progressista-Democratici Popolari-Partito Liberale Italiano joint ticket, 33,250 (1 elected); Unità della Sinistra, 23,909; DC-PSDI-PRI joint ticket, 13,442; MSI-DN, 2,077; Democrazia Nazionale-Costituente di Destra, 824.

a "Other" vote includes: Nuova Sinistra Unità, 294,951; Democrazia Nazionale-Costituente di Destra, 228,453; Partito Popolare Sud Tirolese, 205,007 (4 elected in district number 8, Trento Bolzano); Associazione per Trieste, 65,397 (1 elected in district number 32, Trieste); Movimento Friuli, 35,235; miscellaneous, 61,450.

SOURCE: *Elezioni Politiche del 3 Giugno 1979, Risultati* [Results of the June 3, 1979, parliamentary elections] [Rome: Ministero dell' Interno, 1979)

ITALY: SENATE ELECTION RETURNS, 1979

Region	Total	DC	PCI	PSI	MSI-DN	PSDI	PRI	PLI	PR	Joint Tickets and Other[a]
Abruzzi										
Valid vote	674,531	312,667	213,670	56,568	39,773	15,695	13,577	6,599	11,175	4,807
% of vote		46.4	31.7	8.4	5.9	2.3	2.0	1.0	1.7	.7
Seats	7	4	3	—	—	—	—	—	—	—
Basilicata										
Valid vote	299,950	133,837	87,109	38,176	18,434	12,007	3,306	3,179	—	3,902
% of vote		44.6	29.0	12.7	6.1	4.0	1.1	1.1	—	1.3
Seats	7	4	2	1	—	—	—	—	—	—
Calabria										
Valid vote	913,769	368,625	260,501	139,062	84,217	22,865	12,633	6,152	—	19,714
% of vote		40.3	28.5	15.2	9.2	2.5	1.4	.7	—	2.2
Seats	11	5	3	2	1	—	—	—	—	—
Campania										
Valid vote	2,512,171	984,934	657,744	255,731	270,900	118,204	100,214	38,958	—	85,486
% of vote		39.2	26.2	10.2	10.8	4.7	4.0	1.6	—	3.4
Seats	29	13	8	3	3	1	1	—	—	—

(Table continued on next page)

Italy: Senate Election Returns, 1979 (continued)

Region	Total	DC	PCI	PSI	MSI-DN	PSDI	PRI	PLI	PR	Joint Tickets and Other[a]
Emilia-Romagna										
Valid vote	2,551,956	711,580	1,229,204	224,489	68,404	110,544	114,278	39,583	—	53,874
% of vote		27.9	48.2	8.8	2.7	4.3	4.5	1.6	—	2.1
Seats	22	6	12	2	—		1		—	—
Friuli-Venezia Giulia										
Valid vote	774,039	297,399	184,582	64,872	32,665	45,219	17,871	11,102	23,596	96,733
% of vote		38.4	23.8	8.4	4.2	5.8	2.3	1.4	3.0	12.5
Seats	7	4	2	1	—	—			—	—
Lazio										
Valid vote	2,796,096	1,028,568	864,022	245,380	250,056	104,739	101,452	62,538	124,305	15,036
% of vote		36.8	30.9	8.8	8.9	3.7	3.6	2.2	4.4	.5
Seats	27	11	9	2	2	1	1		1	—
Liguria										
Valid vote	1,156,506	385,723	418,257	136,492	42,987	42,528	42,493	38,521	44,624	4,881
% of vote		33.4	36.2	11.8	3.7	3.7	3.7	3.3	3.9	.4
Seats	10	4	5	1	—	—			—	—
Lombardia										
Valid vote	5,209,969	2,117,789	1,530,781	620,900	186,412	217,704	162,090	156,745	154,257	63,291
% of vote		40.6	29.4	11.9	3.6	4.2	3.1	3.0	3.0	1.2
Seats	48	21	15	6	1	2	1	1	1	—

	Valid vote / % / Seats									
Marche										
Valid vote	848,190	334,444	330,767	71,537	31,609	25,164	29,932	8,294	13,991	2,452
% of vote		39.4	39.0	8.4	3.7	3.0	3.5	1.0	1.6	.3
Seats	8	4	4	—	—	—	—	—	—	—
Molise										
Valid vote	172,060	95,295	39,280	12,716	9,977	4,311	3,876	3,512	2,430	663
% of vote		55.4	22.8	7.4	5.8	2.5	2.3	2.0	1.4	.4
Seats	2	2	—	—	—	—	—	—	—	—
Piemonte										
Valid vote	2,682,834	939,229	854,527	282,547	94,424	152,946	124,819	140,307	—	94,035
% of vote		35.0	31.9	10.5	3.5	5.7	4.7	5.2	—	3.5
Seats	25	9	9	3	1	1	1	1	—	—
Puglia										
Valid vote	1,870,849	776,234	518,333	198,106	186,761	87,805	41,991	24,485	—	37,134
% of vote		41.5	27.7	10.6	10.0	4.7	2.2	1.3	—	2.0
Seats	20	9	6	2	2	1	—	—	—	—
Sardegna										
Valid vote	760,177	301,261	244,427	71,999	51,372	23,406	13,496	11,078	16,417	26,721
% of vote		39.6	32.2	9.5	6.8	3.1	1.8	1.5	2.2	3.5
Seats	8	4	3	1	—	—	—	—	—	—
Sicilia										
Valid vote	2,320,755	934,772	519,190	260,693	225,356	127,759	116,287	49,415	—	87,283
% of vote		40.3	22.4	11.2	9.7	5.5	5.0	2.1	—	3.8
Seats	26	12	6	3	3	1	1	—	—	—

(Table continued on next page)

Region	Total	DC	PCI	PSI	MSI-DN	PSDI	PRI	PLI	PR	Joint Tickets and Other[a]
Toscana										
Valid vote	2,262,602	702,170	1,055,528	234,679	75,575	60,882	64,787	24,787	—	44,194
% of vote		31.0	46.7	10.4	3.3	2.7	2.9	1.1	—	2.0
Seats	20	7	11	2	—	—	—	—	—	—
Trentino-Alto Adige										
Valid vote	480,665	160,634	55,372	32,960	11,706	14,281	—	6,581	15,897	183,234
% of vote		33.4	11.5	6.9	2.4	3.0	—	1.4	3.3	38.1
Seats	7	3	1	—	—	—	—	—	—	3
Umbria										
Valid vote	503,615	153,413	233,211	59,134	22,331	9,457	12,260	3,365	6,752	3,692
% of vote		30.5	46.3	11.7	4.4	1.9	2.4	.7	1.3	.7
Seats	7	2	4	1	—	—	—	—	—	—
Valle D'Aosta										
Valid vote	62,200	—	—	—	2,003	—	—	—	—	60,197
% of vote		—	—	—	3.2	—	—	—	—	96.8
Seats	1	—	—	—	—	—	—	—	—	1
Veneto										
Valid vote	2,477,861	1,272,142	559,446	246,369	75,988	125,213	77,889	56,517	—	64,297
% of vote		51.3	22.6	9.9	3.1	5.1	3.1	2.3	—	2.6
Seats	23	14	6	2	—	1	—	—	—	—

TOTAL

Valid vote	31,330,795	12,010,716	9,855,951	3,252,410	1,780,950	1,320,729	1,053,251	691,718	413,444	951,626
% of vote		38.3	31.5	10.4	5.7	4.2	3.4	2.2	1.3	3.0
Seats	315	138	109	32	13	9	6	2	2	4

NOTE: In addition to the 315 elected senators there are 7 life senators, whose party affiliations are as follows: 1 PSDI, 2 DC, 1 PSI, 1 PLI, 1 independent, and 1 independent left.

[a] "Other" vote includes: Partito Radicale-Nuova Sinistra Unità, 365,954; Democrazia Nazionale-Costituente di Destra, 176,966; Partito Popolare Sud Tirolese, 172,582 (3 elected); Associazione per Trieste e l'Isontino, 61,911; Nuova Sinistra Unità, 44,094; Unione Valdostana-Unione Valdostana Progressista-Democratici Popolari-Partito Liberale Italiano joint ticket, 37,082 (1 elected); other lists and joint tickets, 93,037.

SOURCE: Elezioni Politiche del 3 Giugno 1979, Risultati.

Contributors

Samuel H. Barnes is chairman and professor of political science and program director of the Center for Political Studies of the Institute for Social Research at the University of Michigan. His publications on Italy include *Party Democracy, Representation in Italy,* and chapters in *Political Oppositions in Western Democracies* and *Electoral Behavior: A Comparative Handbook.*

Karen Beckwith is a visiting instructor at Oakland University and a Ph.D. candidate at Syracuse University. She is working on a study of women's political participation in the United States from 1952 to 1976.

Joseph LaPalombara is Arnold Wolfers Professor of Political Science and professor of international management at Yale University. He is the author of *Interest Groups in Italian Politics, Italy: The Politics of Planning* and *Multinational Corporations and National Elites.*

Robert Leonardi is associate professor of political science at DePaul University in Chicago. He received a Fulbright grant to lecture in Italy in 1981 and is currently working on a longitudinal study of the Italian regions.

Patrick McCarthy is associate professor of European studies at Haverford College and visiting professor at the Johns Hopkins School for Advanced International Studies in Washington, D.C. His publications include articles on the French Socialist party and the Italian Communist party.

Gianfranco Pasquino is professor of political science at the University of Bologna, visiting professor of political science at the Bologna Center of the Johns Hopkins University, and editor of the journal

Il Mulino. His most recent book is *Crisi dei partiti e governabilità* (*Crisis of parties and governability*).

WILLIAM E. PORTER is professor of communication at the University of Michigan. The author of *Assault on the Media, the Nixon Years,* he is preparing a study of the Italian journalist.

GIACOMO SANI is professor of political science at the Ohio State University and the author of books and articles on Italian government and politics that have appeared in Europe and the United States. He is working on a comparative analysis of mass political behavior in Italy and Spain.

RICHARD M. SCAMMON, coauthor of *This U.S.A.* and *The Real Majority,* is director of the Elections Research Center in Washington, D.C. He has edited the biennial series *America Votes* since 1956.

SIDNEY TARROW is professor of government at Cornell University. He is the author of *Peasant Communism in Southern Italy* and *Between Center and Periphery: Grassroots Politicians in Italy and France;* the coeditor (with Peter Lange) of *Italy in Transition: Conflict and Consensus;* and (with Donald Blackmer) of *Communism in Italy and France.*

DOUGLAS A. WERTMAN, an analyst in the West Europe/Canada Unit of the United States International Communication Agency's Office of Research, has taught political science at the University of Missouri and the Johns Hopkins Bologna Center. He is working on a study of generational differences in Italian mass attitudes on foreign policy issues.

Index

AEI's *At the Polls* Studies

Australia at the Polls: The National Elections of 1975, Howard R. Penniman, ed.

The Australian National Elections of 1977, Howard R. Penniman, ed.

Britain at the Polls: The Parliamentary Elections of 1974, Howard R. Penniman, ed.

Britain Says Yes: The 1975 Referendum on the Common Market, Anthony King

Britain at the Polls, 1979: A Study of the General Election, Howard R. Penniman, ed.

Canada at the Polls: The General Elections of 1974, Howard R. Penniman, ed.

France at the Polls: The Presidential Elections of 1974, Howard R. Penniman, ed.

The French National Assembly Elections of 1978, Howard R. Penniman, ed.

Germany at the Polls: The Bundestag Election of 1976, Karl Cerny, ed.

India at the Polls: The Parliamentary Elections of 1977, Myron Weiner

Ireland at the Polls: The Dáil Elections of 1977, Howard R. Penniman, ed.

Israel at the Polls: The Knesset Elections of 1977, Howard R. Penniman, ed.

Italy at the Polls: The Parliamentary Elections of 1976, Howard R. Penniman, ed.

Japan at the Polls: The House of Councillors Election of 1974, Michael K. Blaker, ed.

A Season of Voting: The Japanese Elections of 1976 and 1977, Herbert Passin, ed.

New Zealand at the Polls: The General Elections of 1978, Howard R. Penniman, ed.

Scandinavia at the Polls: Recent Political Trends in Denmark, Norway, and Sweden, Karl H. Cerny, ed.

Venezuela at the Polls: The National Elections of 1978, Howard R. Penniman, ed.

Democracy at the Polls: A Comparative Study of Competitive National Elections, David Butler, Howard R. Penniman, and Austin Ranney, eds.

Referendums: A Comparative Study of Practice and Theory, David Butler and Austin Ranney, eds.

Studies are forthcoming on the latest national elections in Belgium, Canada, Denmark, France, Germany, Greece, India, Israel, Jamaica, Japan, the Netherlands, Norway, Portugal, Spain, Sweden, and Switzerland and on the first elections to the European Parliament. Also *The American Elections of 1980*, edited by Austin Ranney.

American Enterprise Institute for Public Policy Research
1150 Seventeenth Street, N.W., Washington, D.C. 20036

A NOTE ON THE BOOK

*The typeface used for the text of this book is
Palatino, designed by Hermann Zapf.
The type was set by
Hendricks-Miller Typographic Company, of Washington.
Thomson-Shore, Inc., of Dexter, Michigan, printed
and bound the book, using Warren's Olde Style paper.
The cover and format were designed by Pat Taylor,
and the figures were drawn by Hördur Karlsson.
The manuscript was edited by
Claudia Winkler, of the AEI
Political and Social Processes Studies staff, and
by Elizabeth Ashooh, of the AEI Publications staff.*

SELECTED AEI PUBLICATIONS

Public Opinion, published bimonthly (one year, $18; two years, $34; single copy, $3.50)

Greece at the Polls: The National Elections of 1974 and 1977, Howard R. Penniman, ed. (220 pp., paper $7.25, cloth $15.25)

The American Elections of 1980, Austin Ranney, ed. (391 pp., paper $8.25, cloth $16.25)

The New Congress, Thomas E. Mann and Norman J. Ornstein, eds. (400 pp., paper $9.25, cloth $17.25)

Youth Crime and Urban Policy: A View from the Inner City, Robert L. Woodson, ed. (154 pp., paper $6.25, cloth $14.25)

The Corporation: A Theological Inquiry, Michael Novak and John W. Cooper, eds. (234 pp., paper $7.25, cloth $15.25)

President vs. Congress: Does the Separation of Powers Still Work? John Charles Daly, mod. (27 pp., $3.75)

Toward a Theology of the Corporation, Michael Novak (57 pages, $4.25)

The State of the Congress: Can It Meet Tomorrow's Challenges? John Charles Daly, mod. (28 pp., $3.75)

Revitalizing America: What Are the Possibilities? John Charles Daly, mod. (33 pp., $3.75)

Prices subject to change without notice.

AEI ASSOCIATES PROGRAM

The American Enterprise Institute invites your participation in the competition of ideas through its AEI Associates Program. This program has two objectives:

The first is to broaden the distribution of AEI studies, conferences, forums, and reviews, and thereby to extend public familiarity with the issues. AEI Associates receive regular information on AEI research and programs, and they can order publications and cassettes at a savings.

The second objective is to increase the research activity of the American Enterprise Institute and the dissemination of its published materials to policy makers, the academic community, journalists, and others who help shape public attitudes. Your contribution, which in most cases is partly tax deductible, will help ensure that decision makers have the benefit of scholarly research on the practical options to be considered before programs are formulated. The issues studied by AEI include:

- Defense Policy
- Economic Policy
- Energy Policy
- Foreign Policy
- Government Regulation

- Health Policy
- Legal Policy
- Political and Social Processes
- Social Security and Retirement Policy
- Tax Policy

For more information, write to:

AMERICAN ENTERPRISE INSTITUTE
1150 Seventeenth Street, N.W.
Washington, D.C. 20036